AGAINST ESSENTIALISM

Against Essentialism

A Theory of Culture and Society

STEPHAN FUCHS

HARVARD UNIVERSITY PRESS

Cambridge, Massachusetts, and London, England

First Harvard University Press paperback edition, 2004

Library of Congress Cataloging-in-Publication Data

Fuchs, Stephan.
Against essentialism : a theory of culture and society / Stephan Fuchs
p. cm.
Includes biblographical references and index.
ISBN 0-674-00610-0 (cloth)
ISBN 0-674-01596-7 (pbk.)
1. Culture.   2. Social groups.   3. Social structure.   I. Title.
HM621 .F83 2001
306—dc21   2001024389

Acknowledgments

My first thanks goes to Randall Collins, friend and fellow traveler. Peggy and Ellen Plass provided shelter and nourishment. Many people have helped make this book what it is; I owe intellectual and other debts to James Davison Hunter, Mel Leffler, Richard Harvey Brown, Robert Merton, Bennett Berger, John Ziman, Peter Weingart, Ansgar Weymann, Charles Case, Steven Shapin, Richard Rorty, Jon Turner, and Mark Schneider. I dedicate this book to the memory of Niklas Luhmann.

Contents

For scientific truth is but that which aspires to be true for all those who *want* scientific truth.

—Max Weber

Introduction

This book is unfinished and incomplete, given that many more puzzles are posed than solved. Worse, most of its puzzles are not really solved, either, in the sense that a solved puzzle actually goes away, does not draw any more attention, or is replaced by new puzzles. This I do not expect. What is found here is a "theory"—a map as to how research on society and culture might be done. There is some evidence marshaled for this theory, and there are also some sketches of how more evidence might be gathered to test it.

The puzzles considered here are basic to many sciences. They include the perennial mysteries of agency, rationality, knowledge, mind, and truth. I will argue that sociology has more tools to solve such puzzles than any other science. As a case in point, there is no physics of physics, and no genetic explanation for Darwinism, despite rather fantastic and utopian proposals to provide them. At present, no physicist can provide a physical explanation of his or her science, and no Darwinist has a genetic and evolutionist story about the rise of Darwinism. There is, however, a sociology of science, which I see as part of the sociology of culture.

The sociology of culture is not cultural sociology, which has become something of a fad lately, and which is closer to postmodernism, literary studies, and deconstruction. In contrast, the sociology of culture is practiced here as a comparative and explanatory theory of differences between observers. Observers are positioned in a culture; they are "cultured" observers. What they see, and do not see, depends on

1

where they are located in the networks of society and culture. I do not believe that there is "A Culture," in the singular, only very many of them, with the numbers still growing. "Modernity" occurs when observers observe themselves and other observers as one possibility among very many others. Observers and cultures are seen in this book as networks of communication and meaning. For those living in these cultures, they appear as forms of life, as ways to make a living, or as lifeworlds. When seen sociologically, cultures are observers in their own right. They observe other cultures, themselves over time, and also their niches in the world.

My major question is how cultures and observers do their work. Unlike cognitive science, I am more interested in differences between modes of relating to the world, not constants or universals. If there are constants, this is because they are being held constant by an observer. When this happens, essences appear, along with things-in-themselves or natural kinds. Essences prosper in the deep cores of cultures, where they house that which they cannot even consider, let alone deconstruct. The literature has many different terms for this core, including paradigm, tacit knowledge, practices, ethnomethods, common sense, and pretheoretical understanding.

Some of the tools and devices in this theory of culture come from the classics in sociology. One can find in the classics a cultural constructivism that is sensitive to variations. This more structural sort of constructivism does not deny the world, truth, or an external reality; rather, it acknowledges variations in the processes and outcomes of constructions. An implication is that while all cultures are constructed, not all of them are constructivist, in the sense of understanding themselves as but one possible culture among others. For sometimes a culture might become so strong and widespread that it turns into a "dominant" or hegemonic culture. It is then more realist about itself, and insists on its being not "just a construct." At other times, under different conditions, cultures are much more fragmented and uncertain about their identities. This structural pluralism supports more relativism and mutual ideological observing.

The postmodernist "discovery" of constructivism is not really a discovery. There is nothing much new in postmodernism; its central topics—for example, the death of the Subject, antifoundationalism, or the critique of representation—can be recovered from the classics, without all the philosophical essentialism of postmodernist critiques. The Subject or Author are not really dead because they are still the ones who receive praise, blame, and royalty checks. True, this does not make persons promising building blocks of social science, but persons remain at the core of commonsense accounts and explanations. An important distinction to consider is when an observer observes in terms of persons, and when a different observer manages to observe without them.

Sociology has the tools for a scientific theory of culture, but they will need a bit of rearranging. What I have in mind is a fusion of systems and network theories, which are each at the cutting edge of some current convergences between sciences of things both social and natural. Systems and networks are relational, not essential—what things are they are for an empirical observer, and what these things can do depends on how they are related to things of a similar sort. The opposite philosophy, essentialism, holds that things are what they are because that is their nature, essence, or definition. Common sense is essentialist in this sense, since it—along with much of social science, philosophy, and cognitive science—validates persons, agency, mental states, free will, and the rest of the humanist and liberal inventory.

Overcoming essentialism in the social sciences might bring them closer to other sciences. The tired old distinction between the Two Cultures of science and the humanities and its derivatives—such as the double hermeneutic, agency philosophy, *Sinnverstehen*, and so on— have become obsolete and unhelpful. The trouble is that there are so many more than just two cultures. A science, say physics, usually has subcultures. And science is just one among many observers, if a very distinctive one. Little can be gained by contemplating the nature of science as such, or the nature of culture. Such contemplation of essences would be metaphysics, but metaphysics becomes improbable after Heidegger, Sartre, and Nietzsche.

Allowing for variation drives one toward explaining differences. This is why the notions of systems and networks appear very promising; they both start with the assumption that everything could be otherwise or different from what it is, and that what things are depends on the other things to which they are connected. What something means, for example, depends on a host of variables, including context, situation, and place. My sort of question is not, for example, whether persons and their actions are, or are not, rational. Instead, I am interested in finding out under what conditions "rationality" emerges as a possibility, and when there is more or less of it, provided we can agree on what it means to be or act rationally.

Variables and their interactions change, generating much turbulence. I see society as a turbulent system, where "order" or "consensus" emerge locally and for the time being, if at all. An order might become more extended and inclusive, but this is, on the face of it, unlikely, and does not happen by itself. Instead, expansion requires much net-work.

Merging systems and network theories yields a theory of social structure that distinguishes four social observers—encounters, groups, organizations, and networks. Society takes place in these modes of association. None of them can be explained in terms of actors, agency, actions, or individual intentions. Much less does it seem possible to reduce social associations to particles, genes, or consciousness. Rather, actions and persons are viewed as observational devices and attributions, chosen by some observers, but not others, to do certain kinds of cultural work on certain actual occasions. Who you are as the person you are differs according to the social and cultural relations around you, and also according to who the observer is in each case where you are being observed and treated in some way. At least, this is what the observer "sociology" is equipped and prepared to observe. Your lover, in sharp contrast, would be very upset if explained by you as an outcome of social forces or, for that matter, genes, neurochemistry, or robotics. Explaining each other scientifically is not the road to love and intimacy.

Variations in social structure correspond to variations in cultures. At this point, the sociology of knowledge comes into the argument. The main empirical illustration I have chosen is degrees of realism or relativism in cultures. This measures how confident and certain a culture is of its mode of making sense of its world or worlds. Very confident cultures "rest" on their foundations, which means that they are not worried about them, or they are unaware of them, much like a blind spot in vision. Less confident cultures are more skeptical and divided about their identity and accomplishments. They are more prone to various degrees and shades of relativism.

Viewed sociologically, as a property of a certain culture at a certain time and place, realism is not primarily a philosophical problem with knowledge. Rather, it is a dependent variable and outcome of certain social structures. So is relativism. Both represent opposite poles in a continuum of culture. That continuum has many aspects or dimensions to it. As a rule, what exists and happens has many "causes," and a "cause" is what it is for the observer who reasons in terms of one set of causes, and not other possible ones. When you get promoted, you explain this as the result of merit, talent, contributions, and such. A sociologist would look instead at the structure of positions in the network that is your place of work. Your critics and competitors might suspect foul play, dispute merit, and attribute your promotion to "mere politics." For the IRS, your promotion might be reason to place you in a different tax bracket. Who is right? Which observer decides what is right? How far does such a decision carry, and for how long does it remain binding?

An important observation in this book, which comes from the sociology of Luhmann, is that there are many observers, who make different observations and deal with different problems in different ways. Following Wittgenstein and the pragmatists, there are no genuinely philosophical problems, only the problems and puzzles that emerge in certain cultures, in certain places and times. Philosophy is but one such culture and observer. As metaphysics, philosophy used to be cherished as a very special observer, but metaphysics has not survived the advance of the sciences. The solutions advanced to fix philosophical problems usually do not work outside of philosophy, and frequently not even there.

Can sociology do better? I think so. An obstacle to sociological advances, it seems to me, is obsession with persons and personhood, with beliefs, plans, goals, and intentions. With some materialists, I share the suspicion that common sense is not a decent scientific theory, and cannot be so, since it is not a scientific theory to begin with. In particular, I am skeptical about agency, mental states, and intentions as explanations for society and culture. Rather, they are approached here as outcomes and results of society and culture, not their causes. A sociological science might get off to a better start without the dogma that it is persons who do, say, or mean something. We will see what happens when persons appear as outcomes of society, rather than its sources, building blocks, or rational designers. Society does not "consist" of persons.

This is not to say that persons are "dead." Far from it. Persons survive, but they appear sociologically, and admittedly unattractively, as bundles of attributions and concessions. This lessens their importance, which is not pleasing to individuals accustomed to seeing themselves as actors and Selves. A sociological morality would recommend modesty about persons, about the difference it makes to society whether or not you are the unique person you feel you are. As a construct, "person" is employed by some social observers, but not others, as a device for making sense and for explanation. Demographers, for example, do not see persons, but aggregates. As a variable, as something that can be different as well as weaker and stronger, personhood has various degrees of depth. Most observers see only a fraction of a surface. A select few intimates are invited backstage.

Generally, how an observer observes depends on how that observer relates to what is being observed. Forests appear in different ways to various modes of behavior. Think of hunters, the EPA, ecoanarchists, or Thoreau. Likewise, personhood is an acquired characteristic, not a constant truth about human nature. It has a history; it varies. Persons and minds are social and cultural institutions, and the question is how these institutions emerge, work, and reproduce.

Allowing for variations is paramount. Much of social science remains stuck in essentialism and natural kinds, or things-in-themselves. The nature of action, the purpose of science, the reality of persons, the essence of mind—all these are examples of pseudomysteries that result from suppressing variation. No progress can be made in this way, this "philosophical" way, as Nietzsche and Wittgenstein realized. Instead, let us point the arrow the other way, toward sociologizing philosophy, and see how metaphysical mysteries might be converted into decidable problems.

Sociology has the tools, but not the identity, to be a great science. But it is a culture unsure of itself. When "hard" scientists look at sociology, they see little but an ideological battlefield prone to deconstruction and antiscience. This is disappointing. The sciences have much to gain from sociology, especially in terms of understanding themselves, which they do not. There is a welter of evidence from science studies suggesting that there is no global logical or methodological unity to science. There is no science "as such." No one has ever done "science in general." Science, with a capital *S,* is an invention of philosophers, and one that does not measure up to the empirical evidence pointing at the disunity of the sciences. Some science critics mistake science for its method, then call this method "positivism," which presumably has something to do with numbers and statistics. These are ideologically and politically suspect.

Another popular myth equates science with instrumental reason and technical control. But the critique of instrumental reason is at home in philosophy, not science. A working device or tool does not "follow" from a science. The great mystery is that anything works at all. What a science does is not the result of a philosophical logic, but its own previous operations and results. A most astonishing accomplishment of a science is nonideological communication. Unlike religions, a science looks forward, not backward. A science cares for itself, not some social cause. If it does anyway, it becomes a social cause, and feudalizes into status groups.

Chapter 1 explores what happens to theory once essentialism is gone. This chapter deals with methodology and issues of theory construction, though not in a formal way. Evidence from about three decades of science studies suggests that science is not its method, that method is not positivism, and positivism is not numbers, statistics, or instrumental reason. A commitment to science entails no commitments to any of these.

The argument departs from Luhmann's constructivist theory of observers to suggest that sociology of culture is a second-level observing of how, not what, first-level observers observe. The distinction between levels of observation helps resolve paradoxes in the theory of ideology, offers a reconciliation to the opposing fronts in the science wars, and destroys the myth of "going native" in interpretivism.

Forget the "new" rules of method and reconsider some older ones, such as the decomposition and recombination of commonsense properties and essences. This methodological reorientation blows a fresh breeze into the old controversies about value-freedom and disinterestedness. Scientists and other cultural workers are very interested—in their work and its outcomes. An observer is an observer in the network into which the observations are to be fed, to make a difference there. A disinterested observer would be careless.

Once variation is allowed, a convergence emerges in classical sociology on a structural constructivism. Unlike textual and idealist postmodern versions, this constructivism has nothing to do with skepticism about reference. It avoids relativism. Systems and network theories are the strongest systematic successors to this classical tradition. They overcome humanism and agency metaphysics in a strong move toward relationalism. "Persons" are not the source or origin of society; rather, they are outcomes of some networks, but not others.

A working "epistemology" combines an antifoundational positivism, pragmatism, and constructivism. This is not an epistemology of the philosophical sort, but a bag of tools to get scientific work done. Positivism says there is nothing nonempirical, transcendental, or universal. An order or agreement might become more global and binding, but this takes work and is not irreversible. Pragmatism reunites empirical science with philosophy. Constructivism adds that that which empirically exists is a construction of some sort, relative to an observer. Both the constructs and the observers are empirical as well, and so vary. They can also be observed, on a second level. Then it becomes clear that modes and outcomes of construction vary in the same way that, for example, the design of public housing projects differs from custom-made residential architecture.

Chapter 2 applies the framework of postessentialist theorizing to a series of perplexing metaphysical puzzles. These are not solved, but dis-solved, or hammered apart. Allowing for variation converts philosophical constants into dependent variables that covary with social structure. There are no general epistemic problems, only the problems that a culture creates and solves for itself, without consulting philosophers. Both traditional and revisionist philosophy are caught in essentialist traps; as a result, they have made no empirical progress.

Unlike philosophy or postmodernism, sociology has the tools to dissect epistemological mysteries and enigmata, such as incommensurability, relativism, or the differences between things and persons. Once variation is allowed on a second level of observation, the dualistic contrasts between realism and relativism, things and persons, commensurability and *in*commensurability, or cumulation versus revolution are linked by an underlying continuum. Cultures move along this continuum, sometimes generating things, then persons, and sometimes running into more troubles with rationality and understanding than at other times, or in different cultures.

Chapter 3 invites rational choice theories to consider what happens if "rationality" is explained as an outcome, rather than a foundation, of certain networks and relations. This implies accounting for the observer to whom something appears as rational. Does rationality structure what happens when two rational choicers fall in love with each other? A thesis that emerges is that rationality frames expectations when the numbers of strangers get very large.

The concept of "bounded" rationality goes in the right direction (toward variation), but not far enough, since the next puzzle is: bounded how, how much, and for how long? Failures of rationality become more likely when a center falls apart—the identity of a person, a central administration, or a quantitative metric. When a caged complexity bursts out of its cage, panic rules, not rational deliberation. Rationality declines as the number of options and alternatives grows rapidly.

A sociology of rational choice explores variations in its classical, and neoclassical, arsenal of concepts—mental states, natural personhood, decisions, utility. These are not natural or primordial givens, but improbable accomplishments of social structure. There are far too many persons doing many things for many reasons for an *empirical* theory of action to be feasible.

Neither natural nor corporate personhood is a ready-made unity of self-conscious beliefs and wants. Rather, some persons and some organizations, on occasion, use "rationality" and "decision" to make sense of what they do. Decisions are not simply acts occurring in the world, but attributions to agency, to halt causal regresses. Rationality is more of an option in a niche that has been simplified and digitized to a large extent. It fails, or falls apart, together with failures in unity and personhood, maybe due to turbulence and uncertainty. It is also easier to be rational when it is all over, when the dust has settled and clear story lines emerge. Goethe said that what matters to life is life, not its results.

Chapter 4 applies postessentialist theorizing to some problems in the sociology of culture. "Culture" is seen as recursive networks of distinctions from other networks. An example is art. Art distinguishes itself from common sense, nonart, or different art. Much like literary criticism or social theory, some art, though not all of it, is visibly constructivist about itself and displays that which turns it into art. When a common object, say a piece of shit (example from Bourdieu [1993]) turns into a piece of art, a network transsubstantiation in this piece occurs. It becomes related to other art, the art that is already there. This cuts off its ties to the drainage networks in which shit usually floats. What a node is in a culture and network depends on its relations, not essential properties.

Cultures occur in large numbers. There is no transcendental observer, or not anymore, and there is no global center, such as a fairly universal Church, where all culture comes together according to a "logic of practice." Increases in diversity are further propelled by distinctions between subcultures, such as administered and avant-garde art. An avant-garde is the velocity of a relation between itself, and that which it moves away from, such as administered or large-batch art.

Cultures give reputations to those contributing to them. Depending on network ranges, reputations are as local as the specialties and professions where you earn them. Under advanced specialization of reputations, the Renaissance intellectual becomes rare. Persons cannot, really, make reputations for themselves; reputations make reputations, and there is very little you can "control" about it. Networks that prize innovations use the device of "creativity," sometimes "genius," to explain to themselves how they make major breakthroughs.

Chapters 5 and 6 argue that sociology can be unified as a theory that distinguishes between four emergent social observers—encounters, groups, organizations, and networks. Persons contribute bodies and brains to society, which has neither. Bodies and brains, though not minds, are the results of Darwinian evolution, not society. At the same time, societies and their modes of association forge different social and cultural relations to minds and bodies.

The four observers are emergent; they occupy "nested levels" of various dimensions, including how far they are removed from the bodies and brains of persons. Encounters register bodies more than bureaucracies. Encounters occur in the massive plural; there is no master encounter, or collective consciousness, that coordinates or controls all of them. Encounters are turbulent, which adds surprises to social life.

Groups are prime observers of personal mental states, while organizations get into trouble for favoritism when they attend to individuality. Persons know their groups, much more so than they understand their organizations. Groups allocate attention to their members, who can now be cared for as individuals. Some groups, cults, freeze their nodes' degrees of freedom by severing ties to the surroundings of the cult. As encounters, groups are archaic and will not go away.

At the next level, complexity increases further, given that organizations "house" very many encounters and groups. This makes organizing less orderly than organization, as it appears on frontstages and in formal structures. Organizations are not per se streamlined and efficient iron cages. They often fail, especially when they are complex and interactive. Organizations employ various means and devices to get a grip on the turbulence from their informal systems, such as scheduling and files, but these techniques do not work all that well. It is a miracle that anything works at all, that organizing does occur.

The "master" concept is networks, which are systems of relations wherein differences can matter, such as good or bad research. First come networks, then nodes. Nodes are the specific "formats" or "versions" that the network constructs of them—they acquire "identities" in the process of getting tenured in a certain network position. Networks have cores and peripheries; inside the core, redundancy and dense coupling reduce degrees of freedom, to the point where tautologies emerge. The core shelters black boxes, routine equipment, and very solid facts.

Networks have resonance and metabolism—they restructure and rearrange that which is being fed into them. A culture goes to work—not on the world at large, but on the outcomes of its previous activities. Networks, by sheer relatedness, create self-similarity; one way in which this is observed is "culture." A culture condenses and converges, in its core, on analytical truths, institutions, and other blind spots.

Chapter 7 explores what this theory can explain about realism and relativism. These are seen as opposite positions on a variable continuum, with most cultures falling somewhere between the extremes. Realism and relativism change over time. Realism can be gained or lost, and it lasts until further notice—for example, until an empire or monopoly falls apart, and with it the "transcendental observer." Likewise, "relativism" does not indicate absence of foundations, but severe ruptures and holes in the networks of cultures and their observers.

Realism is not restricted to the sciences of nature, but likely occurs in any culture under certain structural and organizational conditions, such as an extreme concentration in the material means of cultural production. Realism prospers around routine machines and copresence around the equipment. It is the sign of an imperial culture at the zenith of its reign and expansion. When multiple observers emerge on the scene, and when that scene becomes less centralized, transcendental observers likely turn into empirical ones, occurring in large numbers.

CHAPTER 1

Theory after Essentialism

Nothing complicated enough to be really interesting could have an essence.

—Daniel C. Dennett

A sociological theory of culture and science loses the habit of essentialism, which suffocates much of social science. In its elaborate version as worldview, essentialism is Aristotelian metaphysics. In its mundane version it is common sense, or what phenomenology calls the natural attitude (Hallett 1991:1–9). The Churchlands (1999) refer to common sense as "folk psychology," but their description of it, "a self-conscious rational economy of propositional attitudes," is a better account of rational choice theory than of mundane reasoning.

Essentialism searches for the intrinsic "nature" of things as they are, in and of themselves. The opposite strategy is relationalism. A science gets more scientific as it breaks the hold of common sense and selects more counterintuitive premises (Bachelard [1934] 1984:23, 29–32). A science that does not remove itself from common sense will not advance much; it only produces more or less redundant duplicates of what everyone already knows.

In analytical philosophy, essences are called "natural kinds." Natural kinds are those to which terms and classifications refer when they are true and constant in all possible worlds (van Brakel 1992:255). These terms become what Kripke (1980:55) calls "rigid designators." Natural kinds are things-in-themselves, after they have reached their true state and unfolded their inherent potential. They cannot be imagined otherwise. The preferred logical mode in essentialism is necessity, worked out in formal syllogisms, deductions, definitions, tautologies, and the like. Natural kinds always exist, or seem to exist, independent of relationships, context, time, or observer. The properties of natural kinds are those that make a thing what it essentially is; the rest is "merely accidental," or contingent and historical.

One unresolved problem for natural kinds is their own status (van Brakel 1992:250). Are natural kinds themselves natural kinds? Is it an essential property to have an essential property? Another problem is that, if they do exist, there should not be so much conflict and controversy over which candidate entities are true natural kinds and which are "merely accidental." Yet another problem is change and diversity, because many groups believe in different natural kinds. In the history of science, some natural kinds disappear altogether, or turn out to be nonessential after all. Quine (1992:8) confesses that his "tentative ontology continues to exist of quarks and their compounds, also classes of such things, classes of such classes, and so on, *pending evidence to the contrary*" (my emphasis). Had he gone a bit further toward dissolving essentialism, toward sociology, Quine would have realized that this physicalist and reductionist "ontology" is not really an ontology at all, but the special niche of a rather small, yet influential, sector of science, particle physics. Physicalism is the "regional" ontology of physics. The rest of the world, including some physicists, continues to believe in God, horoscopes, weather predictions, love, cheeseburgers, and television. If modern society were compatible with any genuine ontology at all, it would not be that of particle physics, but common sense, in which the important entities are not really quarks, but include "Harvard Philosophy Department," "the Quine family," and "Boston traffic."

Essentialism makes either / or distinctions, rather than variable distinctions in degree. It posits polar opposites, instead of gradations and empirical continua. Examples abound everywhere. Science is either driven by method *or* not; action is either rational *or* interpretive; the nature of art is to express subjective experience; the nature of technology *is* impersonality; knowledge either corresponds to the world *or* is socially constructed; the mind is either a machine *or* conscious; persons differ from things because things are not reflexive; organizations are bureaucracies *or* anarchies; a social outcome is due to either action *or* structure; this structure *is* macro, not micro; the nature of method in social science is ideographic hermeneutics; society is either Gemeinschaft or Gesellschaft, but not both at the same time; the Middle Ages are all dark, while modernity is illuminated by the bright light of reason. The list goes on.

Consider class. Much effort has been spent on defining what classes really are. Once this is done, the major problems left are operational, instrumental, and conceptual, including how to define away the remaining anomalies, how to refine the current lists of shared attributes, how to fit new groupings into the grids, or how to account for the unexplained variance. In relationalism, classes turn instead into contingent outcomes, into rare and temporary accomplishments. Whether or not classes "exist" is the wrong question, since we should add: exist for whom, when, how much, and under which conditions? Allowing for variation means expecting to observe "class" not as a stable and essential fact about society, but as a variable outcome obtained under certain conditions, but not others, and sometimes obtained to a larger degree than at other times.

The Marxian distinction between classes in themselves and for themselves, elaborated by Bourdieu and others, is a step in the right direction, since this distinction accounts for the observer. Classes in themselves are classes on paper; they are the construct of an outside observer, such as a surveyor, who lumps code sheets together according to his own criteria. In contrast, classes for themselves come closer to actual collective actors. Allowing for variation, the critical problem is now to find the conditions under which this is more or less likely to happen, and the variable degrees of class emergence. Classes turn into variable and temporary accomplishments and outcomes, not independent facts and stable realities of society.

As classes become larger and more diverse, chances are that any "collective action" does not involve the entire collectivity, and does not occur at a constant rate. Instead, delegation and representation shift "collective action" to small clusters within the collectivity—clusters often centered around organizations, if the movement has become somewhat established. Network studies of social movements suggest that participation depends on network connectivity and density, and so is concentrated and energized in smaller local cores (McAdam, McCarthy, and Zald 1988:707). It is these cores and organizations that "act," not the class, as a whole, for itself. As a process and outcome, "classing" is local, changing, temporary, and contested. Any cohesiveness must be accomplished, and extends in space and time only as far as it actually does. None of these matters can be decided in advance. Multiple observers are involved in this process, debating rights to delegation and representation. Sociology is but one of these observers.

In essentialism, the preferred mode of operation is static typologies and rigid classifications, whose grids separate things that are everywhere, and under all circumstances, really separate. Essentialism is often accompanied by a dualistic cosmology that draws deep distinctions between things natural and social, body and mind, behavior and action, cause and intention, agency and structure, mere machines and true all-too-human humans, artificial and natural intelligence, or rules and practices. To get to these essentially different things, essentially different methodologies are necessary. This leads to yet more polar opposites, such as explaining versus understanding, science versus hermeneutics, quantitative versus qualitative research, theory versus narrative, hard versus soft science, and so on.

Operationally, essentialism is the failure to allow for variation. Where nothing is allowed to vary, nothing can be explained. There are two kinds of variation, qualitative and quantitative. The central questions, therefore, are when, and under what conditions, does something happen or not, and when do we get a lot of some thing, and when little. Since variables, and only variables, can be measured, only theories sensitive to variation can be tested according to the standard methods, quantitative or qualitative. Methods are pragmatic tools, well suited for some tasks, but not others.

Allowing for variation means dissolving natural kinds and their essential properties into relationships and forces. Variation is skeptical of Aristotelian substances and commonsense certainties. Historically, antiessentialism turns into an operationalist and instrumentalist philosophy of science with Galileo's later theory of motion and the widespread skepticist distinction between primary and secondary qualities in the Scientific Revolution (Gillispie 1960:355). Darwinism did much to destroy essentialism, "the most insidious of all philosophies" (Mayr 1976:414). Cassirer ([1910] 1969) describes the corresponding rise of relational science over essentialist metaphysics. Essentialist explanations in terms of intrinsic natures, ultimate goals, and true potentials give way to probabilistic descriptions of observable physical behaviors. Empirical observations are no longer commonsensical truisms and universals, as in Aristotle, but recordings of contrived singular experiments (Dear 1995). Scientific explanations might "save the phenomena," but they do not "feign hypotheses"—they do not claim to uncover the essential nature of physical objects and their movements. Theoretical entities may be invoked to economize on explanation costs, but they are pragmatic devices and summaries to account for observations, not actual realities.

In relationalism, things are what they are because of their location and movement in a network or system of forces; they do not assume a fixed and constant position in the network because of their essential properties. A network is a field of relationships between nodes that vary with their relationships. A cell becomes part of the liver, not the brain, not because its inherent nature is to become a part of the liver, but because a complex interaction between the selective activation of its DNA, and the network of other cells to which it becomes linked, makes it so.

Natural kinds exist, or seem to exist, in various areas of culture. They are the "black boxes" of cultures, the central institutions and core foundations on which a network rests, and without which it could not work as it does. But a constant is only a variable whose range of variation has not yet been discovered, or has been fixed and stabilized in some way (Bachelard [1934] 1984:25). An unnecessary restriction is for networks to link persons only. For this is just one case, and never are "persons" linked as complete individual beings. Persons and individuals are not essences and natural kinds, either, but result from relations and constructions. Not all networks are prepared and equipped to observe persons or individuals. Persons are observed by an observer for whom such an "identity" (White 1992:5–9) exists—in a certain situation, under certain circumstances, and until further notice. Persons and actions are flawed building blocks for social theory, not least because most persons, and most of their actions, are not observed by any observer, and they do not make much of a difference in what happens next in society.

Once variation is allowed, an added advantage is that we do not really have to make a philosophical choice for, or against, essentialism. Essentialism itself turns into an outcome of certain networks. Essentialism is how a network works when it protects its foundations. In its essentialist mode, a network condenses its operations into that which it cannot do without, which it cannot imagine otherwise. Essentialism is closure of a network to isolate and shelter its basic certainties and natural kinds.

Both stabilization and change may happen simultaneously in a network, albeit in different segments. The parts specializing in change are less anxious to protect the basic facts and rituals. They are more curious and restless. Over time, some of these new and uncertain things may become natural kinds.

Turning natural kinds into dependent variables leads to an important distinction between modes of classifying: some grids are visible as contingent constructs that could have been constructed otherwise; other grids are so deeply entrenched and embedded in an institutional order that they seem to separate that which is truly and essentially separate. That is, some groups are constructivists about classifications; others are realists. Most are probably somewhere in between and change their location on the continuum over time as well. It makes little *sociological* sense to ask who is right, because constructivism and realism are not either / or alternatives. They are matters of degree, not principle. This relationalist strategy prepares the next step—identifying the social and structural covariates of certainty and institutionalization.

For example, constructivism is more likely when groups compete over proper classifications, when a grid is being hammered out through controversies and conflicts, or when the group is linked to other groups with radically different grids. Conversely, realism is more likely in isolated and inward-turning groups, those with high density and little tolerance for innovation. Such groups are more likely to sacralize their core institutions and protect them by moral prohibitions and reifications.

Accounting for the Observer

One important reason for essentialism is the failure to account for the observer. It is one of the great merits of Luhmann's (1992:chap. 2) work to have revived this central notion in classical sociology of knowledge. The sociology of culture and knowledge can be understood or practiced as the comparative sociology of the observer. Since the world itself contains no information, only unstructured complexity, information is information *for* an observer in this world. For this observer, a certain piece of information is news only once. Observing means using a distinction according to which an observation is an observation of something, and some thing, and not something else, or some other thing. Information is the difference that makes a difference. That is, observing is an observer-dependent and -specific relation *to* the world *in* the world.

Distinctions are not drawn by the world itself, but by observers in it. Unlike religion, science assumes that all observers are empirical, which means that they occur in the world, together with their observations. Empirical observers observe the world in this world, not from outside. As part of the world, observing and observers emerge and disappear at certain places and times. Their empirical status implies that they can also be observed themselves, by other empirical observers or by an observer who observes himself.

Observing by means of distinctions accounts for the infamous "theory-ladenness of observation," though too much has been made of this (Hanson [1958] 1969:7, 30). That observations are theory-laden simply means they occur within a distinction. This distinction is "theoretical," in the sense that it comes not from the world at large, but from an observer in it, who makes other distinctions as well. Distinctions are either constructed or not; if they are not, they do not occur in the world and cannot make a difference to other distinctions. Theory-ladenness does not imply that there is no correspondence, truth, or objectivity. The extent to which observation terms are couched in theoretical interpretations *varies*. For example, observations of new things—the signal received by the telescope might be a new star, an old star doing something new, not a star at all, a measurement error—are more "theoretical" than observations of familiar things (the cat is on the mat).

Distinctions belong in a network of related distinctions. This network *is* the observer. An observer is anything equipped to apply distinctions to the world or, more precisely, that part of the world which is an observer's niche. Observing is a relation within a niche. Or, by means of observers, a niche relates to itself. Observers and niches co-emerge and -disappear. When an observer, say a species, dies, so does its niche and its relations to the world. As one changes, the other changes as well, since an observer is also part of the niche. An observer in the niche cannot see the "niche as such," only some things in it. Observing is contingent and selective—a choice from other options and alternative distinctions.

The niche is where the distinctions and observations of an observer matter and make a difference. "Observer" includes bacteria, immune systems, frogs, lovers, and physics. An observer is not an "entity," much less a "person," but a network of related distinctions. It is this network that "observes." An observation is what it becomes in relation to other observations. It is these relations that matter.

The information obtained by observing according to a distinction is selective, not complete and exhaustive. No network of observation reveals the world as such, or all of it, since a network occurs within this world and its times. If no distinctions are drawn, there is no information; if different distinctions matter, they yield different information. Except for highly stratified societies, where all "privileged" information is concentrated at the top, there are different social observers, located in different positions in a social structure. There are no privileged observers in the philosophical sense anymore in modern society, only observers whose observations make more or less of a difference to *other* observers and *their* observations.

A society has as many observers as its complexity and pluralism allow. New observers emerge all the time, together with novel distinctions and instruments of observing. Nothing guarantees that all of these different observers use the same, or even compatible, distinctions. There is no transcendental unity of all observers, no universal communicative rationality, and no view from nowhere (Nagel 1986). Similarity of distinctions across observers in a society is a contingent and improbable social outcome and accomplishment, not a transcendental a priori.

Self-similarity across a more or less demarcated network of distinctions creates a "culture." An art or science is a network of self-similar distinctions and observations, although degrees of self-similarity vary between the opposite extremes of fragmentation and unity. A culture ends where its distinctions cease to matter. There is no art outside of art, unless a different art makes it so. A culture can extend the range of its networks and distinctions, but this extension must also be done, or does not come about at all.

The distinctions that do matter matter in time and space, there and then, here and now. Past and remote distinctions matter if they are adopted and go to work within a here and now. Distinctions that do not survive become extinctions. When an observer becomes extinct, the world loses this particular niche. Extinct observers can still be observed by surviving observers, but these work in their own niches and according to their own distinctions.

Observing Observers

Since observers can be observed by other observers, just who or what is an observer, and just what the status and relevance of his observations are, is the meat of social and cultural conflict. The important conflicts in modern societies are not restricted to classes and status groups, but concern who is an observer, what this observer can and cannot see, and how significant or binding his observations are for other observers. An observer or observation is nothing in and of itself; it is what it is only in relation to itself, and to other observers and their observations.

An observer capable of observing himself is a "reflexive" observer. Reflexive observers observe themselves and distinguish themselves from other observers, who are themselves reflexive or not. Reflexive observing is not some "higher" or "advanced" mode of observing, as if capable of discovering something very special or unique that is inaccessible to "lower" observers, who are unable to observe themselves. Rather, self-observing shares the restrictions of all observing, such as location in time and place, or dependence on frames and distinctions without which no observation is possible.

A social structure begins to emerge when distinctions are coupled, making what happens in one part of the structure, at some point in time, relevant for another structure, or a different time. With this, a social structure begins to distinguish *itself* from a different social structure, and vice versa. Distinction involves a measure of boundedness and demarcation. A conversation gets going when it distinguishes itself from other conversations, and when the participants follow its emergent flow. All of this is up to the conversation itself, not the state or the ruling class. At any moment, the conversation might fall apart, dissolve into the conversations around it, or degenerate into the noise that results from failures at coupling. Due to multiple contingency, coupling is very improbable, since there is no primary transcendental or universal unity among all observers. What they observe or not is, to a large part, up to them, at least as long as they remain, to some extent, "autonomous" or independent. Nothing guarantees, from the beginning, that coupling will occur. Rather, coupling is itself an empirical outcome and accomplishment of a social structure.

Sociologically, observing is a matter of location in a network. Among other things, network location decides what an observer can and cannot see—as observed by another observer, such as the sociologist of culture, who can also observe only that which can be observed *from there*, from within sociology of culture. Since all locations are "in" the world, which includes society, no observation can ever disclose "the" world as such, as if viewing it from outside. Distinctions remain what they are only until further notice, or until different observers construct different distinctions in the future. Once this future acquires an open extension, the structure of the world can no longer be fixed in advance, once and for all.

Spengler would call this modernity's "destiny," though it no longer has one. In modern society, fundamental and essentialist ontology is bound to fail, at least in the long run. When he had nearly finished *Being and Time,* it began to dawn on the owl Heidegger that because there are only beings, there is no way or position for any of these many beings to reveal "Being" as such. There is no "view from nowhere"— except for *this* view, which also must be somewhere. But where? Right here and now. Where else?

Sociologically, the observer is not a complete and unitary "person," although some observers observe "persons" as sources of agency. A sociological observer observes relations. Then "agency" appears as the myth of the modern self, ritualized in subjective rights, privileged access to their own incorrigible mental states, or personal property claims (White 1992:8). This myth is real—realized in institutions. Even sociological observers cannot simply bypass such institutions. They can use "relation," "structure," or "network" instead of person, but will expect credit for this as persons, too. The person is alive, at least in some contexts, and on some occasions. The identity "Harrison White" would be very upset if credit for "structural equivalence" went to another person, though structural equivalence precisely destroys persons qua persons.

The question, then, is not whether there are, or are not, persons. This is one of the irresolvable and essentialist quasiproblems that plague the social sciences. Instead, observe under what conditions some observers attribute some outcomes to persons, and when they manage to observe without persons. Observing without "person" can be rude and difficult, for example, in small encounters and intimate associations. In such contexts, "person" still does a lot of moral and cultural work. It is persons who fall in love—or is it the habitus falling in love with itself? It is persons who say and do something—or is this an attribution of a structure?

Observing with "person" does not make for good sociology, since one either knows all the persons who can be known or has some prior rule or rationale for excluding and ignoring most of them. There is no such rule; the only filters we do have are structural, not personal, such as "power," "network location," or "habitus." Agency theorizing has not solved its own basic enigmata, including intention, will, decision, and the like.

The observer may be a body, its immune system, or brain. Bodies, brains, and immune systems are the results of natural evolution—for Darwinism, yet another observer. Immune systems perceive and react only to invaders that are hostile or dangerous to the body that houses them. For the immune system as an observer, the world falls into the distinction harmful / harmless—a distinction tailored to the organism for which something can, in fact, be harmful or not. That distinction *is* its world; an immune system has no other, and cannot react to anything that could not be classified as falling on either side of that distinction. Without this organism, this particular distinction would not occur in the world, which is why "environment" is not something apart and outside of an organism or system, but the *interaction* between an observer and its segment of the world, or niche. A niche is just the variable interaction between an observer and that which he observes. If an organism changes, so does its niche and its interactions with it. Its world is then no longer the same as before. One could not describe a niche without referring to its inhabitants. No organism lives "in the world" at large. When a species becomes extinct, the world loses not only this species, but also itself, or that part of itself that once was the world for this species.

An observer can be anything and anyone observed as a unit of observing by itself or other observers. Physicists say an observer is anything equipped to take measurements, or to register something and react to it, or not. If an observer does react, he can do so only in his own terms, though these can change over time with evolution or learning. Observation occurs as soon as a distinction is drawn according to which something falls on either side of the distinction: self / other; true / false; edible / inedible; hostile / friendly; male / female; inside

/ outside. Applying a distinction can be done in countless ways, but it *must* be done, or observation does not happen at all.

Information is a difference that makes a difference—to other observations, and to other observers. Observations are not "attuned" to the world at large. No observer could observe the world as such. Nor would this observation, if possible, inform anyone, since no distinction could be drawn within this observation. In the early Wittgenstein, the world is—everything that is the case. But what about all the events that have yet to happen, and all the cases yet to be made? And what about the case of an observation of something that is the case? Has it not just become part of that which is the case, the case of this observation?

Observations are attuned not to the world as such, but to a niche within it. This niche is home. An important part of the observational niche is other related observations, including past (memory) and present observations. Within an observer, observations are bundled, in many different ways, into clusters (Chokr 1993). These carve out themes or topics. A theme or topic occurs not by itself, but as the outcome of actual couplings and networkings. Coupling is contingent, not necessary, and so can be done in different ways. Observations connected in clusters of related observations "cohere" to varying extents. The degree of coherence is the degree of "truth" in this network, if it has any place for truth. Microbes do not, but their measurements cohere as well. The coherence of measures is the coherence of an observer and his niche.

While all this happens, the rest of the world is still there but does not matter at this particular moment, though it may later, or at the same time for other observers, who observe something else from somewhere else. As Zetterberg and Haferkamp used to say, a way of seeing something is always, and at the same time, a way of *not* seeing something else. An observation does not "reveal" the world; rather, it becomes part of it if, and only if, it is made. An observation does not "disclose" the world, but adds itself to the world. The world is now more, not less, complex than before. A theory might "reduce" the complexity of its world or niche, but it can do so, paradoxically, only by making the world more complex still, since the world now contains itself and this theory.

Observations travel as far as the networks in which they are embedded reach—no farther, and usually not even this far. For example, if a body feels pain, the pain ends where the body ends; it cannot be shared. With the exception of symbiotic relationships, such as pregnancy, one body's pain cannot be felt by other bodies. One cannot die *for* someone else, because that person still has to die as well. Physical pain cannot be eased by propositions or theories, only drugs, and only by drugs that can be fed into the body's ongoing metabolism. Pain can be eased by the performance of communication, but not by its referential content or truth. A mother might relieve the pain of her baby by mumbling to it in a soothing voice, but *what* she says makes no difference. Psychotherapies might ease pain, but this does not prove that their "underlying theories," if there are any, are correct. They might work simply because of a Hawthorne effect, because someone pays attention. Or they might distract from the pain for a while. But the pain remains one's own.

It is possible to communicate about one's pain, but not the pain itself. Communication about pain is not itself physically painful. Communication travels along its own networks, so that only those to whom one is linked can possibly observe one's communicated pain, even though they still cannot feel it. Pain reaches a larger audience only through organizations and their own extended networks. The pain is then no longer a physical sensation, but a communication phrased according to the operations of social structures. In this process, the pain becomes something different entirely. For example, it metamorphoses from the physical sensation of a body into statistics about torture, international political drama, accusations of injustice and human rights violations, and Amnesty International fundraisers (Scarry 1985). As it proceeds along the networks linking different kinds of observers, the event does not remain the same, but changes according to the internal modes of observation and operation of various social structures.

Observations always tell at least as much about the observer as about the referent of observation. Again, observations are what they are only for an observer, and they reach only as far as the networks in which they occur as events.

Levels of Observing

An important distinction in the theory of observation is that between various "levels" of observation (Luhman 1992:chap. 2). There are two basic such levels, the "what" and the "how" of observation, or levels one and two. Level one attributes an observation to the world, or a niche in the world; level two attributes observation to an observer of the world or niche. In this sense, level one is "realist" and level two is "constructivist." No observation can operate on both levels simultaneously, because switching levels takes time. Persistent back-and-forth level-switching triggers adventures in reflexivity, where one authorial voice is not enough, and the linear and monological narrative organization of the text is disturbed by recursiveness, self-commenting footnotes, new literary forms, and the like (Woolgar 1988; Ashmore 1989).

Levels of observation differ in what becomes visible. For example, the mind is aware of some outcomes of conscious operations, but not these operations themselves. The conscious mind cannot become conscious of how consciousness is possible, at least not while it is conscious of something else. The operations of consciousness, its hows, can become a subject only later, for different observers, such as neuroscientists or philosophers of mind. A "theory" of mind deals with its hows, because there is no way to recover the "contents" of what billions of minds actually experience.

On the first level, observation proceeds in a naively "realist" way; it observes what it observes and accepts its content as more or less taken for granted. Significantly, there are no optical illusions or chronic doubts at this level, for one sees what one sees, smells what one smells, and attributes this to the world, not to the observer. It is the flower or pot roast that smells good, not your experience that it does. When someone kicks you in the shin, you do not grab your head. At the first level, one can see something, but not the seeing itself. Optical illusions, for example, can be revealed only later, and only on a different level, which has the first level as its theme. While they observe at this level, first-level observers cannot observe just how they manage to observe. They cannot see the physical, physiological, or social conditions of observing. They also cannot observe just how selective their pattern of observation is, as an actualization of one possibility among alternatives. This becomes an option only at subsequent levels, which have their own conditions for observing.

The first level of observation is the level of common sense and the natural attitude. "Common sense" and "natural attitude" are *modes* of observing, not observations. They do not have a fixed content or reference, since both vary from observer to observer, and over time. The common sense of a twelfth-century monk differs from that of a twenty-first century Wall Street investment banker. What remains more stable and continuous than "content" is the way in which common sense attributes causes and effects. An important attribution is to persons and their intentions, decisions, and actions.

All forms of observation, including science, have their own common sense and natural attitude: that which they consider familiar, in no need of proof, and to be expected from any competent member of the craft. The first level of observation is that which is taken for granted in observing, and that which is "naively" attributed to the world, not the observer. Accordingly, that which some science's common sense takes for granted might be problematic and counterintuitive in other cultures and other sciences, and vice versa.

What is "common" about common sense is not a given and fixed set of actually shared beliefs, opinions, or attitudes. Rather, common sense is common in that no form of observation can proceed without some basic certainties that cannot be questioned at the first level. They remain invisible there and then, for the time being. But certainties and institutions vary from observer to observer, and over time. That is, commonalities exist among *modes* and "hows" of observing, not in *contents* and "whats." Therefore, a theory of observing is a theory of how observing is done, not what observing observes.

Paradoxically, it takes a lot of uncommon and nonintuitive attention to reveal how common sense observes. When made explicit, the implicit becomes more and more improbable and strange. Eventually, the observer falls into the bottomless pit that made the existentialists both worried and giddy with freedom. Examples include Husserl's monumental struggles to explicate immediate apperception, Schutz's reconstruction of everyday reciprocity, Garfinkel's studies of mundane sense making, or Goffman's frame analyses. They all deal with common sense, but their writings are anything but commonsensical. Why should this be? Precisely because common sense is not an observation, but a mode of observing, so that each explication of a piece of common sense reveals yet more common sense, ad infinitum.

The bodies of first-level observers feel pain—not "physiological malfunctions." While they are in pain, they cannot observe *how* their brains manufacture painful sensations from physical information about damages to the body. How the brain does this can only be observed on a second level, for example, scientifically. Neuroscience turns the "hows" of the first level into its own "whats." That is, first-level modes of observing and experience turn into second-level themes or topics. But this second level cannot do without its own "hows," that which *it* takes for granted when it observes what it observes. These "hows" remain invisible and taken for granted at this level as well; they are its own common sense. To observe how the second level observes, we need to switch to a third level, say a sociology of (neuro)science, which also comes with its own modes of operation invisible within this level.

On the second level, the "how" of first-level observation becomes visible. On this level, the second observer does not attribute the observations of the first observer to the things and states that make up the referents in his world, but to this first observer, who is, of course, also located in this world. For example, the unproblematic facticity of the world in common sense can now be seen not as the way the world really is, but as an improbable and selective accomplishment of ethnomethods. The next switch to a higher observational level would reveal ethnomethodology itself as the social construct of an observer, the network of ethnomethodology. At higher levels, the puzzle is not what the observer observes, but how he manages to do so, and how or why his mode of observation differs from that of other observers.

But keep in mind that each level has its own "hows" and certainties invisible *to it*, while it does its own observing. These "hows" might become the "what" of a next level. This is where sociology of culture and science are located. Observing how other observers observe, what they can and cannot see, and what they "bring" to an observation is just what sociology of culture does. The sociology of culture is a comparative sociology of observers. The attribution of observations is to the observer, not the world or the things in it to which the observations refer. Of course, the sociological observer assumes, "naively" as it were, that these observers actually exist, and that his own sociological observations "correspond to" how these observers actually observe.

Therefore, the characteristic mode of operation in sociology of culture is to reveal the selectivity and contingency of first-level observation (Berger 1995:34–36). This often irritates the first-level observers, since they trust that their observations correspond to reality. The subjects of Garfinkel's breaching experiments got as upset by disruptions in this common sense as did the natural scientists reacting to postmodern deconstruction. Lovers hate being told that their love is not what it seems to them, but instead depends on physiological arousal, market exchanges, or historical culture. This sort of irritated and hostile reaction is triggered when second-order observers tell first-order observers that their observations are socially constructed. The first-order observers understand this to mean that their love is not real, their science is not true, or the facts in their world are not really facts. Of course, someone must construct this constructivism as well, or it does not occur at all.

The sociology of culture cannot observe together *with* first-level observers, and it cannot observe *what* they observe. A sociology of love cannot be done while falling in love. A sociology of science has nothing to say about the "truth" of that science, although it does claim truth for its own results. If it did do the former, it would not be sociology of culture, but part of the culture it observes. A sociology of physics is sociology, not physics. It does not observe *what* physics observes, but *how* physics observes. It attributes "physics" not to physical reality, but social structure. The "Science Wars" are due to a failure to distinguish between levels of observation (Fuchs 1996).

Of course, the sociology of culture has its own culture that shapes how it observes other cultures and their observers. Its own culture is the theme of a sociology of sociology. But even if, and as, it observes itself, a culture cannot do without its own natural attitude and common sense. Thus, constructivism has its own natural attitude—when it observes that observations *are,* in fact, constructed. Thus, after thirty years of institutionalization, Shapin (1996:9) turns constructivism into normal science, which takes "*for granted* that science is a historically situated and social activity."

Advancing through the levels of observation is not climbing up the tree of knowledge until the final level has been reached and the whole world itself comes into plain view. There is no such final level, at least not in science, though there certainly is in religion, when all rests forever in God. Instead, second-level observations behave "realistically" when it comes to their *own* observations, whose referents just happen to be different observations on another level. Constructivism believes in the reality of observers and constructions. What comes into view at higher levels is not the final and ultimate truth, but only a different set of restrictions and constraints from which no observer can escape.

Sociology was born with the realization that there is no view from nowhere. Postmodernists of various persuasions think they have discovered something new because they do not know much sociology. The idea of "truth" as an unconstrained or "unsituated" representation of the world as it is, without an observer, is really gone, and gone for good, given the work of Marx, Mannheim, Fleck, and Durkheim. For sociology, observations are made by an empirical observer located in a particular social structure and embedded in a network of related and connected observations that make up a culture. The sociology of culture views observations—including its own, at the next reflexive level—as social and historical events that could be otherwise, or that might not have happened at all.

Sociology might even predict when levels of observation will be switched, when the "what" turns into the "how," or when observation-as-correspondence turns into observation-as-construct. This happens when something "goes wrong" at the first level, such as competition, conflict, and disagreement. Controversies are naturally occurring "autogarfinkels" (Collins 1983:95), because they upset and question first-level certainties. When this happens, observations may turn away from their referents to observe themselves. Mannheim ([1928] 1971:260) correlated the birth of sociology of knowledge with democracy, conflict, and competition. A "sociology of knowledge" is a plain impossibility when there is only one language game in town. Second-order observations start with suspicions, probably first in politics, when the opponents discover "biases" and "interests" in each other's observations. They observe each other's observations not as innocent reflections of the truth, driven by the world itself, but as immersed in "standpoints" and driven by partisan interests. That is, the opponents in debate are often realists about their own classifications, but constructivists about those of their enemies.

Ideological Conflicts in Observation

Does a constructivist sociology of cultural networks have any place for "ideology"? In classical Marxism, ideology is false consciousness, a system of mystifications and reifications emerging from social structure, particularly from the legalistic fictions of civic rights and equality circulating, together with commodities, in markets (Marx [1939–1941] 1972:253, 273). The bourgeois ideology of free exchange and subjective rights is grounded in the surface of distribution, while production is highly stratified and organized as coercion. Markets are the surface of a deeper reality of production; ideologies "reflect" this surface and so conceal the underlying structural realities of industrial capitalism. Since the proletariat experiences this deeper level firsthand, it can see through ideological fabrications and advance, with a little help from its intellectual friends, the truth of historical materialism against the ideological fictions of bourgeois liberalism.

Classical Marxist theory splits into three separate strands. The first is Hegelian Critical Theory, which equates ideology with instrumental and administrative reason and the "repressive desublimation" (Marcuse 1964:56–58) of late capitalist culture industries. According to this paradigm, ideology now also envelops the formerly revolutionary proletariat and is anything that perpetuates and justifies the status quo as the inevitable outcome of technical efficiency and instrumental rationality. The origin of ideology dates way back before the rise of capitalism, to the very origins of working control over nature. There is not much hope for destroying this all-encompassing ideological machinery, because the exploited and oppressed masses have become subsumed under its organized unfreedom as well. The intellectuals escape into negative dialectics and modernist avant-garde art as the only refuges capable of resisting ideological colonization. There cannot be any truth in the false life (Adorno 1951:42), however, so the resistance of critical theorists is admittedly and outspokenly rendered futile and tragic.

In the critical theory of Habermas ([1984] 1987:chap. 4), false consciousness results from the distortions that communication suffers when it is invaded by the systemic imperatives of power, money, and instrumental reason. True consciousness escapes to the fragile and quasitranscendental islands of ideal speech, where discourse responds only to the noncoercive force of the superior argument. Habermas still hopes for emancipation, but his faith is more in new social movements, not the workers of old. Emancipation will be realized when the project of modernity is finally finished and society is modeled after the distinctions residing in formal pragmatics. For it is here, in the formal pragmatics of speech acts, that one can show instrumental reason to be not superior to, but derivative from, communicative reason. Once everyone understands this, we can all discourse ourselves and each other right into complete enlightenment.

The second string in the development of "ideology" moves through Lukács and Gramsci into French structuralist Marxism and Bourdieu (1989). The meaning of "ideology" is generalized to include the operations and outcomes of any ideological apparatus that reproduces cultural hegemony through the organizations of the state, most prominently education and the mass media. The distinction between true and false consciousness does not yet disappear, but fades away and becomes less obvious as "ideology" becomes any systematic form of stratified and organized cultural reproduction. Ideology still serves to rationalize and justify domination, but it is no longer clear and undisputed which, if any, social structure and movement are capable of overcoming ideology and "misrecognition." To the extent that the means of ideological production are decentralized, any group, party, or movement produces its own ideology. But the concept retains its original critical and enlightening spirit in this intellectual lineage; the progressive intellectuals must show how ideologies systematically conceal the real nature of social relations. So ideology is opposed to structural Marxism, or whatever theory the intellectuals happen to endorse at the moment.

As false consciousness, ideology is opposed to true consciousness. But what is false about false consciousness? False consciousness is not simply in error about some state or fact in the world. Such errors could be corrected by learning. Rather, the very notion of "fact" is ideological, since facts are collected by bureaucracies working to subsume the world under their own repressive classifications. Ideological falseness runs much deeper than error; it is a systemic or structural falseness that cannot, and will not, get any of the facts right, since the entire ideological approach is distorted by symbolic violence and cultural hegemony. An ideology is not just a false theory, for its mistakes do not reside in any testable propositions; rather, it is mistaken in its "totality." It conceals its true interests and social location. The social carriers of ideology are themselves trapped in its mystifications.

Coupled to the very notion of ideology is a deep suspicion about ulterior motives. One suspects that those who are trapped in an ideology are neither capable of learning nor willing to do so. They cannot see what they cannot see, and this fallacy cannot be remedied, since those who profess an ideology do so unaware of its true functions. Now emerges the core problem of this entire critical theory of ideology: the social and cultural location from which nonideological observation might still be possible.

This problem eventually replaces the theory of ideology by the sociology of knowledge. In *Ideology and Utopia*, Mannheim ([1929] 1969:135) still thought that, due to their relative autonomy from the major social strata, the intellectuals occupied a privileged and remote position from which they could escape the traps and fallacies of ideological mystifications. But once all knowledge is coupled and related to social location and position, this privileged position, outside and above society, becomes a nowhere land. In his later works, Mannheim annuls the exemption of intellectuals and their worldviews from social conditioning, and an "ideology" becomes any set of ideas and cultural practices that "reflects" an underlying social structure. The distinction between true and false consciousness collapses, and with it the entire project of enlightening and emancipatory *Ideologiekritik*. The sociology of knowledge turns reflexive and now includes a sociology of itself and its intellectuals. In fact, the intellectuals are a supreme challenge to any sociology of knowledge, since they often claim to speak nothing but the truth, to be driven only by the neutral and objective forces of rationality. Such claims must provoke the sociological imagination. In the 1970s, the Strong Program takes one more step and builds a sociology of scientific knowledge as well. Science itself turns into an "ideology"—no longer understood as false consciousness, but as one culture among others and somehow related to social structure, including "interests" and other profane forces.

Where can we go from here with ideology? It seems that two roads can no longer be traveled. A sociology of culture, practiced as a comparative sociology of observers, cannot maintain the distinction between true and false consciousness although, as we have seen, it cannot do without "truth" when accounting for its own operations and outcomes. At the same time, it also cannot exempt any culture, including its own, from sociological explanation. When it explains itself as the outcome of its own social structures, however, it must do so again in the medium of truth. Such is the paradox of reflexive self-observation.

If these two roads are closed, which one should we take? The theory of levels of observation shows a new possibility. Levels of observation differ in the ways that they attribute observation. On the first level, observation proceeds naively, observes what it observes, and attributes its results to the world. It is unaware of construction. On the second level, observation attributes outcomes to the distinctions and constructions of a specific and empirical observer, who can only see that which can be seen from where he is at the moment. When second-order levels are chosen, observations are observed as "ideologies." Ideologies are not false consciousness, but attributions of observations to the variable locations and circumstances of observers—instead of to the world, which of course includes its observers as well. Ideologies are not themselves observations, but *modes* of observing; they cannot be true or false, only operative or not. "Ideology" is the expression for the fact that an observer, *any* observer, cannot observe *how* he observes at the same time as he observes *what* he observes. These modes of observing, however, can become the theme for the observations of different observers. These observers are not themselves exempt from ideology; rather, they have their own modes and hows of observing, which they too cannot observe. In other words, no observer is exempt from ideology, as the old theory claimed.

We can go one step further. To an observer, the ideological modes of his observing are invisible; they are the frames, paradigms, and perspectives outside of which he could observe nothing at all. While observing, these frames are tacit and taken for granted. One might say they are the observer's common sense, his background certainties and obvious truths. This much is true about the old Althusserian adage that ideologies are "lived," not just "believed" (McCarthy 1996:42). To be sure, for another observer who observes this observer, these frames come into view as local and historical constructs, not evident and universal constants. But again, that second observer also cannot observe anything without his own tacit and implicit certainties.

"Ideology," then, belongs to the core of a cultural network, which houses its specific invisibilities and modes of observing. It is here that we find essentialisms, natural kinds, universals, rigid designators, and things-in-themselves. It is here, in the core, that necessity, logic, rationality, basic rules of method, and elementary truisms and tautologies reside. The core nodes and relationships are mapped onto the world and reified as that which remains true in all possible worlds. Cores are eminently realist; they cannot imagine things to be very different from what they are. As we shall see, however, the strength of the core co-varies with other variables, including the structure and connectivity of the overall network. Variation notwithstanding, the core is just how the world *is*—for the cultural network in which it is the core. At the same time, this very attribution of the network's behavior to its own opera-tions cannot be done from within the network, only from the outside, or by a different observer who is himself part of another network with its own core or cores.

What happens when two or more such networks compete and strug-gle against each other? Each network will observe the other's core as a contingent construct, not as a basic natural necessity. They will behave as constructivists about the other's core practices, and as realists about their own. They will debunk each other's core as being composed of "ideologies"—beliefs and ideas suspiciously unaware or deceiptful of their "true" motives and interests—while asserting that their own ideas and beliefs are just right and righteous, and that they capture the em-pirical and moral order of the world as it really is, without any con-struction going on at all.

For a sociology of cultural networks, then, "ideology" attributes the core operations and outcomes of a network to an empirical and histor-ical observer within that network. Such mutual attributions are trig-gered by conflict and controversy between networks and, in some cases, by internal ruptures within a network that is falling apart. To trigger ideological observation, conflict must be intense, leading to mutual suspicions about ulterior motives, concealed interests, and hid-den agendas (Berger 1995:34, 38, 80). As conflict becomes more in-tense, cores are exposed as contingent constructs, not basic natural necessities. There is, then, no nonideological observing on a second level, although first-level observers do not observe their own observa-tions as ideologies. In other words, conflict triggers the switching of levels of observation, so that "ideologies" emerge as attributions of ob-servations to the observer, not to the world. At the same time, the world includes all of its observations as well, and so no observation is possible from without the world. If we discovered another world, that world would become part of our world also.

Once ideologies are observed, they reveal the paradox of all observ-ing. So here is the trick. As long as they are part of science, second-order observations cannot but themselves operate in the medium of truth and objectivity. That is, the scientific revelation that first-order observations are made from a standpoint cannot be communicated as yet another standpoint or, if it is, then *this* observation cannot be so communicated, and so on. This much follows from the fact that the *how* of an observation becomes the *what* at the next level, and so on, without end. The medium of truth operates as science's blind spot; it cannot leave this medium and do something else, if communication is to be any part of science. One can, of course, observe with another distinction, such as male / female, black / white, or imperialist / subaltern. But the result of this is ideological politics, not science. No doubt, ideological politics can become a *subject* for science, and it is indeed a central subject for any sociology of culture and knowledge. But whatever observations sociology offers about ideological politics in science, or elsewhere, those observations cannot themselves be communicated and observed as anything but ideological politics.

Inside and Outside Observers

Observations that occur inside a network behave differently from those occurring outside. This difference becomes most visible when the self-observations of a network are fed into its ongoing operations and outcomes. Then they lose their theoretical and "detached" character and become part of what the network does, and how it does it. These observations matter directly to what happens in the network; they are not "neutral" and "disinterested," because the network uses them for its own activities. This situation is possible when the observations of the network and its operations use the same basic distinctions and frameworks.

Take critics in networks of art or literature. Even if they produce no art or literature themselves, critics are observers whose observations matter directly to the network's behavior. Through their observations, critics focus the attention of the network on that which "deserves" critical recognition. The cultural work of the critic is an integral part of the work that is art. Criticism defines and interprets what art is, relates a piece of art to other art, and so shapes its very production and appreciation. Through criticism, the network makes sense of itself to itself. On this basis, blame and praise can be awarded, traditions of style can be built up, and changes in artistic appreciation can be observed and marked in time.

To accomplish this, criticism adopts the network's mode of operation. That is, it explains the network in its own terms. It cannot choose radically different terms, or only at the risk of becoming irrelevant to the network—of "academic interest" only. For example, networks of art or literature observe persons as origins of communications; it is persons who are "creative." In sharing this mode of attribution, criticism contributes to the foundational myth of the network: that the source of art, music, and literature is the "gifted artist." This source is obscured as a somewhat mysterious mental wellspring of special and extraordinary sensibilities. This attribution to personhood interrupts the causal chains and is no further decomposed and questioned—within this network, at this time. In this way, the network and its self-observations create blind spots and irreducible elements or building blocks. Networks produce such basic certainties to halt the infinite regresses that result from no mover ever being unmoved himself. Where one stops the movement and chains of causation to attribute a cause to a mover says much about the observer, less about the world.

The difference that makes the difference in observers and observations, then, is the network into which observations of a network are to be fed. If these two networks are the same, or use similar and compatible distinctions, observations are part of the ongoing activities of this network. These are inside observations. If they are different, observations have a stake not in the network they observe, but in the network into which they are being fed. These are outside observations. But keep in mind that there is no absolute "outside," for each outside has its own inside. What matters is not simply the place and position of the observer, but the place and position relative to other places and positions. What matters is relationships between positions, not positions taken by themselves. "Position" refers to a space defined entirely by the relationships among positions.

As we shall see later, what matters also is the observer's "velocity," that is, whether he is part of a more stationary or fast-moving network. To anticipate a bit, stationary and fast observers have different senses of history and time.

A special case of an inside observer is the official observer, who often is near and employed by organizations. Official observers are spokespersons representing their organizations in public and to other organizations. They carry a "mandate." In their capacity as representatives, official observers issue pronouncements and statements that are more or less binding, and hence vaguely general to maintain the organization's discretion and room for maneuver, backtracking, and compromise. Official observers enact the frontstage culture of organizations, which consists of rational myths and rituals that celebrate and praise the organization's accomplishments and contributions to the larger good (Meyer and Rowan 1977). Such public ceremonies are often carefully rehearsed displays of solidarity and common purpose. It is here, when the organization goes on holiday from its daily work, that we find values and virtues in action. These are favorite targets for ironists and insiders, who know how to separate the deceptive glamour of official presentations from the actual backstage realities. Official observations do represent the reality of the organization for most outsiders, however. They are not sheer fictions, but officially binding fictions, which make a huge difference in how outside observers make sense of the organization.

Official observations released by organizations to the public condense, summarize, and simplify their referents or messages for broader public consumption. That smoking "causes" cancer can be found as an obvious fact on cigarette boxes, but the closer you get to where cutting-edge research on cancer is being done, the less certain and more controversial this relationship becomes. At the frontiers of cancer science, it might be considered that smoking increases the probability or risk of cancer, but even if this is the case, and even if this increase could be measured and compared to other related or unrelated risk factors, all this would still say nothing firm about what will happen, as opposed to what is "likely" to happen, in the case of an individual smoker.

One does not have to be a Humean to be skeptical toward "real" causation, to notice that attributions of effects to causes vary widely among observers and depend on the occasions where such causes are given, presented, or believed. These variations are the subject of a comparative sociology of the observer, which remains happily agnostic about "ultimate" or essential causes, except of course its own causes, which are social-structural and very real.

The farther an observer moves from the referent or source of an observation, the more he depends on simplified and condensed "official" observations, those that can be more or less trusted because they appear in the news of more or less "serious" sources. One reads that drugs cause violence, that education causes technological advancement, that eating oatmeal reduces cholesterol, or that drunk driving "causes" accidents. Get closer to an actual accident, however, and any number of other causal forces appear operative as well, such as weather, blindness, traffic, road conditions, and so on. More careful—that is, closer to science—is the statement that intoxication "increases the risk" of accidents, but so do many other things, and "risk" is very difficult to quantify, as is the contribution of this one factor, intoxication, to a measurable increase in that risk.

Intoxication might cause delayed attention spans and longer reaction times but, again, so do a host of other variables, such as age, exhaustion, or interactions between drivers and passengers. Some accidents are caused by bad, not drunk, driving. Even if we did find that, all other things being equal(which they never are), intoxication does increase the probability of accidents, and even if we did find that this increase is, compared with the other variables, significant and strong enough to warrant a policy intervention of some sort—even given all of this, nothing has yet been said about what causes intoxication itself, or whether a certain alcohol concentration in the blood has always the same effect on driving, regardless of variations in persons and bodies.

The closer you get to where science is being made, and the more complexities and uncertainties emerge there, the less straightforward and more ambiguous become the "interventions" or "remedies" considered. Here, where a science is made, "causation" is treated with much more care than is invested by a distant observer, who does not have the time, resources, or credentials to handle much complexity. Distant observers have other things to observe and deal with beyond what happens in one science. Popular expositions are very different from what they report; they omit much more than they include and simplify the rest. There is no other way—no news has ever been reported without selections, that is, bias.

Outsiders' bounded rationality limits their tolerance for uncertainty and complexity, and so they plug into the official simplifications of frontstage organizational observers. What else could they do? In this world, smoking causes cancer, intoxication causes accidents, and the

next President will either fix morality or not. In this more orderly, secured, and comfortable web of illusions and half-truths, one can also
make "informed" decisions that make good sense, such as quitting
smoking, or voting for another political candidate.

The status and visibility of frontstage observers covary with the status
and visibility of their organizations vis-à-vis the other organizations in
the field or set. The higher this status, the more official the pronouncements, up to the point where an organization and its official
observers might claim to speak for the entire set of organizations in
that field. In modern society, this sort of leadership includes being authorized to make official and binding statements to the media. The
media are official observers in their own right, with varying degrees of
officialness and legitimacy.

In contrast, an outside observer cannot do what the organization or
network does, because he operates within the confines of his own network. It is this network, not the one referred to in observations, into
which the observations will be fed. Unlike art criticism, a sociology of
art, for example, feeds its observations into sociology, not art. It is not
art, contributes nothing to art, and cannot be understood as art. The
sociology of art cannot independently distinguish between good and
bad art. Most importantly, an outside observer cannot take for granted
the network's basic inside operations and attributions. The outside observer cannot stop where the network stops, but digs deeper into the
layers and chains of causation. Outside observers do not observe first-
level whats, but second-level hows. They see what cannot be seen from
the inside, decomposing the foundational certainties and invisibilities
without which the observed network could not do what it does. That
which appears obvious and necessary to the network appears improbable, variable, and contingent to its outside observers. There will be ten-
sions between inside and outside observers, because outsiders view a
network as just one of many possibilities. Outside observers cannot
make the premises of the network their own premises; that would be
redundant. Instead, they explain them as social and cultural constructs relative to time, location, and structure.

The sociological observer of art, for example, decomposes "creativity" and "originality," and generally refrains from accepting persons as
the ultimate and irreducible source or origin of art. Now the social
structure of art can come into view, whereas art cannot explain itself as

an outcome of social structure—this would be unartistic and "crude." At the same time, of course, the sociology of art has its own blind spots and inviolate levels, which *it* takes for granted when it analyzes art sociologically. Among other things, it takes for granted the efficacy of "social structure" in bringing about cultural outcomes.

Value-Freedom and Disinterestedness

The distinction between inside and outside observers casts a fresh light on the old and unresolved problems of "value-freedom" and "disinterestedness." Often value-freedom is argued, essentialistically, to be attainable in the hard sciences but not the softer ones, since the latter are irremediably caught up in the realities and struggles they have as their themes. Social science is inextricably involved in class interests, ideological conflicts, and social standpoints in ways that the natural sciences are not. Social scientists are subject to the very same forces they try to understand; they cannot be impartial and unprejudiced since the outcomes of their work are, to some extent, fed back into society. A variation on this essentialist theme is that, even if social science could be value-free, it should not be so, since the betterment of society is one of social science's intrinsic goals.

This argument fails for empirical and conceptual reasons. Conceptually, it fails since no science, whether social or natural, can admit the possibility that a value, say preferring Bourbon to Scotch, does have an influence on its outcomes, or on the ways in which it allocates merit and reputation. Empirically, the argument fails because many natural sciences are as involved in moral and ideological debates as the social sciences. A much discussed recent example is genetic engineering. Instead of drawing a dualistic opposition between the social and natural sciences, we should say simply that the social sciences have, on average, less reputational autonomy than the natural sciences, and so are more subject to moral scrutiny by the public at large. They are less able to separate sharply their internal and external concerns, and "technical" questions from "ideological" ones. By and large, the social sciences have a lot of trouble securing a referential and social niche that is exclusively their own. The result is that values and ideologies may shape their internal workings and outcomes. The longer this happens, the more it seems that value-ladenness is an *intrinsic* property of sciences dealing with the social. It is not that the natural sciences have no values or valorizations, but their advanced professionalism has turned these values into those of the profession itself. When this happens, values turn into "technical" and "cognitive" values; they lose their bearings in the values of society at large.

In its more sophisticated neo-Kantian version, the value-argument suggests that, as part of society, a science, natural or social, constitutes its domain according to the *Wertbeziehungen* prevalent in a culture. Weber ([1904] 1982) believed that the most important such value for the modern West was rationality, and especially instrumental reason. In his incarnation as a neo-Marxist Kant, Habermas (1968a:71–72, 221) thought that these *Wertbeziehungen* were a trinity of universal transcendental "interests" hardwired into the very reproduction of the human species. The natural sciences followed an interest in instrumental control over nature, shared by technocratic social engineering. Cultural studies, in contrast, proceeded hermeneutically to maintain communicative understanding across cultures, periods, and texts. The third major interest of humankind was Critical Theory itself, which helps with global emancipation.

Overcoming essentialism turns the fact / value distinction into an empirical outcome of a science's operation. The separation between facts and values is not written on the face of the world, as if the world itself fell into two classes of entities, facts and values, at all times and for all observers. At any point, "factual" is that which can be decided by the normal methods of a science, while "normative" is that which cannot (yet) be so decided. Another science might do just that, however, and so draw its own fact / value distinctions in different ways, with different items falling on either side. One science's facts might be another's values, and vice versa.

When observers are part of the network they observe, their observations matter to what happens in the network. In fact, their observations are part of what the network is and does. As a result, inside observers have a *stake* in the network; they are not value-free and disinterested when it comes to the difference their observations are supposed to make. It would be absurd to claim that Roger Ebert has no interest in the movies, because his observations matter, even to how well or badly movies do at the box office, let alone standards of cinematic distinction and appreciation.

The outside observer, in contrast, has no direct stake in the network he observes, and his observations are not part of that network. They are not fed into the network that they observe. For example, if the network of music is told that music emerges from social structure, it cannot do much with this information, especially make music with it. Music cannot reward any musician for making great music just because a musicologist discovers that "musician" is not a person, but a constitutive fiction of musicians' networks. The observation that music reflects social structure creates no music, and does not improve any music. A sociological observer might identify social-structural conditions of musical breakthroughs, and recommend creating such structures, but even in the unlikely event that this would actually work, what is considered "creative" in a culture other than its own cannot be decided by sociology, only within the networks that make music or art. This puts any "sociology of creativity" in a difficult position; it cannot itself decide who is creative and not, but it also cannot take for granted the accounts of creativity circulating in the field.

Since outside observations make no, or very little, difference to the network they observe, they can afford to be "neutral" and "disinterested"—in that network. But since their observations must be fed into their *own* networks, the outside observers are not neutral and disinterested in *their* outcomes and operations. The question "Can an observer be disinterested?" is faulty in the way it is posed, for the more adequate question continues: disinterested in what?

No observer can be disinterested in the network into which his observations are to be fed. An observer disinterested in his own network would be a very poor observer indeed. He would be care-less. In a sense, he would not even be "in" his network—"interest" comes from inter-esse, being among or between. The observer is interested in what happens to the network in which his observations are supposed to make a difference. When this network *is* class, or gender, or race, the observer practices propaganda, not science. Whatever else an empirical observer might be interested in, he is, first and foremost, interested in the difference his observations make to the network in which he is an observer, and which makes him the observer that he is. Outside of this network, he is not even an observer, least of all an expert and professional.

To summarize, fact / value distinctions are the outcomes of actual operations in a science, not ontological distinctions between natural kinds of statements. A "value" is whatever is currently undecidable, or taken for granted, by a science. Values appear to be more of a problem in the social sciences not because these sciences are intrinsically or essentially biased and subjective, but because of comparatively low professionalism and reputational autonomy. This makes them more sensitive to larger moral and ideological conflicts. More mature sciences are, first and foremost, interested in themselves. They value their science.

The Myth of "Going Native"

Lynch (1992:239) claims ethnomethodology as an exception, due to its presumed ability to merge levels of observation, as well as inside and outside observers. Lynch believes that Garfinkel and Sacks "place sociology squarely within the ordinary society ethnomethodology studies." But this is squarely impossible, leading to some instructive paradoxes and contradictions that will further illustrate the advantages of second-order constructivism.

First, the social fact is that ethnomethodology is done in academia by and for academics, not ordinary society. The ordinary society I am familiar with, including the ordinary society of scientists, would not, and does not, recognize itself in ethnomethodology. If anything, the ethnomethodological instrumentarium, in its hyperempiricism and -complexity, is further removed from everyday experience than the sociological "mainstream." The intellectual origin of ethnomethodology is not common sense, and not ordinary society, but German phenomenology. To common sense, ethnomethodology sounds strange and unfamiliar, remote as a science. Anyone who has ever struggled with *Studies in Ethnomethodology* should confirm this. For those who have not opened its pages since graduate school, here is a quick fix. A 1988 Garfinkel article in *Sociological Theory* is entitled "Evidence for Locally Produced, Naturally Accountable Phenomena of Order, Logic, Reason, Meaning, Method, etc., in and as of the Essential Quiddity of Immortal Ordinary Society."

The paradox is that descriptions claiming closeness to "lived reality" do not resonate well with that reality. This is not just true for ethnomethodology, but also phenomenology, whose accounts of "elementary perception" cannot be perceived by elementary perception. Instead, elaborate philosophical discourse and nonintuitive descriptions are required to do the job. Hence the arcane terminology of a Husserl, whose analyses of ordinary perception and primary experience are anything but ordinary and primary. Another example is the analytical philosophy of action, which has managed to present even rather simple actions, such as opening a window or lifting one's arm, as incredibly complex and sophisticated behaviors. When one reads these descriptions, they estrange ordinary behaviors instead of "reproducing" or "mirroring" them.

It is difficult to recognize one's common actions or perceptions in the ethnomethodological, phenomenological, or analytical accounts of them. Why this paradox? Because science and ethnomethodology cannot go "radically native" all the way. If they did, they would not come back home to their specialties and intellectual networks. Sooner or later, if one wants to remain an academic or scientist, one has to leave the field, read the literature, write a report, and hope that one's peers, not the natives, will find it interesting and relevant enough to cite and celebrate. As it advances, a science removes itself further and further from the common sense around it. Again, this does not mean that a science has no common sense, but its common sense consists of its own certainties and invisibilities.

A second problem is that if ethnomethodology were indeed "placed squarely in ordinary society," as Lynch thinks it is, what could it add that was not already known to its members? Ethnomethodology either adds something or nothing to ordinary society. If it adds nothing to our understanding, there is no reason to do it. If it adds something, it removes itself, in and through this very process of "adding," from its object. That is, we now have ordinary practice and commonsense accounts in addition to ethnomethodological accounts of them. Another observer, ethnomethodology, has been added. On a third level, one could also do an ethnomethodology of ethnomethodology, which follows.

Garfinkel, Lynch, and Livingston (1981) study an inadvertently tape-recorded episode of discovery in an astronomical observatory. The ethnomethodological observers of this episode are not really part of the science they observe, because they lack credentials, expertise, and equipment. Since this trio has no observatory, it can add nothing *astronomical* to the "ordinary society" of astronomers. They are doing not astronomy but ethnomethodology, which comes to astronomy and astronomers from the outside. Astronomers know nothing about it.

But ethnomethodology can still discover something *about* that science and its practitioners. If what it discovers is something already familiar to the scientists, then it is not really a discovery, but simply repeats what is already known. The result would be banalities, such as "science is human." If ethnomethodology does discover something unknown to the science it studies, however, then it becomes, *nolens volens*, a part of an outside "science" of science. This outside science does not faithfully reproduce its reality, but rather estranges it. That is, it decomposes and rearranges whatever it observes according to some theoretical and methodological instrumentarium. This instrumentarium is not part of the observed object or group. Nor does it "mirror" this object or group. Instead, the ethnomethodological tools and devices have their own philosophical traditions and origins, outside of which they do not exist.

In other words, one cannot have it both ways and operate on two levels of observation simultaneously: one has to choose. One can be on the first level, that of science, do what that science does, and observe what that science observes. This is not what Garfinkel, Lynch, and Livingston do. They are not discovering a pulsar, nor do they assist, in any way, in this discovery. To discover a pulsar, reading Garfinkel is neither required nor helpful. Alternatively, one can observe, on the second level, *how* the scientific observations on the first level are being made. In this case, one is doing sociology (or some other science) of science. But there is no level between, above, or underneath these levels.

For ethnomethodology, the distinction between levels of observation means that it cannot go native all the way. Let us stay with the astronomy example. Going native "all the way down" would amount to letting the tape record the conversations between scientists and then simply distributing that entire tape to whomever wants it, without any transcription and interpretation from the observers. Going radically native adds nothing to ordinary society except yet another "member." This is not what ethnomethodology does. Instead, it brings an outside theoretical and methodological apparatus, formulated by Garfinkel and his disciples, to whatever field it is studying. It is this "outsideness" of a theoretical and methodological apparatus that allows ethno-methodology, or any other social or natural science, to make discoveries. It is this apparatus that makes it possible to reveal, say, distinctive "formal properties of ordinary action" not readily available to ordinary members. This apparatus is in a broader sense "scientific," because one cannot get it from members directly, but only from academics and their academic writings. Without this apparatus, there is nothing to do and nothing to write about.

With the help of this apparatus, ethnomethodology discovers something about its object and addresses the outcomes of that research mainly to other ethnomethodologists, not, to stay with the astronomy example, to the astronomers. Even if the scientists read this work, they would not understand it, would not recognize themselves or their work in it, and would not be able to do their jobs better.

Lynch (1992:248) admits that ethnomethodological descriptions of pulsars as "cultural objects" violate scientists' own, more realist, understandings of what they are dealing with. The scientists think that they have discovered an external physical object, which is taken to be the main cause for its discovery. The ethnomethodologists believe that the scientists have manufactured some "cultural object" in the "local historicity of the night's work."

Now, suppose someone had taped the conversations between Garfinkel, Lynch, and Livingston about how they were to write their story about the taped conversations between their scientists. These third-level observers (let them be behaviorists for the sheer fun of it) could then debunk and deconstruct ethnomethodology's debunkings and deconstructions of scientific practice. The scientists think that they are dealing with independent external objects; the ethnomethodologists think that their scientists are constructing cultural objects, and the third-level behaviorists think that their ethnomethodological subjects have simply been conditioned, through training, to release from their brains ethnomethodological accounts of anything and everything, including pulsars, when in the company of reinforcers, especially other ethnomethodologists. Who is right? That is the wrong question, for matters of truth can effectively—that is, sociologically—be decided only *within* each of these levels.

Each of the three observers assumes an independent reality for their objects. This is first-level observing, or "common sense." At this level, observers see objects as existing apart from accounts of these objects. The scientists do not assume they have constructed a cultural object, and the ethnomethodologists do not claim to only have uttered "indexicality" and "accountable orderliness of practical action" according to conditioned reflexes. The scientists assume that they have discovered something important about the external natural world; the ethnomethodologists assume that they have discovered something important about the external social world of astronomy; the behaviorists assume that they have discovered something important about the behavior of ethnomethodologists.

A Few Pretty Old Rules of Method

Methods are tools to do a job, not emblems of ideological partisanship. A method is useful for some purposes, but not others. For example, when the assignment is to analyze the demographic migration patterns of large numbers of persons, understanding a single person's motives or "situated, lived experience" will not suffice. There are simply too many N's to consider. Conversely, when the idea is to get a close grip on the way of life in a small group, thicker descriptions and narrative are possible.

As will be argued later, method has nothing to do with ontology, as if things social or cultural "called for" and "insisted" on being researched differently from things physical. There is no one method in physics, either, and its methods depend on the job or task at hand, as well as on advances in instrumentation and measurement. The standard "covering law" account of physical explanation (Salmon 1989:12–25) belongs in philosophy, not physics, or belongs to areas in physics with much routinization, closure, and outcome predictability. Conversely, novel or strange physical objects and forces call for different tools and devices.

Likewise, when dealing with persons, many different methods and strategies are available, depending, among other things, on what we want to do with or know about persons, on how many persons we want to know something about, and on how deep or thick we plan our understanding to be. The possibilities range from understanding one action of one person to explaining the behaviors of large populations. Much depends also on the *relation* between observer and referent; a lover resists statistical explanations of his beloved, while a survey researcher aggregates and categorizes. Explaining versus understanding is not coextensive with thing versus person, because both are relations and so follow social, not ontological, structure.

A scientific theory of culture and science approaches its domains in the same way that a science approaches its own domains—scientifically. Since Goethe, who resented it, the procedure of science has often been called "decomposition and recombination," although no specific "method" follows from this procedure. Some historians agree that, among other things, the Scientific Revolution has converted substances and essences into functions and relations. Gillispie (1960:352–373) shows how this happened in classical kinematics and in nineteenth-century thermodynamics and mechanics. The latter two dissolve the substances of caloric and ether into energy—itself not seen as a substance, either, but as a difference or relation between states of a system, or between a system and its environment. The essentialist *vis viva* slowly disappears everywhere, as do many of the formerly primordial or primary properties supposedly inherent in the nature of things. With Einstein, the observer and his frame of reference—free-falling with gravity, or inert without gravity—enter the picture.

Scientists are eminently "deconstructionist"—much more so than postmodernists who invert, submerge, and postpone the hierarchies and orders of texts only. Whatever else science might do, it proceeds by decomposing essences into relations between elements that are what they are only in their variable relationships. No science can just repeat and reproduce the entities populating the worlds of common sense. The elements are not essential building blocks, constant in all possible worlds, but sets or spaces of possibilities that are gradually narrowed down as they become embedded in patterns of interaction between elements and forces. Change the interactions and forces, and you change the elements as well. A constant is a constant only in the network or system within which it is, in fact, being *held* constant, and only until changes in the configurations of forces in the network change the nodes and elements as well. Both variation and constancy, difference and sameness, unity and diversity, are accomplishments and outcomes of the network. They last only until further notice.

Decomposition has no natural end when the ultimate constituents of reality will have been discovered. Rather, ultimate and irreducible components of reality remain so only until further notice, until they have been decomposed and reduced as well. In microphysics, the "fundamental" building blocks of matter have become ever smaller and more evanescent as machinery and instrumentation have advanced. Sciences, and observers generally, differ in precisely how and where they interrupt further decompositions and regresses in the chains of causation and emergence. Constructivism sees causation as a variable construct, depending on what sorts of work different observers are trying to accomplish. The causes of promotions will appear different— for a network theorist modeling vacancy chains, for whoever just got promoted, for his rivals, or for his supervisor. Until further notice, an observer's boundaries are the limits of his current decompositions. Observing stops where it stops, but these are its own limits, not the world's, and they will change together with the advances a culture makes.

Unless a science becomes stagnant, or is destroyed, it will continue to make further advances and innovations, including in its foundations and basic building blocks. At least no present science could rule out this possibility in its own future. In a science, decomposition is halted for pragmatic and technical reasons, not metaphysical or ontological ones. That is, the limits of its decompositions are the limits of its current boundaries, practices, and instrumental possibilities. As these boundaries and technologies change, so will the foundations, building blocks, and premises.

Dramatic improvements or breakthroughs in the capabilities of instruments often lead to novel decompositions; one can now observe that a once irreducible substance or quality is really the composite of yet more basic elements. One can try to decompose society into actions, but might also decompose "action" into its constituents, as in the "unit act" of Parsons. Work is always built on premises that are, for the moment, taken for granted, but this does not exclude changes in these premises at some point in the future, or in another network.

Again, allowing for variation, both qualitative and quantitative, is the key rule of method. We can see what something is, and explain how it behaves, by comparing what happens to the other variables when that something is there or not. Weber's comparative explanations of "historical individuals" proceed in this way. We can also compare what difference it makes when there is a lot of that something, as opposed to a little; some organizations are more bureaucratic than others. Staying with this example, the biggest mistakes to avoid are to fix the essential characteristics of bureaucracy in advance, to assume that all organizations are equally bureaucratic, and to expect that all the parts and divisions of a bureaucracy are equally bureaucratic. In any case, we are looking for the difference that makes the difference in an interacting network of variations.

The most important rule of method is to allow for variation, and to turn essences or natural kinds into dependent variables that covary with other variables. One corollary of this rule is that there are no constants, only variables, or that constants are *held* constant within a network of variables chosen by an observer. A constant remains constant only until further notice, or until it is again allowed to vary and regains its degrees of freedom.

The observer "sociology" observes variations in social structure, not particles or genes. Social structure cannot be decomposed any further within the observer "sociology." Observing with "social structure" is that observer's niche, and distinguishes this observer from other observers operating in different niches and with different distinctions. Again, all sciences halt regresses and decomposition at some point, and where they do so marks an observer's current identity, boundary, and limit. Identities, boundaries, and limits change together with changes in the observer, and also with changes in the relations between observers. Many such changes are driven by advances in instrumentation, because improved techniques and tools might allow a science to decompose further that which it has, until now, accepted as its premises, foundational building blocks, and limits.

Allowing for variation replaces static typologies, and dualistic contrasts between essences, with multiple continua and variable locations along such multiple continua. A critical axis of variation is time, since an observer's location on a continuum changes over time, and since the best predictor for the current state of an observer is its immediately preceding state. The continua are degrees of freedom—that is, anything and everything that might matter sociologically to an outcome or dependent variable. For example, if the dependent outcome is degrees of realism in a culture, there will be a series of corresponding sociological variations in social structure and time to explain variable degrees of realism. One difficulty is that variables work together at the same time to produce an outcome, while the analysis of such variations proceeds one step at a time. Therefore, discussion of single variables proceeds ceteris paribus.

Once natural kinds are gone, everything is a matter of degree, not principle. It is not, for example, realism or constructivism, but different degrees thereof, changing over time and responding to many other dimensions of variation. These might themselves be associated with each other, also to varying degrees. What matters is relations, and variations among them, not kinds, essences, things as such, intrinsic properties, or the like.

Think of society as a web or network in time. There are "involutions" in this network—that is, networks within networks, with higher internal than external connectivity (White 1992:75). Networks have bounded clusters inside them, although again, degrees of boundedness and involution vary together with other variables, and over time. Boundedness generates cultures and subcultures. These are networks among self-similar distinctions from other such networks. An encounter, for example, comes into being when it distinguishes itself from other encounters, and when that distinction is itself distinguished from other distinctions. Then an encounter assumes a distinctive "identity"—for itself and for the surrounding encounters. The encounter becomes bounded by focusing inward, toward itself. It reacts to itself and to its flow in time. When it is over, it dissolves its distinctive identity and merges into the networks around it. This specific encounter, which is also a specific observer of itself, now is no more.

A final basic rule of method is that the variations that can come into view depend on units of analysis and frames of comparison, chosen by a particular observer. There are variations between and within such units, depending on what is being compared to what else. One might, for example, compare modern societies to premodern ones, but this broad frame glosses over the many internal variations within each. The danger in such broad comparisons is essentialism, or setting up a dualistic contrast between societal types, as in Gemeinschaft versus Gesellschaft, status versus contract, rationality versus tradition, and so on. The risk is underplaying the continuities and internal variations that make Gesellschaft more similar to Gemeinschaft than essentialism would suggest.

Now watch what happens when we follow these rules of method in a series of illustrations and examples. It turns out that modern society is not all that modern, after all, but still contains tribes, mechanical solidarity, kinship, superstition, and urban villages. It is not that Gesellschaft "replaced" Gemeinschaft; rather, there remain pockets of tribal solidarity within enlarged cosmopolitan networks, and these tribal or neotribal structures link past and present. It is not that rationality replaced enchantment; rather, enchantment continues in popular superstition, such as belief in the mysterious powers of agency. Likewise, rationality is often little more than rational myth and frontstage appearance. In modernity, science does not supersede religion; rather, there emerge more religions than ever before.

Once society is seen as a network, what matters is variations in networks, not polar and dual opposites between "types" of society. Equally absurd, however, is to argue that "we"—whoever that might be—"have never been modern" (Latour 1993), or that there are *no* differences between, say, twelfth-century Europe and contemporary Europe. It is just that there are no *essential* differences between the "natures" of societies. But there are differences just the same, such as in scale, size, range, and diversity of networks. These are differences in degree, not kind, and allowing for variation both between and within networks makes the search for the "essentially modern," as opposed to the "essentially traditional," vacuous and pointless.

Likewise, it makes some sense to compare science to art or religion, but such coarse-grained comparisons run the risk of essentialism again. Coarse comparisons tend to contrast, for example, essentially "subjective" art to "objective" science, or knowledge based on "evidence" to knowledge based on "faith." Such dualisms hold constant and disregard considerable internal diversity and variation *within* a science, religion, or art. Not all sciences are the same—they do not follow a single method or logic, and a science usually has many different specialties, networks, and subcultures inside of it as well. The same can be expected for an art or religion. When these internal variations are observed, they indicate more continuities and similarities between science, art, or religion than broad comparisons between them make visible, especially when these comparisons are part of essentialist dualisms and contrasts.

Consider some possible variations that are common to science, art, and religion. Not all parts of a science are equally rule-driven or objective. The dramatic breakthroughs occurring at the innovative frontiers of a science are frequently the work of charismatic virtuosos, while routine or normal science is more "objective," in the sense of relying on more rigid protocols and methods. A science that is being formed, that is in its "liminal" stage, has its share of prophets and visionaries, much as a new religion or art does (Turner 1974:79–82). The difference that makes the difference is not scientific method versus religious prophecy, but time-dependent degrees of consolidation, routinization, and closure. "Method" appears when repeatedly successful behaviors trigger outcomes with some measure of uniformity and predictability, regardless of whether this happens in a science, an art, or a religion. Because a network takes time to settle down in its niche, method emerges later, after prophecy, vision, personal knowledge, and the like (Fuchs and Ward 1994).

"Faith" is not essential and restricted to religion, as if there were no faith in science, and as if science were solely based on rational argument and empirical evidence. No science can do without some faith, such as trust in reputation and truth, or faith in materialism. The essential difference between science and art is not that science is by nature cold, impersonal, and without passion. Sometimes a supposedly cold and dispassionate science gets very excited and emotional, as happens in priority and property conflicts (Cozzens 1989). Likewise, some art is not so subjective; when it becomes the official aesthetic of a State or Church, it may be regulated by formal doctrines and official compositional rules. The difference that makes the difference is not in the "nature" of art but, among many other variables, the relation of an art to a state, church, or party.

It is not the nature of religion to disregard evidence from empirical observations. Far from it. To the contrary, the intellectual wing of a religion likely responds and reacts to the observations that a science makes when those observations concern that religion's turf and domain. But the religion likely renormalizes a scientific observation into its own networks and culture. This means that some observation or finding might not have the same status in the networks of religion as it does in the networks of science. The "meaning" of that finding will likely differ accordingly in the two networks. A religion does with it what it can do to maintain its own identity and internal coherence.

The intellectuals of the Church may actually do some science themselves, and vice versa, to see how parts of that science fit into religion. Sometimes, networks of religion and networks of science actually overlap to some extent, and then an essentialist religion-science dualism becomes less plausible and poignant still.

When time enters the equations, it adds yet another dimension of variation that cuts across essentialist dualisms and oppositions. A young science might resemble a young art or religion more than an established and firmly institutionalized science. When they are very young, social movements, whether in science, art, or religion, behave differently from advanced and settled movements, those about to turn into bureaucratic organizations (Mullins 1973:21). In the beginning of a movement, there are more degrees of freedom, and more loose coupling, allowing more prophets to offer their charismatic visions of possible futures. Gradually, as a movement consolidates, the prophets may be replaced by textbooks, authoritative scriptures, classical texts, examinations, and bureaucratic structures.

Take another presumably essentialist conflict, that between "logic" and "rhetoric." Allowing for variation, two equivalent mistakes are to be avoided—that there are no differences at all between them, or that they separate natural kinds of reasoning. Instead, ask what happens when logic and rhetoric are seen as gradations along a continuum, as matters of degree rather than principle.

In the beginning of a culture, there is likely much uncertainty and ambiguity in its terms, concepts, and relations. A culture that is young and unsure of itself produces more rhetoric than logic in its self-observations. There are, as yet, few visible successes and solid accomplishments. Logic takes systematic work and time. Formal and rigorous axiomatization come later, as a culture settles in its niche, draws more solid boundaries around itself, and demarcates itself more firmly from other cultures. As a culture repeatedly feeds the outcomes of its previous accomplishments into further outcomes, these outcomes consolidate into facts that are "logical"—for it, for this culture. The difference that makes the difference is degrees of cultural closure and settlement, correlating with time, not essentially opposite kinds of reasoning. One might capture variation in the formula, Logic = rhetoric + repetition → outcome predictability.

Once variation is allowed *tout court,* both between and within units of analysis, essentialist contrasts between natural kinds, separate in all possible worlds, turn into dependent variables and distinctions of degree. Variations within such units cut across variations between, and render more similarities visible between, presumably essentially separate kinds. Mayr (1997:37) notes that "there is more difference between physics and evolutionary biology . . . than between evolutionary biology and history." A critical rule of method is: Replace static typologies and rigid classifications by continua and gradations along continua, possibly shifting their positions over time as well. Distinctions between, say, science and literature are still possible, but must not be mistaken for dualisms of natural kinds, and should remain aware of variations within both, cutting across and dissolving their essential separateness.

Then one might observe that, overall, the levels of professionalization and reputational autonomy are higher in science than literature (variation between), though some sciences are more self-referentially closed than others (variation within), and a young science is generally less professional than a mature one (variation over time). Some historical sciences, such as alchemy, are as "enchanted" as certain areas of contemporary social theory or cultural anthropology (Schneider 1993:chap. 1). That is, the difference that makes the difference is not between things social versus things natural, but between loose and tight coupling, ceteris paribus. Some social sciences that were once softer are now harder because their entry restrictions have grown more severe—economics is one example (Whitley 1984:181).

A major rule of method that follows from variation is that nothing is, in and of itself, the same or different from something else. Sameness and difference depend on net-work and on the observer's choice of frames for comparison. It is networks and cultures that render something similar or different from something else. An art, for example, establishes similarities and differences in ways different from or similar to those of other observers. When an object is recognized as part of an art, it becomes related and similar to the objects that are already there, in the networks of that art. No such similarity existed before; it is an outcome of net-work, not its independent condition.

Something might look the same as something else—until you get very close. You thought there was a firm boundary around a network—until you move closer to see the boundary dissolve into a shifting horizon, moving together with the velocity of the network. It seemed that science was different from religion, until you observe both in their emerging phase, when they are young, visionary, and charismatic. Art seemed to be essentially subjective and private, until a state or Church monopolizes an art for its own official ideological affirmation. Modernity seemed very rational and bureaucratic, until you discover that inside bureaucracies there are tribes and clans that gossip endlessly about persons, much as happens in a small village. It seemed that the modern metropolis alienated strangers from each other in impersonal monetary transactions, until you zoom in very close, into neighborhoods, and perceive a great amount of ethnic and tribal solidarity. On television, inner-city gangs appear as threats to social order and cohesion; move closer, and gangs esteem honor as much as did medieval knights preparing for a crusade.

Observe the observer. For doctors and lawyers, medicine and law are obviously different, but sociologically, they are both professions and, as such, similar in some ways. Move closer to a profession, and its apparent unity is counteracted by variations within, such as those between high- and low-status professionals. Compare now low-status professionals across different professions, and you might observe more similarity among them than among, say, general family physicians and specialist medical researchers in university hospitals. The difference that makes the difference to status in a profession, whether medicine or science, is closeness and involvement in areas of high uncertainty and unknown possible futures.

Observe scientific professions up close, and see that not all areas or subcultures that deal with things social are equally soft, hermeneutic, or interpretive, as the double hermeneutic or Two Cultures argument would suggest. For example, quantitative survey and experimental small-group research appear more methodical and systematic than contemporary social theory, where discourse reigns. Why should this be? Maybe because the former areas of research have comparatively concentrated hardware and highly standardized raw materials, which allow them to be run more as normal sciences, or bureaucracies. Move closer even, and variations appear even within social theory. Rational choice strikes many as more cumulative and mature than ethnomethodology, perhaps because ethnomethodology overlaps mostly with dead German phenomenologists, whereas rational choice is an import of economics, which has high prestige and a Nobel prize.

When you allow for variation, some literature begins to resemble routine and hardened science when it is swallowed by the state and administered by a central cultural bureaucracy (socialist realism). By itself, routinization and normalization do not distinguish science from literature in all possible worlds. Continua and gradations matter, together with changes in the position along a continuum over time. You thought the essential difference between science and philosophy was that philosophy was intrinsically divisive, multiparadigmatic, or nonexact. But then, when the means of mental production are monopolized by the Church to maintain sacred traditions, some philosophy sometimes proceeds very dogmatically and consensually (high scholasticism). By itself, consensus does not distinguish literature from science, since controversial and innovative science has very little consensus as well (Cole 1992:135). Mass-produced movies with many sequels differ, in their cultural phenomenology, from movies made by independent studios for an avant-garde audience of connoisseurs.

The pattern of professional stratification varies between medical science and law, because status in law is more client-driven, decreasing the reputational autonomy of its reward system (Flood 1991). Medical specialists enjoy more prestige than general doctors for reasons similar to status differences between innovative and normal science. Generally, higher discretion goes to those dealing with areas of critical uncertainty and many possible futures. Regardless of any overall differences between science and art, avant-garde artists and scientists doing cutting-edge research are both core groups of charismatic virtuosos who claim personal knowledge, the "hunches" of a "smell" and "nose," to escape the bureaucratic or methodological accountability of their skills. In contrast, rank-and-file workers, in both science and art, are more constrained by bureaucracy, whether they work in colleges or corporations.

Is science always cold and impersonal, by its very nature? Not really. A science heats up its networks for informational gossip very quickly— for example, when news breaks about an impending major discovery. Such networks are structurally and behaviorally similar to those among reporters following critical leads, investment brokers plugging into rumors about corporate takeovers, or jazz musicians experimenting with a new improvisational technique (Fuchs 1995).

Overcoming essentialism, and allowing for variation both between and within units for comparisons, compares that which otherwise, without variation, remains essential, constant, and necessary in all possible worlds. We can now build a coherent and explanatory theory of variations between and within cultures. What is more, we can do so with the same sociological variables and do not need theories of each distinct area of culture. This is the sign of a strong theory: it decomposes natural kinds and essences, rearranging the parts on higher levels of generality with broader explanatory range. Strong theories economize on explanation costs. All this becomes possible once variation is allowed for, essentialism is overcome, and the right frames of comparison are found.

The Classics Revisited, Briefly

Some of the theoretical tools for a sociological theory of culture come from the classics. It is not unfair to say that many leading theorists do not have an actual theory about anything. A great deal of social theory is foundational social philosophy. Alternatively, theory amounts to interpretive exegesis of classical texts. These texts are compared to other texts, and soon reality itself becomes a text while the texts become unreal.

As far as theory and explanation are concerned, "cultural studies" and "cultural sociology" do not fare better. There are some exceptions, such as the Production of Culture approach (Peterson 1994), Becker's (1982) sociology of art worlds, DiMaggio's (1987) research on aesthetic stratification and classification, Schneider's (1993) theory of cultural enchantment, Crane's (1987) network studies of avant-gardes, Berger's (1995) work on ideological rationalization, and Collins's (1998) comparative studies of creativity. Remarkably, these authors are all veteran sociologists, not specialists in cultural studies.

Against the grain of interpretive exegesis and cultural studies, explanatory theory approaches the classics in systematic, not historical, ways. From Marx, I take the idea that variations in the material means of cultural production correspond to variations in cultural forms. It matters to culture whether the means of mental production are expensive and concentrated, such as accelerators and organizational monopolies, or whether they are cheaper and more widely dispersed, such as pencil and paper. Mannheim ([1928] 1971), Peterson and Berger (1975), and Collins (1998) show that, in ideology, popular music, and philosophy, respectively, rates of cultural innovation increase when the monopolies that produce culture break up to allow for some degree of competition. The relationship between organizational structures and innovation appears to be curvilinear; stagnation occurs in both monopolistic and highly fragmented markets. Organizational fragmentation also fragments the attention space, resulting in loosely coupled conversational anarchies with no common focus. In contrast, innovation prospers when small numbers of cultural producers compete within a focused attention space.

Material means also matter because new scientific instruments are discovery-generating devices (Price 1979:79). A culture is also a network among instruments, tools, and devices, not just "theories." Over time, such networks yield cohorts and generations of instruments. Stepwise improvements in instrumentation are a backbone of gradual cumulative advances. Breakthroughs in instrumentation open up opportunities for discovery. The expansion of a science or specialty into new territory is often driven by the export of its instruments, tools, and techniques. In big sciences requiring a lot of expensive and sophisticated hardware, a major part of the work is securing new instruments, linking them together in complex chains and networks, and tinkering with them to detect more direct and straightforward traces of novel phenomena. Such organizations become centers anchoring extensive international networks of cooperation and competition.

In the *German Ideology,* Marx and Engels ([1932] 1972:159) also advance a promising argument about the "relative autonomy" of a culture. Their point is that an idea begins to think itself separate from matter when there appear experts in ideas, who achieve a measure of independence from the rest of society. A culture can no longer be explained as a simple echo or reflection of society when it becomes, to some extent, self-referential and inwardly focused, generating its own puzzles, tools, and solutions. As this happens, a culture produces its own history, self-observations, and modes of causation. Then it can no longer be understood as reflecting, say, economics, class, or politics. Rather, a self-organizing culture decides what matters to it, how it measures and distributes reputation, and how it explains its internal workings. Such cultures become observers, and self-observers, in their own right, and any "explanation" of culture should acknowledge this operational independence.

Weber ([1922] 1980) and Bourdieu (1984:171) suggest some elements of a theory of stratified reputational class cultures, with different amounts and forms of capital. In science, for example, class cultures exist both within and between specialties and their organizations. Internally, specialties are networks divided into highly visible and elitist cores, and more obscure peripheries (Collins 1998:42–46). Externally, a specialty occupies, until further notice, a position within the overall status array of specialties. Reputational class cultures emerge from a variety of status groupings, including position within an organization that pays and employs persons, position of that organization vis-à-vis the organizations in its field or set, location in the core or margins of a specialty, and location or rank of that specialty in relation to other specialties.

The resulting strata of reputations are astonishingly consistent and coherent over time as measured by accumulating advantages and disadvantages (Merton 1973a:457–458, 1988). In a science, much of mobility is sponsored through generations of teachers and students. To a large extent, sciences are still organized as crafts—another argument against their "essential modernity." Stratification relates to how social movements across academic labor markets yield certain cultural outcomes, such as reductionism, cross-fertilization, and interdisciplinary hybrids among specialties and subcultures (Spear 1999). On a micro level, stratification focuses the flow of attention upward, toward that which is being done by the most visible reputations. High reputations confer legitimacy to the work that is being done where these reputations carry weight and influence.

One special and privileged cultural property is closeness to innovation, which separates small elites at the forefront of a culture from more routine and "integrated" practitioners. Becker (1982) has traced this division in art. Innovation, and closeness to where it happens, are the most coveted possessions. Discretion, and the respect or admiration that reputational class cultures draw, covary with the uncertainty of work and the unpredictability of its outcomes. Both discretion and uncertainty shift all the time, as some uncertainties are transformed into routines and new uncertainties emerge with new lines of work.

Durkheim and the neo-Durkheimians (Douglas 1966, 1970; Bloor 1983) link variations in the social structures of such class cultures to variations in cognitive styles. The critical variables are those shaping the texture and connectivity of networks. All other things being equal, isolated groups with high social density and strong moral commitments to tradition tend to reify their sacred cultural tokens in totems and taboos. They do not allow for much internal diversity and dissent. Lacking contact with alternatives, the group's culture acquires logical and moral necessity, mapped onto the very fabric of the world itself. The group's way of life seems to realize the natural order of things.

Such groups have facts and universals, true in all possible worlds. The core cultural possessions are carefully protected and guarded against decay and dissent. Since the important truths are already known, innovators are prosecuted as dangerous heretics straying from the righteous path.

As coupling loosens, density declines, and outside contacts increase, more contingency and alternative possibilities flow into the world. The group increases its tolerance for deviance and dissent. Some nonconformity is rewarded as innovation. Some facts become ambiguous, some universals turn out to be historical individuals, and some moral certainties become less sure of themselves. Criticism emerges and no longer indicates moral failure and irresponsibility. The future becomes more uncertain, not just an extension of the good traditions. Instead, the open future promises more innovations and discoveries; it is a future that needs to be made, and might be made in different ways. More cosmopolitan and decentralized networks sustain more pluralism.

Under certain conditions, loose coupling might lead to decoupling, or fragmentation of communication and interaction. Self-sustaining subcultures emerge, with few or no overlaps. The group's attention space divides into multiple perspectives, whose incommensurability increases with decreasing exchange frequency and density across the borders and boundaries. Contingency turns into arbitrariness, the historical sense into relativism, and each perspective expresses only the idiosyncratic standpoint from which it emerges. Criticism exaggerates into global and foundational skepticism.

The Durkheimian insight is that the first group condition produces realism about facts and universals. The second favors pragmatic innovation and discovery, while the third one leads to conversational and perspectival relativism. Keep in mind that, as usual, there are other variables affecting these outcomes as well, to be discussed in due course. Larger networks might also contain all three structures in different locations. There are also transitions between conditions and phases, depending on time and overall connectivity in the network. Significantly, these conditions and phases are not ideal types, but malleable situations along a variable continuum.

The Durkheimian variables help explain, for example, why some groups fear Kuhnian anomalies, while others celebrate them as a unique opportunity for discovery. Still others, prominently conversational and perspectival hermeneutics, have a hard time distinguishing discoveries and advances from fads and fashions. We expect rigid and exclusive cultural classifications and grids to emerge when density and isolation are high. In contrast, boundaries become more permeable as a network changes in the direction of greater cosmopolitanism. Then, sacredness loses some of its ritual and moral intensity, though it by no means disappears. Some networks change faster than others, accelerating the rate of cultural turnovers.

Durkheim's theory of religion includes a sociological theory of profane / sacred distinctions, even in science; this is another surprise, because science is traditionally seen as the major force of cultural rationalization and occidental disenchantment. The code itself, truth and objectivity, is "sacred," protected by taboos against trespasses and intrusions from the profane. Generations of analytical philosophers have designed elaborate schemas to demarcate science from the rest of life. Much philosophy of science is really a branch of moral philosophy, celebrating a special and unique "ethos" and freedom of science from outside constraints and forces. Violations of the sacred code, intentional misconduct, are punished by ostracism from the tribe (Fuchs and Westervelt 1996).

Mannheim ([1933] 1956:101–139) and Scheler (1924:55–87) add that groups of cultural workers differ in their organizational affiliations. In Scheler's typology, it matters to culture whether it is organized as a bureaucratic and hierarchical church dispensing religious salvation according to official procedures, as a cosmopolitan philosophical academy sustaining a metaphysical "school" around a charismatic leader, or as a corporate profession of employed academic specialists. The intellectuals of a church are closely tied to authoritative traditions in need of preservation and purification. Metaphysical schools typically produce grand and holistic cosmological syntheses covering the heavens, Earth, and everything between and beneath. Metaphysics strives for timeless unity and complete closure, while the many modern sciences either no longer converge on any substantive and final grand cosmology, or make any such convergence local and temporary. The charismatic leader of metaphysics is not a researcher, and not just a teacher, but the edifying moral exemplar and anchor of a shared form of life.

Intellectuals closer to the state and its central bureaucracies enforce stricter canons of political rules and methods than do more self-contained and "detached" cultural workers. Groups of culture workers wrapped tightly around the formal structure of examinations, grades, diplomas, and lectures to novices have more localistic networks and redundant ties to an educational bureaucracy. Theirs is a normal or official culture with known outcomes and procedures. In contrast, more cosmopolitan networks with less redundant ties, and more structural holes, seize discoveries and breakthroughs as their unique cultural capital.

Networks and Systems

The contributions of the classics, and of the explanatory work that builds upon them, can be integrated into a theory of networks and systems. Network and systems theories are on the cutting edge of an emerging synthesis across the old-fashioned natural / social divide. Systems theory has one of its roots in constructivist neuroscience and biological self-organization; network models range from neural nets to kinship and world systems, crossing the great divide into neuroscience and the "tensegrity" of biological structures (Ingber 1998).

I see the most important commonality in systems and network theories as antihumanism—bidding farewell to the agency framework and its derivatives, such as intentionality, the unit act, and rational choice. These instead turn into variable attributions or outcomes of social structure. This means dropping "person," "individual," and "actor" as foundational constructs. It is not that persons and actors were somehow "unreal" or "dead," as some postism thinks (Rosenau 1992:42–52). Far from it, because persons and actors remain prominent devices for making sense of social outcomes, such as blaming the responsible parties, distributing rewards, or acknowledging intellectual property. But neither systems nor networks should use the agency paradigm to do their own explaining.

Instead, systems and network theories start with social emergence and explain persons and actors as *constructs* that some social structures produce to do certain kinds of cultural work. This move turns persons into dependent variables and outcomes, not sources or origins, of society. The result is replacement of agency metaphysics by empirical science. Agency and intentionality are first-order constructs, used to account for outcomes and distributing responsibility in some commonsense situations, such as when stories about persons are told to teach or preserve a moral lesson. Agency happens, or is made to happen, in the natural attitude, the lifeworld, and everyday experience.

On a second level, the sociological observer observes these observers as dependent variables and contingent outcomes of social structure. "Person" is a variable construct of variable observers, not a natural kind, essence, or constant, and not an origin or source of all things social.

System theory's constructivism is much more explicit, elaborate, and deep than it is in networks. Network theory does not occur in its own theory of networks, while systems theory does. In this lies its constructivist radicalness. Systems theory contains an account of itself as part of a social system, science (Luhmann 1997:1128–1142). Network theory is less reflexive; it does not include itself in itself as a construct of certain intellectual and organizational networks. If it did include itself, network theory would appear as an event, or chain of events, within a social network, housed in a specialty, anchored in organizations, and extending through time and space through a generational network.

A second commonality to systems and networks is antiessentialism, or relationalism. In systems theory, the central relational concept is communication; in network theory, it is links or connections between nodes. Both communication and links are constructed as emergent social realities; they are not further reducible, at least not in, or by, sociology. In systems theory, communication is the unity of sending, transmitting, and interpreting information by more than one observer. Nothing becomes socially real or consequential unless it is observed and communicated by any of the many social observers. In fact, who is an observer in society, as well as his status, are outcomes of communication as well.

Insofar as communications use similar distinctions to process thematically related information, a "system" emerges, with its own inside

/ outside distinctions. These distinctions are variable and change together with the operations of a system; they cannot be fixed in advance, or once and for all. As soon as a system of communications gets going, these communications are coupled through recursive networks, such as a scientific specialty or an interaction episode. In this way, systems build up their own internal reality and complexity. It is communications, not persons, that make communications fit into the network of related communications, where they are expected to make a difference. Most of them do not make much of a difference. When they do, coupling occurs, and recursiveness.

A recursive network of communications is internally closed, because it cannot go outside of its own operations. Communication cannot see, smell, or taste anything; for this, it depends on bodies. But that which bodies perceive and experience cannot directly, "as is," enter communication either. Instead, communication "seizes" and directs the perceptions it needs to continue its ongoing operations.

Relationalism in network theory treats the nodes in the network as fully derivative from their connectivity. What a node is and what it does do not follow from any intrinsic properties or categorical characteristics, but from its location, position, and temporality in the network. The best analogy to network emergence is an electric circuit. Here the electricity is not "in" any component of the circuit, much as the behavior of a network is not "in" any of its nodes, say the actions of persons. Nodes are selectively activated by their connections, much as a cell is selectively activated into a neuron or blood cell. Nodes are not connected in their entirety or "totality"; rather, the connection constructs a specific *version* of a node, and it does this according to its own, not the node's, specifications. In the special case of the nodes that happen to be persons, these are not connected in their full and unique biographical wholeness.

A node that travels to another network will be activated by its new surroundings in ways different from before. It will not be the same node. The criteria for similarity and dissimilarity are network-dependent, too, so that no two things are similar or dissimilar in and of themselves, or in all possible worlds, for all possible observers. It is observers in recursive networks, not the world, that make things similar or dissimilar.

As opposed to systems theory, network theory can point to an impressive array of empirical corroborations and applications (Wellman and Berkowitz 1988). The basic framework has proved useful in predicting mobility paths and promotions, political participation, state formations and breakdowns, or the distribution of market opportunities. There are networks of kinship and scientific reputations. Networks are where tribal kinship and the modern metropolis come together. Fleck ([1935] 1979:83–84, 94–95) and Latour (1988:25, 42) use networks to explain the emergence of stable facts. Networks are the building blocks of social structure; they link not only people in local cliques and clusters of intimate relationships, but also organizations and firms in "embedded" social markets (Granovetter 1985). Networks link groups within and between organizations and states. States themselves are the intersections where multiple networks among organizations overlap to become observed as "politics" (Laumann and Knoke 1987:380–381).

Networks are good where systems are weak, that is, in areas of explanatory generalizations with empirical content. Systems theory tends to get bogged down in dialectical subtleties, which might stem from its formal, though not material, family resemblance to the *Subjektphilosophie* of Fichte. Systems theory transforms everything into dependent variables for an observer, including "action" and "structure," but network theory is better at actually explaining variations among them.

To be sure, network theory is not without its own problems. One problem is not realizing its power. The main reason for this failure appears to be that networks are frequently equated with social networks among persons. But this is only one special case, and never are persons, in their full biographical totality, linked to other such persons. It would be more accurate to say that networks link encounters between persons; Randall Collins's (1988:chap. 6) theory of interaction ritual chains moves in this direction. Relationally speaking, networks do not "consist" of persons, and the actions of persons do not aggregate to produce the network's outcomes.

Worse than person is the essentialist assumption, made in much network exchange theory (Cook 1987), that the persons in networks act "rationally." Network models should start not with persons and their rational agency, but with the emergent behavior of a network, and then approach "rationality" as an occasioned mode of network sensemaking and operation. The challenge in network analysis is to discover some fundamental properties and regularities of networks, regardless of whether they occur in natural or social life, are small or large, or consist of cells, people, statements, instruments, or organizations.

Some Elements of a Working Epistemology

Constructivism

There is a large variety of constructivisms in fields as diverse as biological and cybernetic epistemology, autopoiesis and self-reference, sociological interactionism and phenomenology, transcendental idealism, and science / technology studies (Knorr-Cetina 1999). What they hold in common is that culture must somehow be constructed, or does not come about at all. Some constructivisms go a step further and insist that whatever exists exists for an observer, who is himself a construct of some kind. Second-order constructivism emerges when that observer can also be observed, so that constructivism is itself constructed.

One obstacle to more widespread acceptance of constructivism is its equation with referential inadequacy. But to say that something is constructed, or exists for an observer, is *not* paramount to saying that it does not really exist, or is somehow less real, objective, and true. Take social institutions. That they are constructed does not make them less real; to the contrary, institutions appear solid and external, especially when they have been around for some time. Likewise, to say that particles are constructs of particle physics says nothing about their "real" existence or correspondence. Constructivism does not debunk physicists' belief that particles are real. That markets and states are constructed does not mean they do not exist, either.

Constructivism emerges with classical sociology. I see classical sociology converging on a constructivism that is sensitive to variations in constructs. Some constructs are weaker than others; the weaker constructs are more visible as constructs, whereas stronger constructs acquire a stability that suggests realism. Sociology is constructivism about science and culture. One of the earliest writers to extend constructivism to science was Fleck ([1935] 1979), whose epistemology is thoroughly sociological and who, unlike young Mannheim and Durkheim, did not lose his sociological nerve when explaining scientific knowledge.

Cultures are networks that construct themselves out of net-work.

Not all constructions, however, are constructiv*ist*, because constructions vary in their stability. Very solid and established constructs appear altogether unconstructed; they are mapped onto reality itself. Expect to find much realism, universalism, and transcendence here. But even coherence is local and temporary, not total or holistic, as some neopragmatists say.

Pragmatism

The valuable contribution of the older pragmatism was to put epistemology back into practice, out of the hands of self-appointed philosophical guardians of rationality. The early pragmatists realized that there were no properly "philosophical" problems, and no properly "philosophical" methods, apart from empirical problems and methods. Pragmatism is not so much a philosophy as a transformation of philosophy into a science—experimental psychology, in this case. Likewise, the experimental neopragmatism of a Hacking (1983) or Galison (1987) stays close to the equipment and apparatus. These scholars emphasize that doing science is much more than deducing predictions from bodies of theory. Doing science is much like practicing a craft; the skills necessary to separate order from noise come not from textbooks and theories, but from socialization into a practice, handed down through generational ties between masters and apprentices. The culture and practice of science is not homogeneous and linear; rather, it resembles a patchwork or tapestry woven from many disparate strands, without a unifying logic or method.

Pragmatism is opposed to epistemology as such. A science does not do its actual work by following procedures, although codifications of method do tend to surface on some frontstage occasions. When it comes to method, pragmatists allow for opportunism and flexibility, acknowledging the empirical diversity of the many methods in different sciences. Some prominent liberal, bourgeois, and postmodern neopragmatists ironize truth (Rorty 1989), but this irony belongs to very remote and distant second-order observations, not where science is actually being made.

Putting epistemology back into practice, pragmatism highlights the adaptations in methods that follow scientific work through trials and errors. A common misunderstanding of pragmatism likens truth to success in instrumental or technological applications: Truth is whatever "works." But the pragmatic "working" is the working of a network, not some technical device, though this may be part of the network. Pragmatism does relate truth to process and outcome, but these are the processes and outcomes of a network itself. Nothing guarantees that such outcomes will lead to a technically useful device. Even networks without technical applications "work"; they produce outcomes, and explanations for these outcomes, as part of their truth stories.

Truth happens in the network, not in the world at large, although the network is part of the world as well. Truth is the internal accomplishment of such a network, not external correspondence, although, as we have seen, some stable constructions are mapped onto the fabric of the world in an act of ontological externalization. The contribution of pragmatism is to take truth away from philosophy and put it back into science.

Positivism

I see positivism culminating in the principle that there is nothing nonempirical or transcendental. There is nothing absolute, universal, or foundational. Better, any universality, including truth, is one of variable degree and range. If it were complete and final, it could not even be observed, because it would be the perfect a priori. Once an a priori becomes visible as an a priori, it is no longer a true a priori. For then it is being distinguished from non–a prioris, from other a prioris, and from contingencies. In this process, the a priori gradually loses its special force and exemption from revision.

In the "history of Western metaphysics"—if there is such a thing— this process marks the transition from Catholic Realism, to Kant, Durkheim, and the sociology of knowledge. Durkheim sociologizes transcendence and pulls it from the lofty skies of idealism down to society. Universality does not descend from above into the heads of philosophers. It does not exist by itself. It must be accomplished by starting small and locally, it reaches only as far as it does, and it acquires binding status only gradually, if at all. Some universals expand, some shrink, and some universals that were not so universal to begin with disappear altogether, such as classical Greek civilization, the Roman Empire, and medieval Catholicism. At least sociology has good network theory reasons for this claim, reasons that are themselves the outcome of a more or less local network.

In positivism, there are no natural kinds, true essences, or final causes. Whatever exists does so not because of its inherent nature or intrinsic properties, but because of variable relations and forces. What things do reveals nothing about their essential being or destiny, but much about the variable forces and interactions to which these things are subject. Accounts of these forces are themselves empirical; they either exist or not. This is where positivism becomes naturalist. Something is actually observed and fed, via communication, into a science to make a difference there. That science will decide whether such communications are viable or not. Such decisions are themselves structured by the operation of the code, which demands, at a minimum, that good reasons and evidence are given for claims and counterclaims.

If there are no natural kinds and essences, science itself is not a natural kind, either, but a historical and empirical reality. Positivism's mistake was to grant science natural-kind status in the "unity of science" movement. When it comes, reflexively, to science, constructivism fares better than positivism. Constructivism goes beyond positivism; it is no longer an "epistemology" that opposes realism for philosophical reasons, but explains both itself and realism as the behavior and outcome of culture. Positivism opposes realism, but does not explain it.

To explain science scientifically as the behavior of an actual network is "naturalism." Naturalism prefers that science be explained scientifically, not philosophically. Unlike physicalism, naturalism allows the possibility that many sciences—sociology, psychology, anthropology, and so on—contribute to explaining science, not just physics. In fact, physics may be least prepared to do so, because there is no current physics that explains itself as the result of physical forces.

Naturalism is a metaphysics or program, not a science. One can be for or against it, even offer reasons in support of one's position, but I do not see how this metaphysics could be justified naturalistically or scientifically. One can do a science, and then there are certain networks and their constraints already in place. But there are many other things one might do instead.

CHAPTER 2

How to Sociologize with a Hammer

Philosophy has made little, if any, progress in resolving its foundational enigmas. The reason for this is not that philosophical problems are naturally or essentially perennial in some deep and mysterious way; rather, such perennialism is an outcome of continuing lack of success. A problem turns perennial, seemingly tied to the human condition itself, if it does not go away; it does not persist because it is fundamentally perplexing and universal.

Nietzsche and Wittgenstein do not solve, but dis-solve, philosophical mysteries. They do not bring philosophical puzzles closer to a solution, but break them apart. Then there is nothing much left for philosophy to do except exegesis, commentary, criticism, or edification. A *systematic* philosophy, however, one that explains something, cannot really ignore the various sciences in its domain, at least not anymore. It senses this and calls itself "naturalism," but naturalism is ideological advocacy of science, not a particular science. Some philosophy turns into sociology, or some other social science, and discovers history and contingency. When history and contingency are allowed, and when variations matter, no "genuinely philosophical problems" are left. Once variations arrive, there is little left to do but describe and explain them.

The Crisis of Representation

Some postmodernist theory claims that Culture, with a capital C, suffers from a general crisis of representation (Ward 1996:chap. 2).

About truth there seems to be no truth. There are many conflicting accounts of what truth is, how it can be secured, for which cultural items it might be claimed, and so on (Schmitt 1995; Skirbekk 1980). Philosophical notions related to truth, such as objectivity, progress, or rationality, have become more controversial as well (Forman 1995).

The "Science Wars" have recently energized and polarized the debate on truth (Fuchs 1996). At issue is, roughly, whether science captures the truth about the world, or whether science and truth are local, historical, social, and cultural. In one camp one finds "realists" of various shades; the opposite camp is constructivist, sometimes also relativist and antifoundationalist. Polarization has done much to simplify the opposition between constructivism and realism; there are really many shades of each, and all sorts of positions on truth between the extremes. Such subtleties, however, tend to get buried when polarized ideological conflict drives the camps into more homogeneity. By and large, the realists are said to believe in the ability of Science—note the singular—to discover the external and objective world as it really is and make cumulative progress toward this goal. In contrast, "constructivists" or "skeptics" are those who think science is a local and temporal construct, one culture among others, without any special "privileges."

Where does this "crisis of representation" strike? No hard or mature science is experiencing it. A mature science must be told from the outside that it has no foundations, method, or truth; it does not arrive at such conclusions on its own. To be sure, a science might be in a "crisis" of some sort, but it is not likely that such a crisis is triggered by philosophical problems and epistemological critique. A science is in real, not philosophical, trouble when its resource base dries up, when it is being invaded and colonized by another science, when it is being destroyed from outside, or when it runs out of new discoveries to make. These crises are not remedied by philosophical means.

There is a lot more to a science than representations, that is, theories and statements. A big part of a science is its material means, including instruments, detection devices, experimental apparatus, data-processing and imaging devices, and so on. It is hard to see how the hardware could undergo a philosophical crisis. Instruments may become outdated, but this is reason to obtain instruments with higher powers of resolution, not cause for philosophical worries. There will be anomalies and holes in theories, but these are seized as opportunities for further improvement and discovery, not taken as warrants for global skepticism about truth.

Skepticism does not mix well with grant applications, multiple choice exams, frontstage justifications, celebrations of past accomplishments, or promises of great discoveries to be made in the near future, as soon as more money is given. Skepticism is more suited to the remote and ironic observer, located in "idle" language games that do not get much actual work done, in the sense of normal and steady puzzle solving.

The "crisis of representation" affects primarily fragmented and conversational fields with very loose coupling, not much hardware, and little interactive overlap (Weimann 1996:8–9, 29). This is where postmodernism is concentrated (Collins and Waller 1994). Many areas of social theory and literary criticism are skepticist and antifoundationalist strongholds as well. Here the main mode of intellectual production is exegesis, commentary, anecdote, and storytelling. A very popular genre now is the anecdotal autobiographical narrative.

Fragmented networks with little coherence tend to be very constructivist, attributing their outcomes to the many independent and discretionary observers inside of them, not to their world or niche in the world. Semantics swallows reference. Loose coupling is conducive to relativism and standpoint epistemologies, especially when outside social movements invade an academic profession's attention space to push their own distinctions to the fore.

From inside fragmented conversational fields, the crisis of representation is generalized into a global "postmodern" condition of culture (Lyotard 1984). But there is no "general culture" that could experience a "general crisis," and if there were, it would not be a genuinely philosophical crisis, and could not be overcome by means of philosophical argument. A local crisis can become more general, to be sure, maybe even revolutionary, but this happens rather infrequently; for example, due to multiple and interacting failures in social and cultural networks (Perrow 1984). There is no sign of an impending global crisis in science and culture.

Not all is well in "traditional" philosophy, either. Both postmodernism and the "tradition" are trapped in constants. They both do not allow for variation—science either corresponds to reality or not; it either has a method or not; it makes cumulative progress or not; it either has foundations or not; and so on. Instead, a more tractable and empirical puzzle is when do such outcomes obtain, and why do they occur to varying degrees. Then essentialist opposites turn into variable positions along a continuum.

Accept that "truth" is the outcome of a network that cares about truth. Sociologically, from the perspective of second-level observing, the truth of a science is its truth, not the truth of science as such. A science has only the foundations it builds for itself, and it has those until further notice, until it changes these foundations. A science can expand its truth and foundations, but this requires extension of its networks, and does not happen by itself, or as a result of philosophical analysis. Conversational and fragmented textual fields happen to rest on no, or very shaky, foundations, but this is an argument not against foundations, or against method, but for a sociology of foundations that explains them, or their absence, as a result of variable network couplings and configurations. In this approach, antifoundationalism and skepticism signal a local fragmentation in social solidarity within "weak" cultures, not a global and philosophical crisis of representation.

The alternative between secure foundations and arbitrary contingency should be replaced by a continuum of various degrees of closure and institutionalization. When this is done, expect some cultures to behave *as if* they were built on secure and universal foundations. Some cultures are so loosely coupled and diversified that they doubt the very possibility of foundations. But this is *their* problem, not the problem of culture in general. Foundationalism covaries with differences in social structure and culture. How this happens is the sociological problem.

Underdetermination and Theory-Ladenness

The Duhem / Quine thesis of underdetermination (Duhem [1906]91:150–158, 183–188; Quine 1964:42–43) paved part of the intellectual road for the sociology of scientific knowledge, and is frequently cited as a strong warrant against realism (Knorr-Cetina and Mulkay 1983:5). Theories—or, more accurately, choices between theories—are held to be underdetermined by the available evidence when that evidence is compatible with different interpretations. Reality is never strong and clear enough to force science into but one true representation. The result is "interpretive flexibility," one of the favorite themes in the more idealist and textual wings of science studies (Mulkay 1985). There is a "looseness of fit" between the word and the world. There are always many alternative and viable responses to surprises, anomalies, or contradictions. What happens when an anomaly challenges a theoretical structure is not decided by that anomaly itself, but by the behavior of the theoretical structure, which includes social processes and network dynamics.

So far, so good. The trouble starts when underdetermination is seen *philosophically*, that is, as a constant and universal problem for all of science, as warrant for a general skepticism, or when underdetermination is exaggerated into undetermination. Dietrich (1993) raises two important questions about underdetermination. First, it is not an exclusively epistemic problem, but occurs in many decisions, such as economic choices, which are underdetermined by their important parameters as well. This observation is helpful, since underdetermination can now be compared across a variety of settings and contexts in which decisions are made. Such comparisons help turn underdetermination into a dependent variable. Expect varying degrees of underdetermination, correlating with the empirical constraints working in a decision situation.

One example comes from decisions in organizations. Organizational neo-institutionalism questions that goals, actions, information, and outcomes usually have a clear causal order, or combine into a preferred rule or algorithm for deciding (March and Olsen 1984). Much information is never used, goals are ambiguous and controversial, actions lead to unexpected outcomes. Information may be open to multiple readings. Occasionally the reasons for an action are not its effective causes but are made up after the fact to distribute praise and blame.

Not all decision situations are structured alike. Some are more open and ambiguous, inviting underdetermination and flexibility. Others are more closed, fixing more behavioral parameters in advance. Think of this as a continuum, not a duality. The more routine a choice situation, and the more familiar the variables affecting the likely outcomes, the fewer problems there are with underdetermination and interpretive flexibility. Conversely, such problems increase in novel and unfamiliar territory, when it is controversial or not known which parameters matter most to choices and their outcomes.

In some cultural fields, such as social theory or literary criticism, underdetermination is very high, while in others, such as routine medical diagnosis, it is pretty low. When it is high, there is much discretion, many alternative ways of dealing with a problem, and many conflicting interpretations of the evidence. When it is low, choices become invisible as decisions that could have been made otherwise. In familiar machines, or machine-like behaviors, some routines are black-boxed or hardwired into the equipment and institutions. Routines become defaults, or eigenvalues. In its routine mode, a network follows what appear to it as a few simple and basic rules of reality and logic. This is its algorithmic, not interpretive, mode.

Degrees of determination change over time as well. As novel results and techniques gradually become more secure and accepted, they lose many of their former degrees of freedom. At the same time, the innovative sectors of a network move on to the next uncertainty and controversy.

Organizations work on underdetermination. They taylorize some activities, digitizing and simplifying parts of their world (Simon 1976:chap. 4). "Bureaucracy" means little underdetermination, though degrees of bureaucratization vary as well. Some tasks and areas in an organization escape a great deal of bureaucratization, at least for the time being. These areas are often the province and niche of high-status professionals dealing with high uncertainty, and less bureaucracy affords them much discretion over their work. We would expect "interpretive flexibility" and "underdetermination" to increase together with uncertainty.

Once variation replaces essentialism, underdetermination disappears as a philosophical problem and dissolves as an argument for skepticism. The attention can now turn, on a second level of observation, to the variables that constrain choice situations on various occasions, and in different kinds of networks and organizations. Skepticism about working machines and machinelike routines is idle and implausible. When they have long been working as expected, machines do not "draw" skepticism. To repeat, skepticism settles more around texts and interpretations in loosely coupled conversational areas.

The thesis of underdetermination is often coupled to the argument that observation statements or protocol sentences are not neutral records of the actual facts, but depend on an underlying theoretical apparatus. The locus classicus for this point is provided by Hanson[1]

([1958] 1969:30). The theoretical and instrumental apparatus influences what is being observed, how the observations are made, and how they are being recorded and reported. There is nothing objectionable about this; observations are indeed embedded not only in previous and related observations, but also in nonobservational structures of the overall network that is a scientific culture.

The trouble starts, again, when the theory-ladenness of observation statements supports the skepticist philosophical conclusion that theories cannot really be tested against the evidence, that the evidence is "never" neutral to theory, or even that two theories are "incommensurable" in their interpretations of the data. Expect theory-ladenness to be more of a problem under certain conditions than others. The theory-ladenness of observation is variable. When everyone sees the same, and when what one sees is what the group expects one to see, or when what one sees is what the instruments indicate, then seeing simply appears as registering what is "out there." Conversely, when not everyone sees the same, when there is disagreement and low certainty, and especially when one sees something new and unfamiliar, the observer and his "constructions" become more active and visible.

As underdetermination, theory-ladenness is more pressing when novel objects and forces are involved. When there are controversies over innovations, the observations themselves are likely controversial, which pushes them closer to the theoretical or conjectural realm. Under high uncertainty, the border between observable and theoretical becomes fuzzy; there is, as yet, no solid empirical bedrock. The "neutrality" of that bedrock does not imply that observations are logically independent from theory in all possible worlds, but that a culture converges on its foundations as a matter of fact. Neutrality is not absence of location in a cultural framework or paradigm; rather, it is the outcome of stabilization, closure, and convergence. A factual bedrock does not exist by itself, but only as the result of successful cultural work, which establishes a network of facts and institutions as its basic realities.

Objects or entities are not observable, or unobservable, in themselves. This is an essentialist mistake as well. More researchable is the assumption that observation is a relation or interaction between observer and observed. That which can, or cannot, currently be observed varies from science to science, and also together with advances and changes in instrumentation. Something may be unobservable, but only until further notice—given the limits of current tools of observation and measurement. The line between observables and unobservables is not rigorous and logically clear-cut, but shifts all the time, together with advances in detection devices. An actual science will not respect philosophical limits on what it can, and cannot, observe "in principle."

An advancing science will try to shorten the indirect inferential links between its observations and their referents since the longer such links and chains, the more susceptible they become to objections and deconstructions. A shortening of the distance between referents and detectors seems to occur, for example, with the current advances in cosmological astronomy, where higher-resolution telescopes and satellites bring more direct evidence for objects formerly inferred from complex and long chains of indirect indicators, such as gravitational disturbances in planetary trajectories, or Doppler redshift. A science will try to couple the elements and relations of its culture more closely together through networking, thereby reducing possible weaknesses, holes, and soft spots.

In sum, the distinction between theoretical and observable is a variable and changing *outcome* of scientific work. It is not really a philosophical problem, should not be used to make any epistemological points, and cannot be "solved" by philosophical methods. Instead of looking for universal and logical "criteria" that will always separate theory from facts, philosophers should observe how actual technological advances redraw the lines between realism and positivism all the time. Of course, they would have to stop doing philosophy first.

The Indeterminacy of Translation

The indeterminacy of translation combines many relativistic themes, such as underdetermination, incommensurability, and theory-ladenness. It has advanced as a core theme in "interpretive" social sciences and humanities (Bohman 1991:1–19, chap. 3). In its classical statement by Quine (1969b), the indeterminacy of translation means that members of different groups or cultures can never be sure when they have translated each other's terms and practices "accurately." Quine's favorite example is the translation of a seemingly simple ostensively used term such as "rabbit" from one language into another, when the rest of that language and culture is still unknown. Then the translator cannot decide by simple ostension whether his translation of "rabbit" refers to an individual animal, to parts of that animal, to its states, or to certain of its behaviors. This is so because each time ostension and conditioning of ostension occur, the observers point at the same thing, so that ostension alone cannot decide to which of these facts about rabbits reference occurs. Quine acknowledges that a translator, after much probing, revising, and adjusting, would likely be able to distinguish correctly between various extensions. As a philosopher, however, he is not content with translation occurring eventually in practice. He wants to settle translation in principle.

To do that, one would have to show that no other grid of translated extensional terms could fit equally well with the observations. We are back now at underdetermination since, "in principle," there are always multiple possible accounts of the same phenomena. It is just this "in principle" that carves out a unique space for philosophical reflection. For in practice, translation either happens or not, and if it does happen, other possible translations are, in fact, discarded, at least for the time being. This is an empirical, not philosophical, observation, but Quine continues to search for the abstract conditions for the possibility of translation in principle. There is no such thing, only actual translations.

For Quine, the grave philosophical problem here is that it is not just meaning or intension, but reference and extension, that are problematic. Intensions have long been recognized as dependent on cultural context, but extensions appeared to provide a solid common grid for slicing up the world into discrete chunks that are really there under all circumstances. In the ambiguity of meaning, reference was supposed to be solid, firm, and universal, especially for natural kinds that remain the same in all possible worlds. But the indeterminacy of translation "cuts across intension and extension alike" (Quine 1969b:35), with the result that reference itself becomes inscrutable.

Once we allow for variation to sociologize philosophy, the mysterious indeterminacy of translation and the inscrutability of reference all but disappear, and become an actual empirical problem only under very rare circumstances. They are irresolvable only within philosophy. What is being translated is never isolated single terms such as "rabbit";

rather, translations make use of entire networks of related cultural expressions and behaviors. In this sense, understanding is "holistic" because it proceeds in "hermeneutic circles" and translates single terms according to implicit understandings of related terms within a network of prior interpretations. Translation never starts with single terms; rather, it starts within a tradition of prior interpretations and feeds its results into those that are already there. Being not just a philosopher, but also a physicalist, Quine comes close to solving his own problem:

> Within the parochial limits of our own language, we can continue as always to find extensional talk clearer than intensional. For the indeterminacy between "rabbit," "rabbit stage," and the rest depended only on a correlative indeterminacy of translation of the English apparatus of individuation—the apparatus of pronouns, pluralization, identity, numerals, and so on. *No such indeterminacy obtrudes as long as we think of this apparatus as fixed.* Given this apparatus, there is no mystery about extension; terms have the same extension when true of the same things. At the level of radical translation, on the other hand, extension itself goes inscrutable. (Quine 1969b:35, my emphasis)

The crucial distinction Quine makes here is that between "radical" translation and "normal" translation within a "fixed apparatus." Radical translations of cultural items are those with many degrees of interpretive freedom—those that are unfamiliar, strange, or highly innovative. These items occur in the uncertain regions of a cultural network, where terms are ambiguous and relationships between items are few and obscure, subject to alternative possibilities and interpretations. In contrast, when a cultural apparatus is "fixed," interpretation is more normal and routine, and rarely stumbles into perplexing surprises. Examples are traffic lights or speed bumps. Here the world is better known and familiar, and interpretation makes unproblematic and unreflected use of the available methods and conventions.

Radical translation has much in common with revolutionary incommensurability (Kuhn [1962] 1970:198–201), and they are equally rare. It is not the "normal" behavior of culture, but the sign of a severe disruption of communication. The resulting crisis is not primarily a philosophical one; rather, it increases with social distance, structural holes, and severe ruptures in the networks. When there is very little actual empirical interaction and overlap between cultures or paradigms, controversies over translation and reference are notoriously difficult to settle. When two cultures interact and overlap to a great degree, problems of translation and reference become less severe, until they move into the area where the cores of networks merge. Here, translation and reference turn into institutions, such as natural kinds, logical rules, tautologies, and definitions. In the core, rabbits are rabbits, rabbit stages are stages, not rabbits, and they behave according to the fundamental laws of our science (see Chapter 7).

In the core of a cultural network, which includes networks among networks, the indeterminacy of translation disappears and reference is eminently scrutable, to the point where natural kinds seem to exist in all possible worlds. Natural kinds are the *outcome* of having moved into the core, not its cause. That is, a cultural item is not intrinsically certain and unproblematic, but gradually becomes fixed upon being embedded in the core and habitual routines of a culture. Variation matters.

In interpretive cultural anthropology, the indeterminacy of translation is coupled to the problem of rationality (see Wilson 1970; Hollis and Lukes 1982). The lines of conflict here are very similar to those in the sociology and philosophy of science. The rationalists believe in rational universals that unite all cultures. These universals not only make translation possible, but also can serve as yardsticks for the comparative assessment of epistemic merits, including truth and progress. In this camp, we find Lukes, Horton, Hollis, and Habermas. The opposing camp is composed of relativists of various shades, for whom the very attempt at understanding, let alone evaluating, an alien culture is ethnocentric and leads to false projections and conceptual violence that echoes the real violence of colonization. The most prominent original representative of this position is Winch.

Rationalists and universalists argue that the very possibility of understanding requires a common ground that underlies all cultures. This common ground is usually conceived as some neutral "primary theory" or observation language, maybe a "rational foundation" or elementary logic that all intelligent minds are compelled to follow. For some, a Chomskian grammar, hardwired into the mental apparatus, makes translation possible across cultures. Rationalists acknowledge that there is much empirical diversity, but this shared foundation unites humankind in conversation.

Relativists counter that such a foundation is likely to be construed from the unique and local perspective of Western rationalism. Even if there were such a thing as a universal observation language or logical core of reasoning, this would not assure proper understanding. Cultures are forms of life; observations and reasoning may assume radically different positions, depending on how they fit into the overall network that is a culture. Validation and truth happen only locally; they are not independent from context and cultural traditions.

Between rationalism and relativism is historical hermeneutics. For Gadamer ([1960] 1975:261–269), understanding is always contextual, and so constrained by the "prejudices" of those trying to understand. But sustained dialogue with alien cultures leads to a gradual deepening of understanding; two cultural "horizons" begin to merge as a result of an ongoing practice of understanding. This rapprochement is easier when the two cultures are part of a common *Wirkungsgeschichte* (Gadamer [1960] 1975:283–290). Then the hermeneutic circle becomes productive; understanding moves back and forth, and eventually up toward a better sense of what the alien culture is about. This process is never ending. There is no "one accurate understanding," but neither is correct understanding "impossible."

Danto (1968:11) adds that understanding continues as long as history does. Understanding will change with history and future observers, so that as long as history continues, there cannot ever be a "final" account, never to be revised. Instead, history itself continues to produce the novel and changing hindsights that modify past accounts of history. As a result, there is no "complete" historical episode, and one cannot describe it in full. A new hindsight may reveal aspects and effects of an episode that could not have been observed before.

Gadamer and Danto deserve credit for moving the problem of translation and understanding beyond philosophy. As soon, and as long, as communication is going on, two cultures do not remain closed universes for each other. To understand strange meaning, no universal criteria or methods are needed; such criteria or methods are themselves the *outcome,* not the foundation, of actual communication. At the same time, keep in mind that an observer of a culture is not its participant. The "participant observer" is a temporary and unstable hybrid; either he leaves academics and starts living the native life for good, or he eventually leaves the field to return to academia to write up some report. This report must be fed not into the culture it is about, but into the culture of previous academic reports. Only here can its "validity" be established, and only here can it make a difference to subsequent reports. "Member validation" (M. Bloor 1983) is another unstable and temporary hybrid; the fact that members might assent to the interpretations of their behavior, or accept the ethnographer as a "virtual" member, might make a difference, but only as a warrant used to support an argument *within* academics. If academic specialties are to some extent professionalized, then what matters to them, and in them, is decided within that profession, not by amateurs and lay folk.

To be sure, it is excellent methodological advice not to think that the whole world is just a faded copy of or incomplete pre-stage to the modern West. It is also sound scholarly practice not to generalize one's own prejudices to the rest of the world. To understand how life appears from somewhere else, from a different standpoint or culture, is a most worthy goal. But a caution must be added. There is no position for an observer other than the actual empirical positions he assumes in his culture, organization, or group. A position can change, but only into another position, since there is no position above all positions. A culture makes an observer what he is. He is recognized there. From it, he receives status and reputation, training and credentials, knowledge and skills.

An interpretation remains that of an observer. If he is part of a professional specialty with other observers, it is those other observers, not the natives, who make the difference in what happens to an observer's contributions. The behavior of interpretations is determined not by the reality or extension of their referents, but by the behavior of the network of other interpretations into which they are being fed. It is this network that decides on matters of truth, progress, and misunderstanding. The more professionalized and autonomous this network, the more important will the peer system be in determining the merits and rewards for cultural studies.

Instead of debating the "general philosophical nature" of rationality, then, we should expect variation, and start with the premise that communication is an actual empirical process. This process can either go on or not. If it does, it will lead to some results, which are fed into the other related and connected results accumulated in, and by, a network. These results are not fixed and constant, but change together with the activity of the network as it produces new results. In this process, some interpretations, say of foreign or alien cultures, will turn out to be mistakes—not in the culture being observed, but in the professional culture of the respective observers. There is nothing special about understanding foreign cultures, as opposed to figuring out how some ocean turtles manage to navigate according to the earth's magnetic fields. The fact that foreign cultures interpret themselves, while turtles apparently do not, is just another fact about culture and does not make science impossible.

As soon as we allow for variation, we can go a step further and analyze under what conditions understanding will come more easily, or when divergent interpretations might eventually converge on "the truth" about a culture. Understanding is less problematic when there is less social distance between two cultures, when there are network overlaps, frequent interactions, maybe emotional solidarity. The more remote the common origin and ancestry of two cultures, the longer it takes to get from point A to point B, and the stranger and more distant or foreign A and B appear to each other. This occurs in natural evolution as well—as the inability of two species to cross-breed. Now *that's* incommensurability.

Understanding runs into more trouble as social distance increases, to the point when two separate cultures are completely isolated and sealed off from each other. Then they tend to think of each other as barbarian noncultures living on the edge of the world, outside of civilization proper. In today's world society, complete insulation and isolation happen less and less, and so it is modern society, not some universal rationality or philosophical method of interpretation, that solves the mysteries of interpretation in practice.

Empiricizing Contexts and Demarcations

Still another metaphysical pseudoproblem is the "demarcation" of science from other cultures. A "demarcation criterion," or set of criteria, is supposed to separate Science, in the singular, from the rest of culture in all possible worlds, thereby highlighting that which is essentially special, rational, or objective about science. There have been many candidates for this criterion, all of which have failed, including science's "empirical basis," its superior rationality, capacity for cumulative progress, objective truth, unique ethos, or method. These efforts have failed so miserably that Laudan (1996:23) laments the "demarcation debacle."

Once empirical and historical variations between sciences are allowed, none of these criteria, let alone some combination of them, remains constant and without counterexamples. Once a philosopher thinks he has identified that which separates science from other cultures in all possible worlds, some actual science will do something that violates this criterion, such as theorize about singularities and unobservables. Alternatively, some nonscience will do something scientific, such as cumulate (home electronics). In any case, the behavior of a science cannot be fixed in advance by some philosophical "criterion." Instead, a science creates and destroys its own criteria as the result of its own operations, not those of philosophy. It makes and remakes "criteria" as it moves along and fixes its problems. The result is an empirical proliferation of criteria, not their unity.

Demarcation criteria are revisable cultural markers identifying the core entities and domains of a specialty; they will change as the result of advances within a specialty, and of tectonic shifts in the overall configuration of specialties within the larger networks. Demarcations belong to the actual process of specialty formation, change, destruction, or expansion. They are not the foundation of any science or culture, but their variable results and outcomes, to be replaced by different results and outcomes, which will do the work of demarcation in different ways.

Demarcations and boundary markers are important devices to direct and focus the attention of a science to what currently matters to it. At the same time, boundaries filter out vast sources of possible information without further consideration or justification. To repeat, specialty markers are variable and changing; they differ not only from science to science, and culture to culture, but over time as well.

Under conditions of advanced specialization, that which any science actually deals with is a very narrow selection from an immense array of other possibilities. A science makes progress on its problems if it narrows its attention to a very limited set of variables. The rate of advance in a science depends on its ignorance—not just about the world in general, but about most other sciences as well. The commonsensical and philosophical image of science as open skepticism, where little or nothing is excluded, is dead wrong.

A science ignores most of the world, and also most other science, "blind" and flat out—that is, without good reasons. This is very risky, since no one can rule out that the excluded possibilities might hold the key to progress, discoveries, and advances. But inactivity and paralysis come from information overload, not scarcity. More accurately, they come from being unable to exclude, discriminate, and narrow down. Learning and ignorance are not opposites; rather, they are mutually enabling. One can learn something only when one does not try to learn, at the same time, and all at once, all the other things that could also be learned. When everything seems to matter, nothing can.

In this situation, a science uses various cultural and structural markers to distinguish between that which is relevant and irrelevant to its work—at the moment, and until further notice. There are ambiguities and controversies about such distinctions, but these concern not the distinction between relevant and irrelevant itself, but how and where it should be drawn, to include this or that.

The temporary, variable, and observer-dependent distinctions between "matters" and "does not matter" or decidable and undecidable always leave more things out than in: If you decide to research this problem, then all the other possibilities are thereby excluded, although you could not list most of them. Their negation is unspecific and open-ended. If you say "yes," you commit yourself more than by saying "no," since a "no" is still compatible with a "yes" to many things, while a "yes" affirms *this* suggestion, no other.

Observers draw distinctions that leave much more out than in. To focus attention means to *increase* the excluded world, about which indifference or ignorance rules, or where different observers observe. A science uses markers to draw such distinctions. These markers include (in the order of decreasing amounts of what is being ignored and left out) code, time, specialty, and reputation.

Codes

A science uses the code of objectivity and truth to explain to itself how it does its work (Luhmann 1984:chap. 4). As a medium, objectivity is a mode of attribution. It attributes a science's outcomes and results to the world, not the observer. If something is true and objective, it is so not because of power, standpoint, or interest, but because the world makes it so. If a science advances, it does so because it is learning more, making progress, not because of historical accidents and contingencies. A science rewards contributions for their merits, not their authorial origin or one's personal likings. For the most part, objectivity and truth attribute false statements and errors to honest mistakes, not ideological blindness or wicked deception. If a statement is false, then someone has made a mistake, and that mistake can be corrected by learning. If a statement is true, it is so regardless of kinship, sexual attraction, or party membership.

That which is considered objective and true changes all the time in the history of a science. To say that objectivity operates as a science's code is not to say that its outcomes are actually "objective" in a philosophical or metaphysical sense. Likewise, to argue that truth is working as a code in a science has nothing to do with any specific truth claim circulating in that science. Rather, truth and objectivity are modes of attributing what a network does to actual states and forces in the world. In this attribution, however, the code is very strict and tolerates no exceptions. The outcomes of a science are either true or false, subjective or objective; they cannot be anything else, say politically correct, feminist, or emancipatory. If they are false or subjective, this is reason to do it better the next time around, not to deconstruct the code itself, question the "possibility" of truth, or investigate the ideological "desirability" of objectivity.

As codes, truth and objectivity "happen" in a science, or not. They are empirical attributions and explanations a science uses to make sense of how it does its work and what matters to it as it does so. There is nothing transcendental or metaphysical about truth and objectivity. They are empirical modes of observing, not necessary or essential facts about science. In fact, truth and objectivity are rather improbable accomplishments. They have a complex and turbulent cultural history in which the semantics of truth and objectivity undergo various cultural changes (Daston 1992; Shapin 1994).

As modes of attributing a science's outcomes to the world, truth and objectivity are modes of first-order observing. This raises the possibility of observing them on a second level as empirical and contingent facts about a culture, science. The second-level observer does not repeat what the first-level observer does, which is attribute the outcomes to actual states in the world. Rather, the second-order observer observes what cannot be observed at the first level, that is, that the outcomes of a science are its own outcomes, including the code. At the second level, truth and objectivity are internal accomplishments of a network that externalizes these accomplishments to the world.

A special and reflexive situation arises when the second-order observer is also part of a science, say sociology (Ashmore 1989). Then that observer is also bound by objectivity and truth on his own first level of observing. A sociology of science tells the objective truth about the science that it has as its external referent. If it does not tell the truth, or if it is biased and partial, then it needs to be corrected by a better sociology. As a science, sociology does not celebrate error, bias, and partiality as cognitive virtues, or as essential necessities in all ways of knowing. Rather, as a science, sociology of science advances its own claims to truth and objectivity; when these turn out not to be true and objective after all, then the mistakes have to be corrected.

Since codes are empirical, however, and not necessary, they can be disturbed, irritated, or abandoned entirely. The science in which this happens begins to question whether it is, indeed, a science, or something else, say activism or propaganda. Its modes of observing and attribution change then as well; it no longer attributes its outcomes to reality, but to the multiple observers within itself. The science that does this is on its way to becoming an ideology, attributing its outcomes to standpoints, feminine ways of knowing, postcolonial emancipation, and so on. In ideological observing, biases and errors are intrinsically linked to social status, so that they cannot be overcome by corrections and learning.

Time

Time is a marker that mature and progressive sciences, those with rapidly moving research fronts and high information turnover, use to ignore anything that is much older than about two years, which is the average half-life of scientific papers, some citation classics notwithstanding (Price 1986:72). The attention is focused on what happens now and, even more importantly, on what is about to happen. This focus excludes—by fact, not intention—the vastness of past science in the archives. For an observer, this systematic amnesia appears incredibly risky, since nothing rules out that some forgotten past science might hold the key to current and future advances. This has happened quite frequently in the history of science, but the temporal frame of rapidly advancing sciences turns this possibility into an accident or serendipity.

Mature sciences leave their history to historians, and separate systematic from historical matters. They do not cultivate much of a historical "sense," but are eager to forget and overcome their past. That past reappears in rational reconstructions or frontstage occasions for celebrating breakthroughs, advances, and linear progress. Less mature and bookish humanities and social sciences engage in hero worship and classics religion. They tend to look backward, not forward, interpreting and reinterpreting their origins, foundations, and trajectories. They make very little progress and breed skepticism about the very idea of progress. Very little can be excluded out of hand in this way, or the very idea of "exclusion" turns ideologically suspicious.

Specialty

Specialty is a science's way to deal with bounded rationality. A specialty focuses the attention of its specialists on the puzzles and problems that this specialty creates for itself. This set of puzzles, problems, methods, and techniques is a tiny subset of "all" scientific puzzles and techniques. As a specialty turns inward, toward its focus, it thereby excludes most of that which could matter as well. The more specialties there are, and the narrower their foci of attention, the more any particular specialty ignores the rest of the world de facto. This operational ignorance or indifference includes the niches and foci of most other specialties as well, for which the same is true.

A specialty claims and defends its own unique turf and niche as its legitimate intellectual property. Specialties are usually emergentist about their operations and niches, claiming they cannot be "reduced" to competing specialties. Among other things, specialties are professions, or professions within professions. In this lies their "autonomy," although autonomy does not imply absence of empirical interactions and interdependencies with the specialty's multiple environments. Rather, "autonomy" means a variable degree of closure, self-reference, and recursivity in a specialty's operations. That is, it uses its previous outcomes as the premises or material for future outcomes. A specialty creates its own problems and solutions to problems. These can still originate somewhere else, outside of the specialty, but just *how* the problem is being dealt with is up to the specialty—given a degree of professional and reputational closure (Ben-David [1972] 1991:187–209). A specialty decides what matters to it and what makes a difference to how it does its work.

A specialty also decides who competes against whom over what. It settles such competitions, distributing reputations in the process. The specialty ends where the reputation it distributes ceases to make an actual difference. Some reputations become more "global," extending beyond the specialty in which they were originally acquired, but this is comparatively rare and hardly extends to all specialties. This means that experts in a specialty are amateurs in all the specialties outside of their expertise. The reputation that a highly visible expert might have in a specialty other than his own is more like a general popularity, not an expert reputation, which is given only to contributions to that specialty.

Not all specialties are equally professionalized. An advanced degree of professionalization means that you cannot acquire a reputation in a specialty without making a contribution to it that is recognized as such within that specialty. Further, to make such a contribution requires, in most cases, that you already have some specialist reputation, if only as a promise or potential borrowed from professional credentials, teachers, laboratories, or affiliations with renowned persons.

Specialties are connected to related specialties in networks, but these networks are not homogeneous or unified. They are full of structural holes, or absent ties, until such a tie is actually forged (Burt 1992:18–49). The relationships between specialties change all the time. So do the boundaries around them and, with these boundaries, that which captures a specialty's attention—its turf, territory, and property. Some specialties emerge, some die, and other specialties merge into joint ventures.

In all of this, however, "specialty" does not appear on the verge of disappearing as a mode of networking and organizing. I suspect that "interdisciplinarity" is often little more than a rhetorical device to impress deans and funding agencies. They like "interdisciplinarity" because of its openness, pluralism, and fairness. But when it comes to doing the actual work, and organizing its outcomes, "interdisciplinarity" is structured as yet another specialty whose span of attention just happens to extend to more than one specialty. Interdisciplinary programs are thus organized as specialties as well, housed in their own separate institutions. Bounded rationality predicts just this—that the operative focus of a science has to be restricted and narrowed somehow, and "specialty" is the result.

Membership in a specialty usually comes with membership in organizations. A specialty has its own organizations and professional associations, and its members usually draw payments from the organization they are working in. Organizations own property and issue payments to their workers. Scientific organizations—universities, corporate research departments, government labs—own the material means of scientific production. This means one must be there, in the organization, to do one's work. At least this is so when the equipment becomes too expensive or large to be housed at home. When the equipment gets very expensive, only a few organizations can afford it, which tends to concentrate the material means at a few sites. Only those who are at the site, at least sometimes, or are connected to that site, can do research there.

Finally, reputation in a specialty further directs and focuses the attention of a specialty. As networks, specialties are highly stratified according to visibility and reputation. Reputation accumulates and concentrates in the core, dropping off as one moves from the core outward to the peripheries and margins, which are more obscure and less active. One pays attention to the activities of leaders, which can be persons, organizations, departments, or labs. Location in the core means closeness to where the important advances and breakthroughs occur. The farther a location is from the core, the more time it takes for the news to travel there, and the more other locations will already have heard the news as well (Fuchs 1995).

When a specialty moves very fast, the disadvantages from being not in the core accumulate over time (Merton 1988). Marginality is self-fulfilling and self-reproducing, as is location in the core, or centrality. The core is small, elitist, and intensely competitive. To make a difference to what happens there, it helps a great deal to be connected to the core. The longer you are not so connected, the smaller become the chances that you will eventually contribute to the major breakthroughs and discoveries occurring in the core.

In sum, "demarcation" is a social, not logical, activity. There are no "criteria" for demarcation, above and beyond that which actual sciences and specialties do to construct and protect their identities. Demarcation is a response to bounded rationality. It focuses the attention space on that which matters to a science or specialty, and on that which matters to it *most*. As always, demarcation does its work only until further notice, until a specialty changes, dies, or merges with another one. Demarcations, that is, are outcomes, not foundations. They cannot be decided in philosophy, once and for all, nor can they be researched there.

Incommensurability

Still another major philosophical mystery to be hammered apart here is incommensurability. A difference between traditional and revisionist philosophers is that traditional philosophers abhor incommensurability, while revisionists celebrate it. Traditionalists worry that incommensurability means relativism, absence of standards, or the end of rationality. Revisionists hope that incommensurability will support multicultural divergence. In neither philosophy can incommensurability be explained.

Incommensurability has become a popular theme in skepticism with Kuhn ([1962] 1970), despite Kuhn's frequent disclaimers that he was not a Kuhnian. The theme comes in varyingly radical versions. The most radical version, meaning-incommensurability, has it that different cultures or forms of life make sense only in their own terms, and cannot really be understood, let alone evaluated, from the outside. Incommensurable forms of life pass each other like ships in the night. Meaning-incommensurability often draws support from interpretivism in cultural anthropology and ethnography. Standpoint epistemologies endorse incommensurability as well, as do anarchist critics of method and some romantic hermeneutics. The result of meaning-incommensurability is a multicultural relativism of "practices" (Turner 1994:119).

Relativists are entirely correct to be skeptical of universal rules or algorithms for interpreting meaning and translating between cultures. There are very likely no such rules, for who would be their ruler? The absence of transcendental rules, however, says nothing about actual empirical constraints and institutional habits. Much less does it imply that "anything goes." To be clear, such constraints are the actual local and temporary outcomes of communication, not its universal foundation. They result from "sedimentations" in the ongoing process of communication, and last only until further notice (Tolbert and Zucker 1995:17). As empirical facts, such constraints either emerge or not, but when they do, not everything is equally possible or probable anymore. Likewise, to say that the law is no longer grounded in Nature is not to say that the law is "arbitrary," since only bills that pass legislation become law.

Many misconceptions surround incommensurability. To begin with, incommensurability is not opposed to communication, but actually encourages and energizes it, by irritating the background certainties and institutional invisibilities taken for granted in each of the interacting cultures. When communication encounters severe barriers to understanding, these turn into themes for further communication. When a different culture says or does something very strange and unusual, another culture may realize that its own necessities are actually contingent. This stimulates communication, rather than rendering it fruitless or impossible. As long as communication continues, there is no radical incommensurability, only empirical obstacles to understanding, to be overcome as communication goes on.

If communication does break down and cease, it does so locally and temporarily. For example, one walks away from an annoying or insulting conversation only to talk to someone else. Or one stops reading a worthless book, and picks up another one. At the same time, all the other conversations or readings go on undisturbed, experiencing no incommensurability, or only their own local and temporal difficulties, which they either overcome or not.

Incommensurability is not simply misunderstanding, since any understanding understands what it does according to its own terms; there is no other way. Misunderstandings occur all the time, and sometimes they are observed as such and then repaired on-site, as communication proceeds—toward the next (mis)understanding. One might also go to a third party and communicate indirectly, gossip, or wait until some time has passed, at which point the atmosphere will have cleared and communication can be resumed. There may also be "trading zones," where otherwise separate groups and networks overlap and interact enough to sustain communication in hybrid cultures (Galison 1997:138).

Two cultures or observers completely unaware of each other's existence could not even experience incommensurability. This shows that incommensurability is not the cause, but the result, of a breakdown in communication. Again, such breakdowns are more likely temporary and local; they are not universal and global, as if affecting entire cultures. If there had been no communication to begin with, no exchanges and interactions, no incommensurability could have been diagnosed. Incommensurability may be used by an observer to explain communicative failure after the fact, but does not really become available as an explanation until communication actually does break down.

Since incommensurability could not occur without some prior communication or mutual observation, it is not sheer silence or otherness. Once two cultures observe each other, communication gets going, however one-sided and "centered" at first. To some extent, "ethnocentrism" is unavoidable, since the observations that a culture makes of another are part of its own culture, not the observed culture. How could it be otherwise? As a rule of method, avoiding ethnocentrism, or practicing hermeneutic charity, is entirely sensible and informs the precaution not to assume that everything in the world looks like home. At first, however, everything does look like home, for one must start from here, from one's own location.

Incommensurability does not end communication—the end of communication causes incommensurability. What, then, does end an ongoing communication? Two real communication stoppers are physical violence and ideological suspicion. Ideological suspicion knows the enemy's real motive better than the enemy does, and can see through his deceptive maneuvers from the more enlightened and elevated vantage point of its own righteous perspective or standpoint. There is no real point in even talking to the enemy, since he is deeply and existentially caught in his own web of deception. Ideological suspicion is the modus operandi in standpoint epistemologies, for example. At its most extreme, incommensurability is military or ideological warfare, energized by antagonistic sacred objects, such as embryos for right-to-lifers versus the adult liberal self for pro-choicers. For scientific communication, that is, communication in the code of truth and objectivity, ideological incommensurability is a state of emergency, not cause for celebrating multicultural diversity. In a science, multiculturalism is a fact to be observed, not a ritual to be performed. Multiculturalism is good for music, dance, and food, not for science.

As long as nonideological communication continues, the distinction between incommensurability and commensurability is best replaced by varying degrees of commensurability, resulting from other variables, including social distance, interaction density, cultural isolation, and derivation from common ancestors. Incommensurability decreases with exogamy, cross-breeding, common ancestors, and lack of incest taboos. Commensurability decreases as the networks fold inward into cliques, then cults and sects, whose total and greedy institutions cut off ties to the environment and moralize distinctions between inside and outside into distinctions between good and evil.

As a variable, incommensurability is rather rare and not the standard case in society, science, or culture. Therefore, it cannot well be used to make general philosophical points about the abstract or logical "possibility" of understanding. A degree of incommensurability may follow from revolutionary upheavals, but revolutions are very rare as well. If a revolution happens in a science, the other sciences may, or may not, follow suit. If they do, they might take much longer to change than the science where the revolution started. Like everything else, revolutions start locally; nothing guarantees that they will spread into more "global" events. Much business goes on as usual, despite the revolution. Revolutionaries also have stakes in exaggerating discontinuity and incommensurability with the ancien régime. Once the revolution eats its children, later historians often discover more continuities and commensurability than admitted by the prophets of revolution.

To sum up, incommensurability is the variable outcome, not cause, of social and cultural separation. It is the consequence of communicative breakdowns and exhaustion, and then contributes to increased alienation as well. It is not a philosophical problem, or at least not originally, and should therefore not be used to make a general philosophical point for relativism. It cannot be remedied by any "philosophical methods" or "conceptual analysis," only by actual and ongoing interaction and communication. As long as two networks do overlap, if only slightly, no radical incommensurability occurs.

The Double Hermeneutic

In dualism, the world falls naturally apart into two separate kinds of being—silent material objects, governed by mechanical and causal forces, versus speaking and acting humans, equipped with language, free will, and intentionality. The physical world exists as an independent "out there," by itself, while the social and cultural world exists only by virtue of construction, interpretation, and attribution. Somehow this is taken to mean that the social world is less real than nature. Nature is hard and resistant; society and culture are soft and malleable. Physical facts are discovered, while social facts are created.

Fleck ([1935] 1979:98) counters that there is no essential difference between social and natural facts. There are strong facts and weak constructs, but they form a continuum that cuts across the social / natural divide. A "fact" is whatever moves closer to the core of a network, where its certainties and institutions are housed and protected. A fact is a construct whose constructedness has become all but invisible. It makes no difference whether a fact concerns social or natural realities. What does make a difference, however, is whether the culture or network in which facts are produced is strong or weak (Latour 1987:44).

Sociologically, both social and natural facts are constructed. How could they occur otherwise? A dualist, Searle (1995) thinks that only social facts are constructed, while natural facts are just there, as discovered by physics, chemistry, and biology. But this says little more than that Searle is most impressed by these sciences, given their higher prestige and reputation. But do not some social facts—for example, that persons act according to their intentions—actually appear more unconstructed and taken for granted than, say, superstrings and wormholes?

Dualism leads to the double hermeneutic, faced only, so the argument goes, by the sciences of society and culture. Often the double hermeneutic is cited as a warrant for claims that machines, computers, or expert systems can never do what humans do, since machines lack "essentially human" skills, including tacit knowledge, common sense, or Wittgensteinian "practices." Humans have practices; computers have algorithms, and practices cannot ever be fully compressed or condensed into algorithms (Collins 1990:8, 39, 60).

Two separate methodologies are required to study things social and natural. The behavior of physical objects can be explained nomologically by universal mechanical laws, while the actions of humans have reasons that must be understood from within. Taylor (1971) believes that interpretation is, intrinsically, subjective and personal, whereas explanation is rigid, objective, and formatted. Interpretation varies with the location of an observer, while true explanations remain true, regardless of context or time.

Constructivistically, there is no essential difference between things social and natural. The fact that humans talk or interpret themselves and each other is just that—a fact about society, to be reckoned with by explanatory science. But this fact does not make society somehow special and exempt from science. As another fact about society, interpretation and meaning do not make human society more special than ants communicating by chemical traces. Both are interesting facts about a society, and neither fact means that we cannot have a science of ants or society.

Sociology allows for variation and explains under which conditions an entity moves closer to a thing physical than a thing social. Rorty (1979:349) might lead the way. He argues that hermeneutics is a problem of morality, not methodology. Hermeneutics is a way of paying respect to the liberal and humanist Self, admired as a knowledgeable and capable inventor and creator of the social world. The double hermeneutic is a leftover from religion. Originally, hermeneutics was the decoding of sacred texts and divine messages. It remained coupled to biblical exegesis until humanism and historism, which generalized hermeneutics into a secular philology. But hermeneutics never quite lost its religious bearings. Revealingly, Collins (1998) calls socialness "applied soul."

Intentionality

A powerful constructivist and antiessentialist objection against the double hermeneutic comes from Dennett's (1987:15) "intentional stance." For Dennett, intentionality is not a special and essential fact about human actors, but a variable and contingent device used by some observers when they encounter systems whose behavior can best be explained with the assumption that these systems do, in fact, have intentions driving their actions. Persons are assumed to act and to have reasons for what they are doing. The intentional stance is deeply engrained in common sense, but rules much social science as well, from Weberian intentionalist hermeneutics to interactionism and rational choice. This is unfortunate since, as we have seen, a science cannot take off on its path toward discovery if its premises remain stuck in what everyone knows already, in the obvious and seemingly natural.

Since intentions are presumably in the heads or minds of persons, we might ask the neurosciences for help. They have not found any intentions in the brain, however, and some "eliminative materialists" suggest getting rid of the concept altogether (Churchland 1992). But this is both unrealistic and premature, since common sense is not about to react to the latest scientific findings, and since intentionality continues to do much important cultural work. In any case, even if neuroscience did succeed in explaining intentionality in purely physical terms, this would not bring any social science closer to explaining society. Even if there were a physical solution to the enigma of intentions, we would still know nothing about anyone's intentions in particular, let alone about all the intentions of all the persons, dead or alive or unborn, in whose actions a science might be interested. This is why rational choice "solves" intentionality by a breathtaking fiat: All actions of all persons at all times follow not just from intentions, but from *rational* intentions.

Sociologically, even if we did know someone's intentions, we would still be very far from explaining any social outcomes, since the most relevant outcomes may not be intended by anyone in particular. This embarrasses even the state, whose allegedly all-controlling instrumental and administrative reason runs "permanently failing" social policies and interventions (Meyer and Zucker 1989). One might say that social outcomes result from many actions, through some process of aggregation. But "aggregation" has remained a metaphor that does not show how this actually works—how we get, say, from a conversation to the world system. There are so many persons doing so many things for so many different and unknown reasons that nothing empirical and reliable can be said about all of them. Within the agency or intentionalist framework, the best one can do is say that other persons are probably doing something, and that there is a possibility that they might have some reasons for whatever it is they are doing. To philosophize about the nature of "agency" in general goes back to essentialism (Emirbayer and Mische 1998).

Instead of getting bogged down in agency metaphysics, sociology might switch to second-level constructivism and deal with "intention" as an outcome, not a cause, of social attributions, by various observers located in networks and social structures. A first clue comes from Mills (1940:904):

> As over against the inferential conception of motives as subjective "springs" of action, motives may be considered as typical vocabularies having ascertainable functions in delimited societal situations. Rather than fixed elements "in" an individual, motives are the terms with which interpretation of conduct by social actors proceeds. This imputation *and* avowal of motives by actors are social phenomena to be explained. (my emphasis)

Now the sociological problem is to find out under which conditions an observer likely takes the intentional stance to explain an event, and when observation proceeds without assuming or expecting intentionality. Whether or not persons really do have intentions, whether these intentions do cause actions, or whether intentions are really in the brain—all these enigmata are bracketed. Instead, the more tractable puzzle is considered: explaining variations in the distribution of "intentionality," conceptualized and operationalized as an observable and empirical device for making sense across a variety of social observers.

In this way, we can avoid two opposite, yet equivalent, essentialist fallacies: either to assume that persons are natural kinds with intrinsic mental faculties, or to announce the "death" of the person, which is an equally bad move since "person" continues to do a lot of real cultural work for various observers, including social scientists when they are not observing scientifically. This is the observer commonly called "common sense," although there are immense intensional and extensional difficulties with this notion. Common sense may not be very common, and the sense that it makes is likely not a constant, either.

Until further notice, I assume that "common sense" or "folk psychology" takes the intentional stance. It believes that persons are real, that they have intentions, and that these intentions explain their actions. This grid structures "ordinary" social interactions. There are variations, however, and these are critical since a sociological science cannot stop where common sense does. With Goffman and ethnomethodology, "person" is an attributional frame, occasioned by some situations, but not others. The "same" person may be a body on an operating table getting prepared for surgical intervention, a complex bundle of hidden libidinal forces on a psychiatrist's couch, or a case file in the drawers of a bureaucracy. How much can be understood about such variations when "person" is held constant as an essential property of all humans?

Much as human bodies in physical interaction grant each other some protection against improper closeness, "subjectivity" respects a person's mental privacy. Except for degradation rituals and intense conflicts, one does not "get into someone's face." To assume that persons have subjective mental states is to respect their mental privacy. One expects other persons to have an inner life, though how this life feels to them is unknown, except when more closeness between intimates raises the expectation that this inner life is to be shared in some ways, through mutual empathy. Persons experience, think, and feel something. Philosophers of mind call these sensations "qualia," which are now known as the "hard problem" of their profession (Chalmers 1996:4). They argue with their reductionist peers over whether qualia really exist. Nothing has been gained by this essentialism, since it leads to metaphysical undecidables such as whether trees have mental states as well, or what it feels like to be a philosopher wondering what it feels like to be a bat.

Qualia are social constructs, not natural kinds. At least, sociology has nothing to contribute to research on brain properties. This is best done by neuroscience. Sociology can, however, think of qualia as social attributions and outcomes. As an observational device, a person credited with qualia is granted the moral privilege to know best himself what it feels like to live his inner life, what it feels like to be this person, not someone else, and what are the contents of his experiences, thoughts, and feelings. When it comes to mental states and inner lives, one cannot "usually" claim that another person misunderstands, misexperiences, and misfeels his own mental states. But this obstacle is a moral and social one, not a property of minds. It is an obstacle established and reinforced by certain forms and patterns of sociality, not nature.

Through qualia, we pay each other respect as selves. These authors of their own biographies are in sovereign charge of their lives and aware of their surroundings. Liberal selves are in-dividuals—they cannot be divided, that is, decomposed and recombined, by an outsider such as a scientist. One must not make an object of another person, at least not while interacting with him, though maybe in gossip. Qualia establish a private zone of protection against unwanted intrusions; they keep those strangers and scientists out who claim it is possible for someone else to know us better than we do.

Computers

A sort of cultural work similar to that done by qualia is performed by distinctions between human minds and computers. Too often, debates on artificial intelligence and expert systems are bogged down by ontological or metaphysical essentialism and dualism, which search for an opposition between natural kinds and things-in-themselves. In essentialism, the core problem is what makes humans essentially different from computers, meaning that there are some things that humans can do, but not machines. Since they are, in essence, just machines, the machines can also never learn to do these things, due to limitations from their nature. In Dreyfus's ([1972] 1992:293–297) terms, machines will never be able to engage in "nonformal" behaviors—the essential stuff that everyday life is made of.

Allowing for variation, and accounting for the observer, turn distinctions between minds and machines into a matter of degree, not kind, and into a dependent variable. The question of whether the mind "is" or "is not" a computer is ill-posed. More researchable is the hypothesis that some human minds process some cultural tropes to claim ways in which they are, indeed, different from computers, special in some way, irreducible to binary codes and algorithms because of consciousness, social practices, background or tacit knowledge, soul, and the rest of the dualist arsenal of metaphors. In this empirically driven approach, mind / computer, mind / body, and person / thing distinctions are of the Bourdieu type: they are observable patterns of forging an identity and discriminating that identity from others.

At this second-order level of observing observers, the next step would be to explain variations in such distinctions. Which observers, for example, are more likely to "reduce" mind to body, machine, or computer? When and where do such reductions occur, and how far do they extend in a social structure or culture? Who, in contrast, is more likely to insist on persons having some special and emergent qualities that make them unique and irreducible? This insistence is related to the old problem of "free will."

Free Will

The philosophical concept of free will is contradictory and paradoxical. In the tradition of moral philosophy, this contradiction is captured in the uneasy definition of freedom as insight into necessity, coupled to the idea of uncaused causation (Dennett 1984). For sociology, "free will" is not an essential property of humans, but the respectful gesture of an observer granting an actor some measure of control over his actions—no matter what these might be. Free will does not lead to any particular action; it is part of the very meaning of intentionality, not an explanation for it. Whatever an actor does, the expectation is that he could have done something different, and did what he did because he "decided" to do it, maybe even after some "imaginative rehearsal" or "preference ranking." Free will does not explain anything; it is a general capacity that leads nowhere in particular. We still may want to explain why someone did what he did, but the expectation that he did so "freely" adds nothing to that explanation. Since free will explains nothing, it is the unexplained residual from incomplete attempts at explanation or prediction. Indeed, the paradox of free will is similar to that of God, inasmuch as He is the uncaused cause and unmoved mover. The great mystery is that He did what He did for a reason, but could have done otherwise, decided not to do so, all the while remaining unbounded by His own decisions.

Free will is the label for the willingness to assume that human reasons are not natural causes (Rosenberg 1995:33–36). The mystery of consciousness is supposed to signify how these two modes of causation differ. In free will, a moral assurance is given that persons, and what they decide, matter. Liberal selves have a hard time considering the possibility that what they do next might already be fixed and unavoidable, or that in the larger scheme of things it does not matter much what they do. Without free will, something is lacking, something that hopefully makes us humans special and different (Ryle [1949] 1984:196). Free will provides moral assurance that, after all that can be explained is indeed explained, humans are still special, since they could have done otherwise, at least in theory. If an actor had, in fact, done something different, the same puzzle would recur: Why did he not do something else still? Free will is never something, but always something else. It cannot be decomposed and recombined, and so is not a useful concept in a science.

As opposed to essentialism and agency metaphysics, the sociological problem is not free will, but variable amounts of elbow room and discretion granted by various social structures. Discretion is a variable, from operators on an assembly line to charismatic genius. The assembly line tries to curb free will; the genius exemplifies its most awesome mystique. Perinbanayagam (1991:19, 22) notes that the self depends on the initiative to take action—expect, then, more attributions of special personhood to go to positions affording a lot of discretion, elbow room, and agency effects. Under different conditions, say more bureaucratic containment, persons will more likely be observed as Meadian "Me's" acting out roles and scripts, not Sartrean "I's" with spontaneity, creativity, and initiative.

Some cultures, such as those rewarding creativity and innovation, are well prepared to observe and encourage a great deal of individualism. More taylorized and routinized areas, in contrast, work toward canceling and averaging agency effects. Bureaucracies generally cannot deal with individuals, much less their mental states and qualia. Bureaucracies condense, summarize, and quantify. They have little use for free will, especially when they are very large. If they did observe what is special and unique about persons, they would get in trouble for exemptions, exceptions, and favoritism.

We should, then, replace the philosophical mystery of free will with a variable continuum in degrees of constraint. The critical rule of method is to observe the observer, when or which observers use free will as a device, and which other observers manage to observe without it, only to observe with another device, in another network and culture. There is very little that free will can do, for example, when a fire breaks out in a crowded theater. Free will is more at ease when leisure allows for contemplation of alternatives. Free will is a celebrated quality in artists, but a problem of social control in elementary schools and prisons. In surveys, the idea is to aggregate and quantify people's responses to standard questions, and regress the results on social forces. Ethnographies can handle a bit more agency and interpretive flexibility, but not because they are in line with the essential nature of agency and social life, whereas surveyors are not. Rather, ethnographies deal with fewer persons over longer periods of time, making room for agency effects. It is the matrix of the ethnographic research grid, not the nature of social life, that makes room for observing more discretion, free will, and agency.

Things and Persons

From a sociological perspective, things social and things natural are not separated by a grand ontological divide, but by more or less contingent, though never arbitrary, social distinctions. These distinctions distribute intentional and causal effects unequally across the landscape of various populations. Sociology, practiced as structural second-order constructivism, can identify some variables that make a difference in such attributions. Since there are many variables operating at the same time, the effect of each depends on the effects of all the others, so that all following arguments obtain only ceteris paribus.

The basic antiessentialist premise is that "action" and "behavior," "persons" and "things," "nature" and "society," "science" and "humanism," and the other dichotomies are indeed not opposite poles of Being, separated by an unbridgeable essentialist gap. Rather, they are social devices of description and explanation that covary with other sociological variables, such as the status of observers, the conditions of observing, and the degree to which an observed system has been rendered predictable through normal science.

All other things being equal—which they never are—intentional interpretations and *Verstehen* are more likely to occur when observers and observed are socially close, and when the observed are few in number. Then the observer is more likely to use "soft" and very time-consuming methods. One can *verstehen*—but not that many people. Therefore, when observer and observed are separated by some large distance, and when there are very many systems to be observed, the observer is more likely to conceive of the observed behaviors and effects as driven by impersonal causal forces, to be measured by quantitative formulas and explained by general theory. Distance and size are, of course, variables, which means that we are dealing with a continuum here, bracketed by "understanding" and "explanation" as opposite ideal types. One extreme pole is the pure understanding of one person: love. The opposite extreme pole is pure explanation of all organisms: genetics and molecular biology.

Allowing for variation makes it possible to explain when systems move across the continuum, when they tend to become more person-like or more thing-like, and when they occupy some intermediate position. In addition to distance and size, another factor is time. Over time, some systems tend to get better understood and routine, and so move closer to the mechanistic and deterministic thing-pole. Their behavior gets more predictable and, as a result, "intentionality" and "free will" or "decision" decrease. At the same time, time will be counteracted by social closeness and moral boundaries around groups (Smiley 1992:12, 114). Within those boundaries, intentionality is a stronger assumption than outside. Whatever is far outside the moral boundaries separating "us" from "them" acquires a more thing-like character, implying that "they" cannot participate as equals in "our" constructions of "their" behaviors. The reason we are not sure what bats feel is that bats are not pets, while dogs are—and so Searle (1992:74) is ready to grant consciousness to dogs, but not "fleas, grasshoppers, crabs, or snails." But Searle may change his mind.

Such mutual reifications are characteristic of ideological observing, for example. Ideological observing moves the observed closer to the thing-pole of the continuum. The opponent is caused by social forces without being aware of them. If "they" are stuck in ideology, they are unwilling or unable to see through their maze of deception and need to be explained from the outside. Then "they" become a target for "our" science and explanation, not equal hermeneutic partners in conversation. The explanations that ideological enemies give for themselves are symptoms of deception, and so cannot be "in the truth."

The cases at the borders are ambivalent and ambiguous—these are Simmel's strangers and Kuhn's anomalies or Latour's hybrids. On the one hand, strangers are not well known; their mysteriousness and exoticism call for interpretation, rather than explanation. On the other hand, they are not really part of the group, and so are *objects* rather than subjects, or some of both. That is, object and subject status are ascribed, but ascriptions covary with other variables, such as time and distance, which implies that ascriptions will change over time, and with interaction.

Consider a more concrete example. One does not normally understand one's spouse as an impersonal system driven by causal forces, and irresponsible or unaccountable for her actions. This does not mean that her actions cannot be explained by science, only that science does not reach into love. What the spouse does may indeed be explainable as the result of chemistry, neuroscience, or social class, but explanations of this kind do not *work* in close and intimate relations. Here "individuals" occur, and each is supposed to appreciate and understand the other as "special," not "just" as a particular configuration and outcome of empirical forces and causes. In intimacy, agency terms are more expected and appropriate; not even the hardest-nosed neuroreductionists could approach their families as a neural network, algorithm, or artificial intelligence—at least not during intimate encounters and interactions. As an intimate relationship breaks up, of course, mutual explanations and attributions may change, moving once again closer to the thing-pole.

Scientific explanations of spouses and other intimates may become more serviceable when making sense of some behavior according to common agency terms becomes increasingly difficult. "Insanity" is one concept that signals a breakup of a moral community, when insiders who used to have special privileges in accounting for their own behaviors turn, to some extent, into outsiders and objects for some sort of "scientific" explanation. When social scientists explain the behavior of large crowds, or of structural systems such as states, they conceive of reality as more object-like and physical. What matters are not the essential properties of different natural kinds, but the social contexts in which different observers attribute different faculties to systems for different pragmatic purposes.

Interpretation and explanation also vary with the amount of perceived uncertainty. When an observer is very uncertain about the erratic behaviors of some rather hard-to-predict system, he is more likely to assume that that system has an internal center where it makes decisions and choices according to unobservable rules, beliefs, and preferences. In the movie *Backdraft,* the fire inspector, played by Robert de Niro, muses that a fire does not grow because of the physics of flammable liquids, but because it "wants to." Agency is attributed here to the behavior of fires as a result and expression of uncertainty and unpredictability. Another way of saying this is that "agency" is the expected or observed capacity of a system to surprise its observers. Upon being surprised, the observer might try to get closer to this system by softer and more interpretive methods. He might try to develop a "feeling for the organism" and to understand this system "from the inside"—as if it had agency. "Agency" is a moral capacity that a system receives from an observer who is not, at present, entitled or able to make sense of that system in deterministic terms.

Outside of close relationships, most observers will probably try to construct deterministic explanations first, because these are simpler, faster, and more generalizable across classes of systems. Deterministic explanations economize on explanation costs. They are more accommodating to the "bounded rationality" of all observers, or their limited ability to deal with complexity and novelty. This is especially so for organizational observers, because the organization sets the parameters for how and what its workers are supposed to observe, what they are expected to ignore, and because organizations try to simplify and routinize as much as they can. But when this proves infeasible or inappropriate for some reason, when exceptions and surprises accumulate, these very same systems may be granted faculties such as "spontaneity," "creativity," and "originality." In this case, the organization and its observers make special amendments to the rules and routines, such as special programs for "gifted" students, who stand out and refuse to be processed by the routine methods.

In contrast, the observer will tend to become a "scientist" explaining the behavior of his systems from the outside when that behavior can be accounted for unproblematically as simple, repetitive, and invariant across time and place. For this, it does not matter whether the system is a person or a thing, since "personhood" and "thingness" are the outcomes, not causes, of observations, attributions, and cultural work. At least, *this* particular way of assigning causes is the specific contribution of sociological constructivism.

An example for an account located toward the middle of the thing-person continuum is rational choice. Rational choice conceives of actors as "persings," combining the "soft" ambiguity and uncertainty of individual preferences with the "hard" maxim that all actors will optimize. Rational-choice-type explanations arose when markets increased the numbers of actors with which one had to deal. To assume that everyone is behaving "rationally," regardless of individual differences and idiosyncrasies, is a strategy chosen when it is no longer possible or necessary to "empathize" with all of one's partners in exchange. The algorithmic machine of rational action is a radically simplified construct that can be chosen in circumstances when one observes and interacts with very large numbers of strangers. One cannot possibly know or care what all of them actually think or feel, and so everyone assumes that everyone is behaving rationally.

In contrast, "thicker" descriptions and explanations will be chosen when the observer and observed are socially close, or even intimate. In such cases, an objectifying attitude would violate the moral expectations and taboos of such associations. One grants the other a "rich inner life" that cannot easily be algorithmically compressed into a standard formula such as self-interest or stimulus-response. This rich inner life also allows for surprises, which preserve the "magic" of the relationship. This magic is a vital Durkheimian sacred object, which would be violated by a "scientific" attitude. This may be the reason why scientists are not considered perfect spouses. In a variation of Black's (1976:41) law of law, we could say that there is more explanation between strangers, and there is more hermeneutics between intimates.

Some strangers deserve an interpretive ethnography, however. This happens when there are not very many of them, and when their cultures are very exotic and mysterious. In any case, personhood and thingness are outcomes, not causes, of social processes of attribution. People tend to take the intentional stance toward their own pets, granting them some amount of agency and taking a more interpretive approach toward making sense of them. Pets acquire some of the "rich inner life" normally reserved for persons, whereas persons with Alzheimer's stop being observed as having a rich inner life. Such former persons move closer to becoming physical objects in beds, to be handled much as other physical objects. The important *sociological* difference is not between things and people, but between the attribution of interpretivism or determinism.

Pets move closer to personhood on the person-thing continuum, especially when they have been around long enough to become an integral part of a close moral community, such as a family. Then they even acquire "character," which imposes some structure and consistency on behaviors, makes sense of them in terms of a network of "characteristic" dispositions, and fits them into a schema that makes prediction more possible. Over time, "character" may reify and generalize into "stereotype." This happens when explanations of behaviors move back along the continuum, closer to the object-pole. Non-pets, or other people's pets, are not part of one's intimate circle of associates, and so are treated more as physical objects and biological organisms. Such organisms may live in one's house, such as spiders, or even in one's body, such as bacteria, but they are not part of a moral community, and so do not acquire the privileges of agency. Their behaviors do not express "character," but must be explained by the methods of hard science.

The choice of methods, stances, and approaches is indeed not governed by intrinsic differences between things social and things natural. Rather, "social" or "natural" are the *consequences* of processes of attribution that vary from observer to observer, across time and space. Nothing is natural or social in itself. There is no *Ding an sich*. Rorty's (1979:321) great insight is that science and hermeneutics are not coextensive with nature and culture, but that science turns into hermeneutics when there is a lot of uncertainty, and when the "normal" methods do not seem to work anymore. This happens, for example, in episodes of "revolutionary" science. Hermeneutics is also a tribute to the modern self and its celebrated capacities to invest the world with meaning.

Conversely, there are very routine areas of culture, such as large-batch manufacturing or elementary public-school teaching. In such routine bureaucracies, there is little hermeneutics, but much method, for dealing with many things or thing-like persons that are constructed as roughly similar before they are subjected to the same treatments. As a matter of fact, thing-like persons are routinely perceived as standard cases, holders of ID numbers, and fully describable by bureaucratic formulas and classifications. This changes when there are fewer and richer students in smaller classes—for example, in elite liberal arts colleges. Such organizations are paid and equipped to perceive more individualism. Parents expect teachers to make sure that their children are all special in some way. Due to small size, this is now possible. Larger public educational bureaucracies have no way of dealing with all these individuals; they process large numbers of people through standard sequences of courses and examinations, one cohort after another.

To sum up, we do not need a new metaphysics to overcome essentialism and dualism if we make full use of the sociological arsenal. In fact, a new metaphysics does not solve any problems, but simply displaces them to another level, such as the middle kingdom of collectives of quasi-objects (Latour 1993:77–79). Instead, once we allow for variation, we can observe nature and society, subject and object, persons and things, interpretation and explanation, or hermeneutics and science as the poles in a continuum of social attribution and construction. Processes of attribution and construction depend themselves on other variables, such as size, time, uncertainty, or moral boundaries. This displaces the metaphysical problematic. The next question, then, is how are these variables chosen and distinguished, and by whom?

CHAPTER 3

Cultural Rationality

> Operations of thought are like cavalry changes in a battle—they
> are strictly limited in number, they require fresh horses, and must
> only be made at decisive moments.
> —Alfred North Whitehead

Depending on ideological tastes and political affiliations, "rationality" is seen as either the crown achievement or the chief vice of societal and cultural modernity. Few would disagree that modernity is "rational," though it is not clear what exactly this means and implies. Rationality appears exemplified by modern science and science-based social or technical engineering. Rationality demarcates scientific from other ways of knowing, and modern from premodern and non-Western society and culture. A society or culture is "rational" to the extent that it has been engineered according to scientific and technological principles. Accordingly, rational societies and cultures can be reengineered if science improves on existing knowledge. It is rational to learn from mistakes and superior insights.

In the tradition connecting Weber, Parsons, and Habermas, rationality is celebrated as the unique virtue of Western modernity. The demystification and disenchantment of the world turn society and culture into an empirical and historical fact to be made and unmade at human will. Social and technical engineering are no longer retarded or prohibited by sacred taboos, dignified traditions, and unchanging values. Rationalization turns all institutions into contingent and conventional social arrangements that can be rearranged according to plans and decisions. Rational societies rely less and less on primordial and ascriptive orders; they delegate more and more activities or functions to purposively created organizations. Organizations are "rational" to the extent that they operate as well-engineered administrative machines. Rational societies can be managed and changed to realize whatever values and utilities are set by collective decisions. As a result, they are, in a technical sense, "superior" to other societies, whose religious taboos and sacred traditions limit social and political engineering and adaptation (Hirschman 1977:48–56).

In the intellectual lineage connecting conservative romantic social philosophy, earlier Critical Theory, the existentialist Weber, Foucault, and various multicultural postisms, rationality is a vice, not a virtue. Instrumental rationality leads to alienation and unfreedom, not emancipation. Technological and social engineering build a totalitarian and unbrotherly cage of instrumental control over outer and inner nature. With the assistance of science, rational society forges regimes of discipline and control. Technical rationality forces life into a straitjacket of efficiency and bureaucratic classification.

As either virtue or vice, modern rationality is not substantive, but procedural. A distinction can be drawn between the rationality of action and the rationality of belief (Rescher 1988:2–14). Actions are rational when they achieve a given goal in the most effective and efficient way. Goals are derived from ranked preferences or personal tastes that cannot themselves be formed and decided upon rationally. Preferences are arbitrary and contingent, while derivations of goals from preferences can be logically consistent or not. Rational actions are deliberate choices from a set of options. To calculate expected payoffs, possible future outcomes of actions must be rehearsed. Rational actors converge on a superior decision or dominant strategy. They act according to their decisions, but are able to learn when their decisions turn out to be mistakes.

The rationality of belief consists of the consistency among various parameters of cognition. Beliefs are rational when they reflect true states of the world, correspond to established facts, and are consonant with other true or corroborated beliefs. The most rational beliefs are scientific, since science follows methods that eliminate bias and reveal objective truth. Estimates of probable future states of the world are rational when they are based on the most reliable information and forecasts. A system of beliefs is rational when it has been structured intellectually to avoid internal inconsistencies and contradictions. Rational beliefs make good and effective reasons for acting. A rational system of good reasons is well-ordered, clear, parsimonious, and objective.

Actions are rational when their various parameters and reasons are closely coupled and logically integrated with given preferences and obtained outcomes. Rationality decreases when actions do not follow from preferences, when they produce unintended effects, and when they are less optimal or more costly than an available alternative. The most rational action is that which optimizes a given utility function under the prevailing circumstances. Since some outcomes cannot be known in advance, and since objective probabilities may not be available, the most rational action is the one that is subjectively expected to yield maximum payoffs. This cannot happen when the beliefs guiding action are unwarranted and empirically false (Elster 1989:22–29).

Rationality, then, is procedural, methodical, and algorithmic. Rationality yields unique, or "dominant," outcomes that can be generalized across contexts and situations. What varies idiosyncratically are preferences and tastes, but the rules and methods for rational action and belief remain more or less in place. To rationalize action, its components are isolated and rearranged, much as in scientific management and taylorization. A perfectly rational actor does what another perfectly rational actor would also do, or would expect him to do, given his tastes and likes. This makes rational actions more predictable and accountable than other types, which was Weber's main reason for the construction of ideal types. Effective and efficient actions are eminently intelligible and accountable; they "make sense" in an immediately plausible way. People do what they need to do to likely get what they want most, and they will try to invest as little as possible to get it. Under this assumption, actions of a different kind, such as emotional or compulsive behaviors, can be explained as deviations from the ideally or perfectly rational model.

Rational actors are either natural or corporate persons. Both are legal entities, equipped with rights and capacities for action. They are both seen as unified and homogeneous, with a central utility function governing an action or sequence of actions. Rational persons are autonomous agents carrying subjective rights and private inclinations. They act rationally in a variety of areas. The Cartesian cognitive actor arrives at indubitable logical truisms and certainties by systematic reasoning. The Kantian moral actor follows generalizable moral principles. The Hobbesian political actor contracts with other actors to create a sovereign body politic. The Smithsian economic actor invests his resources prudently to maximize selfish gains; in the long run, this will make the commonwealth prosper as well.

Rational actors interact through contracts to negotiate mutual obligations and benefits. They do so within competitive markets, regulated by prices, which aggregate and quantify information about market opportunities. Prices make opportunities commensurate and comparable and, under equilibrium, clear the market. Competition eliminates suboptimal strategies and reduces problems with the distortion of price mechanisms typical for small-numbers bargaining and market-access restrictions (Marsden 1983). Since actors are selfish and opportunistic, they will lie, steal, and cheat. Perfect and unrestricted competition among rational and strategic actors cancels—in the long run, and on average—the effects of opportunism by damaging the reputations of cheats.

A special problem for rational choice is collective action to produce public goods. Since rational actors are selfish, and have no inherent commitments to any normative orders, they will enjoy collective goods without contributing to them. People listen to public radio without making a pledge. Under these conditions, public goods require either taxes or sanctions to punish the deadbeats, or selective incentives to reward those who do contribute something, according to the relative value of their contribution.

Action rationality requires rational social orders, since only rational orders can create a predictable and accountable legal-political environment in which markets can prosper. The basic idea in economic liberalism is to keep outside interferences and interventions in markets to a minimum. Rational orders are mostly conventional and voluntary associations, with a minimum of inherited privilege, coercion, and sanctions. Rationality thrives within protected and pacified environments. These provide those resources and frameworks for rational actions that cannot be generated by contracts among persons, such as internal and external security. The external conditions for markets consist of nonexclusive and indivisible public goods or services that free riders will not deliver—especially when there are very many of them, a situation that obscures the difference any single actor's contributions might make to the collective efforts.

Many free riders acting rationally and selfishly tragically destroy the commons and produce suboptimal outcomes in prisoners' dilemmas.

Such dilemmas result when optimal or dominating strategies yield a deficient and suboptimal equilibrium. A fine example comes from Dawes (1991:20–21). Since deans do not read or fully understand scholarly papers, they count quantity, and so faculty write as many of them as possible, driving down the value and quality of each paper. The result is a lot of mediocre papers that are worth less and less. The classical corrections to free riding are sanctions and selective incentives, while suboptimal collective outcomes can be prevented by iteration of bargaining episodes, or in assurance games that allow for some communication and negotiation among the parties.

After Reason

Unlike many critics, I do not see idealization and generalization as the central problems of rational choice theory (RCT), although rational choice does tend to offer tautologies, especially in the doctrine of "revealed preferences" (Sen 1990:29). But many sciences "idealize" by controlling and simplifying the conditions under which their laws and explanations work (Cartwright 1983). Theories usually come with ceteris paribus clauses that protect their core assumptions against falsification. Strong theories also have a will to generality; they expand their range as far as possible. There is nothing wrong with this. Theories calibrate a balance between explanatory power or range, and empirical realism or naturalism. That RCT is "unrealistic" is commonly understood, at least since Weber's ([1922] 1980:190–192) "Objectivity" essay. Power and realism cannot both be increased at the same time, and one increases at the expense of the other. No theory explains its events and observations "as they actually occur," but only as they occur under a certain description, which is guided by theory and ignores much empirical complexity.

Rather than its "model Platonism" (Hans Albert), I see the core problem of RCT in its essentialism, or the failure to allow for variation (Tolbert and Zucker 1995:5). Like all essentialism, RCT does not account for the observer who uses "rationality" as a central category and distinction. Instead of introducing rationality as a constant and normative postulate, a sociological theory sensitive to variation would explain "rationality" as a dependent variable that covaries with arrangements in social structures and also with the specific observers for whom actions appear "rational" under the standard model described earlier. A sociological theory of rationality examines the conditions under which "rationality" and "rational actor" appear as a schema used by an observer to account for an outcome. Such a theory will not follow Weber in the construction of ideal types, whose "essence" is to be contrasted and demarcated from "essentially different" types of action, but will expect *varieties* of behavior and observation to follow from underlying variations in social structures.

As a dependent variable, rationality more likely emerges under some conditions than others, and is used by some observers in some social relationships, but not others. Expect variations in the *degrees* of rationality as well. The challenge for explanatory theory is to find out when these variable outcomes will prevail over different possible outcomes.

Sociologically, "rationality" and "rational actor" are arbitrary interruptions of causal chains, performed by an observer who decides (rationally?) to stop asking further questions about why actors do what they do. Needless to say, all science interrupts causal chains somewhere, and sciences differ precisely in how and where they do this. The boundary and identity of a "specialty" depend on how it limits and justifies its specific interruptions of causal regresses. This is the "blind spot" of specialty, or its metaphysics—that which cannot be questioned if the specialty is to do its normal work. The problem is not that RCT produces such a blind spot as well, but that *sociology* cannot interrupt the causal connections and patterns at the same point as RCT does.

Causes and Reasons

One paradox in RCT follows from ambiguities in the distinctions between reasons and causes, and between actual and good reasons. RCT intends to explain actions by their reasons. Where do these come from, and whose reasons are they? They are not the actual reasons that empirical persons might give for their actions in natural settings and occasions. RCT does not "go native" to uncover the "actor's point of view." If it did, it would likely find that actors usually give many reasons for what they do, that the reasons given depend on who is asking, that actors often forget why they did what they did, and that remembered reasons are as much due to the actual reasons effective at the time of acting as to the very process of remembering them in a specific here and now.

Instead, the reasons in RCT are *good* reasons, that is, those that optimize expected utilities. In other words, RCT's reasons are not those of actors, but result from an attribution to "actors" by RCT. They are constructs of an observer who observes not actual or empirical reasons, but idealizations of reasons. This observer is RCT itself, a specialty and culture formed around core institutions such as Becker's faculty seminar in rational choice at the University of Chicago. Correspondingly, the "actors" in RCT are not actual or empirical persons, since these come only in the manifest and immense plural, not in the singular, as in "the" rational actor. "The" rational actor is not an actual person, but a highly simplified construct and attribution.

This construct is equipped with free will and the capacity to decide. Actors with free will have good reasons to act selfishly. But how do these reasons "cause" an action? By and large, RCT assumes that the reasons it constructs have a real causal force—that persons act in some way *because* they have good reasons to do so. This leads to the old puzzle of freedom and necessity. How can actions be caused, empirically, by freely chosen reasons? Does not "causation" contradict "free will"? Can one freely decide not to act according to one's free will? What causes such decisions? A decision or cause?

RCT stops asking further questions when it has reached the "actor" with his tastes, beliefs, reasons, and actions. This is not a decision that social reality itself made, but one that depends on an institution or specialty that separates the foundational dogmas of RCT from the foundational dogmas of other specialties, including sociology. When it observes social structure, sociology does not stop where RCT does. Instead, it goes back further in the causal chains, behind the "actor" and "rationality." Sociology deconstructs the core metaphors of RCT and turns them into dependent outcomes of social structure. Then the very notions of "actor," "self," and "person" turn into problematic constructs that some, but not other, observers will employ to explain some, but not different, outcomes (Hirsch, Michaels, and Friedman 1990:45).

For sociology, RCT does not explain actors and actions, but celebrates them out of respect for the liberal self and private autonomy. The liberal self is celebrated as the mysterious origin and wellspring of agency and cognition—a sacred taboo that must not be decomposed into its elements and reduced to social forces (Coleman 1990:503). The "knowledgeable and capable agent" is a powerful moral fiction with strong institutional supports and anchors, such as civic and subjective rights and competencies. The liberal self is in charge and control of what he wants and does. He likes what he likes, wants what he wants, and knows what he must do to get it. In this control lies his responsibility and accountability. Without control, the actor would not be an actor. To end causation there, as RCT does, is to uphold these moral fictions instead of explaining their social force.

Powerful moral and constitutional fictions come at great explanatory costs. Paradoxically, to interrupt causation at actors and agency is to advance a very impoverished and unitarian view of the self. In RCT, the self is an abstract calculus, molded from one piece and differing from other selves only in contingent and accidental desires and opinions. In contrast, the sociological and psychological evidence suggests multilayered and scrappy selves with disparate needs, cognitive dissonance, and ambiguous beliefs—bundles of heterogeneous forces, not sovereign origins of force (Wiley 1994:29). Likewise, for corporate actors, the evidence suggests not one principal with integrated utility functions, but conflicting coalitions and alliances advancing multiple and changing goals and agendas (Hall 1991:115–116). When organizations are founded, their goals differ from those acquired later. In this way, organizations "relieve themselves from the conditions under which they were originally founded" (Gehlen [1956] 1964:84).

Organizations also spend much time finding out just who is in charge, and of what. "Being in charge" is also not a "given." Sociologically, one cannot just accept that the leaders are those who are formally in charge, according to the organizational charts. Often, coalitions fight over "principality." There may be different principals in the formal and informal systems.

At the same time, sociology avoids the opposite essentialist mistake, which is to view persons and organizations as "essentially" or "naturally" disorderly. This opposite mistake is often committed by "interpretive" accounts of persons and organizations. For them, there is a mysterious and irreducible space of "practical reasoning" or "forms of life" that cannot ever be structured algorithmically. Computers and artificial expert systems must always and necessarily fail to simulate this

human, all-too-human, sort of action, since they can only mimic behavior that is completely and uniquely describable by rules (Turner
1994:1–11).

Sociologically, this elusive and opaque realm of practices is a leftover
from religion and morality. There remains a boundary between humans and computers in some cultures, but this boundary is not a natural one that separates that which is essentially separate. Rather, on a
second level of observation, this boundary is a social, moral, and technical distinction that shifts together with changes in social structure. A
culture finds ways to be different from another one, and some cultures
might continue to find new reasons why humans are still more special
than computers. A different culture, in contrast, is busy breaking down
the boundaries separating humans from computers in all possible
worlds.

It is these variations that a second level of constructivist observing
can explain. This second level leaves undecided the metaphysical mystery of whether computers "really are" different from persons in all
possible worlds, and for all possible observers, at all times. Sometimes,
some persons can be observed as having a capacity for interpretation,
practical reasoning, and reflexivity, but much of what they do under
conditions of low uncertainty and simple habits is not that interpretive
and reflexive. When allowing for variation, and seen as opposite poles
of a continuum, not as separate ideal types, interpretivism captures ac-
tion-in-the-making under high uncertainty; rationality captures ready-
made action when most behavioral parameters are given. Clarke
(1992:31) is right: "Perhaps economic decision theory is least useful in
situations involving choices regarding important risks."

The Unity of Persons

Sociology rejects both rationalist and interpretivist essentialism to
examine the conditions under which persons and organizations do,
in fact, sometimes construct possible unities out of heterogeneous
sources and materials. The puzzle that follows from this is no longer
"Is action rational or not?" or "Is there a unified self or not?" Instead,
the puzzle is how persons or organizations manage to accomplish
some degree of rationality and unity, and when they are less able to do
so. A related puzzle is how long a unity lasts, how it is repaired when it

fails or breaks down, and at what times rationality surfaces for a particular observer.

For sociology, "person" and "organization" are not givens, but variable accomplishments of social orders. They are not simply entities that occur in the world, but come into temporary being as the result of certain kinds of cultural work. Persons and organizations do sometimes appear as unities, but that unity is accomplished and preserved against disorder and incoherence. Unity lasts until further notice, that is, until persons and organizations fall apart or fail. Then they also lose any integrated utility functions they might have had at some point.

Unity is unstable and sensitive to disturbance and time. Unity likely breaks down under very stressful and turbulent conditions; it can be repaired and reestablished, but if some measure and appearance of unity are reestablished, they will likely differ in form and substance from previous states. Persons and organizations change, and with them their goals, tastes, beliefs, and identities. Expect more unity in some segments or layers of persons or organizations than in others; as an example, accounting is more orderly and integrated than research and development (Lawrence and Lorsch [1967] 1986:30–39).

As for persons, a sleeping person's unity may fall apart in dreaming. It can be regained upon waking, but this takes a little work and time as well. Some days are better than others; our intimates know this about us. More distant observers of a person likely exaggerate that person's unity, sovereignty, and rational conduct (March and Shapira 1992:279). Frontstage behavior is dedicated to confirming expectations that we are in charge of our lives, have a solid grip on reality, and can be relied upon to act coherently. We tend to see others in more simple and abstract terms than they use to observe themselves, or than we employ to observe ourselves.

Further, link unity to certain kinds of observers, and to certain relationships they have with the observed unity. For example, strangers to persons and outsiders to organizations do not experience and participate in their internal complexity and autopoiesis. Persons know how difficult it can be for them to maintain face and continuity, particularly in stressful and turbulent phases that disrupt the familiar routines and increase uncertainty. Organizations operating in multiple and rapidly changing environments respond by internal differentiation and decentralization, to the point where their "unity" exists only in property, and on paper.

Just like persons, organizations are not of one piece; location and status within the formal and informal networks structure how the world is being perceived and "enacted," and which parts or aspects of the world are relevant for this or that particular niche within an organization's internal environments (Weick 1979:130–131). On backstages, and in the informal systems, there is usually less order and coherence to organizing. The leaders make irrational mistakes all the time, and their "decisions" are, at best, loosely coupled to the outcomes and consequences (Clarke 1992:36). In a series of case studies on how organizations make choices, Thomas (1992:216) finds that no organization had any "strategy" directing choices. Ethnomethodological accounts of repairs to disrupted habits reveal an anxious and uncertain self that has little in common with the sovereign and confident self-made man of RCT. They are desperate—not to realize their selfish interests, but to restore some measure of facticity and normalcy to their interactions.

Most casual observers of persons in normal frontstage situations, including survey research, see only the polished and finished results, a snapshot that freezes activity into prestructured and orderly measures and categories. But this orderliness is as much an artifact of the interactional parameters of observing under these special conditions and assumptions as it is a "true" indicator of an underlying unity. That persons "have" certain wants and beliefs is, to begin with, part of an observational and attributional operation, not a given primordial reality. A different observer could just as well attribute wants and beliefs to not persons, but groups, the subconscious, or the "gaze" of an observer who sees persons as fundamental and irreducible "units of analysis."

Once this unity is constructed, it may include wants and beliefs, possibly rank-ordered, scaled, and quantified. But the point is that this unity must somehow be accomplished and constructed or does not come about at all. Sociology cannot take unity at face value, or as a given and essential fact about persons. Instead, its problem is to explain under what conditions, and in what social processes, this unity emerges, and how long it lasts. Accounting for variations in outcomes also includes the possibility that "unity" can be constructed in different ways.

Likewise, when organizations communicate with outsiders, they pretend to have more unity, rationality, and method than they actually do (DiMaggio and Powell 1983). This is not because they are dishonest and deceptive, but because no outsider could process and deal with the full actual complexity of an organization's internal operations. If he could, he would no longer be an outsider. Organizations and persons invent models and accounts of themselves that gloss over and summarize the complexities of their internal operations for an outside observer. This observer will perceive more rationality and unity than actually exist. Depending on who the observer is, he will be presented with varying accounts of a person's or organization's unity.

Unlike RCT, sociology cannot simply take for granted the "fact" that persons are natural kinds who "have" certain wants, reasons, and beliefs in the same way that they "have" hair and limbs. Actions do not simply "follow from" wants and beliefs, because reasons may not be causes, and because some actions may only be loosely coupled with wants and beliefs. Much less can it be taken for granted that actors and action are rational—that is, that the reasons are "good" reasons, that the preferences are ranked in an orderly way, or that the beliefs are empirically warranted.

An observer cannot participate in the internal mental operations of a single person, let alone billions of them. Intimacy does not alter this fact, since one cannot live another's life or die another's death. We have no idea what goes on inside other people's minds. We cannot plug into their internal lives. Some very few persons might tell us what they think and do, but their thinking and doing remains theirs, while our thinking and doing remains ours. We may try to think their thoughts, or feel their feelings, but we can only think and feel according to our thoughts of their thoughts and feelings.

As for the large rest who do not tell us anything about themselves, we do not know what they do, or why they do it. We might assume that they have reasons for whatever it is that they may be doing, but this is an observer's assumption, not an elementary fact about action. Luhmann once remarked to me that he would expect me to pick him up at his hotel until I did not show up, and that he would then assume that I had some reason for not showing.

Reasons are the properties of cultures, not persons. They are standard accounts acceptable and available in a culture for making sense. They are clustered and networked into stories and accounts—the stuff from which everyday life is made. Some liberal modern cultures have expanded the elbow room for persons, allowing them to communicate self-interest, on occasion, as an acceptable reason for doing something (Hirschman 1977:42). This does not imply that they actually do act out of self-interest, only that they are allowed or expected to *communicate* self-interest as a legitimate motive—as opposed to, say, witchcraft, oracles, or totemic spirits. To assume that selfish intentions effectively "cause" action is, again, an observer's assumption, not a basic fact about action.

There is, at present, no way to observe that a reason causes an action or how that might happen. There is also no way to decide which actions of which persons one should observe. It is impossible to observe all of them, and so an observer who wants to hold fast to a theory of action must decide, without recourse to any actual or empirical actions, how to conceptualize "action" as a theoretical tool. It is this explanatory tool of an observer, not the actions of persons, that sociology addresses—with its own tools, to be sure, those of "social structure."

The problems with action run deeper still. Once we "analyze" action to find out what its basic components are, it becomes more and more difficult to define just what an "action" is, how long it lasts, and when a new action begins. This much can be gathered from the rather dreary debates in the analytical philosophy of action, where even supposedly simple actions—the standard cases being opening doors and closing windows—turn out to lack exact referential and temporal extension (Beckermann 1977). Neuroscientific reductionists question that minds and actions exist at all; for them, explanations that make use of "mentalese"—intentions, wants, beliefs—are irrational superstitions of folk psychology. Eliminative materialists would dump "reasons" onto the trashheap of dualist and mentalist Cartesian metaphysics (Rudder Baker 1987:chap. 1).

What Do Persons Want and Believe?

RCT has no sociology of status groups, tastes, and knowledge (Bourdieu 1980). Stigler and Becker (1990:191) go so far as to postulate that "tastes neither change capriciously nor differ importantly between people." RCT assumes that natural and corporate persons come equipped with wants and beliefs. These are private, that is, independent from others. What is more, these wants and beliefs are consonant with the demanding standards of rationality. This does not explain their contents, but does place formal and logical restrictions on the sets of wants and beliefs that still meet rational specifications. RCT assumes that rationality is best defined when actors are separate and independent, and when they have correct and complete information about current and future states of the world. Arrow (1992:72) calls RCT "a stochastic form of perfect foresight." Choices and decisions are internal accomplishments of mental or bureaucratic calculations and assessments. Rational actors are strong-willed; once they have made the decision that is best for them, they follow up on it.

Sociology questions the realism of these assumptions. To begin with, "wants" and "beliefs" are not internal states or attributes of personal minds, but result from observations and self-observations. These may condense and crystallize into discrete "wants" and "beliefs" when an occasion or situation calls for this to happen, as when respondents check opinion and attitude boxes on a questionnaire. Ethnomethodologists would say that beliefs and wants are not independent properties of private mental states, but "occasioned" accounts of such states. Ethnomethodology shows persons to spend a great deal of time and effort explaining to others just what they believe, and just what they want. Sociologically, "actions," "beliefs," and "wants" are not given facts about persons, but communicative and interactional devices for making sense of, and accounting for, mutual observations. One cannot observe mental states as such, and so assumes that others have certain wants and beliefs, and that they will act accordingly.

As a result, there is a rather large gap between rational choice models of calculation and empirical studies of actual or practical reasoning. To begin with, RCT seems unable to accommodate a rather large variety of behaviors altogether, such as dreams, emotions, or neurotic compulsions. Conversations would immediately grind to a halt if they occurred between rational actors. In conversations that "flow" rhythmically, what one says next follows from the conversation itself, not from decisions made from selfish interests (Turner 1974:87–90). One can try to manipulate conversations strategically, but when a strategic interest is suspected or perceived by others, the intent to manipulate may backfire, working against the interests and strategies.

If they occur as part of a science, conversations assume persons to be *disinterested* in the outcome, and to not act out of ulterior selfish motives. One expects these conversations to be interested in the truth alone. When ulterior motives are observed in science, they are perceived as misconduct, that is, as an abhorrent violation of trust in truth. When two rational choicers talk about the merits of rational choice theory, they will assume that they speak the truth about the truth. When rational choice theorists talk about selfish interests, they mean those of others, not their own. They mean to say that "rational choice" is a *true* account of social action, not a selfish one. Deciding to endorse rational choice theory cannot be observed as a rational decision, but as a decision resulting from comparative assessments of epistemic merit.

Take another example, writing. Writing follows more from previous writing and writings than from rational deliberation or calculation. The best writing is probably done in selfless dedication to a task, or even a calling. Selfishness is not opposed to altruism; the all-encompassing commitment to a task or calling might appear selfish in light of other obligations, but it is the work that controls and uses the person to get itself done, not the other way around. When one is deeply immersed in a task, one's utilitarian well-being recedes behind the demands of the task itself, or its *Sachzwang*. With Dennett, one might say that a scholar is a library's way of producing more books, much as an organism is a genome's way of producing more genes.

Persons often do not know what they want, how to get it, and where to get it cheapest. They do not make many decisions deliberately. "Making a decision" is more likely when some routines of everyday life have been upset. Then actors may switch to a second level, try to figure out what went wrong, and correct or avoid the mistake the next time around. Decisions are second-level interruptions of what used to be first-order certainties. Persons wait with their decisions until something goes wrong, or until what used to work works no more. Why fix it if it ain't broke?

When too many things go wrong at the same time, and there is much ambiguity and uncertainty, persons tend to lose their rational cool and start to panic (Orbell 1993:130). Gehlen ([1956] 1964:54) shows that what followed from the feast of alternatives in the disruption of institutions during the French Revolution was the "grande peur," not the grand rational actor.

Persons do not, as a rule, have integrated and commensurate utility functions, especially not when they cannot draw on reliable prices that aggregate and quantify various parameters of choice. They have many beliefs that could not be judged "rational" under any of the standard assumptions, such as corroboration and consistency. Wants and beliefs are not independent, but interact to produce wishful thinking. Some people just want what they believe others have—not because they really want it, but because they want to be like others. Irrational beliefs coexist with rational ones, even in adults. There are adults who have no trouble believing in alien abductions, the surgeon general, and the lottery. Many of them will not see any contradiction until it is pointed out to them. Again, this is so because beliefs are occasioned by varying situations and contexts, and at different times; they are not simultaneous neighboring states in a person's mind.

Most persons have a hard time assigning probabilities to future outcomes. They are easily fooled by different framings and formulations of what amounts to the same choices. They tend to be overly optimistic in sequential planning and programming, yet not pessimistic enough when it comes to connected accidents, since the probabilities are multiplicative in programming and additive in accidents (Tversky and Kahneman 1990a, 1990b). Facing risky and uncertain situations, actual behavior moves further and further from rationality. If they are being asked, which is unlikely, persons usually can tell you some reasons for what they do or did, but they often make those up, with the benefit of hindsight, to fulfill assumed or perceived expectations of reasonability and sensibility.

There are many good reasons for doing opposite things, and there is no unique and objective way to distinguish good from bad reasons. Not even the spooky shadow world of Habermasian discourse can assure nonideological outcomes, since the distinction between ideological and nonideological outcomes requires yet another discourse, and so on. We often jump to conclusions and generalize with abandon across time and situations, regardless of sample size. Scientists do this as well, particularly when confronted with puzzles outside of their expertise. People sometimes choose from alternatives, but the more alternatives they consider, the harder a decision gets, up to the point of inertia and indecision. Ryle ([1949] 1984:176–178) shows why rationality, when applied to itself, would lead to blockage of action, not its improvement.

Decisions, decisions. It is difficult to decide how much more information to obtain before making a decision to act. Information is costly, takes time to obtain, and is often unreliable or biased. Exploring the options may take so much time that the choice situation disappears altogether, or others have already moved ahead. Most information is gathered from sources other than direct and personal observation, necessitating yet more decisions on whom to trust. Trusting becomes more problematic still when information about future states is uncertain, spotty, and loaded with agency problems.

The most important choice situations are often those where something needs to be done fast; in these situations, one is better off using practical experience than rational choice algorithms. Impending traffic accidents are an example, as are decisions of organizations in turbulent and rapidly changing environments. RCT never allows for variation in the *kinds* of choices that are more amenable to rational calculation. Reflex moves in critical situations show that some of the most important decisions are not really "made" at all. In turbulent and uncertain environments, actors often have little to go by but "instinct." The most innovative scientists, presumably the bright idols of reason, often say they follow their "hunches," or that someone has a "nose" for where promising solutions might lie. Many decisions are made in good faith, but then forgotten or ignored. The flesh is weak, and the temptations strong and abundant. Some people like to be told what to do since they cannot make up their own minds. Information gathered may be used not to make a better decision, but to impress clients or customers with elaborate charts and confident forecasts. Many problems are solved not by any rational strategies, but because they disappear or are replaced by new, or more urgent, problems.

Decisions, Decisions

The standard scenario in RCT is that of an actor deliberately considering and weighing alternatives, deciding on a course of action that promises the best returns, and acting accordingly. At the same time, the actor is flexible and willing to learn, revising strategies according to experiences. It would be irrational to stick to a decision that is not yielding the expected payoffs. Rational persons can decide when to decide, and they tend to decide to make more decisions, since decisions are the glorious moments in the drama of the rational actor. He is truest to himself when choosing among alternatives. When there are none, and no decisions to make, the actor succumbs to destiny or outside causality. It cannot be rational to avoid choice, or to decide not to decide (Collins 1993:63).

The model is inexcusably unrealistic. It is probably fair to say that most decisions are made in fact without awareness that one was deciding anything at all. Margolis (1993:11) notes that "cases of explicit judgment are some tiny fraction of all the choices we make." One does something, which later turns out to have been only one option among others. An actor may not be aware of the options at the time, and is later told, by an observer, that he did have a choice. An observer, say a historian, sees more or different alternatives than does an actor.

In this light, "decision" is a schema for assigning organizational responsibilities and allocating praise and blame. Depending on the actual outcomes, there are typically conflicts over who has made which decision, and who is responsible for it and its consequences. Conflicts reveal how problematic and difficult it is to pinpoint a decision in time, or decide who decided, what the intentions were, and which outcomes can, and cannot, be attributed to the decision and its makers. There is widespread finger-pointing and denial when things go wrong, and competitive jockeying for credit and recognition when they go right. When things go wrong, no one is responsible; when they go right, everyone wants to be. Who is to decide all of this responsibility as well? In many cases, one cannot locate precisely when, and by whom, some decision has been made, and so assumes that decisions must have originated in the "office" that "usually" makes decisions of this or that kind.

"Leadership" in organizations generalizes and simplifies the search for the responsible parties. Leadership interrupts the causal chains and concentrates agency effects at the top, while all the others simply do as they are told. Leaders receive a disproportionate share of praise *and* blame. "Everyone knows" that the leaders have the power to make the decisions, and so that is where one starts searching for causes and agency.

This myth says little about where, and how, decisions are actually made. The causal impacts of leadership are vastly overrated in common sense. Presidents cannot "fix" the problems in their companies or countries. Rather, problems do, in fact, get fixed or not, and then

"President" is a mode of observing who is responsible, and who gets credit. Leaders' decisions depend on previous decisions, and on information that they cannot verify or gather themselves. Neither can they determine what happens once they have made a decision. How will a decision be understood and implemented? In complex and large organizations, the elusiveness of decision gets worse.

Precisely since they are so elusive and invisible, important decisions in organizations are often ritualized and set aside for special occasions and meetings. Everyone present there is expected to know that a decision must be made. But what happens in encounters is so much more, and so much less, than "making a decision" or "resolving a problem." In fact, processes that are not decisions can become so dominant in an encounter that, in the end, there is no time left to make the decision, and it must be postponed until the next meeting, by which time the world is not the same anymore. When the next meeting comes around, there are different matters to be decided, and some of these decisions will also be never made, forgotten, or pushed away by more urgent business. Some of those present in meetings pay no attention to what is going on, concentrate on things other than the business at hand, fall asleep, or watch what the others are doing before making their own moves. When groups make decisions, they enjoy or suffer from sheer togetherness and sociability as much as they decide anything. The order and timing of various topics and choices in a decision situation are not accidental to the outcomes, as standard RCT would suggest. Much depends on how decisions are framed, on who writes the agenda, and on who speaks first. Frequently, the people needed to make a decision do not show up. Much time is spent not on deciding, but on defining what the meeting is about and how it fits in with previous meetings. One spends a lot of time explaining to others what one is saying. Even if an official decision has been reached, it remains unclear what it means, how it is to be carried out, and by whom. Decisions are social processes and dramas, not mere instrumental steps in the realization of preferences.

Decisions and actions may sometimes be coupled, but to varying degrees. RCT expects close coupling, where decisions follow from wants and beliefs, and where decisions "lead to" an outcome. Soon we shall see why this is a very rare and unusual case. The extent of coupling is a variable, and should not be held constant as part of a definition of rationality. That is, we expect some decisions to lead nowhere, other decisions to be the outcome, not the cause, of actions, and still other decisions to lead to some outcome, though maybe not the intended one. Decisions, actions, and outcomes are not, as a rule, independent, since attribution of some decisions to a responsible party is itself an action.

"Decision," then, is a highly simplified and controversial means for observing organizational causality, and for allocating praise and blame. Organizations use this observational and attributional device to carry out their business. They cannot do their work unless they can observe where decisions are being made. But different observers may decide to observe with a different schema. A good example for a different observer is sociology, which can observe what organizations cannot observe, such as "unintended outcomes" or "unanticipated consequences" of organizational action. These two constructs show that "decision" is much more difficult and problematic than is visible from inside the organization. The sociological observer can interrupt the causal chains somewhere else and argue that decisions are not the origins, sources, or unmoved movers of outcomes and events. Neither do they appear as "the last word" for an outside observer. Instead, he can, for example, extend the time frame to the long run and analyze historical processes and structures of organizational change that cannot be pinpointed in time or neatly reduced to any specific decisions. Alternatively, the observer might expand the realm of possibilities and explore what would have happened if someone had made a different decision.

For Weber ([1906] 1982), such counterfactuals lie at the very heart of historical explanations. An observer can ask what caused a decision to move causality backward in time. He can also observe, on a second level, "decision" as a first-order schema for observing organizational events and outcomes, and analyze how such self-observations covary with structural variables that escape the frame of internal organizational observers.

It makes a big difference whether an organization observes itself, or whether it is being observed from outside, including by other organizations. Observing itself, it cannot go much further behind decisions and actions, backward in time and causality. Despite their reputation for alienation and impersonality, organizations are actually sites for intense and ongoing talk about persons, including moralistic gossip about character faults, scandals, and private adventures. When they observe themselves, organizations perceive persons, offices, rules, decisions, and actions. They cannot handle much more historical and structural complexity, since the result of their inside observations is fed into the ongoing organizational operations (Chapter 1). An outside observer can use a different framework for observing, but his results are his results, not the organization's. If an organization is told, for example, that its structure is the result of social forces, not decisions, or that its leaders cannot really decide all that much, or that "decision" is a simplified fiction, or that the organization perpetuates the dominance of ruling elites—all of these observations cannot really be fed into an organization's ongoing internal operations. They can be fed into the ongoing operations of another observer, however, such as Marxist class analysis.

How to Locate Rationality

A central conclusion from these arguments is that "rationality" is a property not of actions by persons, but of *observing* and communicating about action, practiced within the social and cultural networks of "rational choice theory" and its relatives. RCT does not observe actual persons, since there are too many of them doing too many different things for too many different reasons. RCT certainly does not observe "individuals," since those whom one knows and deals with to some extent, including one's fellow rational choicers, would be insulted if observed as selfish opportunists. Actual persons, if they exist, do not reason well, or at least they reason differently than rational actors are supposed to reason.

The "rationality" of RCT, then, is a framework for observing and communicating that circulates within the networks that are RCT. *Doing* RCT means assuming rationality. In this way, RCT's identity is defined and demarcated against other sciences and specialties. For RCT, assuming rationality is not itself an option among others, to be arrived at after rational deliberation and calculation. Instead, for RCT, rationality is its unique cultural and disciplinary possession. Rationality is the core of this network's institutions; it is immune against falsification and achieves a normative status as that which cannot be suspended without discontinuing the practice of the specialty. The rationality of RCT, like that of other institutional cores, is the blind spot of observing within its parameters. Rationality is the *how* of this observing, not its *whats*.

In this, RCT does not differ from other basic institutions in other scientific and cultural networks. Like all science, it observes according to its own constructs, and so observes a piece of itself when observing its referents. Rationality is not an essential property of action, but a contingent device for observing action. What remains to be seen is how this device should be used to explain empirical outcomes. Like all devices, it will work better in some situations, and for some tasks, than others. The notion of "bounded" rationality leads the way into converting rationality from an essential property of action into a dependent variable. At least, this is what sociology does when observing rationality and RCT.

Some Covariates of Rationality

Allowing for variation, we should not fall into the opposite trap from RCT and declare that "action" is essentially irrational, emotional, habitual, inscrutable, tacit, interpretive, and so on. This would lead to polar dichotomous metaphysics, not an empirical continuum of rationality. Assuming a continuum of action, rather than incompatible natural "types" or kinds, paves the road for solving "rationality" as an empirical puzzle, not as a foundational postulate. Where nothing can vary, nothing can be explained, and the result is irresolvable debates between various metaphysical and ideological standpoints. Sociology should not contribute to these, but instead examine under which conditions "rationality" is more likely to structure action than "interpretation" or "emotion." These should not be seen as mutually exclusive, but as gradients along a continuum.

Bounded Rationality

Simon ([1945] 1976:79–83, 100–103) says that organizations "bound" rationality to structure behaviors that "satisfice," rather than maximize. Williamson (1975) sees bounded rationality as one of the prime reasons for internalizing formerly market-driven transactions within organizations. By dividing labor, and by structuring communication flows, organizations reduce and bundle complexity into divisions, units, levels, offices, and rules. These bounded internal environments deal with digestible "chunks" of a partitioned and classified administrative reality. They form the structural premises for decisions. Within a niche, these premises are exempt from decisions; they constitute a background world of already reduced complexity that is taken for granted when a niche does its work.

In this way, organizations limit the amount of uncertainty and information that need to be taken into account when making decisions. Most of the world can be safely ignored; what matters is a very small segment of that world, and the things and events of that world have already been "cooked" to some extent. They do not appear in their "raw" complexity, but have already been digested and metabolized in the past, or in a different niche of the organization. A niche or division focuses the attention space on a prestructured world of facts and givens. It is this highly restricted focus that makes a modest degree of rationality possible. The facts and givens do not have to be decided upon, or be decided anew each time a decision comes up.

To be sure, facts and givens can be changed—for example, according to decisions at another level or location in the overall structure. But these decisions are also the work of a routinized and structured niche. Actors are structurally relieved from pressures to decide anything that falls out of the narrowed confines of their task environment. This structural relief from intentions and decisions is built into the institutional "habits" of an organizational niche. Those who are "acting out" such habits do not have to find incentives and motivations within themselves (Gehlen [1956] 1964:53–55). Rather, behavioral adjustments to niche environments are grounded in the material ecology of such niches—one sits down at one's desk to write or work on a file, and the very material conditions and objects-at-hand in the workplace trigger sequences of behavior that a person need not rehearse, decide, or calculate every time anew. In this way, habits outlast persons, become indifferent to individuals, and account for the temporal continuity of an "office."

At the same time, keep in mind that the extent of structuring and limitation is variable and depends on other organizational variables. Structuring is more narrow and rigid in simple and repetitive niches with low uncertainty; it decreases gradually as status and discretion expand the range of options in more diverse, changing, and uncertain niches of the organization (Lawrence and Lorsch [1967] 1986:151–159).

Simon's account of bounded rationality corresponds well to psychological evidence on actual reasoning and decision-making. Paradoxically, rationality improves not as a function of increased alternatives and information, as standard RCT would suggest. To the contrary, rationality becomes an option as more and more of the world is being held constant as given and already decided. Then, rationality can operate on a tiny segment of the world within a niche that forms the context and background of such operations. Much as in adaptive advances in natural evolution, which are mostly gradual improvements of an already existing and working device, organizational rationality is local and temporary, not universal and long-lasting.

Rationality fares best when the parameters for decision are digitized into simple yes / no options, and when information is quantified to make it commensurable across times and locations. Quantification also gives preferences a common metric within which they might be compared and ranked. A good example is grades and the decisions based upon them. One can make "rational" decisions about, say, scholarships or recruitment because performances have been standardized into preset categories, and because these categories are assumed not to vary from location to location and over time. All else being equal, ten publications signal higher productivity than two publications. Everything depends on this "all else being equal"—since it never is, and so must be *made* equal, or *held* constant, both of which are contingent operations of an observer. Then, and only then, is an A always and everywhere better than a B, and deserves more credit than a B, in economics as well as physics. Ignoring the complexity involved in actual grading, grades digitize and simplify the world, and are assumed to measure true differences in actual performance. At the time of grading, or of processing grades, this simplified fiction is itself not open to decision. It is possible to deconstruct grading somewhere else, but if this operation is also coupled to grades, they structure decisions there as well.

In a digitized and quantified world, it is easier to act "rationally." As always, "rationality" refers to procedure, not substance. Organizations and particularly bureaucracies are so keen on numbers because numbers summarize and gloss over actual complexity. They can be handled and manipulated *as if* they were independent from context and time. Since they are not, in fact, independent from context and time, organizational numbers, statistics, and rationality can fail. There may be disagreements about what the numbers actually show, whose numbers they are, or how they got assembled. The numbers always leave something out—and that is the way to attack them, or come up with alternative numbers.

The success of organizational numbers and statistics depends on the construction and maintenance of commensurability (Herzfeld 1992:65–66). Numbers will face the opposition of local traditions, and especially of entrenched elites whose discretionary powers would be curbed by quantification and accountability. The worst enemies of quantification are not the oppressed masses, but local estates, with their byzantine arrangements of special traditions, privileges, and exemptions. Quantification requires the work of abstraction and decontextualization, and so remains reversible. The Simmelian ([1908] 1977:chap. 6) triad of numbers, money, and abstract concepts disappears when central administrations collapse. The opposite of numbers is not liberation from alienation and individualism, but feudalization and inherited corporate privilege. Despite their reputation for rigid instrumental and disciplinarian control, organizational measures and numbers are actually fragile and tenuous. This is so precisely because they ignore most of the actual complexity that they bundle and summarize. Recover context and time, and the numbers become problematic, ambiguous, and controversial once again.

Rationality is less of an option when information is vague, qualitative, and contested. This happens in conflicts over definitions of reality, or when innovations increase uncertainty. Since uncertainty and innovation are concentrated at the top of organizations, we would expect fewer numbers and bureaucratic protocols there (Morrill 1995:65). In a very aristocratic manner, high-status virtuosos claim exemption from quantification; they protest and resist the taylorization and digitization of their skills (Porter 1995:75). These are mystified as the special possession of a gift or talent that some persons just have, while others do not. Numbers and quantification are actually much more "democratic" and accountable than virtuosity and charisma. Incidentally, it is yet another empirical mistake of some postmodernism to expect liberation *from* the numbers.

As risk and uncertainty overload rules and capacities for rationality, discretionary judgment and "personal knowledge" appear. The true aristocrat of "personal knowledge" is Polanyi ([1958] 1964), with his matching elitist distaste for bureaucratic control and regulation. Adorno is likewise self-enchanted. As it confronts high uncertainty and innovation, virtuoso behavior gradually becomes more "interpretive," flexible, and "underdetermined." One can avoid the opposite essentialist mistake—that persons and organizations are not, and never, rational. Expect some organizations, or some of their segments, to behave in a more disorderly way when dealing with high uncertainty and controversy. They probably behave more rationally and bureaucratically when working on well-defined and routine tasks within a stable or stabilized environment.

Powell (1985) compares academic publishing and public TV, and finds that public TV works more as a garbage can than does academic publishing, since television extends into multiple turbulent environments where preferences and beliefs cannot easily be reconciled and aggregated. Textbook publishing is more orderly and bureaucratic than the publishing of scholarly papers and monographs, since textbooks are more consensual and standardized (Levitt and Nass 1989). Complex organizations are usually not either bureaucracies or garbage cans, but both, at different times and locations.

Rationality as Social Relation

When are persons and organizations expected to act selfishly? Not when they are in love, dreaming, having fun, or getting loose. Markets do increase the range of expected rationality, but not all markets and not at all times. An important finding in sociological economics is that markets condense into networks and niches of "embedded" relationships (Burt 1992). These networks are neither markets nor hierarchies; they have more organization than markets, but less than hierarchies, since there is no unified chain of command.

Rationality prospers when strangers expect each other to have interests and selfish intentions. Perrow (1986b:16–17) outlines the market conditions under which this happens, and Hirschman (1977:48–49) shows that "rational interest" emerges as a mode of observing when the numbers of strangers get very large. Since their "real" interests, wants, and beliefs are unknown and unknowable, the expectation is that strangers will act selfishly and rationally. One assumes that strangers have reasons for what they do, and that they could explain their actions in a rational way. Since they are rational, rational actors will act rationally in the future as well. As a mode of observing and attribution, "rationality" and "interest" render the world more accountable, maybe even predictable. Until further notice, the expectation is that others know what they are doing.

The social relation of rationality is tautological. We know what strangers will do, since they are rational and selfish. They have wants and beliefs. These can be inferred from what they actually do. This tautology is at the heart of "folk reasoning" or common sense; it constitutes the inviolate and unfalsifiable grid of treating strangers as persons, that is, entities making decisions and acting accordingly. Deviations from rationality can then be treated as such—as deviations that do not question the integrity of this agency metaphysics.

Strangers are those on the outside, wherever this may be. Inside a group or organization, one is a member, and as such is expected to keep selfishness at bay, especially when there are high moral and ritual densities (Marshall 1999). As an outsider, one may be a competitor or enemy, and as such is expected to act strategically for one's own benefits. Outsides, however, have their own insides, and so there is honor among thieves. Rationality is an expected strategy for "in-between" transactions; solidarity and trust are "within" transactions. Solidarity and trust become stronger as density and ritualization increase. If we assume that persons have multiple selves, an interesting problem emerges: when do these selves trust each other, as in a within-relationship, and when do they eye each other suspiciously, maybe as rational strangers within oneself, so that one does not trust oneself?

In sum, rationality is a variable, not a constant. It is a mode of observing and communicating about action, not a natural property of acting itself. Rationality prospers when the relevant world has been simplified and quantified, concentrating the attention space on a small and domesticated set of well-understood variables and parameters. Rationality appears shakier as uncertainty and turbulence disturb the familiar routines. As a social relation, rationality formats expectations toward strangers, particularly when there appear to be very many of them. Strangers cannot be trusted; they will do what is in their best interest. In contrast, within groups and the informal systems of organizations, solidarity and trust curb agency effects.

CHAPTER 4

Foundations of Culture

Culture is not value consensus. The most visible and influential consensus theory of society comes from Habermas ([1984] 1987 94–102). Habermas thinks that the lifeworld is held together by communicative action, which has the intrinsic purpose of rational agreement on validity claims. The foundation and arbiter of communicative action is discourse, where reasons are considered without immediate pressures to decide or do anything.

But consensus tends to break down when probed and examined in more and more detail (Gilbert and Mulkay 1984:138). Everyone agrees that racism is bad, but what follows from this basic value is far more controversial. The official measures of consensus are aggregates or artifacts of method; they outline groups in the computer, or on paper. But consensus breaks if stretched too far. You believe your own reasonable opinions are held by other reasonable people as well—until you discover that they have good reasons to believe otherwise. Consensus is more of a generalized expectation than an actual state of agreement on anything in particular.

Likewise, "values" occur as part of frontstage rhetoric when consensus is inflated to mask divisions. A case in point is "family values," which are not the actual values of any family in particular. Such slogans work precisely to the extent that their concrete content is left unspecified. Only then can they pretend to express a general and shared concern. Were such values to be specified in some detail, they would likely become divisive, not integrating. How much of what a family does in a day is the outcome of its "values"?

Never Minds

Maybe culture is in the mind or consciousness, as beliefs or knowledge. After all, it is persons who know and do something. For example, Sperber (1996:56–97) believes that cultures are sets of beliefs stored in the mind's "belief box."

But culture is not in the mind. Minds may contribute something to culture, but only after a culture has trained and prepared them. That which a mind can "know" is limited. A mind can do very little; networks a lot. The mind can focus on something, such as writing or reading this text here and now, but there are also all the other minds, belonging to different persons, who focus on something different. The mind's focus is also quickly changed or lost—for example, by a loud noise, a different focus, getting tired, and so on. In the meantime, the network continues its work.

There is no aggregate mind or collective consciousness. There is no direct way for one mind to feed its sensations and perceptions into another mind, though copresence around art, sex, or ritual do come closer to close coupling of several minds. Sex and ritual, however, depend on small numbers. Larger numbers tend to break up the common attention space into smaller separate clusters.

A mind does not know all that is attributed to it as, for example, its mental or intellectual property. Those products are on disks, on paper, in books and articles—not in the head. It is also not correct to say that they were in the head *before* they were also on paper, or that what was in the head duplicated itself on disk. For once an intellectual or mental product is on paper, or some other medium, author and intentions become immaterial to what happens next. If a contribution does get noticed, it will be reconfigured in the process of reception, interpretation, and subsequent usage. Some theories of interpretation go as far as to say that meaning is not just coconstructed, but solely due to reading and perception.

Indeed, authors have very limited control over their work. Once that work is published, or publicly accessible, authors can do little to make sure that their own interpretations prevail. The longer a work is noticed, and the larger the radius within which this happens, the more distant a work gets from its source, and the more it will be interpreted in relation not to the author, but to similar or connected works, to which the same applies.

Consider the possibility that authors do not write books; books write themselves, in the sense that the books that have already been written are a better, if still very poor, predictor for which other books will be written next than the brain states or thoughts of persons. When something gets written in a book or article, or when something is inserted into the flow of a conversation, the surrounding sentences or utterances are better predictors for what happens next than are mental states. Previous books are imperfect predictors for future books, but they will fare better at prediction than brain states. No author is the sole origin of communications.

Classical works can even less be understood from their authors' point of view. They become embedded in extensive networks of commentary and related classics. Who is the real Shakespeare? Classics are institutions or exemplars. Much like institutions generally, they dissociate from their original purposes and meanings. Not even the God who complains that His Bible is not being read right has any way to make sure this will not happen again.

Rarely, in simple cases, is information the objective transmission of some fixed and identical content between a sender and receiver. For a signal, or bit of information, to be transmitted more or less "as is," without meaning changes, that signal's content and message are reduced, formatted, and tailored into a very simple and narrow stimulus. Traffic lights fit this pattern, but not *Faust*. Some numbers and bureaucracies come closer to rather drastic reductions in variability than many other transmissions, but even they are not completely indifferent to context, culture, or usage.

To assure reliability of transmission, it helps to protect a signal by prohibitions and taboos, since such moral controls make deviant interpretations morally risky or offensive. One way to do this is through liturgy and ritual, and by securing the means of liturgical production in the hands of an exclusive elite. This elite also concentrates culture within certain settings and times, where control over practice can more easily be maintained.

But even in very dense and small groups, there is still no megamind, no operational unity of all the different consciousnesses involved in information and communication. Minds still read what they read, understand what they understand, and think what they think.

This suggests modesty about minds and persons. Most of what a mind knows is based on selective and partial *hearsayread,* fed into it by various sources over long periods of time. Soon a mind starts forgetting where the news came from, or which news came from which source, and may finally decide that an idea is really "his." Innovation is often a polite term for memory loss, unawareness of the literature, or conveniently selective forgetfulness. It is this very event or process of forgetting that gives rise to the idea that persons "have" ideas. I prefer to say that ideas "have" or "seize" persons. When they become emotionally charged in interaction with others, ideas can even "consume" a person, who then becomes their driven executive, rather than sovereign source.

As author, the mind celebrates itself as the ultimate source of insight and creativity. When the network, or part thereof, joins in the celebration, prizes can be awarded to intellectual leaders, and citations can be given to authors by their names. The practice of citation by personal name *creates* the myth that persons are the authors of their own ideas. Citation in fact leads to authors as the results of network activities and attributions; authors are not the independent or foundational source, origin, or cause of a network. For each reference to a person points not to a certain individual, but beyond that individual to a network of further citations, so that "author" is a drastic abbreviation and summary of this network.

Sociologically, ideas "belong" to networks, not persons, although authors emerge as nodes in this network. It is networks, not persons, that settle controversial and uncertain matters of authorship, such as priority conflicts, plagiarism, degrees of authorial creativity, and the like. It is networks, not persons, that attribute authorship to persons, thus pinpointing the source or origin of culture in the minds of persons. Such attributions are contingent, not necessary, and so come with a history. Oral cultures do not know authors in the way that literate and print cultures do. As in any network, the nodes are what they become as outcomes of the network activities, relations, and connections.

Rather than saying, with common sense or agency metaphysics, that culture is "in" the mind, it is more sociological to say that minds are what a culture uses to produce more culture. A scholar is, in Dennett's (1996:346) words, the way in which a library produces more books. Strong versions of neo-Darwinism see an organism as the way in which genes make more copies of themselves.

Maybe knowledge is, indeed, not in a person's mind, but in a collective mind, as the shared knowledge of a group, for example. But the whole notion of "collective consciousness" is misleading, since only individual persons have brains that might be conscious of something. Nowhere in the networks of culture do we find a masterbrain or megamind as the seat for the consciousness of an entire network. Much less is there a consciousness to entire societies.

As far as we know from neuroscience, consciousness is a property of neural nets, and neural nets alone. Neural nets occur only in brains, and brains exist only in the very massive plural. Until further notice from telepathy, one cannot feed one's own conscious operations directly into another consciousness, let alone into very many of them. Even telepathy, if indeed real, occurs only between very few persons, for a brief moment, and involves few experiences.

Consciousness cannot be shared. One can say what one thinks or feels, but then communication takes over to interpret such utterances in its own ways—that is, according to prior communications, not consciousness. What happens in communication and interaction does not follow from the experiences and sensations of any individual consciousness in particular. The results of the mind, say a thought, are what they become upon being fed into ongoing communication. By far the most thoughts never enter communication to begin with. Those that do become restructured and renormalized in this process. By means of communication and networking, a thought or idea becomes linked to other ideas and thoughts. What happens to them next, in the course of communication, is hard or impossible for any one mind to anticipate. This might, however, be accomplished in retrospect, and with the benefit of hindsight simplifications, which present an episode of conversation or communication as the gradual and linear unfolding and consequence of an idea or purpose.

Nor does the behavior of communication follow from the sum of all the consciousnesses involved, since there is no such sum or unity. Even if there were, the massive simultaneity of such a giant unified consciousness would result in the immediate breakdown of interaction, due to information overload and unstructured noise. It seems more realistic to say that an ongoing interaction selectively directs the attention of copresent consciousnesses to its own flow. If an interaction cannot manage to get this done, it soon falls apart and loses its focus, releasing the persons with their minds into the environment.

The consciousnesses involved in an interaction remain on their own. They can be addressed by an interaction's ongoing history, but never completely so, or without rest. The consciousnesses involved in an interaction do not merge into one. The minds of persons can focus their attention on a common conversational theme, but it is the conversation itself, not the minds, that directs this attention, with varying degrees of success. The conversation itself is not in anyone's head in particular, but constitutes an emergent flow that structures what the minds of participating persons contribute to it. If this direction or focus disintegrates, the conversation decays and falls apart.

Consciousness might be a "stream," but if so, there are very many such streams, and they do not merge into a mental delta. To be possible at all, communication and interaction direct mental attention, not the other way around. Even literary and artistic experiments with expressing the "totality" of a stream of consciousness, as it actually happens and unfolds (as in *Ulysses*), format experience according to communicative and literary, not conscious, sequences, tropes, and patterns. *Ulysses* is a book, not a conscious stream. It unfolds through writing, which must be read, not experienced "as is"—as a stream of consciousness in someone else's, James Joyce's, mind. That which Joyce experienced as he was writing his book is completely and irrevocably lost and unrecoverable.

To mimic in writing an actual stream of consciousness, complete with qualia, is to create a work that borders on unintelligible. An understanding of what is written relies on other writings and readings, on interpretation and criticism, not consciousness. A "total" expression of "pure" consciousness is never total and pure, but selective, and this selectivity can be introduced by writing, which has its own flows and rhythms independent of consciousness and mental experience. Husserl's phenomenology struggles mightily to recover primordial experience, but manages to do so only on extremely abstract levels, which are as remote from primordial experience as one can find. Husserl tried this again and again, which is why he wrote so many Introductions to Phenomenology, up to his last major work. In this perspective, claiming to recover someone's "lived and situated experience" is hubris unless it happens between intimates.

This separation of consciousnesses from each other is a bit alleviated among copresent and interacting persons, since they can at least assume or expect that the other is experiencing the same world—seeing the same things standing around in the here and now of a space, listening to the same sounds, smelling the same scents, and so on. For a brief episode, an encounter synchronizes time and space—but only for the very few persons who are there while it happens, and only as long as the encounter or episode lasts. Once this episode is over, the persons go their own separate ways again, taking with them their lived experience. Interaction among copresent persons and their minds breaks down when too many persons participate. A face-to-face interaction cannot deal with many minds expressing their internal states as they actually occur.

In fact, an interaction cannot reach too deeply into the few minds that are present, either. The great Freudian theme is that minds are bottomless pits and know themselves not all that well. An interaction would derail quickly if minds communicated "freely," running wild, without formatting themselves according to the topics, themes, rhythms, and sequencing of the ongoing interaction.

Interaction is more sluggish than the participating minds. It moves more slowly, overflowing when too much comes too fast. During an interaction, the minds can "wander" somewhere else; the interaction cannot, and remains in the here and now. One consequence of this limitation is that a conversation, as it goes on, cannot initiate and sustain a running commentary on itself. In contrast, the minds can dissociate themselves from a conversation a bit to think, for example, that they had better leave this conversation. A conversation might recognize this withdrawal of a mind from the conversation, however, and make it its explicit theme as soon as that mind exits, so that gossip may commence. But as you are there, in this conversation, nothing you do, or do not do, is exempt from possible observation and thematization.

Again, its topics may be remote, but the conversation itself stays right where it is, or where it moves. As communication goes on, focusing on a theme or topic, the minds involved can think of something else, think that this conversation is really boring, and withdraw into their own imagination—all the while pretending to remain engaged and occupied by the conversation. Conversations also take longer than minds to switch levels of observation, as in conversing about conversation. A mind can run faster and wilder than a conversation.

An interaction can, of course, react to the expression of a mental state, but this takes time, and the minds do not stop experiencing something new and different while the interaction still deals with this earlier expression of a mental state. A mind can jump levels, switch frames, or ironize much more quickly than any interaction could handle.

An interaction has its own sequences and turns to observe; it cannot expose itself to too many irritations from minds, especially when those minds bounce from this to that idea or sensation. A conversation can handle only one contribution and theme at a time, while the minds involved in conversation can process more sensations in parallel, or simultaneously. As long as it continues, the conversation itself makes more or less sure that the participating minds do not become too absent or too agitated. It notices when someone present falls asleep, faints, or pays no attention to the conversation. Conversations break apart soon after their focus is gone, as would happen if everyone started talking about what they really felt right now. After such an interaction breaks down and falls apart, it might reform into smaller separate conversations.

In written communication, it is even less possible to know what happened in the consciousness of a writer as he wrote something. Writers and readers are separated by space and time, and cannot deeply probe into each others' intentions, subjective meanings, and mental states. The difficulties get worse once authors are dead. Since one can no longer ask them about their intentions, one would have to infer them somehow, maybe from the very work that one tries to understand in terms of intentions. In any case, intentions are accessible only by communication and interpretation, and so it would be more correct to say that the meaning of intentions comes from communication, not the other way around. As we shall see shortly, the same applies to culture generally, since its meanings also do not reside in anyone's head in particular.

Even if intentions could be retrieved somehow, this would not help much with understanding what is written and read. A book or work of art cannot be understood by understanding the intentions of its author, since the work or text does not follow from such intentions, at least not in any planned or linear way. When asked where his ideas came from, Mozart is reported to have responded that he had little to do with his ideas. What did Mozart intend as he wrote the *Requiem*? Even if this could be known, chances are that he intended to write it, that his intentions changed as he did so, and that, at some point, the music that was there already took over to pressure Mozart's intentions into finishing what he had started. The same thing happens to texts; one resumes writing in the morning where one stopped last night, and what was written last night is the best, if still poor, predictor for what gets written next, not personal states, intentions, or mental plans.

As a result, authors and composers lose control over their work, and over its reception, once it is finished and made public. As long as they live, authors and composers can say what they meant, deny some interpretations, and claim to be misunderstood. They actually have to do this to encourage further interpretations, which can then be denied also, extending the time a work and its author get from the relevant networks. Declarations of authorial intent will not put an end to the interpretations that beg to differ. The work of interpretation and commentary goes mostly to critics, who would put themselves out of business if authorial intention were final or one interpretation prevailed. Final interpretive closure by the authority of an author would put subsequent critics and criticisms out of work.

Very large and complex works are particularly likely to support diverse and controversial interpretations. I count, for example, at least "three Webers"—romantic, conflict, and rationalist—sometimes on the same page. The romantic Weber dislikes the soullessness of rational culture; the conflict Weber is a realist analyst of politics; the rationalist Weber is a herald of disenchantment. The authors of classical oeuvres likely forget some of what they created in the past, and have no idea what they intended when they wrote down this or that passage. And why should authors always be right when it comes to how their work should be read, and who decides whether they are or not? Is it not true that, sometimes, an author or composer is a rather poor judge or interpreter of his own work? The poverty of the author makes room for the critics.

The "meaning" of a book or composition, then, resides not in anyone's head, but in the ongoing communications that have it as its theme. This is why meanings can change, why great works are never finished, and why subsequent communication can discover new and surprising meanings, unintended and unanticipated by authors. To say that a work means what its author intended it to mean is just to grant the author a special liberal and humanist privilege. It is a decision to grant a person control over his productions and their reception. But no author has, in social fact, such sovereignty; even the most original and creative minds do not start from scratch, in a vacuum, all by themselves. Authors and their works belong to synchronic and diachronic networks, and one might say that these networks energize themselves through authors.

"Authorship" has a history of its own, and emerges together with the solidification of early modern print culture. In the early phases of that culture, authorship is contested, uncertain, and weak. Only later can printed works be attributed directly to their "obvious" authors—those whose names, and later photographs, appear on the cover (Johns 1998:624).

Who Knows? No Idea!

A consequence is that "knowledge" has no personal and empirical subject that "had" this knowledge in its possession. Popper's (1972:chap. 3) observation, that culture is knowledge without a knowing subject, is on target, but the problem remains just where this knowledge is to be found, what this knowledge covers, and how long it lasts.

Take the notion of "scientific knowledge." It has no directly observable referent. Scientific knowledge is not the knowledge shared by all scientists, since not all scientists know all of it, and might not know what they know until somebody asks them. Specialization exacerbates this problem; we are all amateurs now about most things that could be known—even, or especially, the experts in one specialty. When responding to knowledge-eliciting questions, experts do not produce "scientific knowledge" per se, but bits and pieces of it, tailored to the specific contexts, situations, and audiences to whom such presentations are being addressed. Garfinkel (1967) says knowledge is "occasioned"—it is not the neutral and faithful expression of a mental or cognitive state, but the outcome of a social situation and interaction. This is especially so for "certified" knowledge, which is its own institution and, as such, not "in" the mind at all, but a social fact "out there."

As we have seen, it is also inaccurate to say that scientific knowledge is somehow the sum or average of all the knowledge held by all the individual scientists. For this would exclude, for example, highly concentrated innovations being made at the active frontiers of specialties.

Only a very few scientists are involved in those, and those scientists who are involved do not contribute to most other discoveries. When do discoveries become knowledge? When they are being made? When they pass peer review? When they are accepted for publication? Or when they make it into the textbooks?

More difficult even is to locate tacit knowledge, know-how, skills, and intuition. Common sense attributes these to persons as well, and for good reason, since doing so enables and justifies hiring decisions, for example. But skills are not really the property of persons at all, if this means that they know what they know and can state their knowledge. The significance of tacit knowledge is, precisely, that persons cannot seem to state or express how they manage to do something. Obviously, a skill would disappear without any persons at all, but if a skill "belongs" to anyone, it belongs to the generations through which it is being passed on, not to a particular person.

Saying that skill is "embodied" points in the right direction. A skill is "embodied" because it cannot spring into action without familiar clues from a familiar setting (Heidegger [1927] 1979:87, 150; Stinchcombe 1990:33). The exercise of skill depends on a familiar ecology and terrain. One can derail a skillful performance fairly easily by changing apparently minor details of a familiar performance environment or setting. Take a gifted lecturer out of the seminar room and observe how presentational fluency is disturbed in an unfamiliar setting lacking blackboards, students, rows of chairs, and so on. None of this should matter if skill were somewhere in the head or mind. Some writers need a unique *genius loci* so badly that they cannot write anywhere else. Deprive a musician of his beloved instrument, take Lucille away from B. B. King, and much of the skill and thrill are gone as well. To do any writing and thinking, the basics have to be taken care of so one can sit down and find pen, paper, and yesterday's work. When the writing goes well, it turns into a flow, sometimes a trance—the opposite from reflexivity and discursiveness.

The insistence on just the right configuration of performance ecologies may be observed as picky or snobbish vanity and self-obsession. But the reverse is true. The skillful worker senses that exercising skill is dependent on such settings, which includes the trusted availability of tools and means. He knows that he cannot rely on mind, natural talent, inner faculties, and such. The skill moves so smoothly precisely because it relieves persons from figuring out how to get something done, from thinking about the next step, or wondering whether this needed piece of equipment is still working right (Gehlen [1956] 1964). When there is a disruption in the familiar backgrounds or contexts that occasion creativity, the skill gets disrupted too, and may be replaced by (skilled) search behavior. Attributing skills to persons gets some jobs done, but a skill works more smoothly as the persons involved, their awareness and intentionality, retreat into tacitness and invisibility.

Next, consider the popular belief that "knowledge" is the consensus within a specialty. But "consensus" is not without its problems, either, as discussed before. It has often been claimed that physics is a high-consensus science, but this impression arises from a large distance between physics and its observer. Zoom in closer and physics divides into many specialties and subcultures. Reduce the distance even further, and networks emerge that are flexibly partitioned into routine and innovative sectors. In an active science, or in its innovative pockets, the normal state of affairs is not consensus, but uncertainty and controversy. In fact, those areas in a science where more consensus does exist—including textbooks, exemplars, teaching, and piecemeal extension of previous outcomes—are the least interesting and coldest ones.

In a science, consensus is often exaggerated by scientists as well, maybe in an attempt at solidifying one's own positions (Gilbert and Mulkay 1984). Probe in much detail, and there will likely be less consensus than initially claimed and expected. Consensus is shallow and hollow; dig deeper into just what is being agreed upon and disagreement, ambiguity, and uncertainty will surface once more. This much follows from the cultural force of competition, which initiates mutual distinctions, not consensus. There may also be differences in rates and amounts of consensus across specialties and subcultures within specialties. In any case, scientific consensus is an unstable and disappointment-prone expectation, not an independent and unproblematic fact that distinguishes, essentially, hard from soft sciences, say according to the intrinsic properties of their respective niches. Against essentialism, high levels of consensus do not naturally emerge when the world itself is simple and unchanging.

Maybe scientific knowledge is what is written in the books and journals, but this "passive" knowledge is not socially real until it is activated somehow in current communication and starts making a difference in the production of new knowledge or the rearrangement of previous knowledge. Nobody knows what is in the archives, and so nobody knows the knowledge contained in them. A speaking library would not communicate knowledge, but sheer noise.

At this point, we should again switch levels of observation and think of knowledge not as a fact about knowing minds, much less as what all these minds know in common, but as an attribution or expectation of a network. It is a network that "knows," when it is being asked to pause and consider what has firmly been established thus far. To do this, it presents a condensed and selective summary of its current state, say to an interrogator or audience. A network cannot tell all it knows, only a very small part of it. This happens, for example, in reviews or grant reports, when one's own research is being related to and distinguished from what is already known from past contributions.

One might say that knowledge is accomplished or "occasioned." It happens at certain places and times. A speaker or lecturer "displays" knowledge in a certain setting and performance. Knowledge can be found on frontstages. "Shared" knowledge is often the construct of a bureaucratic office, an expectation rather than actual reality. In examination and grading rituals, the candidate expects his teachers to expect him to "know" the field. On such occasions can one find Standard Models, laws, propositions, and ideas. Cultural networks are not primarily composed of "mental stuff" such as ideas, although they do contain such stuff in some of their more elaborate and codified parts.

The Meanings of Meaning

Culture has to do with meaning. But where do meanings reside? Prominent traditional candidates include intentions and rules in heads or minds, objects in external reality, and communities with their "practices." But language games are too idealistic and nonbinding to serve as a good account of very strong institutions. Strong institutions are not really games at all; they are the only game in town, and so have already lost their gamelike arbitrariness and conventionality. The proof that all knowledge is "conventional," though logically unobjectionable, sits well only with newer or weaker conventions whose conventionality and contingency are exposed and made visible. While all games are either constructed or do not exist at all, modes of construction differ greatly from site to site.

Not all meanings are rule-driven intentions in the head (whose?), although some hardened and congealed meanings—those close to direct ostension and common sense—are described fairly well in this way. But "GNP" or "wave-particle duality" are very remote from direct ostension, and no clear picture in the mind emerges. Meanings become like mental pictures of things when their social uses are very restricted and standardized. Repetition and drill accelerate this process of semantic taylorization and Fordism.

Such meanings become like traffic lights—they are usually in no need of interpretation and commentary. Instead they are designed for quick action, assumed valid for everyone who participates in traffic, easy to generalize across settings, and not very susceptible to cultural diversity. In the terms of linguistics, such meanings collapse sense and reference: they are what they stand for, cause what they symbolize, and show what they mean by collapsing the word and the world into one. Traffic lights are still conventions and constructs, but their conventional and constructed character has become all but invisible.

In contrast, there are more experimental meanings that have not yet settled into something like a concrete picture or definition. Such meanings make sense only in context as indexical expressions that need further elaboration when used outside of that context. Meanings have different meanings—depending on how novel or controversial they are, on how much they have been digitized and routinized, and on how close they are to the basic practices of a culture.

Habits no longer need interpretation. The reflexive agent and the judgmental dope are not two "essentially different" kinds of actors; rather, they are two sides of the same coin, tending to surface in different kinds of situations. The reflexive self emerges and prospers, for example, in psychoanalytic encounters, but is at pains to distinguish himself from the other selves waiting in a DMV line. When cashiers meet customers in large supermarkets, the mutual assumption that both are reflexive agents who are going to interpret the situation and its rules in imaginative ways is rather useless. But when lovers fall in love, agency is delightful.

Observing Culture and Cultural Observers

A sociology of culture should expect some hostility from the cultures it observes, and the more so when a culture is relatively "mature," prestigious, and professional. Sociological analyses are "disenchanting" to the observers they observe. Lovers, for example, do not want to hear about marriage markets, at least not as lovers or while they love. They love each other thinking that their love is special, not an epiphenomenon or effect of market structures and dynamics. Likewise, religion resents a sociology of religion as a disrespectful assault on all that is sacred. Mozart fans think that no sociology of music could ever account for "that spark." Suspicion and hostility result when a culture notices its being explained by another culture in terms and ways foreign and incongruent with its own. Hostility toward second-order observation belongs to ideological politics and conflict. The sociology of science has experienced this hostility in the "Science Wars."

At issue is whose distinctions count as fundamental. If a culture's distinctions are secondary or derivative from the more basic and elementary distinctions of another culture, the first culture declines as a separate field. If there were nothing to music but sociology and social structure, for example, there would be no music left, or so it seems to music and musicians. No culture can consider itself as "just" social structure. When sociology observes music, these observations are not music, contribute nothing to music, and are fed not into music, but sociology. To make a difference in an art, one has to learn and practice it, and be recognized as an artist by other artists.

Again, this varies with professionalization and reputational autonomy. But no professional and autonomous art explains itself in sociological terms. A mature art will resist outside explanations as unwelcome intrusions, crude misinterpretations, or ignorance about what "really" matters in art. Such resentments are part of cultural and professional distinctions also; they defend turf and property, insist on uniqueness and emergence, and defend a culture against reductionist threats from other cultures.

A professionalized culture observes itself "internally," that is, as the result of its own specific distinctions and modes of operation. Self-observation is part of professionalization. It generates rational myths. At the same time, to a culture its central constructs and modes of observing are not fictions. Observing itself, a culture will ground its accomplishments in a reality outside of itself. Except for disappearing and disintegrating cultures, a culture cannot observe itself as a sheer accident and contingency. Or, if it does allow this observation, then *this* observation cannot count as merely contingent.

Observing itself, a culture will, with varying degrees of controversy and certainty, assume that its core institutions are sound and reasonable, that contributions to this culture have merit, that one cannot get a reputation in it without meritorious contributions, that its accepted claims are generally legitimate, that the distinction between sound and faulty contributions can be known, and so on. This in no way excludes conflict and disagreement, but it does exclude the position that whatever these conflicts and disagreements are about is not worth pursuing. Self-observation is also incompatible with the conviction that no outcomes of conflict and disagreement have anything to do with merit, or that reputations are built by accident. If such convictions harden nevertheless and become widespread, skeptical cultures likely self-deconstruct.

In contrast, outside observers are not part of the culture they observe. Their observations are not to be fed into the referent culture. This includes the observations of participant observers, insofar as these are fed into academic, not native, networks. It is these academic networks that decide the reputational fate of ethnographers and ethnographies, not the indigenous folk. Outsiders are free to draw different distinctions and explain a culture's self-accounts as rational myths. Such observations are also fed into their *own* culture, however, where different myths and institutions work. No outsider can explain a culture as an insider would—without becoming one.

Do not take the official self-descriptions of a culture for granted, since this would amount to repeating and confirming its celebratory myths. Sociological observers refrain from such hero worship as, for example, that van Gogh was creative because he "had" special talents or inspiration naturally missing in other persons (Heinich 1996:37,65). Neither can sociology decide how reputation and creativity should be allocated in any culture but its own. It can explain how creativity behaves, but it cannot decide who deserves reputation outside of its own networks.

Within a culture, merit is obvious and tautological—reputation goes to those doing the best work. A sociology of that culture cannot start with this assumption, however. It introduces its own variables, social structures, to observe what that culture itself cannot observe. Then one might observe that reputation accumulates as capital, is inherited from previous reputations, or is concentrated into status. But at no point can "objective merit" enter a sociological explanation, since sociology has no independent way to assess or measure merit in any culture but its own.

Prolonged and sustained reflexivity of an observer is the cultural result of structural decentralization and fragmentation. As a network fragments or breaks apart, its self-observations lose their unity as well, and the inside becomes many outsides. Its own fragmentation makes it possible for the sociology of culture to see that all cultures, including its own, are constructed.

Most varieties of constructivism do not allow for enough variation. That all cultures, including science, are constructed is true enough, but there is no reason or evidence to assume that processes of construction do not vary, and covary with other variables. Essentialism needs to be overcome here as well. Modes of construction vary—depending, for example, on the status and location of the various observers of a culture, on the material means of cultural production, and on the density of networks.

Some cultures, particularly those with strong coherence and emotional solidarity, actually appear unconstructed and "obviously natural" to themselves. This tendency gets stronger as there are fewer competitors and challenges from outside. The extreme scenario is a strong and homogeneous cultural monopoly at the zenith of its imperial extension and confidence. The opposite extreme is a loosely coupled anarchy.

The sociology of culture, then, remains aware of the conditions for its own observing. If it does not, it runs the risk of extending its own constructivism to other cultures as well, or to all culture. All cultures are indeed constructed, but only some cultures, those with high internal diversity and fragmentation, are constructivist. That things might be otherwise or contingent is easier to see from without than within; if the outside observer is himself part of a fragmented low-density network, he is even more likely to ironicize the cultural necessities that do exist for the insiders of some more realist cultures. A good indicator for the state of a culture is how much irony it allows about its core institutions. Realist cultures are pretty serious about themselves; constructivist cultures tolerate more playfulness.

Cultures are observers; they observe themselves, their niches, and other cultures. Like all observers, cultural observers observe in the terms of their own culture, although the degrees of cultural homogeneity and network coherence are variable. Cultures differ significantly in how much internal multicultural diversity they allow; less "mature" cultures have less unity and house more subcultures, which may be observers in their own right. When such subcultures gain a great deal of independence, the culture fragments or breaks apart altogether.

It is this culture, their culture, that makes observers who or what they are. Cultural observers are also *cultured* observers; they come with a "habitus," which means that observers are trained and accustomed to using the distinctions of their own culture. It is this culture, theirs, that provides observers with the material and symbolic means of observation. It is their culture that gives observers reputation and status. Their observations are most likely to make a difference here, in their culture. Without it, an observer would not be the observer he is.

What Is in a Culture?

A persistent problem of "culture," as a concept, is its extension—what is, and is *not*, "culture"? Does a culture consist of symbols only, or also of things, as in "material culture"? Two definitions seem no longer satisfactory. The first one restricts "culture" normatively to a certain kind of culture—that of the upper strata in society, the owners of "legitimate" or "high" culture, who listen to "serious" music and do not go to monster truck races. Cultural stratification remains, but does not go so far as to deny culture altogether to all that which exists outside of the ruling class, palace, or temple. One example for the erosion of cultural privilege comes from DeNora (1991), who traces the decline of aristocratic control over musical appreciation and legitimacy in Beethoven's Vienna to a social broadening in the institutional means of cultural patronage and consumption.

The second implausible definition restricts culture to the so-called higher mental pursuits, such as arts, poetry, or philosophy. An ethnocentric string of this view adds the distinction advanced / primitive. In this old-fashioned view, composing a symphony is indeed "culture," while fixing a screen door is not. Instead, the conventional wisdom now holds that "culture" can be found in everyday life as well, in ordinary objects, mundane practices, or trash. Cultural anthropology has contributed much to the extension of culture to all sorts of everyday practices and objects. It seems no longer plausible to deny "culture" to certain social strata, to entire societies, or to certain objects.

The disadvantage of increasing conceptual democracy is decreasing sharpness, since the difficulty is now to separate culture from nonculture. The best I can do, for now, is switch to a second level of observation and observe how distinctions and demarcations are actually handled by empirical cultures.

Assume that a "culture" is a recursive network of self-observations and -distinctions from other cultures or noncultures. Distinctions create boundaries of varying sharpness and permeability. They produce an inside and outside, separating that which belongs to a culture from that which does not belong, does not yet belong, or belongs to a different culture. Sometimes there is much movement across the frontiers, making it more difficult to separate inside from out. This uncertainty increases when a cultural network becomes restless, turbulent, or innovative. The inside / outside distinction is a variable accomplishment of a culture as it observes and demarcates itself from other networks. It is never finished or irreversible, although some networks generate more teleological finalism—for example, at the climax of their imperial reign and extension, when a culture thinks of itself as the completion or end of history.

But distinctions change all the time. Rarely are they stable and uncontested within a culture. Sometimes, internal controversies and conflicts generate subdistinctions and subcultures, each with their own internal solidarities. But without any distinction at all, a culture would be indistinguishable to itself and so would have no "self" to begin with. This may happen to very young networks being formed, or to very old networks about to dissolve and disintegrate. They might have doubts about their "identity," including their intension, extension, past, and future.

As always, allowing for variation on all dimensions that might matter is critical. One variable is boundedness, or the degree to which a network turns inward, closing itself off from its environment and focusing attention on itself. More bounded networks are more selective; they restrict and restructure more of what they admit and allow inside. An example is cults. There are fewer degrees of freedom here than in more loosely coupled networks, which generate more ambiguous identities and permeable boundaries. A network with fewer degrees of freedom is more "in its place" than a low-density network, which is more restlessly searching for what its place might be. A network that is "afloat" in this way has a hard time anchoring itself in a stable reality and generates much internal constructivism, contingency, or skepticism. An example is social theory.

The inside of the network is to some extent coherent, and it produces and maintains that coherence against entropy and dissolution—until it does, in fact, disintegrate. Coherence is not consensus, but the outcome of sheer connectivity within the network. Networks have higher internal than external connectivity, though this proportion varies also from network to network. Since networks consist of bounded relations, however, they produce some measure of self-similarity; nothing more is implied by "coherence." A network is more coherent than the world at large, the world as such, or the *Ding an sich*. It is also simpler or, with Luhmann, less complex than the world. A network "knows" who and what belongs inside, although membership can be uncertain, ambiguous, and controversial. Networks are not of one piece, since they have subdivisions, clusters, holes, and cores. Some areas are more certain about membership and insiders than others. But to have a network means to have more internal than external connectivity. Self-similarity and boundaries result, including internal boundaries around subcultures.

The nodes in the network are what they become as the result of their movement and location in various positions and patterns of relationships. Their doings and meanings depend on patterns and modes of connectivity. Only when a node has been somewhere for a long time does it acquire solid properties, characteristics, and identity. A neuron does what it does depending on the other neurons to which it is linked. Link it to different neural nets in different configurations, and it does different things, or "learns." After a while, in later stages of organismic development and maturation, a neuron cannot do anything, or even survive, outside of a brain. Its status hardens, becoming less flexible and having fewer degrees of freedom. It ages and slows down. In contrast, shortly after conception, there is little differentiation and fixation, but many possibilities. At this point, there are only cells—not liver cells, skin cells, brain cells, and so on.

Let us inspect the components of the earlier definition for culture more closely. "Recursive network" suggests a degree of closure, maybe even circularity and tautology. For an art, only the art that is already there can decide what is to become part of it, although there are variations in the degree of autonomy an art may have in exercising discretion over its terrain. We should also expect some uncertainty and controversy over what is, and is not, a piece of art, especially in the innovative or avant-garde sectors of the network.

Something is "art" to the extent that it is recognized as such by the network of art. What is, and what is not, a piece of art can be decided more compactly and securely given an advanced degree of institutionalization and internal network closure. In this, an art behaves much like a science: In the beginning, when a science is in the process of separating itself from other cultures—from different sciences, popular magic, scholastic philosophy, or religion—it is much less certain what is, and what is not, "science," and who is, and is not, a scientist (Ben-David [1960] 1991). Such "roles," if you will, have to be accomplished, established, and separated from other roles and activities. Later on, when and if some degree of internal closure and recursiveness has been secured, a science becomes what its scientists will do.

Circularity and tautology are signs that doing a science, or an art, have become institutionalized to a degree. Sociologically, circularity is not an essential logical property, accruing to the nature of certain statements as such, but an empirical and variable outcome of network activity and connectivity. As we shall see, networks establish circularities in their cores by close coupling and redundant ties. This is more likely to happen under some conditions than others (qualitative variation), and happens to various degrees (quantitative variation). Nothing guarantees that such an outcome will be obtained. But if it does, it does not occur by necessity, by itself, or for transcendental reasons. This is Quine's (1964:20–37) main warrant for collapsing the analytic / synthetic and empirical / transcendental distinctions. Treating circularity as an empirical, rather than logical, network outcome yields some benefits for theorizing culture: antiessentialism, temporalization, and sociological minimalism.

First, there is nothing intrinsic or essential about an object, practice, or activity that would make it "automatically" part of a distinct culture such as art. Likewise, there is nothing inherent in an object or activity that would prevent it from ever becoming art, from losing that status in the future of an art, or from having been part of some art in the past of the same, or another, culture. Anything may become an art—if, and only if, it can be fed into an existing artistic network. This condition excludes complete artistic or aesthetic relativism and arbitrariness.

Not just anything goes—only that which can be fed into an art can become part of it. If there were no restrictions at all, there would be no art, since no operative distinction would be in place to distinguish art from non-art or different art.

The second benefit, temporalization, allows for changes within and between the networks that are various arts. Part of the dynamism of an art is to change its modes of operation, which include distinctions between art and non-art, traditional and cutting-edge art, or actual and possible art. As always, the best predictor for what will be considered art in the future is the present behavior of the network, but predictions likely break down when large time spans are considered.

Finally, allowing for variation in culture provides the benefit of sociological minimalism when it comes to defining what art is. Minimally, art is what artists do—not what they say. A more substantive definition runs the risk of legislating, from outside, some fixed content of a specific art, or interpretation of art, as a constant. To suggest a more substantive definition would be part of art, not sociology. The sociology of art, however, is not an art, but a science. This means that less minimalist definitions are left to the artists, and sociologists observe, on a second level, how these definitions change over time, how controversies over definitions are settled, how some definitions acquire more authority, and so on. To explain such variations, sociology has "social structure," not art or aesthetic theory.

Cultural Stratification

Unlike Bourdieu, I do not think it is possible to reduce all variables and distinctions to the ultimate megadistinctions of class and capital. In Bourdieu, culture is a rather closed and self-similar series of structural homologies, arranged in a hierarchy of mutually corresponding and reinforcing divisions within fields: "Thus the space of judgments on the theatre is homologous with the space of the newspapers for which they are produced and which disseminate them and also with the space of the theaters and plays about which they are formulated, these homologies and all the games they allow being made possible by the homology between each of these spaces and the space of the dominant class" (Bourdieu 1993:89).

It is an essentialist mistake to posit one master dichotomy that "remains structurally invariant in different fields and in the same field at different moments" (p. 89). Even if we did have a clear idea who, or what, dominates whom and how, the degree to which one master dichotomy, dominant / dominated, penetrates into the behavior of all fields, at all times, is variable, not constant. Dominant / dominated is itself a continuum, not a dichotomy; the very definition of "dominance" follows Hegel's master / slave dialectic. How strong domination is, how far it extends, and how long it lasts—these are empirical puzzles, with strong relational and network arguments suggesting that the very ideas of "dominance" and "power" may have to be rethought (Chapter 6).

It is also uncertain just which behaviors of fields can be explained as the result of alignments between dominant / dominated positions, dispositions, and discourses. These are also empirical, not conceptual, matters. They can be expected to vary within fields, between them, and over time. There is no "mysterious ontological complicity," no "cunning of reason," that established a dichotomous opposition between dominant and dominated and then made sure somehow that the "logic" of all fields corresponded, in more or less perfect harmony, to this one grand opposition.

It seems more reasonable to expect such high Bourdieuesque degrees of social, structural, and cultural closure and reproduction to occur only rarely—for example, when a society is rigidly stratified, especially in its educational system, where legitimacy and consecration happen, to be sure, but also desecration and deligitimation. Very hierarchical and centralized societies are, in fact, more likely to structure all of their relations, including cultures, in coherent and mutually reinforcing ways. Such societies and cultures are circular and tautological in their foundations, with each segment or distinction pointing to similar segments and distinctions in an endless mutual alignment, definition, and confirmation. From Douglas (1966, 1970), we know that high-group and high-grid societies enforce conformist caste cultures, in which all matters and manners of life follow homogeneous classifications and divisions, both in society and nature. The various fields of such societies are, indeed, more likely closely coupled around a central authority, which imposes its own distinctions on these fields. As a result, one core distinction—such as dominant / dominated, cultured / primitive, inside / outside, or rich / poor—imposes itself on all other major distinctions. For such societies, the following tautology might apply:

> It is impossible to understand how dispositions come to be adjusted to positions (so that the journalist is adjusted to his newspaper and consequently to that paper's readership, and the readers are adjusted to the paper and so to the journalist) unless one is aware that the objective structures of the field of production give rise to categories of perception which structure the perception and appreciation of its products. (Bourdieu 1993:95)

Dispositions come to be adjusted to positions because the positions, the "objective structures of the field of production," create the dispositions ("categories of perception") in the first place. To be sure, such tautologies are not meaningless, and not necessarily false—as long as one understands Quine's point, that tautologies are comparatively rare, signaling an advanced degree of cultural closure and consolidation.

Bourdieu's constructivism does not go far enough; the dominant / dominated distinction is not a sheer social fact, but an accomplishment that either happens or not, or happens to varying degrees. Bourdieu's theory needs a dose of antiessentialism. Societies differ; field autonomy is indeed relative, but this relativity, or variation, includes the force and extension of "dominant / dominated." We still need stratification, but the *grip* of stratification varies. Part of relative field autonomy is drawing distinctions in a different way, including the degree to which the distinctions in many fields correspond to each other, and to one master distinction. Bourdieu's theory rings more true for high-group and high-grid societies; it is less plausible for pluralistic societies with many cultures, which draw their own distinctions without respect for stratification—reducible, "in the last analysis," to capital. There is no such last analysis anymore. There are only various observers doing their work in the terms of their own cultures. This does not mean that status and stratification are irrelevant to culture, only that these are variables among others. It remains to be seen just how much variance in cultures capital can explain.

Phrased simply, there can be as many distinctions as there are cultures to sustain them, and no cunning "logic of practice" guarantees that all of the myriad distinctions drawn in all of the actual cultures can be subsumed, ultimately, under the distinction of rich versus poor. Bourdieu's theory of culture may be more adequate for a comparatively closed and centered society, say one with an Académie française, but likely does less well, empirically and conceptually, when the ruling class no longer commands a monopoly on legitimate habits and taste everywhere, in all the myriad cultures and subcultures trying to stay afloat. It is not even certain whether there is a ruling or dominant class, who is part of it, how far this rule extends, or just how strongly it rules and dominates. How, for example, does the ruling class enforce true / false distinctions in physics? In sociology? In Bourdieu's own sociology of culture? Even if one considers only science, there is not much unity to it, but many specialties and areas proceeding on their own, without the firm grip of a unified method, logic, interest, or metadistinction.

Bourdieu has not enough constructivism about his theory. When it comes to science, and his own work, Bourdieu is surprisingly old-fashioned and realist. "Cruelly unmasking the truth of artistic practice," Bourdieu (1993:79) finds, for example, that "painters and writers are deeply self-interested, calculating, obsessed with money and ready to do anything to succeed." The distinctions drawn in other cultures are seen as contingent and arbitrary constructs of a regime of symbolic violence and collective misrecognition, whereas the distinctions drawn in his own sociology capture the true state of society objectively. A thorough and self-including constructivism cannot allow such exemptions from its own doctrine. A reflexive constructivism would account for the conditions of its own observing, and this would mean to place Bourdieu's own distinctions into the network where they make an actual difference—that is, not into society as such, but that part of it which is, in fact, governed by Bourdieu's distinctions.

The very fact of a "sociology of culture" already suggests the presence of a certain kind of culture—one without concentration of all culture at the top (palace or temple), in one stratum (nobility), in one place (royal court), or in one special mode of cultural production (high culture). If there is only one observer, or even a "privileged" observer, there can be no sociology of culture—for then there is simply one, and only one, culture, and it is not to be explained from the outside (since the outside has no culture, or its culture is derivative and inferior to the one true culture at the top, or in the center). Explaining it sociologically, or in some other way, would amount to a profane intrusion into the realm of the sacred, a violation of taboo.

Explaining something means approaching it from a distance, and as a variable—as something that might be there or not, or as something that might be otherwise. If there is only one culture, however, its mode of operation is necessity, not contingency. It has, or tolerates, no observer outside of itself, or thinks of the other observers that do exist as a natural hierarchy of levels, with itself at the apex or center, and the others secondary and derivative. A cultural monopoly regards itself as a natural and universal fact, as a given and obvious reality. True monopolies are rare and unstable, however, and even they have some internal strife or heresy. Regardless, only when a monopoly is breaking up into a number of pluralistic and competitive cultures can a sociology of culture become an option.

When a cultural monopoly reigns, all that can be done, from a distance, is to admire and emulate this one culture. One either has this culture or not, and having it usually requires being born into it or marrying into it. Such a culture is unbrotherly and aristocratic. If one does not have it, and cannot get it, one simply has no culture, or an inferior one, and does not belong to cultured society. From this marginal position, it is inconceivable to explain the one true culture as merely one possibility among others. Once this happens, the monopoly has already lost some of its authority and universality. But where necessity reigns, nothing must be explained, since explanation presupposes variation, and with it contingency.

In other words, the very presence of a "sociology of culture" indicates that there is no "culture" in the singular, at least not anymore. Instead, there is a plurality of cultures, following the myriad divisions, subdivisions, and cross-divisions of status, politics, profession, ethnicity, materials, technologies, and so on. This Weberian "plurality of value spheres" is typical for the modern condition. While there remain status differences between cultures, none is so obviously and inherently superior to all the others that explaining it at all, let alone as one culture among others, would amount to sacrilege (Hannerz 1992:82). To be sure, cultural insiders might still resent outside explanations of their culture as cynical disrespect and a call to ideological arms, but once cultures appear in the manifest plural, everyone becomes an outsider to most cultures, and mutual explanations become commonplace.

As Mannheim ([1928] 1971:260) observed, the sociology of culture and its predecessor, the sociology of knowledge, emerge together with, and as a result of, pluralistic ideological politics. Once the privileged and true culture of the center or top is gone, or very much weakened, multiple cultures compete over normative and empirical claims and get ready to explain and disenchant each other. Cultures are observed as dependent variables by other cultures when their claims to legitimacy and validity are no longer obvious and self-evident, but compete with rival claims advanced by different cultures. When cultural certainty comes to an end, outside observers—who are always insiders of their own culture—are prepared to perceive another culture as driven by unacknowledged forces deeper than its own awareness, such as economic interests, partisan politics, social location, latent sexual motives, and so on.

Historically, the sociology of culture is both an engine and result of cultural pluralism and competitive ideological politics. Its mode of observation is fundamentally "suspicious"; it suspects that a culture is not what it seems and claims to be, and that its seemingly innocent truths and values conceal a deeper level of hard interests and narrow standpoints. The sociology of culture is also irreverent; as a mode of second-order observation, it brackets a culture's claims to validity and examines how these claims are "actually" being assembled and constructed. Most inside and official observers take their own culture for granted; outside observers cannot do so without observing redundantly or becoming insiders as well.

The sociology of culture, then, is not the invention of sociology, but is being practiced whenever pluralistic social conflict breeds ideological suspicion and disenchantment. Whenever a culture is explained by another culture as the outcome of latent and invisible forces, we have a rudimentary sociology or psychology of culture. One of the great forerunners of this mode of observation is Nietzsche, who searches grimly for the dark roots of bright ideas. As a loner, wanderer, and perpetual outsider, Nietzsche leans toward nihilism and solipsism, but this is only because he never wanted to be an insider to any network.

Art

A recognizable, and recognizably different, art emerges when an aesthetic culture becomes professionalized. Professionalization is not a linear and irreversible path, guaranteed outcome, normative consensus, or steady state (Abbott 1988). Rather, professionalization is a relation or configuration within various professions, among these professions, and also between professional and amateur cultures. It is no longer possible to define "amateur" without considering the specific professions from which he is excluded, and whose very exclusiveness makes him the amateur that he is. For all of us are amateurs now—in relation to most existing expert cultures. So even experts are amateurs to all areas of expertise other than their own.

Professions are not, as a rule of method, unitary or monolithic, and the relations between them change all the time. Some areas are becoming professionalized; others are being taylorized and deprofessionalized. Even as parts of organizations, some professions retain much discretion and self-governance. Professions also change as a result of technological advances (for example, new instruments in a science), labor market migrations (such as migrations of scientists from one area to another), and changing reward and reputational structures (as when an artistic avant-garde moves away from "mere commerce").

What, then, happens as a profession is emerging? It turns inward—it becomes more selective in what it admits as a contribution and whom it admits as a professional. A professionalizing art will allocate reputation according to ever more "internal" criteria of "artistic merit." While forming, such an art begins to observe itself and distinguish itself from other arts, previous art, and non-art. Origin myths and enchanting stories of breakthroughs might emerge, together with utopian manifestos, charismatic intellectual pathfinders, and promises of change and improvement. Heroes and prophets will be credited with the foundational breakthroughs and discoveries that brought an art into being. There might be some programmatic announcements, strong rhetoric and passion, or philosophical justifications (Mullins 1973:21).

Professionalization is an ongoing process; it is never complete, final, or secure. There is some evidence that there may be some "steps" in this process, but even more evidence that such steps or stages are not linear, irreversible, or necessary (Abbott 1988:30). That is, the process can be interrupted or reversed, accounting for the widely observed "liability of newness" and high mortality rates throughout professional and organizational adolescence (Hannan and Freeman 1989:245). If professionalization does continue, some institutions might emerge in the network cores, signaling a hardening or normalization of some segments of the network as it establishes routines, formats, methods, doctrines, standard techniques, and other "black boxes."

There are variations, however, in the degrees to which a culture turns inward to become an art. Boundaries around cultures vary in their permeability and interactions with other cultures. Important also is the connectedness of a culture to other cultures, in both time and space. Nevertheless, a culture becomes professional to the extent that it is recognized as a profession and recognizes itself as such. A profession places variable formal and informal restrictions on who counts as an observer or producer in this culture, how these observers are to be trained, and on what sorts of observations or contributions are perceived as belonging to this culture.

Art must be recognized as such within the network that is art. This rarely happens consensually, but involves much conflict and disagreement. A piece of art is anything that has a recognized position within the network that is an art. To have a position in the network means being connected to other artists and pieces of art. Networks exist not just between artists, but also link their works, modes of display, styles, and organizations. For example, there are networks among museums and recording studios that are independent of the flows of workers and personnel, although transactions with persons are an important part of the overall structure. Flows of persons are not the only activity of that structure, however. Reputations also flow within the network, as do communications, things, money, and the means of artistic production.

The "meaning" of a piece of art depends on just how it is connected within these networks. Status correlates across various scales and metrics, but the strength of that correlation is an empirical matter, likely different from art to art and over time. What a piece of art "means" is the result of its location in the various networks of other pieces of art, persons, reputations, criticism, creative sites, and tradition. Meaning is a relation within a network, not an intention in the head. It comes from related and different meanings, and also from constructed physical surroundings, critical commentaries, and youth or age.

Meaning changes go along with changes in connectivity. It matters to a piece of art, and its meaning, whether it circulates primarily among commodities and markets, or along networks of cutting-edge galleries. It matters to an art whether it is highly dependent on a temple or court, or whether it has managed to create its own markets. It also matters to meaning changes in a piece of art how long and uninterrupted has been its tenure, if any, in the rare networks of classics.

Art is an acquired status. That status can be lost, changed, and regained. While much prestigious contemporary art is constructivist about itself, some art produces more realism in its self-descriptions, as happens when an art becomes closely coupled to a political, clerical, or ideological monopoly (Chapter 7). Such a "privileged" art might think of itself as an expression of aesthetic universals and constants. The artists then retreat behind their official mission, and rewards go to those conserving the tradition and dogmatics of a central authority. Here there is not much room for aesthetic risk, experiment, and provocation, although the avant-gardes might migrate into an underground, which actually intensifies charisma through secrecy and rumor. An example is the samizdat movement in the former Soviet Union.

Sociology, an observer at the second level, is constructivist about art and refrains from defining what art is. (Only art can decide what art is.) What sociology can do, however, is observe how social structure works in art. This involves switching from "what" to "how" questions, from "what is art" to "how is the art that is already there made, displayed, produced, and understood," or "how does a novel art distinguish itself from previous art." Such how questions overcome essentialism, since the interesting problem is now to explain variations in arts as the result and outcome of networks.

Much of modern art is constructivist about itself; teasing, playing with, and provoking an audience by exploding conventional definitions and criteria of art. This goes to the heart of the matter of how something can be art at all. The traditional criteria—beauty, edification, ecstacy, realism, or moral improvement—no longer seem acceptable, since they belong to an essentialist past in which the intrinsic nature of art could be known. This is no longer plausible, since it belongs to the very dynamism of a modern art to keep changing the definitions and identifications of something as art. This activity belongs to artistic professionalism, and so can be expected to vary together with, for example, the degree of artistic professionalization.

The most visible mode of aesthetic constructivism occurs when acquiring artistic and aesthetic status within the networks of an art requires taking an object or entity (such as an altar or kitchen) out of its previous context and placing it inside an art. Then it is stripped of its original significance and meaning, and acquires new meanings as a piece of art. Often, this is perceived as shocking or provocative, depending on the audience. Moral and aesthetic conflicts may result, and it is these very conflicts that settle whether something is art or not, what makes it so, and who decides. Artists who sell buckets of artists' shit are either artists or not, depending on whether the existing or forming networks of art recognize this as art or not. If I did this, such recognition would be unlikely, since I have no status or reputation in the networks of art. If Picasso did this, or if the shit buckets were displayed in a gallery, instead of a street, chances are that the networks of art would spring into action.

Likewise, whether a sculpture of Jesus defecating on the Mother Mary is art, an outrageous sacrilege, or a waste of money depends on who the observer is and on whose observations will prevail. Observe the observer. In all cases, art is the outcome, not cause, of the relevant negotiations and conflicts. Constructivism expects that outcome to change all the time, and the more so when an art has an innovative core where frequent advances are happening. Then it becomes the business of that avant-garde to change what it considers art, much as it is the business of research frontiers in a science to develop what will become discoveries and inventions. No outside observer can participate or contribute anything to this unless he has, in fact, network connections to the centers of artistic influence, maybe as a critic or curator.

In the beginning, such switching of contexts and networks will require elaborate theorizing and commentary, especially when a piece of art-in-the-making has had a long tenure outside of art, or keeps that tenure afterward as well, so that it now has multiple statuses and identities. Under such conditions, the networks of interpretation and criticism get very excited by novelty and uncertainty. When "ordinary" objects suddenly claim to become art, there will be suspicions, for example, on the part of the observer's "common sense," that this is phony, offensive, meaningless, or sheer nonsense. Such suspicions are the price art pays for a radical constructivism that recognizes that nothing intrinsic makes an object art.

Sociologically, however, the constructivist contingency of art does not imply arbitrariness, since not just anything can become art. Only that which is actually recognized and renormalized into art can, in social fact, become art. Likewise, no art is merely "subjective" or "imaginary"; if it were, it could not be part of society and communication, and it could not be recognized and appreciated by anyone but the artist who made it. An art may be "esoteric," but it is still recognized, appreciated, and celebrated within its esoteric circle, which reduces its subjectiveness. Hence, the popular distinctions between science as essentially objective and impersonal, and art as essentially personal and visionary, should be discarded as well.

Actually, the fact that ordinary objects can also become objects of art illustrates just how selective art remains, despite constructivism. For by far the most ordinary objects never make it into art. The highly selective, restricted, and focused attention and activity of the artistic networks are required for the production and consumption of something as art, and by far the most things that could be art never make it since the attention and capacity of the network are bounded and limited. Phrased differently, while anything could in philosophical principle become art, most things do not. But if the network does, indeed, pay attention, even the denial that there is art at all—or that some objects are intrinsically not art—becomes then and there an event or occurrence within art.

Some variables make it more likely that something will, indeed, be recognized as art, especially when that art has managed to professionalize to some degree. As in science, reputation is critical, since a product by an artist who is already well-known as an artist has a good chance of becoming art as well. Reputation extends not just to persons, but also to organizations and institutions, so that galleries and museums occupy positions in certain reputational strata. If something is on display in a space recognized for its past aesthetic achievements, art is more likely to emerge than in the anonymous privacy of an un-known artist's workplace. If the networks of criticism and commentary direct their attention to a person or work, it is this very attention that contributes to making art more likely, and to make it an art of a certain kind, say "highbrow" as opposed to "popular" art. Shrum (1991:367–368) finds that the mere fact of attention by critics, rather than what they have to say, stratifies an art into "serious" or not-so-serious. Van Rees and Vermunt (1995) report that attention by critics is a good pre-dictor for attention by academics, and that both variables together ex-plain much of the variance in careers in the "serious" sector of the Dutch literary market.

Possibly the strongest resistance against upward mobility to artistic nobility is faced by artists who have already been labeled "commer-cial." They can pretty much write or paint anything—chances are they will not be taken seriously within the artistic profession, which per-ceives them as "popular," "commercial," and "sell-outs." Too much commercial success draws the suspicion and disdain of the profession, which has its own capital, reputation, which is given not by markets, but peers. Reputation generalizes not only the network's attention, but its inattention as well, so that an artistic worker or producer labeled commercial in the past can be ignored by the profession, no matter the "actual" merits of subsequent work. Stephen King, for example, could write the great drama of the millennium, but no one would know it, since his immense commercial success is sufficient warrant not to deconstruct his works in Duke University doctoral seminars on literary criticism.

As in science, and any profession, reputation in art follows the Mat-thew effect and the principle of accumulative advantage (Merton 1988). The earlier in a career a label consolidates, the more that label is likely to stick in the future as well. When an art has become pro-fessionalized to some degree, you can first make a name as a serious artist, and *then* start making some money, but not the other way around. This might be the revenge of those who have very little capital other than their reputation, honor, and "integrity."

Contexts and Clues

There are, then, very strict and specific standards for recognizing something as a piece of art. Only common sense thinks otherwise, that anything goes in art, and that it is arbitrary. But the opposite holds true, since an art will, especially as it grows, restrict more and more what it allows as internal possibilities. This is a process of institutionalization, which turns some pieces of art into exemplars for what art is all about. Such exemplars and classics are much harder to deconstruct, since they are firmly embedded in the core of the network, protected and buffered against deconstruction (Thompson 1967:20).

Institutionalization is critical, especially for an art that tries to evade it and aims at exploding conventional standards. But even a revolutionary aesthetic breakthrough relies on contexts and clues that affirm that revolutionary art is still art, and not, say, science or religion. In a revolution, not everything can change drastically at the same time, since a revolution still distinguishes itself from the tradition, which is thereby held constant, summarized, and opposed as that which must be overcome. Moreover, a revolutionary art or science will still proceed, to some degree, in the old footsteps, since it takes place in a here and now, which is created in a past. One can do science differently, or a different science, or a science with different means—but all this must still be recognizable as "science," not something else.

And so for art. For one thing, a piece of art can be recognized as such only in a certain context, such as a museum, gallery, or special performance. An art happens somewhere, and at some time. If it escapes the museums and galleries and goes into the streets, it must still be distinguished as something special and artistic from traffic, pedestrians, and vendors. This is especially so when the art in question has a program of exploding conventional standards and criteria, or when it aims to disturb routine expectations. Such novel contexts and clues must then be negotiated and recognized afresh. If theater experiments with leveling the difference between actors and audiences, stages and life, this still happens within theater, not in society at large, and so remains a "theatrical" performance and event. It does not escape the networks of art; if it did, it would be altogether indistinguishable from non-art.

Art happens in certain places, and at certain times. All art is such a social happening or occurrence, but the challenge is to account for variations in such happenings. Eventually, as it becomes more established and secure as art, an art becomes housed in designated areas, which support the expectation that an art is, in fact, occurring or happening here. Art becomes art in much the same way as a Durkheimian ritual transforms a profane object into a sacred one—it is the very ritual itself, or the attention and recognition of something as art, that loads an object or performance with sacred or artistic significance. Outside of these contexts, and outside of these expectations, a piece of art reverts back to its pre- or non-art status, much as a sacred object loses its special powers when it is no longer the target of worship and consecration.

Recognizing a piece of art as art relies on such circumstantial clues, which form a network of their own. An equivalent from science would be a laboratory since laboratories are networks of instruments and equipment, linked together in chains of interaction and communication. An instrument becomes a "scientific" instrument when it is housed and used in a laboratory, and when it is coupled to other such scientific instruments. Many of the instruments used in laboratories during the Scientific Revolution had already been available in some form in the craft shops of instrument makers or in artisans' studios, but science took off only when these instruments were taken out of their previous contexts and placed inside the laboratory, where they became linked to other such instruments. When this happens more frequently, and with some regularity, a network sets itself apart from other networks and becomes more similar to itself. When they are connected to each other in networks, and are moved from one network and context to another, instruments acquire a new "meaning."

Hankins and Silverman (1995:3–8, 37–38) show how the new networks among instruments in seventeenth-century experimental science accomplished cultural distinction and emergence. Some of these instruments were also used in the demonstration experiments in popular entertainment and natural magic; putting them into a new context demarcated their "scientific" uses from magic. The displays of popular magic produced wonders; the experiments of the new science produced matters of fact. In magic, instruments work by analogy to generate emblems; in science, instruments work by analysis and dissection. Whether an instrument produces one or the other is flexible and variable. What matters is location in a network and context, and self-similarity among the network components, whose very linkages pull the nodes toward mutual compatibility and resemblance.

The more such contextual clues are present, and the more closely and coherently they are (and remain) related to each other, the more confident is the recognition of something as a specific culture—say, art or non-art. This is when a tradition emerges with its classics and exemplars. With Kuhn, one might call this "normal" art. Typically, such art is on display in museums, which are prime sites for highly institutionalized and recognized networks of contextual clues for confident and quick aesthetic recognition. If a work is in the museum, it must be art, since all the other stuff on display in the museum is also art. Often, art objects are on loan from other museums, a practice that ties museums together in networks and, with them, the art objects that move along the network ties.

In a museum, there are many contextual clues supporting expectations that art is happening there and should be recognized correspondingly. A museum says it is a museum. Starting at the entrance, it has "museum" written all over it. There are uniformed guards, which means that the art there is truly valuable and precious, and so must be protected. There are signs that point to exhibitions and encased displays. Traditions come from repetitiveness within a variably fixed framework of relations, contexts, clues, and occasions. The art that is housed in such frameworks is easier to recognize as art than, say, very novel art, which might be on display only in the artist's studio or workplace. The museum janitor who—accidentally or aesthetically?—tossed a Beuys sculpture ("ball of lard with fleece hat") into the garbage did so when the museum was closed.

Place a Rodin sculpture on a busy interstate, and it becomes a traffic hazard for the observers in cars. No art is supposed to be happening on interstates; if it does so nevertheless, maybe in an attempt at aesthetic disturbance and irritation, it must be especially announced, designated, and physically separated from the routine flow of traffic. To produce, perform, or display art on an interstate, one must get special permission from the authorities. It is, again, these very distinctions of art from non-art, including happenings and occasions, that constitute art in the first place. No distinctions, no art, and the more strange and unusual an art gets, the more vocal, explicit, and elaborate are the distinctions made from non-art, or previous art.

Surely, much modern art experiments with switching or estranging the distinctions and contexts within which something can be recognized as art. But this switching is still done within a network that recognizes art. An art can declare that there is no such thing as non-art, that all is art, or that all art is not really art at all. But this must still happen within art, or it would draw no attention and would not be recognized as part of art. Whether the can of Campbell's soup is a can of soup or a "Warhol" depends not on the "intrinsic" or essential characteristics of an object, but on whether it circulates in the networks of food or art.

It also helps to see whether the can has been signed or not. A signature is one of the most important contextual clues assisting recognition of art. This is especially so when an artist, and his signature, already have an established status within the networks. Signing does several things; it authenticates, identifies ownership, and readies the work for public exposure and circulation. If an artist signs a lot of things that turn out to have a major impact, his "signature" evolves, with attributions of style and "school"—including, very importantly, distinctions from different styles and schools. Then the network becomes a network of family resemblances, which are what they become in opposition to other such resemblances and groupings.

At some point, the constructivism of signature, which turns a piece of art into more than just another piece of art, may be ridiculed in various ways, such as declaring that anyone the artist shakes hands with is, henceforth, an artist also. But the fact remains that such ridicule remains an artistic performance and statement, or is not recognized as art. Reflexive constructivist irony belongs to art as well if, and only if, it becomes recognized as such, which requires feeding irony into the networks of aesthetic self-observation. But then it turns more "serious" already, since this irony now happens inside art, as part of it, not outside of it.

Signing also celebrates and invents the artist as a creator, maybe even a genius. Signing is frivolous, vain, or even sinful when an art has little internal leeway, maybe because it is closely coupled to a dominant or hegemonic religion. Then what matters in art is not up to art, but religion or ideology, maybe the state. The concern is not so much with artistic innovation but preservation, going back to a sacred or pure revolutionary or charismatic origin when the state, religion, or ideology were first founded and announced. In this, persons play a minor role; they are faithful and docile servants of a power much higher than they. As persons, artists disappear into very solid institutions, becoming invisible as individuals. What matters is the execution, continuation, and reproduction of glorious tradition.

Medieval scribes sometimes signed their copies of authoritative texts and added traces of their authorship, but this was risky, up to the threat of excommunication (Drogin 1983). Signature is the recognition of individualism and the celebration of creative agency. It emerges together with the invention of the modern person and author. The outcome of this recognition and celebration—a piece of art that has status in art—is then reattributed backward to the self, in whom a special faculty is believed to reside, and who is now credited with the very emergence of art. This faculty may be interpreted as immortality, soul, genius, or creativity—in each case, there is more permissible individualism than in medieval scribing and copying of sacred texts.

When a piece of art becomes secured by the ties linking it to various networks of related art, its status hardens. Generally, the stronger and denser these ties, the more secure an object can be in its assumption that it is, indeed, art. Latour (1987) sees net-work in the making of facts and black boxes. Facts emerge from repetitive embedding in a network of related facts. Metaphorically speaking, by means of all this attention, care, and admiration, an art object becomes self-confident and exudes that confidence when placed in its proper space and time. Much like a totem, it becomes loaded with a special energy, charisma, or force, which radiates back at the ones looking at it in the gallery— though that still leaves the truckers and haulers unimpressed. For them, museum art is heavy stuff, not sacred objects. They have their own totems, though, too. What distinguishes an archaic totem from modern art is degree of intensity, and size and structure of the group, not natural kind or essence. Bourdieu (1993) speaks of the "social alchemy" that makes, and is, a modern art.

Some art becomes authorized, authenticated, and officially "consecrated," as Bourdieu would say. It travels between museums and galleries. It hangs on walls with other art. This art is talked about in the relevant circles and media, which shift together with different sorts of art. Making art is, again, the work of an esoteric network of its own kind, consisting of artists, critics, curators, and other professionals.

Without the approval and stamp of this professional network, nothing can become art. Of course, an established profession may be confronted by an opposition, resulting in countercultures, avant-gardes, possibly even revolutions. But such countercultures and avant-gardes also distinguish themselves, and their art, from what appears to them bad art, tired art, elitist art, non-art, and so on.

The more an art tries to level the distinctions between art and non-art, the more it relies on an esoteric "theory" to explain this very leveling. The less solid the status and recognition of something as art, the more verbose the surrounding culture, since what is not (yet) obviously art must be debated and negotiated. Critics advance various reasons for why they consider something art or not, while the *Mona Lisa* does not need any theorists or theories anymore to warrant its claim to art. When there is more uncertainty about novel art, however, academic and intellectual critics heed their call.

Critics have their own more or less esoteric networks. The status an artwork will attain depends also on these networks of criticism and commentary. If they have high status, the status of the art being talked about in these networks might increase as well. The correlations of status and visibility tend to be stronger when the respective networks are themselves closely coupled, so that more uniform and homogeneous cultural reproduction results. If artists, critics, curators, galleries, audiences, and locations all overlap, their parameters get mutually reinforced and consolidated, so that the famous structuralist homologies emerge. But recall that homologies are empirical events, not rules of method. Homologies make it possible to start from one point in one network and go directly from there to an equivalent point in a different network and back. Homologies map networks onto each other in similar ways, across a variety of arts and entire cultures.

Instead of holding homology constant, or turning it into a rule of method or principle of analysis, we should treat it as a variable outcome dependent on the extent to which various networks are, in fact, closely coupled. In the case of close coupling, there is more coherence and convergence across various networks on what art is, on what makes it good or even pathbreaking. The networks of artists, art, critics, curators, criticism, and audience overlap so much that they become redundant and self-perpetuating, with little room for change. One can then "deduce" the status of an artist, for example, from the status of his critics, the status of the places where his art is on display, or the status of the spectators attending to his art. This is a comparatively closed social universe, with a high degree of centralization and integration—Douglas's (1985) "high grid / high group" condition.

The other extreme is a loosely coupled anarchy of pluralist and contentious cultures and subcultures, criss-crossing over several dimensions of membership in more loosely coupled and weakly policed networks. The result is more uncertainty about art, including distinctions between serious and popular culture, high and low art, commerce and avant-garde. Much contemporary American art experiments with these very distinctions.

In contrast, classics and exemplars need less theory, elaboration, and explanation than avant-gardes. They need no special philosophy, or not anymore. They have "art" written all over them, due to their long tenure in the networks of art, especially their strong links to other classics. "Everyone knows," or can be expected to know, that the *Venus de Milo* is art, really. If someone does not know this, one has some right to deride him as culturally illiterate, meaning that "illiteracy" and "not knowing the *Venus de Milo* is art" have become, to some extent, mutually defining and tautological. A sure sign of advanced institutionalization is logical criteria emerging, so that one can use a piece of art for *defining* what art is all about, what its substance is, and who is culturally literate.

But this is not, at least not sociologically, because the *Venus de Milo* has something of the eternal essence of art. Rather, there is a hardening in status as art over time. In the beginning, when an art is about to form, it is more difficult to decide whether something is a certain kind of art, or art at all. This difficulty ignites controversy and debate. New definitions, labels, and criteria are needed. In periods of uncertainty, theorists, critics, and commentators get very busy, since it is, in part, up to them whether an art forms or not.

Classic works of art, on the other hand, exude more confidence in themselves. They travel better than avant-garde art, since avant-garde art is more local and dependent on local support and recognition. The dernier cri happens, at first, for a few select inside observers who convince each other that something significant or dramatic is happening around and among them. There may be a charismatic leader, followed and admired by a few faithfuls. But this is as far as it goes until the circles of recognition expand. Explaining how this expansion happens, why it happens so rarely, and why it happens to some artworks but not others, is one of the biggest challenges in network theory.

If a local and fragile avant-garde movement does extend over space and time, which is unlikely, it does so gradually and not without some changes within it. Outside of its origin, a piece of novel art cannot (yet) draw on the relations and appreciations that make it the art it eventually becomes, or not. It is art only somewhere local. Elsewhere, it is nothing much yet, maybe only a rumor in art-observing circles that something important or exciting is going on somewhere. Scientific discoveries behave in much the same way, as do newsbreaks generally (Fuchs 1995).

Difficulties with extensions, we learn from Collins (1985:73–74), also occur when novel or complex scientific instruments leave their home laboratories. They have a hard time working somewhere else, and so does avant-garde art, until both become ready-made black boxes, or routines in the network core. The chances of making it into the core of the art network are very slim, considering how much art there is and how few classics there are. The same happens in science, where most contributions either never get noticed at all, or very little, but rarely become a citation classic, textbook equation, or routine piece of equipment.

Burdened by the liability of newness, most avant-gardes, much as new scientific specialties, probably disappear soon after forming. When an art is very turbulent, undergoing many transformations very fast, upstarts are even more likely to fail. Not so for classics. It is as if, upon looking at them, they reflect back all the previous admiration that has already recognized and affirmed them as "great art." Classics do not need critics and theorists anymore, since their status as art is more solid and secure. At least the talk about them is more self-assured, as when a person is born into a habitus, exuding the confidence coming from a long tenure inside this habitus. The longer, and more frequently, a piece of art has been established and affirmed as art, the less dependent it becomes on context, locale, clues, and occasions. Such art moves into the core of the network, where its basic institutions and facts are being housed.

It is as if a classical work of art had assimilated the contexts and clues that make it art into itself, allowing it to move and switch contexts or frames with more ease and security—much as, Adorno says, a beautiful woman seems to have absorbed all the admiring and desiring stares already leveled at her and now radiates them back as her "aura." This does not mean that beauty will last forever, only that it is more sure of itself when it has been acknowledged for awhile already.

Displays and Performances

An important difference that makes a difference to how an art becomes part of society is modes of reception and consumption. This
much we can learn from recent theories of texts and reading. But
there is something more going on here than just coconstruction of a
text or artwork in the act of reception by an audience. Contrast the
more or less solitary observation of pictures at a museum exhibition
with live concerts. Live concerts have much higher ritual intensity, due
to Durkheimian copresence and mutual awareness of the audience,
which focuses attention on the same performance, at the same time,
in the here and now. There may be dancing and shared rhythm or
movement, further fueling the build-up of emotional energy and ecstasy. Live concerts, especially rock and roll, are probably the closest
contemporary counterpart to archaic tribal ritual. Crowd intoxication
intensifies the collective experience. In contemporary culture, rock
and roll has a strong grip on the material means of ecstasy, and on the
ways in which the moods of crowds can be altered. Sometimes such
concerts play a role in initiating, energizing, or regrouping social
movements. Examples are the 1960s concerts in Golden Gate Park and
at Woodstock.

The special "magic" of live events comes from the evidence of sheer
togetherness they generate and produce, as they go on and build up
energy. To some extent, such events overcome the mutual separation
of consciousnesses and minds, if only for a while. When it is all over,
your own mind returns and senses a shallow emptiness, which is the
crowds and music moving out of the brain, going their separate ways.
This is the postconcert letdown experienced by musicians and audiences alike and sung about many times. Rock and roll circumvents
consciousness and mind, going straight for the bodies. The bodies
take over; they move together in close physical contact. Much the same
sensation occurs at live athletic events, where the crowd produces
waves and cheers. For high-density events, there is no substitute for actually "being there." The liberal self feels uneasy here, though.

A similar, if much less intense, experience sometimes occurs when
conversations achieve a high degree of rhythmic coordination and
"flow" (Csikszentmihalyi 1990). Such flow is more physical than cere-
bral, or more performative than propositional. The "how" of conversation moves up front, ahead of its themes or topics. Such conversations

become emotionally charged, in the sense of coupling bodies, voices, and gestures to the same rhythms (R. Collins 1988:chap. 6). Such conversations come closer to making music together. This is the "art" of conversation—finding not the right thing to say as much as saying it in the right way, sensing the flow of conversation more than being aware of it, and swinging to its emergent beat.

Toward the other pole of the continuum from rock and roll is the lonely gazing at pictures at an exhibition, or the solitary reading of a poem. There may be others around, but there is not much cohesion, since the others who are also present are doing something else. The experience becomes more inward. Correspondingly, the expression of that experience needs more words to be able to communicate itself than does live rock and roll. Viewing pictures is more abstract and intellectual; it lacks the social physics of bodies close together, swaying to the beat.

Administered and Innovative Art

Much like a science, an art is likely to house some routine, or "normal," sectors, as well as more innovative and experimental ones (DiMaggio 1987). Becker (1982:228–246) draws a distinction between the artwork of "mavericks" and that of "integrated professionals." These professionals are likely employees of organizations whose primary work is not art, but commerce, advertising, packaging, and the like.

Sometimes, the distinction between maverick and professional is co-extensive with that between unit and large-batch production. Mavericks create one piece at a time; large-batch work is more taylorized and repetitive, allowing only small deviations from what has worked successfully before. Large-batch, or mass, production makes many like copies or replicas of one thing; unit production is more individualistic, creative, and sensitive to variations—for example, in raw materials, sites, or skill.

The accuracy of predictions of cultural outcomes will increase with the amount of cultural standardization and large-batch production. Predicting an episode of a TV series will likely be more successful than predicting a movie; predicting the sequel to a Hollywood blockbuster is easier than predicting the next winner of the Cannes film festival. In

Cannes, academically minded critics worry about what should matter to themselves.

Unit production technologies tend to co-occur with flat structures and decentralized networks, while mass production occurs in large organizations, with more bureaucracy, hierarchy, and formal structure (Woodward [1965] 1980). Of course, both technology and structure are variables, with unit and mass marking the opposite poles of a continuum. Unit and mass technologies can also occur within the same overall site, giving rise to multiple and diverse internal structures.

Temporalization of culture is itself variable: Innovative sectors of the network are more restless and turbulent, and they deal with more uncertainty during shorter time frames than the routine areas, which more likely conserve and expand that which has already been accomplished, or repeat that which has worked in the past. Innovative work is unit production par excellence, since the next piece is supposed to differ from all previous ones. Routine or normal work is more large batch, such as elementary instruction of large numbers of novices, or gradual and stepwise extension and application of more or less known outcomes. The respective time frames differ correspondingly, with unit work moving much more quickly, so that one has to move with it just to remain in place. High status tends to go to unit workers, such as medical specialists, discovering scientists and avant-gardes, or pathbreaking architects, as opposed to the state employees who design public housing projects.

Organization science finds this structure in nonartistic organizations, which suggests generalizability (Lawrence and Lorsch [1967] 1986). Variable temporalization also explains Bourdieu's (1993:52) keen observation that poetry, one of the most avant-garde forms of cultural production, "lives in the hectic rhythm of the aesthetic revolutions which divide the continuum of ages into extremely brief literary *generations.*" A fast pace follows from competition over novelty. In contrast, routine sectors move much more slowly and sluggishly. But it is here, in the foundational and institutional core of the network, that orderly cumulation and gradual improvements can occur.

Large-batch art becomes commercially driven and bureaucratically administered. In commercial art, the most critical risk is economic uncertainty, especially when the financial cycles are fast, so that an ongoing cash flow has to be sustained at all times. This adds an extra pressure on small firms with little slack and reserves. These conditions are not favorable to artistic discretion, innovation, and self-referential inwardness. Large-batch artistic production is scheduled to appear in advance; an example is TV sitcoms programmed to air at certain regular times and intervals throughout a season, or until no one watches anymore. Sitcoms are taken off the air when they presumably generate no more commerce. As a result, sitcoms are more standardized than, say, avant-garde independent cinema, which is produced irregularly, and in small units, for an audience of cineasts, literati, and virtuosi—including, very importantly, other independent filmmakers.

The cultural outcome is that sitcoms resemble each other, and themselves over time, more than independent movies do. Sitcoms are repetitive and simple, interrupted all the time by commercials (or possibly the other way around). They form their plots from a very limited stock of materials and themes. Upstart sitcoms copy the successful sitcoms, further reducing variability. Upstarts are usually variations on a single and simple theme, with predictable plot lines and preassigned pauses for laughter. With each passing week, the sitcom becomes more like itself and, if it survives, may turn into a staple or exemplar for many sitcoms to follow. Due to the law of large numbers, sitcoms eventually move toward the mean, their center of gravity. There is still some faddish novelty every now and then, but few genuine breakthroughs. Aesthetic risks cannot be taken if the economic risks prevail.

If an avant-garde moves toward the mean, into the mainstream, it is no longer avant-garde and must move on immediately. To turn into masters themselves, epigones have to abandon their own masters. If they do not, they will not stay avant-garde. Independent movies bargain on being innovative and different, which is risky in its own way, since by far most innovations will not be noticed or recognized.

In avant-gardes, the major risk is the feasibility of artistic experimentation and innovation. Once an art becomes fully commercialized, the economic risks gain priority over the risks of artistic advances and creativity. Some observers fear that this will happen to science as well, as it becomes part of large industrial organizations. A greater danger to autonomy, though, might come from the state, when it turns into the sole or most important supplier of funds. This has been happening, for example, to German sociology, which is mostly done in state-funded "research projects," whose outcome is then another such project, and so on. While the personnel changes all the time, projects follow each other in three-year intervals. This adds a lot of bureaucracy, paperwork, and supervision, with the result that all these projects become similar, and workers can move from one project to another easily.

Of course, even independent unit-producers of art sell their art. "Independent" filmmakers are not that independent; they are highly dependent on each other and on their esoteric audiences and sponsors—probably even more so than commercial filmmakers, whose audiences are much larger, more diffuse, and less exclusive or discriminating in their tastes. An avant-garde audience is small, picky, and opinionated. It has confidence in its judgments, and lets them be known. The artist who produces for such an audience confronts fairly specific expectations from a small group of people, many of whom know the artist, and each other, personally. This niche is very small and specialized. Opinionated audiences pressure an artist to stay avant-garde. If he does not, he disappears or starts doing his work for a different, possibly larger and commercial, audience. This happened when Bob Dylan went electric in his 1967 British concert series, to the outrage of his purist folkish admirers. Judas!

Independent musicians or filmmakers are "independent" only from the big commercial studios, to a degree, until they become "corrupted" into the mainstream and start "selling out." In this lies the dialectic of their success—the more recognized and visible they become as avant-garde artists, the more likely the mainstream is to pay attention also, and so the less interesting they become to avant-garde audiences as a self-identifying cultural emblem or icon. Charismatic virtuosity does not survive large-scale commercialization very well. It does not flourish when cultural workers are employed or contracted by large organizations, since such organizations tend to divide the artistic labor, format standards for such labor, and practice some hierarchical outcome inspections.

Administration of culture also destroys the artistic mystique and myths of creativity. Large-batch cultural production observes more anonymously and impersonally than unit production, with the result that many commercial composers, sitcom writers, or industrial designers are not known in person. Avant-garde artists, in contrast, cannot prosper without some personality cult.

If artists become commercially successful, they are no longer considered avant-garde by the remaining avant-garde, and lose that fraction of their prestige and reputation that is due to avant-garde recognition. Their former followers are often outraged and feel betrayed. In any case, commercialization is a variable and a process, not a dichotomy, as in Bourdieu's "left bank" and "right bank" theater. Ceteris paribus, as commercialization increases, artistic autonomy and innovation decrease.

So although cultural critics bemoan the "total" commercialization of art and popular culture, commercialization will never be complete, universal, or irreversible. Rather, we would expect the innovative avant-gardes to move away from an art, or part thereof, as and when that art becomes more commercial. In the same way, the innovative clusters of a scientific specialty move away from that specialty's core when the opportunities for further discoveries decrease. An avant-garde is not a fixed fact or stable set; it exists only as a variable relation and position. An avant-garde is what it is only in relation to what it does not want to be—for example, commercial or industrial art. It cannot exist without distinguishing itself, but that which it distinguishes itself from also changes, making further distinctions necessary. More accurately, the avant-garde just *is* this ongoing process of demarcation from non-avant-garde. Staying avant-garde is exhausting, as is remaining on the cutting edge of a science. These are observers with very high velocities, as opposed to more stationary ones.

Expect, then, ongoing distinctions of avant-gardes from non-avant-gardes, as different segments of an art world become commercial and so are no longer attractive and promising to avant-gardes. Then the avant-garde will be on the move again, exploring new territory and new ways to be "different" and "provocative." In this dynamic, even commercial art can be appropriated, with some irony, into avant-garde art (Warhol).

As long as avant-gardes can sustain themselves, the process of commercialization is not complete and final. Some areas of culture are indeed being "McDonaldized," but others are not, and new cultures emerge all the time, on initially small scales. In fact, commercial penetration and expansion of artistic markets also create new specialized niches for novel work and products. Within such small and narrow niches, avant-gardes might emerge to distinguish themselves from the very commercial forces that helped produce their niches in the first place. Overall, markets probably allow for more, not less, artistic discretion, autonomy, and pluralism than did aristocratic sponsors, courts, or a wealthy bourgeois patron.

Reputation

The degree to which a culture is professionalized correlates with the degree to which it generates and distributes its own reputations. There is a continuum here as well, ranging from the openness and lack of distinction in contested semiprofessions, all the way to full closure. The more closed a profession, the less is it possible for an outsider to get a reputation there and to influence someone else's standing in that profession.

In common nonsociological sense, reputation, much as agency, is something that persons "have" and that they get by making valuable contributions, performing honorable deeds, or living a respectable life. Common sense centers reputation on what persons do, and thinks of reputation as a property of persons.

Sociologically, however, reputation belongs to a structure or network, although persons can be credited with reputation when a network takes the intentional stance. In a network, reputation acts as a selective filter, focusing the attention of a field and reacting to bounded rationality. Reputation is a specialty's way of reducing its own self-produced internal complexity by drawing attention to the communications of its leaders. Reputation directs attention to those who have accumulated a credit of trustworthiness in doing what matters to a profession or culture. Reputation can become a self-fulfilling prophecy, feeding the Matthew effect (Merton 1988).

Such personal attributions conceal the fact that persons do not "make" reputations for themselves. They cannot really "control" their reputations, since reputation depends on recognition and appreciation within a network. Reputation is not a personal quality, something that persons carry around with them wherever they go. In most cases, a reputation makes a difference only in a fairly small specialty, circle, or network. When persons leave the network in which they "have" a reputation, that reputation no longer makes much of a difference, although some rare reputations extend beyond the boundaries of the network in which they were obtained originally.

Reputation is not a thing or property, but a relation within a network through which reputation circulates. A reputation exists not by itself, but only in relation to other reputations. Reputation is just this difference or relation, making it a network, not personal, possession. Networks grant or withdraw recognition, and bestow or strip someone of reputation. It is networks that make some reputations higher than others; a person who is alone in claiming a reputation for himself has no reputation at all. One might complain that one's reputation is not what it should be, or that someone else's reputation is undeserved or inflated. But such complaints are largely idle; they do very little, if anything, to change the actual configuration of reputations in the network. In reputational networks, no one is completely without reputation, and one's own reputation is what it is only relative to someone else's reputation. Reputation is not a "thing," but this difference.

Persons can do little, networks a lot; and most of what networks do does not follow from the intentional actions of persons. It is not just that other persons make one's own reputation, although this is a bit more accurate already. But not just any other person will do, and a certain person's appreciation of your efforts goes a longer way in making your reputation than that of others. To make a reputation, you have to "have" some reputation as well. That is, reputations make reputations, and only previous reputation can increase subsequent reputation. This explains the empirical stability of reputational rankings over time. Much like honor, reputation does not get bestowed by one's peers, but by their own honor or reputations. The more reputation they "have," the more they can do for someone else's reputation. This explains why reputation grows by accumulative advantage (Merton 1973a): the best way to draw more recognition and admiration to oneself is to be recognized and admired already, for whatever reason.

Reputation is built up by communication, both formal and informal, and both local and cosmopolitan (Fuchs 1995). Reputation starts out locally, at a specific place and time. In expert cultures, the largest amount of reputation one has at the beginning of a career is reputation borrowed from the reputations of mentors, departments, labs, and so on. But one has to make good on this promise. Since reputations are properties of networks, not persons, they can survive persons and, to a degree, be transferred between persons, through horizontal and vertical interaction chains and network ties (Collins 1998). To some extent, reputation can be transmitted through master-apprentice ties, not unlike charisma, where the leader passes some of his extraordinary capacities on to his followers.

Though reputation is a property not of persons, but networks, some networks condense their observations of themselves into certain "sources" and points of origin, to explain where contributions come from and to reward the contributors. "Authorship" is a simplified scheme a network uses to attribute contributions to certain persons but not others. Such schemes are conventional, but never arbitrary, interruptions of causality and temporal regress. It is often possible, if only in principle, to go back further in the causal and temporal chains and investigate the influences on an author. As this is done, the author as person or agent becomes embedded in a larger structure or context and loses at least some of his sovereign agency and discretion. This more structural mode of observing is what historians or sociologists of science might do; they do not stop at "person" or "author," but examine the context and structure behind agency. At the same time, a historian or sociologist might receive an award for this work in his or her own field, and then assume full credit as actor, person, and author as well.

Observational schemes and attributions can be contested by other observers, causing conflicts over property and priority in various expert cultures. It is often possible to claim, if not show, that some idea, technique, or discovery actually originated elsewhere, in a different person, or at another time. Interruptions of causal and temporal chains are contingent, but actual conflicts over authorship will sooner or later be settled within, and by, the network in which they occur. Once a prize has officially been awarded, and authorship established, an envious rival cannot long continue to insist that he should have been awarded the prize. At least, such continuing complaints become idle or annoying after a while, and probably damage the plaintiff's reputation more than increase it.

From Creativity to Genius

Genius and creativity are dramatized and unusual forms of reputation. While everyone has a reputation, fewer seem to be creative, and genius is much rarer still. Sometimes the flow of reputation through a network forms an eddy, swirling around persons being elevated to extraordinary heights in this way. Some positions in a network, those in the core, are more likely to be caught up in such eddies. "Creative" minds have diverse currents of communication flowing through them; these currents get tangled up and redivided in the process, so that something new might emerge in the process. For creativity, awareness and intentionality are secondary—as they are in that prime creative force, evolution, which goes to work on mutations through decomposition and recombination, without any plan or intention whatever. Sociology recommends modesty not just for persons generally, but also geniuses, since their accomplishments are not up to them.

Sociologically, creativity does not belong to persons, but travels in groups; it is concentrated in space and time, leading to unusually creative periods and schools (Collins 1998). Not all reputations go to creativity, however. Reputations are attributed to creativity when the network looks forward in time, toward changing its outcomes and making new advances and discoveries. When a network looks back instead, toward a sacred origin or creation, as most religions do, creativity is not an asset but an idle and vain temptation. In innovative networks, however, "creativity" is taken to be the cause and justification for reputation. Awards are Durkheimian ritual ceremonies, elevating those who are credited with "having" creativity into charismatic figures.

Creativity and genius do not start out as facts. Both grow gradually, and genius grows more suddenly than creativity or reputation. If a contribution turns out to make a big splash, its author might be observed as someone creative, and interest in this person increases, drawing attention to him. But this attention needs to build up before it can be directed to the personality of genius. In very rare cases of dramatic breakthroughs, genius appears much in the same way as charismatic prophecy, that is, very suddenly and seemingly out of the blue. At least, this is what followers of genius or prophet experience. For them, the surprise is part of the magic. If they could predict their own prophet, that prophet would not emerge, or would lose some of his mystique.

Despite popular images of geniuses as weird loners, genius cannot command the recognition that builds it up. One can think of oneself, privately, as a genius, but if no one else pays any attention, and no network reacts, such insistence will be inconsequential and observed as a personal idiosyncrasy or disorder. Then the person claiming to be a genius turns a bit tragic, or comic, and protests by blaming the network for its inattentiveness. The longer this goes on, the shriller the tone and the more majestic the great silence and indifference of the network. Alternatively, one might hope to still make it in the distant future; currently unrecognized genius likes to think it is being misunderstood—a mistake for which the network will pay dearly when the day of recognition and celebration finally dawns.

Genius also seems related to the history of a network; it produces more genius in the beginning and end. In between, there is a long period of institutionalization, maturity, systematization, and normal science (Mullins 1973:24–25). That is, genius either makes new, or destroys old, worlds, or both. Newton was a genius because he, among others, is credited with creating the mechanical mass-in-motion universe; Nietzsche is admired as a genius because he destroyed metaphysics. With Spengler ([1923] 1993:143–145), genius belongs to the spring or winter of a culture.

Genius is an increase in selectivity and rarity of reputation. Genius must be rare, since a network full of them would have conflicts over who is the "true" or "real" genius. There are innovative and synthesizing geniuses. The Great Synthesizer unifies a culture into a coherent and confident orthodoxy, at the height of its reign. In innovative cultures, genius goes to those credited with major breakthroughs or revolutions. Here, genius is the simplified and abbreviated way in which the network observes and explains how it produces its most dramatic breakthroughs.

To itself, and to common sense, genius appears as the opposite of rules and method; it is "personal knowledge" par excellence (Polanyi [1958] 1964). Genius cannot be taught; it cannot be formalized in textbooks and manuals. Genius escapes procedure and formalization. It thrives in ambiguity, ambivalence, and uncertainty. Genius has a disdain for routine and accountability. The genius cannot explain how he does what he does, contributing to the religious enigma that surrounds him (Rosen 1998:105–128).

Sociologically, genius is not the cause, but the retrospective outcome, of major ruptures and transformations in a culture. These may happen for structural reasons, such as normal accidents, network fragmentation, or organizational revolutions in the modes of cultural production. At least, this is what a sociological observer looks for, since he cannot simply repeat, or contribute to, the official celebrations of "genius" within the network he studies. Neither can sociology decide who is, and who is not, a genius in any field other than its own.

Sometimes, though even more rarely, genius can travel across several networks, producing Renaissance intellectuals. This probability decreases as specialization and differentiation increase, because this restricts reputation to more narrow areas of expertise. Outside of the culture that made him the genius he is, the genius is—at first, and until further notice—just another amateur: "For Galileo, Nature was written in mathematical language, but with all his genius, he could not read the plain sociological messages from his old friend the Pope" (Ziman [1978] 1991:41).

CHAPTER 5

Modes of Social Association I:
Encounters, Groups, and Organizations

The theory worked out in the next two chapters distinguishes four emergent modes of society: encounters, groups, organizations, and networks. All of these are observers. In one sense, networks are not distinct, since encounters, groups, and organizations are all also networks in their own right. The "master" concept is networks, since networks link all the other modes, as well as themselves, into larger networks. There are networks among encounters, groups, organizations, and networks.

Networks do not link "whole" persons, much less unique individuals. Intimate associations come closer to linking "whole" persons, but not many of them, and how this happens varies with such associations. Networks also link not actions, but interactions and communications. Rather than connecting persons, networks link their encounters, both across space and over time. A special case of such chains among encounters is Randall Collins's (1988:chap. 6) "interaction ritual chains." Networks among encounters can lead to groups; networks among groups can result in social movements, and networks among organizations constitute markets and states. Finally, the society of the modern world emerges as networks among networks.

Networks come first. Encounters, groups, and organizations are variable and temporary "involutions" or condensations of networks (White 1992:35). One might compare them to the eddies in rivers. They emerge as certain segments and clusters of a network turn inward, separating themselves to some degree from the overall structure and from the rest of the world. By means of distinctions, an involution might even acquire an "identity" for itself, and for other identities. Network involutions create or construct their own internal realities. Of course, while all this happens the rest of the world is still there. Some of this rest, though not everything, might become a theme or topic in encounters, groups, or organizations. Encounters, groups, and organizations generate their own foci, and also change these foci themselves. Therefore, an outside observer, say a sociologist, might find out *how* encounters happen, but can hardly predict *what*, specifically, encounters will choose as their focus. This is impossible, if only because of the sheer numbers of encounters—past, present, and in the future.

Involution produces an inside and an outside. The outside is all that is not inside, and so is incomparably larger, and lasts much longer, than any inside. The outside is also more complex and undetermined, if only because the outside contains many more insides than any of these insides. The world itself is unspecific. Each new encounter, for example, adds something to the world. The world is "there," but never *here*. It cannot be known itself, or in its entirety.

The result of involution is higher internal than external connectivity and coupling. A contribution to a conversation is a contribution to that conversation, not to another one. The other conversations, going on at the same or different times, do not know or react to most of what is being said elsewhere. An encounter pays more attention to itself than to other encounters. So do groups and organizations. One cannot walk into a group and pretend one had been part of it since the very first hour. One cannot join a faculty meeting in a department without being employed there.

Inwardness has nothing to do with actual or empirical self-sufficiency or independence. But encounters, groups, and organizations fall apart if there is no distinction whatever between inside and out, between what or who belongs to either side, or between the theme of this encounter, as opposed to the themes of all the other encounters happening at the same time. To be sure, encounters can change their themes and participants, but then a new focus of attention emerges, one distinct from other foci and other participants in different encounters. Of course, encounters do fall apart all the time, only to reform into different encounters in the swirl of the network. Groups disband as well, as do organizations, but both last longer than any particular encounter.

The Bodies and Brains of Persons

Persons, their bodies, and their actions belong to society's environment, although "person" and "action" can be outcomes of social attributions and intentional stances, and there are variable degrees of "overlap" between society, persons, and bodies. These variations depend on the "greediness" and inclusiveness of institutional structures, and on the closeness or reactivity of social arrangements to persons. Seeking to swallow persons whole, cults are greedier and more inclusive than voluntary associations. Face-to-face interactions are more sensitive to irritations by bodies, such as loud burps, than are states and world systems. Rigid structures, such as total institutions, give persons little independence and privacy, and the inmates will have a hard time defending a modicum of space against invasion. For the most part, total and coercive institutions perceive persons as potential threats to discipline, and as sources of trouble and disruption. They constrain them into uni-forms. They are suspicious of privacy and brooding. Cults try to cut off ties to the outside world, and go through elaborate initiation rituals to achieve a metamorphosis of their members-to-be.

With Luhmann, society does not consist of persons, but it can construct and observe "personhood" in various ways, depending on time, context, and locale. But persons contribute bodies and brains to society, which has neither. Society cannot think, perceive, or feel anything, though it can react to thoughts or feelings—if, and only if, they are communicated in some way. As part of society's environment, bodies and brains cannot produce society, and society cannot produce bodies or brains. They are not of society's making, but the result of evolution. Bodies and brains can only be produced by other bodies and brains. As a result, there are variable technological and political limits to what a society can do to persons, their bodies, and their brains.

Society cannot produce human beings as biological organisms. A culture might find ways to alter this biology in some way—for example, by means of breeding, domestication, agriculture, or engineering. But life is always already there; it is not made from scratch, and the life that is already there constrains what can be done or changed about it.

Of course, society relates to persons, bodies, and brains. An important dimension of variation in cultures has to do with how they conceive of, and relate to, the body and brain. Different cultures and observers employ different "root metaphors" in their various dealings with bodies and brains. Bodies can be targets of erotic attraction, objects on surgery tables, or carriers of habitus. They can be seen as heat engines, temporary DNA hosts, or systems of humors. Brains may be seats of an immortal soul, the unconscious, or rational decision-making, or devices for information processing. Bodies get clothed in some way, made-up and readied for encounters. Brains acquire minds as persons get socialized. All this covaries with social structure and time.

Still, bodies and brains are, as biological systems, the result of natural evolution, not society. Or so it appears in Darwinism. Therefore, there are limits to what any society can do to bodies and brains, although these limits are not "natural" or unchanging. Brains can be trained, but they still forget a lot, and even more as they age. Someday, neuroscience might find out how the brain "works," but I do not think any neuroscience will ever be able to explain what it felt like to be Robert Johnson composing "Kind-Hearted Woman Blues." Once brains are dead, they cannot be revived. Society cannot replace them or continue to socialize them. Neither can society expect further contributions from dead brains.

Likewise, organs can be transplanted, but must be accepted by the body of the host. Society can produce theories of life, but not life. There are test-tube babies, frozen embryos, and sperm banks, but to make a human you still need an egg and a sperm. While it may be possible to "cure" some diseases by genetic alteration, the diseases might continue to mutate, and the altered genes must still interact with the previous genes to produce any results. Pregnancy has vastly different status in different societies and cultures, but the same pregnancy cannot be shared by other women. Society can communicate about the brain, but it cannot experience its sensations. There is a philosophy of consciousness in some societies, but that philosophy is itself not conscious, and has no mental states.

Genetics and neuroscience are part of society, but brains and genes are not. Genetics can engineer genes, but only according to the workings of genes, not the workings of genetics. Society can teach brains and socialize minds, but will continue to be surprised by some of what some persons do, say, and think. As a result of evolution, persons with their bodies and brains remain, to some extent, foreign and alien to society.

Take emotions. As brain states, emotions belong to persons, not society, and our novelists, poets, composers, and painters are much better at expressing or mimicking the phenomenology of emotions than is any available science, including sociology.

Society can communicate about emotions, but not feel or share them. Nor can another person share your emotions, because she continues to have her own, even while striving for empathy. If you feel empathy with someone, that is still your feeling, and your empathy—not that someone's. How long can empathy last? Empathy is rare and restricted to a very few intimates. The experience lasts as long as the encounter in which it is offered and displayed, and then persons go their separate ways again, carrying their emotions with them. Another person can *say* she knows how you feel, but this is a communication, not an emotion. Persons can also assume that they feel "with" others, but that remains an assumption. Except when coming from intimates, empathy can become an unwanted intrusion, since strangers have no entitlements to your emotions. As more strangers appear, it becomes ever more preposterous to claim to know what all of them feel or experience.

Take grief. One can grieve with others, but not very many of them—maybe close kin and friends. The others' grief is their own, and so is yours, since no one can grieve *for* you. Since sociology is not a person, it cannot share or experience grief. What it can do, however, is observe under which conditions "emotion" becomes a way of framing, phrasing, or interpreting certain interactions and communications. Sociology can observe "emotion" as an attribute and outcome of social relations; it cannot deal with emotional states as such: "Mourning is not a natural movement of private feelings wounded by a cruel loss; it is a duty imposed by the group" (Durkheim [1912] 1965:443).

A fascinating sociological topic is how socially displayed and observed emotions structure and restructure social relations, as they do in encounters and groups. Let us stay with grief. The grieving are treated differently; they receive more attention, better care, and special liberties or exemptions. Since they are grieving, they are somewhat buffered and protected from still more insults, at least until the grief can be expected to be over. There may be customs as to how long grief is supposed to last. When the mourning period is over, you cannot expect to be treated as a raw egg anymore. While it lasts, you cannot really question the authenticity of someone's grief, at least not to their grieving faces. If you do this nevertheless, you risk provocation, insult, and a call to arms. The grieving do not want strangers telling them that they know what it feels like to be in this grief, *their* grief. The grief is their special exemption and status, making them a bit sacrosanct and immune from criticism.

If a person's body is severely handicapped, sick, in severe pain, or dying, grief can turn into a virtuous and righteous terror—a Nietzschean conversion of weakness into strength, by way of virtue. It is even more impossible to feel someone's pain than to feel their grief. Pain is all one's own. The person in much pain is rarely wrong. Sometimes there is so much pain that it consumes the person, and then the pain rules his relationships as well, uncompromisingly. It dominates the surrounding encounters, if only as an acknowledged avoidance or forced absence. Pain turns into an "agency"—it is now the pain, not the person, doing all the explaining, excusing, and talking. Pain diminishes former personhood by becoming its own person, one who is quite a dictator. Those who are not in pain, and cannot do anything to make it stop hurting, are not in charge either, at least not anymore, since they really do not know what the pain feels like. If they claim to know this all the same, that claim sounds phony and insulting, lacking proper deference to the pain, who is its own sole judge. Pain grants virtue; if you did wrong, it must have been the pain. Your critics shut up.

Sociologically, then, "emotion" is a device used to communicate mental states. It is not that mental state itself. For sociology, emotion becomes important when it enters interactions and communications in some way—as a theme or topic, industry, ritual, or mode of interaction. One can talk about emotions, and about the organizations that market them. Emotions can be outcomes of encounters or groups, and they can turn encounters and groups into emotions, as happens in sex, dance, or music.

Emotional Selves

When they do get communicated, emotions are more "privileged" and private than thoughts. They carve out an area of personal discretion and taboo that thoughts cannot enjoy to the same extent. Goffman (1981:10) notes that when an encounter comes to questions about emotional states, only the persons presumed to be having them are entitled to reply and answer to such questions.

Communication is more ruthless to persons' thoughts than to their emotions. It is possible to disagree with a thought, but not an emotion. If someone tells you that the capital of France is London, you can disagree, with no harm done. If someone tells you they feel sad, you cannot reply, "No, you do not." You can privately disbelieve, of course, but if you question the authenticity of an emotion point blank, you risk having no further encounters with this person.

Emotions are social entitlements protecting the private self; intrude into this inviolate space when you are not invited, and you offend and insult. An emotion entitles its owner to a certain amount of respect for his inner life. As an outsider, you cannot just enter this private space, but must be invited. Only intimates carry a more or less permanent backstage pass. "Tact" is the respect for the distance thus created to a person's inner mental space; "embarrassment" happens when this space is opened for observation by those who are not really entitled to be there but nevertheless witness what happens in that space.

On backstages, you are who you are—whoever you are. "Deep" emotions happen here, and moods, and sensations. You are the ultimate judge of how all of this feels to you, creating a distance from most others, who are the judges of their own feelings. The few intimates who are allowed backstage contribute more to judging who you really are, but they are and remain their own persons as well.

"Deep" emotions thrive when the numbers are small, the spaces private, and the relations intimate. On these occasions, persons are expected to have, display, and somehow share their feelings with those select and few others who are expected to do the same in return. Words may no longer be required for communication and, in fact, disrupt and hinder it, when emotion becomes a *mode* of interaction itself. Then one is expected to understand without words.

When the numbers grow, the spaces become more public, and social relations care less about persons and their possible emotional states. There are still "emotions" in this area, but they turn into manufactured and packaged clichés and stereotypical cultural framings. Such "emotions" are even further removed from any actual mental states of persons; they are the business of special industries and organizations within the various sectors and segments of "popular culture," for example. Popular culture employs emotions as stylized expectations and attributions—generalized modes of communication about emotions, rather than actual emotional states of empirical persons.

The social outcome or construct of ritual attention to personhood is the "modern self." "Emotion" is one of its central possessions, a pillar of self-identity. Emotions, and more importantly "moods," define how you, and only you, experience the world, and what this feels like to you. Your *Befindlichkeit* makes you special and unique, more so than your thoughts do, since thoughts link persons to publics more closely than their emotions do. There are other properties of this modern self as well, including subjective rights, liberties, and "natural" or intrinsic faculties for will and representation (Chapter 3).

Sociologically, this self is not the ultimate or foundational source, but an outcome, of society. The liberalism and humanism that place the self at the center of agency, meaning, and culture are morally driven exaggerations of the importance of persons. In the sociological lens, this masterful and autonomous self gets smaller and smaller, especially as the numbers grow. Paulos (1998:40–41) shows that persons depend on relative frequencies and statistical relations. As persons, we tend to be convinced that we are all special in some way, whereas we see others as pretty typical and average. As parents, we think that our children are unique, while other parents' children are rather normal and ordinary. Stereotyping grows more and more stereotypical as the target grows in size. One stereotypes others, not oneself, and not so much one's intimate associates, who are also special. It is all the others, assembled into "the mass," who are carriers of standard and average traits. They can more or less completely or sufficiently be described as various categories, sets, classes, or populations. But you—you are the outlier.

We all feel powerless and alienated sometimes because statistically all of us receive many more insults than we can dish out to others. In a group of three, if everyone dished out five insults to the others in the group, each would receive ten insults. And that's just a group of three. Each person is a small minority, and the smaller a minority, the more likely it is the target of various insults on its integrity or identity. You might seem so important to yourself that you actually believe that the most noteworthy thing others do is make an appearance in your life.

If sociology implied any moral stance, it might be modesty about the difference a person, as a person, can make to society. Persons make a difference to those very few very close to them, but this difference decreases rapidly as size, radius, and distance increase. What is even a dictator going to do when his generals refuse to execute his orders?

Levels of Society

The four levels of society—encounters, groups, organizations, and networks—are seen here as emergent, mostly for the pragmatic reason that there is no good reductionist theory available at this time that shows otherwise. The closest we have to an actual reduction is from networks "down"; at least, I think the chances for reduction are better in this direction than, say, from encounters to organizations, or even world systems. To be sure, there are some propagandistic declarations to the contrary, promising reduction, typically with the irrefutable argument that reduction must be possible "in principle," because no higher-order things could exist in the absence of lower-order things. Such "in principle" arguments, however, do not get any real work done, and they are irrefutable in principle. They often confound levels of reality ("persons could not live without brains") with levels of explanation—"the behavior of persons follows from their brain states."

One should try to reduce something to something else if this yields more powerful and simpler explanations, and if reduction can do *all* of the work on the level being reduced. At present, this is impossible for the majority of sciences. In fact, it seems that the reductionist propaganda gets shriller as the possibilities and opportunities for true— that is, empirical, not conceptual or logical—reductions decline. In part, this is due to the sheer number of research areas and specialties. As professions, all of these areas are busy carving out unique niches for themselves, which includes developing arguments and exemplars showing and demonstrating their intellectual property to be uniquely and irreducibly theirs. Reductionism, despite its modern materialist manifestations, is deeply religious, because it still searches for ultimate foundations and First Principles.

Emergence does not mean that there can be organizations without groups, or encounters without persons. There are no persons without brains, brains without quarks, or quarks without Joyce and Gell-Mann. Closing the circle, there is no Gell-Mann without society. But the difference between necessary and sufficient conditions remains. The fact that communication needs brains does not get us an inch closer to predicting who communicates what to whom, and when, in terms of brain states. It is also currently infeasible to explain brain states by reducing them to the four elementary forces. Likewise, the fact that organizations "contain" groups and encounters does not mean that we can presently "reduce" organizations to groups and encounters.

Short of a powerful reductionist theory, the best we can do for now, I believe, is to assume that the four levels are "nested" within each other, and differ in the way that they organize and link their components. As I understand it, "nesting" is not an ontological term. It makes no assumptions about foundational or ultimate realities or hierarchies. Nesting denies that, say, encounters are somehow more real, or more basic, than organizations, or that networks can somehow be "aggregated" from encounters.

"Nesting" means that "higher" levels of association are increasingly inclusive, in a variety of ways. First, higher levels "contain" lower levels. Encounters and groups contain no organizations, but organizations contain or house many of both. As a result, organizations deal with more, and more complex, social outcomes than do encounters and groups. Despite the common philosophical and critical prejudice by Weber, Marcuse, and Foucault that organizations are streamlined and efficient iron cages, most organizations are more chaotic and disorderly than most groups and encounters, because organizations deal with many more internal environments, including groups and encounters, than do groups and encounters. Large organizations with many units, divisions, and departments are more turbulent still.

Encounters and groups do not have as many internal environments as organizations do. In organizations, thousands of encounters may happen simultaneously, at any one moment. Except for the bodies and minds of persons, encounters have no separate internal environments to speak of. When encounters do produce internal environments—that is, encounters within one encounter—the encounter breaks up into separate encounters, or persons. Groups have separate encounters and episodes as their own internal environments, and very likely have cliques as well if they are significantly larger than dyads. Once they grow beyond a certain critical mass, however, say about thirty or so members, they cease to be groups. Organizations "contain" groups, but are not groups themselves; networks "contain" organizations, but are not organizations themselves.

By and large, fewer internal environments produce fewer social outcomes and events. On average, and in the long run, two groups will produce more events and outcomes than one group. Organizations, which house many groups, produce more events and outcomes still. It is impossible to know during any particular encounter what goes on in all the other encounters, groups, organizations, and networks. The more outcomes that are produced, the more selective and formatted their subsequent perception and processing will tend to be, all the way to bureaucracy.

Increasing inclusiveness has nothing to do with more democracy, unity, consensus, or coherence. To the contrary, world society is much more stratified and conflictual than an encounter or group. Inclusiveness does acknowledge, however, that only a vanishingly small subset of the world's population can be a part of any given encounter, while everyone is a member of society. At higher levels, communication becomes increasingly and massively parallel. Encounters process contributions sequentially, one at a time, so that not everyone talks and communicates at the same time. In a network, by contrast, countless encounters, groups, and organizations are "happening" at the same time, all the time.

One consequence is that no encounter, group, or organization in society can "match" or "grasp" that entire society itself. This includes encounters or organizations of professional specialists in society; they can produce a "theory" of society, but this theory is just another "happening" *within* society, and a pretty small and insignificant one at that.

Another consequence of nesting might be that modes of association can more readily interact within their own levels, whereas there is looser coupling between levels. Groups do not end when one of their encounters does, unless it's a farewell. Organizations can easily perceive and react to other organizations, especially those in their own sets, but lack the sensitivity to persons characteristic of encounters and groups.

"Higher" levels of social organization are also increasingly further removed from the body, and its various own levels of organization and outcomes, than are "lower" levels. An encounter, for example, will somehow register if someone present coughs a lot; an organization would disintegrate if it could or did. Phrased differently, information provided by, and contained in, the body—say, in the form of sensory perceptions, genes, or brain states—becomes less and less material in explaining what goes on at higher social and cultural levels. Knowing about genetic makeup and brain states becomes more and more irrelevant as an observer switches from the body to encounters and all the way up to geopolitical power transformations in the world system. While groups will be sensitive to variations between persons, especially to the exit and entry of new members (or their new hairdos), organizations are less so, and networks among organizations less still. Keep in mind, however, that organizations house groups, which *are* sensitive to such variations.

At higher levels, communication becomes more "abstract," while encounters can still rely on the shared here and now of a physical setting. At higher levels, the world appears increasingly "constructed," that is, dependent on prior constructions, not on bodily sensations or direct personal experiences. In bureaucracies, for example, the language becomes more quantitative, impersonal, or legal as that language bridges local idiosyncrasies and struggles against context to produce summary representations that can be understood across locales and offices. Against postmodernism, the increasing remoteness of communication from any "embodied" primordial reality has nothing to do with a sudden "crisis of representation," or with a new "semiotic" reality of signs. Rather, the remoteness of communication from persons and their bodies is a simple consequence of increasingly nested levels of association and communication.

At higher levels, persons are less and less able to "influence" social events and outcomes. They can easily disrupt some encounters—that is, those in which they participate—but not so easily organizations, and hardly world systems. An important aspect of nesting is the time it takes for persons to make a difference to society at some level. At the level of encounters between physically copresent persons, almost anything they do or say, or do not do or say, can make a difference to that encounter, as long as it is being observed and recognized there in some way. It is difficult for encounters to ignore anything that gets said or done by someone who is present. Encounters are also extremely sensitive to irritations from their direct surroundings. They move indoors when it starts to rain, they register distracting noises, and they recognize when someone present talks too much.

An important antiphilosophical consequence of nesting is that there are no such uplifting and edifying institutions as a universal human dialogue, an all-encompassing discourse, or a conversation among humankind. These are romantic illusions of talk-philosophy. The fact is that the vast majority of persons will never be part of the vast majority of all conversations. Even fewer will ever be part of any conversations among philosophers, and only a very few of the conversations that philosophers have are about philosophy. The philosophers are convinced that their conversations among each other about philosophy are the conversation of humankind itself. There is no such single conversation. As you read this, there are billions of conversations going on, in which you can never participate, which do not mention you, and certainly do not "care" about you. Encounters occur in the very massive and parallel plural. There is not one master encounter or conversation among all of us.

Encounters

Encounters are face-to-face interactions driven by copresence and mutual awareness or observation. While not all interactions are encounters, some research suggests that interactions over a distance, without copresence, remain dependent on encounters in several ways. Despite romantic communitarian fears, the telephone did not abolish encounters and community, but actually cemented them, providing a way for encounters to continue and extend themselves even without actual copresence (Fischer 1992:5). One rarely calls complete strangers, except by accident, but those one knows already from encounters. Likewise, some studies suggest that computer-mediated interactions do not replace or supersede encounters, but are, often redundantly, used to reinforce, initiate, summarize, or prepare for them (Wellman and

Gulia 1995). One sends much electronic mail to friends, family, and acquaintances. One can chat with perfect strangers in electronic chat rooms but eventually may want to meet in person. One can use any number of computerized or mail dating services, but I do not believe that anyone has yet gotten married without any prior encounters. Even formal organizations continue to rely on encounters, probably even more so now than before, given all the recent emphasis on human relations, teamwork, and human-faced management.

Encounters are here to stay. They are archaic. Encounters link society to the body and its perceptions and sensations, and through the body to the material world of physical things and objects. Encounters are the stuff that everyday life is made of, as it appears to common sense. At this level, there is a fundamental and irrevocable familiarity with the ordinary world of others and things, without much reflexivity. Others and things are what or who they are. One can be wrong and make mistakes, but common sense cannot be corrected and replaced as a whole. Common sense is not a falsifiable theory, or even a set of beliefs. This is why it is so difficult to say just what common sense believes in. The closest I can get is that common sense is essentialist folk psychology: It believes in primary properties and natural kinds for things, and in intentions or purposes for persons.

In any case, common sense cannot be replaced, wholesale, by a scientifically more accurate account. Common sense can react to some scientific result, but only on its own terms, that is, by rearranging and renormalizing such a result into its own edifice. Common sense cannot consider that nothing, and no one, are what they seem.

In encounters, the reality of the local and available world in which the encounter happens cannot really be questioned, or only at the very high cost of absurdity, mutual offense, insult, or violation of trust. This is the realm of the "natural attitude." Two skeptical philosophers conversing about their skeptical philosophies can be skeptical about existence and being at large, or in general, but not about *their* existence and being. They cannot deny, for example, that they are really having the conversation, that they are both present, or that they are both philosophers.

Encounters are close and sensitive to the body and, through its perceptions, to the world. Unlike writing and reading, encounters allow for a "duality of perception and communication" (Luhmann

1997:chap. 13). Communication among copresents can assume and rely on the facticity and reality of the world nearby. Things in this world can be identified by ostension. Writing and reading are more abstract, lonesome, and distant. Bodies sense the world around them as it is, right now and right here, not as it might or could be, or how it is constructed by the body as observer. There is not much tolerance or room for ambiguity, contingency, and alternative possibilities at this level, although "higher" levels can be more reflexive.

Many encounters begin on the level of bodies; this level is the social physics of encounters. Bodies register and tax other bodies for clues as to what to expect in case the encounter gets going. This visceral recognition happens very quickly. It is similar to dogs sniffing each other, trying to sense possible troubles or hostility. There is a German phrase, "Ich kann ihn nicht riechen"—I cannot stand his smell. Bodies give each other a quick once over, trying to figure out the possibilities or desirability of a prolonged interaction. Probably most encounters never make it past the level of social physics; they remain ephemeral glances, a maneuvering through a crowd of persons, a smile, or "hello."

If a prolonged encounter does begin, the bodies of the participants place themselves in relation to each other, often forming an eddy or circle in the surrounding stream. Once an encounter is happening, it identifies and shields itself from an outside, including different encounters. Outsiders can now be expected to know that an encounter is going on here and now. Depending on this encounter's amount of closure, outsiders wait for it to "open"—maybe through a nod or an invitation to join—before they can participate as well. If not, outsiders run the risk of being perceived as intrusive, nosy, or rude.

Those already in the encounter can also address some outsiders, opening the circle, then closing it again, to signal the presence of a new member. More closed and ceremonial encounters might use formal introductions, maybe by a host or designated floater, who targets the lonesome. Besides various stages and cultures of clothing, one measure of formality is how much distance there is between the copresent bodies. Except for degradation rituals, such as a drill sergeant leaning "into the face" of a recruit, maintaining a distance recognizes the privacy of selves—even, or especially, in a face-to-face encounter. Unwelcome intrusions into private space are registered as offenses or provocations. Bumping into another body often calls for excuses.

The more intimate the relationship, the lower the distance, and the more of the body becomes visible or relevant. Then the body and its responses to select other bodies become actual ways and modes of the relationship, as in erotic attraction, for example. As an observer in its own right, the body either feels this attraction to others or not; there is little the reflexive self can do about it, except seek or avoid closeness once this attraction is noticed. When the bodies of strangers get very close to each other, as in a crowded elevator, special precautions assure that this closeness is not to be mistaken for intimacy—people stare at the ground or ceiling, signaling that physical closeness should not be taken as an invitation to intimacy. All this happens without awareness, by means of the encounter itself.

There is not much room for sustained skepticism and chronic doubt at this level, probably in part because this is the level of elementary physical survival, orientation, and reproduction. The reality of other bodies and persons in an encounter, and the material ecology of that which is around, or at hand, is taken for granted. It is real. The natural attitude is more practical than theoretical, although disruptions or disturbances in the routines can generate pauses, inviting more "contemplation" and "thought."

This basic confidence in the world can be upset by experimental interventions, such as breaching, but for these the same is true, insofar as they are also encounters, or embedded in encounters. That is, breaching experimenters and other phenomenological bracketeers will assume, for example, the existence of Garfinkel, the reality of the seminar where they discuss these experiments, the physical geography of the building they are in, and so on.

In large part, the certainty of the natural attitude is due to the closeness of encounters to the body and, through it, to the real world, including other human bodies. When a body feels or experiences something—hunger, urges, pain—it does not doubt this. Even when your eyes are being tricked by an optical illusion, they still see what they see, not an illusion.

Encounters get ready to happen when bodies perceive other bodies in their vicinity. Encounters begin when these perceptions are also perceived themselves. Encounters do not happen simply when several bodies are present. They happen when copresence entails mutual recognition. Encounters do not just occur, but occur when a co-occurrence is noted, and when this co-occurrence makes a difference in what happens next.

Given how many persons there are, and how many encounters between them are possible, the probability of any single encounter between any two, or more, of all persons is vanishingly small. You will never have an encounter with most others. This makes love improbable and risky, since becoming and remaining convinced that you have met the one and only Other rubs up against the fact that most of the others never even got a chance to show you just how much they could have loved you.

The probability of encounters increases with spatial and temporal confinement, since being together in the same space, at the same time, is a requirement for encounters to get going. To be part of an encounter, you not only have to be there, when and as it happens, but your presence must also be noted by the others who are present as well. Your presence must make a difference to the others present. Passengers on a crowded bus do not usually encounter all of the other passengers; there is a size limit to what encounters can still handle before breaking up or apart into separate encounters.

An encounter gets going between some of the passengers only upon mutual recognition, and when this mutual recognition is distinguished from engagement with nonparticipants, or from different encounters. You sit by yourself in a train compartment; someone else enters, and the difference that this makes *is* the encounter. It gets going as a mutual acknowledgment of presence, maybe as a glance or nod. Once this happens, it is impossible to deny that someone else is present, or this silent denial will itself be understood as a very loud and meaningful provocation, hostility, or rudeness.

While the chances of any one particular encounter happening are very small, once the conditions for an encounter are present, it is almost impossible not to have one. Then anything you do or say, or do not do or say, is part of this encounter, *nolens volens,* until you are by yourself again. This makes encounters more "terrorist" than liberating or emancipatory. As we shall see shortly, a "pure" bureaucracy would have no copresence in it at all, since copresence and encounters lead to informal systems.

Other persons, and their different encounters, can still make a difference to a focal encounter, since those who are close by might be observing you or your encounter. An encounter takes also place if this possibility of being observed is recognized, and if this possibility makes a difference to what happens next. It makes a difference if you are talking to someone where you feel sure no one else can observe this, or whether you are talking to someone in a crowded restaurant. Much like eddies in a river, encounters can shrink or expand, to the point of losing their inwardness and focus.

Conversations

Many longer encounters are conversations, as long as we keep in mind that most conversations are not exchanges of ideas, communicative action, or discourse. The performative activities of an encounter are, sociologically, much more significant than its representations, let alone its validity claims (Goffman 1981:10, 19, 48). Within limits, the *hows* of communication, including its "art" and "etiquette," outweigh its *whats*, at least in sociological significance.

At this performative level, having a conversation is more like making music together than having a discourse, with attunement of nonverbal gestures and behaviors, such as smile, voice pitch and speed, or the posturing and movement of bodies in relation to each other. In oral societies, talk, rhythm, and dance are a poetic unity, especially when the group or collective faces critical challenges (Havelock 1986:74). At this bodily and emotional level, conversations do not consist of representational talk, let alone very focused and narrow thematic talk, as might occur in a seminar or public debate.

In fact, this nonverbal level of communication is more primordial, more certain of sharing the same experience, and evolutionarily closer to the grooming rituals that Dunbar (1996) believes are the origin of gossip. A grunt or moan can sometimes say it all, and say it with great force and authority. Once words are exchanged, this primordial certainty breaks down, because it feeds off the isomorphism of reality and sound. Such sounds are themselves "things," not signs that refer to things. The blues started with plantation slaves humming a tune together. The early encounters between parents and infants are very "musical" as well; the words are sounds, not representations. Later, words introduce higher levels of intensionality, and with it the possibility of deception and controversy over meanings.

Higher certainty occurs when the ontic levels of the sign and its referent collapse, as in sounds, sleeping policemen, ostentation, or response cries. Unawareness, or inattention to, intension is also the unique possibility of music and dance as communication. As they happen, music and dance are nonreferential to those engaged and absorbed in them. They might acquire "meaning" later, in the words of critics and commentators, but as performances, music and dance do not "refer" to anything in the world, as do words. Once words arrive on the scene, ambiguity and uncertainty are not far away.

As performances, encounters and conversations have a deep and unaware syntax of turns, opening and closing formats, repairs of breakdowns, or pauses between sequences or frame changes (Schegloff 1992). This high level of structuring or ritualization protects encounters from the more unpredictable and disorderly mental states of their participating persons. Conversations are not such orderly affairs because they somehow manage to "coordinate" the mental states of participants. Mental states are much too nervous, irritable, and unstable to explain the surprising orderliness of conversational grammars and ground rules. Coordination of mental states also becomes impossible as the number of participants increases. More participants experience more, and more different, mental states.

Rather, entertain the possibility that conversations use persons, their bodies, and their brains, to continue themselves. Persons do not "have" conversations, but conversations may refer to persons, and how they do this is up to them, not persons. It is the ongoing encounter that "directs" mental states, not the other way around. Encounters would quickly derail if they were coupled closely to mental states. Conversations do not "follow" from mental states, including what persons might be thinking about, while they are having a conversation. A previous episode or sequence in an encounter predicts what happens next much better than mental states or intentions, although very imperfectly still.

This account of thinking differs from standard Mead. Thinking is not "internal conversation." Thinking is best done alone, without others present. When you think by yourself, you do not have to wait for others to catch up, and you do not have to focus on what someone else is saying. While thinking, one might "simulate" a conversation with imagined or textual others, but a simulated conversation is not a real conversation, much as a textual dialogue is not a real dialogue. It is *you* who is doing the simulation, not the one you are simulating.

Thoughts are wilder than conversations, and less caged by social structure. In an encounter, you cannot just say whatever you think. You can also not "mean" what you say, since meaning is a result of communication, not its antecedent cause. Thinking by yourself, *die Gedanken sind frei* [thoughts are free]. Thoughts can risk more than conversations; they are also much faster than any conversation could handle without derailing.

Turbulence

Encounters are "turbulent" in several ways. First, there are very many of them, and very many encounters happen at the same time. There is no invisible hand capable of "coordinating" or "controlling" all of these encounters. Encounters emerge and proceed "autopoietically," that is, they form when they do, and when they do form, they select and can change their focus. There is no central planning or scheduling center that could decide and determine who meets whom, when, for how long, and what will transpire there and then. There is no steering board where all the encounters, or their results, could be summarized and aggregated. Any such aggregation or scheduling may occur locally, but then imperfectly, as happens in formally scheduled and official organizational encounters.

Prisons, for example, do a better job of planning and controlling encounters than corporations, but even, or especially, prisons have their own informal systems, backstages, and hidden networks. Prisons can isolate inmates, prevent some unwanted encounters, segregate men from women, and make sure that persons remain locked up. Still prisons cannot tame completely the turbulence from encounters, so that "underground" realities thrive. Expect riots to come from unscheduled and unplanned encounters and groups. A fine literary account of prison backstages can be found in chapter 17 ("Epictetus Comes to da House") of Tom Wolfe's 1998 novel *A Man in Full*.

Counting very ephemeral encounters, including mutual glances, by far the most encounters during the average day a person spends in

public are not "planned," or scheduled in advance. Encounters introduce surprises into social life. This does not mean that they happen
randomly, only that it is hard to predict, from somewhere else,
whether an encounter is about to happen here and now, with whom it
will take place, how long it will last, or what it will be about, if anything.
As we shall see, a great deal of work in organizations consists of scheduling and formatting encounters in advance, so that the organization
"knows" which of the countless encounters it houses produce results
that may become important to it.

The second reason for turbulence from encounters is that encounters take place in the here and now, among copresent persons and
their bodies in a concrete physical setting. For this reason, they are
very susceptible to changes in that setting, including the exits and en-
tries of persons. For starters, one can only talk about persons who are
not present. Conversations are easily disrupted by events in the here
and now, because they cannot easily ignore, let alone control, what
goes on in their environment and vicinity. This makes them turbulent,
sometimes chaotic, especially when the surroundings are unstable and
rapidly changing. Since they link perceiving bodies, anything percepti-
ble might disturb conversations or turn into a theme of communication: a slamming door, surrounding conversations, nervous ticks, or
bad breath. Encounters are sensitive also to the bodies and brains of
persons, including their various and changing mental states. Brains
are *nervous* systems; they cannot stick to one sensation for very long,
but continue to experience something different as heads move this
and that way, focusing on novel impressions. Not many of these states
make it into an encounter, where they get recognized when expressed
in some way. But when this does happen, an encounter cannot ignore
this expression, but reacts to it. Then, and for the moment, it cannot
register or notice much of anything else.

How do groups and organizations manage to tame some of this turbulence from their encounters?

Groups

When encounters happen "repeatedly," among more or less the
"same" persons, groups might emerge. "Repeatedly" and "same" are in
quotation marks, since groups are not really extended, prolonged, or

repetitive encounters. An encounter is over when it is over. It cannot, strictly, be repeated, since one cannot have the same encounter twice. One can prolong an encounter, but this just means it goes on longer than expected or scheduled, but then ends as well. What gets repeated or prolonged is not an encounter, but the expectation that the end of a group's encounter is not the end of the group itself.

The persons in groups do not remain the "same," either. "Person" is the way in which some networks—but not all of them, and not in the same ways—observe their nodes, which happen to be human bodies with brains, as far as encounters and groups are concerned. Structurally speaking, however, "person" is an outcome, not a source or cause, of social relations. A group formats a specific "version" of its personal nodes; who is what sort of person varies across groups. It is not the persons who are being connected, but these "versions." Persons are attributions that some observers use to do certain kinds of cultural and social work, such as blaming or firing someone. The work "person" does varies from network to network, and context to context. The "identity" of persons is their difference from and relation to other such identities, and to themselves at earlier times in their lives, when they were different persons (which is to say, nodes in different relations).

While an encounter may be over, the group is still there—on background alert, so to speak—waiting to happen again. Groups do not come to an end when one of their encounters ends, unless it is the very last one, the famous final scene. If there are no more group encounters, ever, the group ceases to observe itself, and be observed by others, as a distinctive identity. As this happens, it fades out of existence, or turns into a memory, which former members have alone. To try to assure that the end of an encounter is not the end of the group itself, there are several modes of stabilization and temporal extension. These give group membership its characteristic certainty or confidence. You know your own groups, and you know that there are other groups to whom you do not belong. The latter set of groups is incomparably larger than the first set.

Arguably, the most obvious stabilization is still kinship, particularly the core kin groups such as nuclear families. Despite the many changes in family structure, and externalization of some previous family tasks, it still matters whether someone is your own spouse or child, or someone else's. Your home is also not someone else's home. A home is the place where encounters among family usually take place; it is more difficult to ignore your family if you are living together under the same roof. A family can have different homes, but each of these is then a home as well.

Whatever else they may be—property networks, role systems, units of sexual reproduction, domestic workplaces, or sites of struggles over generational and sexual inequality—families are also Darwinian arenas for competition over care and attention to persons (Sulloway 1996:chap. 4). In groups, care for individuals can be given, including their physical and emotional states. No person can personally extend "deep" care to a great many others; I would guess that ten or so persons is the maximum, over which limit care becomes more communicated, scheduled, or organized. For example, one then makes a donation to an organization that is paid to care.

In such Darwinian arenas, at issue is how the always limited attention and care space to selves is to be divided among the selves. Groups are sites where weakness can turn into strength by presenting itself as a reason for more attention. Groups differ from organizations in many ways, but an important difference is the degree of sensitivity and attention to personhood, itself a historical and sociological variable (Arditi 1998:40). As members of groups, persons expect attention and care for themselves; they expect to be recognized and treated as "individuals." To a group, it makes a huge difference whether or not you are there, among the group, while organizations, especially large bureaucracies, can afford more indifference and alienation. At the same time, organizations also house many groups, which *are* more sensitive to the exit and entry of persons.

Groups are the units of Durkheimian ritual and solidarity. It is here that a sense of belonging is cultivated and experienced. To recharge the batteries of solidarity, groups will have to arrange recurrent encounters. An important part of being together is talking about the next time. There are very strict distinctions between members and nonmembers; you cannot show up for a Thanksgiving dinner at a family home that is not your own and expect to be treated as kin. Needless to say, there are variations in the degrees of exclusiveness but, by and large, neither encounters nor organizations have boundaries as sharply policed as those of groups. The only way to enter a kin group is by birth or marriage; the only way to enter a nonkin group, especially a tight one, is by admission or invitation. In both cases, special privileges, status, and credits tend to go to those who have been with the group for a long time—founders, elders, and ancestors.

Nonkin groups are frequently formed around workplaces in organizations. Going back to the discovery of the informal system in human relations, organizations provide opportunities for regular encounters with those who work there also, especially those physically close by. Going to work daily also means seeing many of the same persons as yesterday. Again, once opportunities for encounters are present, they will be taken, and so interactions among coworkers might lead to groups of varying density, boundedness, and connectivity to other groups, in the same or different organization. Groups in organizations have their own networks as well; the class cultures within and between organizations are made up of such stratified networks of groups, with their own cultures, habitus, and solidarity (R. Collins 1988:208–225).

Groups are historical networks of encounters, not persons, although groups pay much attention to persons. To say they are "historical" means that links also exist between present and past encounters within the group. Interaction, not action, is critical. What matters is hanging around, gossip, and sociability with the "usual suspects." Groups of usual suspects establish mutual trust, reality, loyalty, and personhood. Groups are "the lifeworld," as seen from a person at its center. Persons know their groups very well, much more so than they know their organizations.

Groups are a source of selfhood and *Befindlichkeit*. There is nothing especially romantic or cozy about them, however. Sometimes, groups may provide a sense of Gemeinschaft but, depending on how closely coupled they are, they can also suffocate and consume persons. A Gemeinschaft may also be a major source of hostility to other such Gemeinschaften, especially when they believe themselves to have opposite true values. Some groups are very competitive and individualistic; think of a group of scientists making a discovery or breakthrough.

Different groups are more conformist and collectivist; these connect their members in redundant ways, and embed or sink them more deeply into their social and cultural fabric. This is what cults do, for example, or very greedy and total institutions. Since groups are linked to other groups in networks as well, groups differ according to the configuration or signature of their networks.

As compared to organizations, and especially bureaucracies, groups have more time for attention to their members as unique or special individuals. The members of a group feel that they make a difference and count in the group. Though not necessarily happy, they are at home there. Small size encourages this sentiment, because it makes free riding less of an option, and because the difference that any one member can make becomes smaller with increasing size. The group would not be the same if its specific members were not part of it. The members cannot really be replaced once they are dead. Again, this does not mean that the group is dead, too, but it will never be the same again, and knows this. Hence, very close groups intensely ritualize birth and death.

Groups cope with much personal drama and expressiveness; they are prime observers and managers of mental states and emotions, especially when they allow for, and delight in, individualism. Some of those groups come close to networks among therapeutic encounters, probing the depths and subtleties of selves. Such groups elevate the self into a cherished object of attention and care. Not all groups do this, however. Some groups are more concerned about themselves than their members, expecting from them intense dedication and commitment to the common or sacred cause.

Cults

An important dimension of variation in groups is density, coupling, and boundedness. High-density groups swallow persons whole, leaving less room for distinction and individualism. This trend gets reinforced if the group is cut off from the rest of society, and if this isolation persists for some time. Such "high" groups have rigid and closed cultures with a strong sense of moral righteousness and uncompromising principles, going back to sacred origins and traditions (Douglas 1992a:76). The culture is relatively settled, institutionalized, and unwilling to change much. The grids of that culture are "realist"—they are mapped onto the essences and natural kinds seen in the world, much as Durkheimian totems. The culture is not seen as "constructed," and is not to be ironized from within.

Cults are high-density groups, especially when they are based on communal living relationships within a "compound" or other restricted area. Cults are greedy and total. One knows who belongs, and who is the enemy. Relations extending outside the cult are severed or severely curtailed, reducing the "drift" of the nodes or members that comes from them being also members of other groups (Berg 1997:421). The followers are all there, most of the time. Outsiders are suspicious. If they are to be admitted, it helps to have links to the inside. Still, new members are stripped of their old identity and networks, assuming new names and identities inside (Zerubavel 1991:32–60). A frequent strategy in cults is to produce and raise their own offspring, which generates kinship links in the network as well and fortifies it against the nonkin outside even further. Exposure to the cult can then be lifelong and all-consuming.

Cults institutionalize more or less complete cultural transsubstantiations and conversions, which are embodied most perfectly in the charismatic heroes, founders, and leaders. Krieger's (1992:8–15) work on how physics gets a grip on the world emphasizes the importance of "walls" in this process; walls, or boundaries, are significant accomplishments for groups as well. Walls create two sides of a distinction, inside and out. They establish distance, defining what is near or far. What is near is "us," what is far is "them." With a wall in place, events on one side affect others on the same side more than can get through the wall, to the outside. Walls rarely isolate perfectly, but they do structure or restructure that which can pass through them, or not. Walls occasionally need repairs, adjustments, and reinforcements; if these are not done, the wall breaks down, and with it the inside / outside structure. Walls are not given, natural, permanent, or constant; they must be built to exist and maintained to persist.

As variables, walls can be of various materials, shapes, strengths, and durations. When they are very new, or in the process of being constructed, walls let much pass through them uninspected and unobserved. The same happens to walls that are never cared for. Walls are better at keeping some things and forces out, or in, than other things and forces. As a wall thickens, the coupling between inside and outside gets looser, and the inside starts to behave or observe itself as an inside, where less is possible than in the world at large. This world includes, of course, all the other walls, and all the many different insides and outsides that they produce.

By distinguishing or separating itself from that which it is not, or not anymore, an inside establishes a measure of self-similarity and sameness among its parts, elements, and relations. Sociologically, what happens here is a network in formation. Through its connections, the network holds its components "in place," at least until further notice—until a wall collapses, for example, and the inside becomes indistinguishable to itself and its observers. When a network collapses, its nodes are set free from the connections that used to hold them in place, defined who or what these nodes were, and decided what they could or could not do. The longer a node has been in the same structural position within the network, the more that node is "in its place." It may acquire the status of natural kind, essence, constant, or basic and fundamental building block. This loss in flexibility, or "character" in persons, means fewer degrees of freedom and more trouble for attempts at changing the aging node and its overall position.

Krieger (1992:33) likens this process to building a clock, since the clock's parts have more degrees of freedom when they are not, or no longer, part of the clock: "Each part's degrees of freedom are then [when the clock is ticking] rather severely limited by the interaction of the component parts." Degrees of freedom are variables that can be manipulated to see what happens. Reducing degrees of freedom means "taming" the other variables that might make a difference to the results: screening out background noise, for example, as well as alternative explanations of the observed outcomes. No degrees of freedom means necessity; infinite degrees of freedom indicates utter arbitrariness. Most networks are somewhere in between, or contingent, sometimes moving closer to necessity, sometimes to arbitrariness. Everything depends on other dependencies.

Networks reduce degrees of freedom by their links. As the nodes become linked, the patterns of these links, and the patterns of their absence, give a network its texture or signature, and define the place and possibilities of the nodes, at least for the time being, until the signature changes. Very dense and redundant networks reinforce links by mutually consolidating various parameters of membership (Blau and Schwartz 1984:84–89). This happens in the network core, where the nodes are linked over and over again to the same other nodes in many coherent, consistent, and mutually supportive ways. Think of textbooks, black boxes, normal science, institutional certainties, tautologies, and constructions that appear unconstructed. Thompson's (1967:11) account of "technical cores" in organizations fits this model as well; for him, the way to buffer and protect the core is to "reduce the number of variables operating on it."

The result is less freedom and ambiguity in a core than is typical for loosely coupled networks, which are full of nonlinks or structural holes (Burt 1992:18–20). Localistic networks are dense and redundant; cosmopolitan networks are more loosely coupled, ill-defined, and expansive, with shifting boundaries and highly permeable walls.

By means of their walls or boundaries, and by training up a network, groups "define" their members by putting them in places or positions in this network. Places and positions are what, and where, they are only in relation to other positions and places. Bourdieu (1989) calls such networks "fields." The places and positions can be changed or filled with different personnel, but the overall structure or configuration of the network remains in place longer, taking more time to change than do individual nodes or connections. The cores of theories, for example, are more robust and slow to change than are its peripheral sectors, which react more nervously and quickly to empirical surprises and anomalies. Kuhn ([1962] 1970) calls such cores "paradigms," in Holton (1973:chap. 2) they are "themata," in Polanyi ([1958] 1964:59–64) "presuppositions," and Quine (1964) calls them analytical truths. Most cultures have such cores as their institutions, lifeworld, common sense, tacit background, or "practices."

To some extent, walls and networks cancel internal irregularities and nonuniformities. To the extent that this does happen, the network acquires a separate and distinct "identity." That is to say, the network's identity begins to be distinguished from the identities of other networks, and also from the identities of its nodes. The nodes—for example, group members—become settled or stuck in their place and position, with their own identity. Mutual expectations and definitions of the situation become firmer. The members' degrees of freedom decline together with their network's degrees of freedom, as the network curtails its own possibilities—including the options of being another group, no group at all, or a group of a different sort. When all this is settled, for now, then "the group" comes into reality, presenting itself as something that can be observed, that is, distinguished, and as something of an observer in its own right. This may include self-observation and observation of the environment, such as other groups, or organizations. As an observer in its own right, the group develops its own culture, sense of reality, and niche in the world. For the group, the world is what it has become after the group was formed. Before, the world was a different world, since it lacked the new group, together with this group's modes of culture and relations to the world.

Degrees of freedom decline when connections are made to other nodes and *their* connections. You marry your wife and her family, as well as, to some extent, their relations and positions. As this network forms, it develops its own behavior, but keep in mind that descriptions and explanations of behavior will vary together with the group's observers, including its self-observations and -identifications. Groups become stronger as they survive various trials and tribulations, much as a stable physical object emerges when it survives various "insults" on its integrity (Krieger 1992:18).

The longer a group persists, the more its attributions and constructs tend to turn into its common sense and natural kinds, which capture the world as it is, for the group. Then the group develops institutions, such as rituals, with their characteristic taken-for-grantedness and blind spots. Such invisibilities are housed and protected in the core of its culture. They become that which the group cannot do or imagine otherwise without actually falling apart, without losing its identity and distinctiveness. Groups disappear when they have no inside at all anymore, or when it becomes impossible to distinguish between inside and out.

The behavior of the group becomes distinguishable from the behavior of its members when this distinction is drawn by an empirical observer who uses this distinction to make his observations. For example, the group, as its own observer, will attribute some events and outcomes to itself, while attributing other events and outcomes to its members, insofar as they are also members of other groups, organizations, and networks. As Simmel ([1908] 1971) observes, individualism increases as such connections to many different modes of association increase. For this increase also decreases the hold or grip that any particular association has on its inside and insiders. Very loosely coupled and poorly enclosed or defined groups will tend to have a weak identity and observe their members more as private and independent individuals who are members of many other and different groups also, though the details of these memberships are not known, or only vaguely.

These are groups of "entrepreneurs," whose other and outside motives and commitments are largely their own business. One could say such groups do not know their own members, or do not know them very well. Groups whose networks are not inwardly focused very often, or not very intensely, have weak identities. They fall apart, but also reform quickly and frequently, much as Maffesoli's ([1988] 1996:11) postmodern tribes.

In contrast, very dense, cohesive, and isolated groups will tend to attribute most events or outcomes to themselves, and then to the totems and "higher powers" that the group represents, but not so much to their members. They do not make much room for observing individual agency, idiosyncrasy, or narcissism. The group puts its own welfare above its members', demanding strict loyalty and dedication to a sacred cause, up to the point of suicide, or death in battle. Such is the behavior of cults: "The morning after the rite, the savage wakes up with a bad hangover and a deeply internalized concept" (Gellner 1992:37).

Structural Fortification

Cults erect very thick and selective walls around themselves, fortified by suspicious guards and protected by strict taboos and filters. Their inside / outside distinctions are rigid and uncompromising, tolerating little ambiguity, uncertainty, controversy, or innovation. The outside is populated by evil strangers who plot and conspire to destroy the cult or infiltrate it. Promptly, the FBI or ATF starts blaring bad music at the compound. On the inside, there are a select few chosen ones, united by the right purpose and heroes, battling against evil and immorality. Inside a cult, the degrees of freedom are very severely restricted, due to dense and redundant ties and connections. Often ties are made stronger still by endogamy, kinship, and common descent (Douglas 1992b).

Cults have a very strong and sharp collective identity, partly because their nodes have little identity apart from the cult. Total and selfless dedication to the common cause is the prime virtue; self-distinction is vanity. Except for the charismatic founder or leader, who differs from everyone so much that he is not really an ordinary mortal, members differ little from each other, or are encouraged to be more like the others. There is not much room or tolerance for internal diversity and dissent, for idiosyncratic expressivism or exhibitionism, or for discoveries (Bloor 1983:140–145). Much less is there room for irony about foundations. Cults have a very secure handle and grip on their insides, much as the physicist gets when using a routinized piece of equipment, technique, proven measure, or in Krieger's (1992:20) words, a "regime of stability." This regime or grip becomes stronger as ties to the outside are cut off, since the absence of such ties means that no forces are pulling at the members from elsewhere, or from far away. In cults, "near" and "far" are so certain that the distinction becomes, literally, reified—as walls around the compound, cloister, or commune.

A medieval environment is probably more conducive to cults than a modern one, since modernity makes it more difficult to sever all ties to the outside completely and for a very long time (even centuries in medieval times). This has nothing to do with modernity's rationality or disenchantment. Rather, as mutual accessibility increases, even over large distances, the odds of surviving as a stable endogamy, autarchy, and unknown island worsen. Resource dependency creates some ties to the environment, as do recruitment, television, radio, or the Web. In modernity, it becomes less plausible to deny that there are other worlds out there.

The grip of a cult is rare and improbable, fighting the forces of time and, in modernity, the rapid acceleration of time. Most networks are not cults complete with rock-solid walls, securely domesticated variables or forces, and very little freedom. Most groups are not cults, either, and their institutions are less greedy or total. Many once strong groups disappear, or become weaker, as their members fade into distant and different groups and organizations. Even families cannot remember their dead for long, at most two or three generations, beyond which "membership" is rarely remembered or activated anymore. Modernity still has some tribes, and maybe more tribes than ever before, but these tribes come and go, form and reform, at much higher speeds, without usually crystallizing into cults.

Will Technology End Groups?

Much like encounters, groups are here to stay. They will not disappear altogether as the result of TV, the Web, the telephone, or email. Wellman and Gulia (1995:11) observe that "despite all the talk about virtual community transcending time and space *sui generis,* much contact is between people who see each other in person and live locally." Groups and networks assimilate into their own fabric novel devices for communicating, doing with them whatever they can to keep themselves up and running. If this proves infeasible or cumbersome, a group might discard or remain indifferent toward a new technology or tool of communication. But such a tool cannot really "destroy" groups, since communicating and interacting are precisely what they do best. Technologies are incorporated into a social structure, and such incorporations happen according to the terms of that structure, not (just) the terms of technology. This much is now commonplace in science and technology studies. The cotton mill does not produce capitalism; sever it from all its manifold ties, human and nonhuman, and the mill just sits there, doing nothing and getting nothing done.

This does not mean that technology cannot "change" society, but the mysterious conversion that utopian technofetishists expect will not happen. This utopianism is not a credible analytical or empirical account; it rather belongs to the frontstage rhetoric of the professions and interests that push some technology. As a technology moves frontstage, fantastic promises are being made about all the good it will do to society, or the users. Put PCs in every office, and the American workplace will never be the same, productivity will increase, and paper will disappear. Get everyone hooked into the Web, and soon race will no longer matter and all hierarchy will crumble. Link persons to global networks of communication, and—poof!—there go local identities, disparities, and conflicts. None of this is happening, because of social structure.

The hapless users are derided as an irritation or disturbance to this utopia; they are labeled slow, stupid, or inflexible. It is their fault if the utopia takes more time to materialize than planned. Nevertheless, the users either use something or not. If they do not, or if no one does, there is no demand for a technology, and it cannot make any profits. If users do use a technology, it will be on their own terms, for their own needs and work.

Social Movements

Social movements are networks as well. Much of the behavior of movements can be accounted for by network models, though variations complicate the task here, too (McAdam, McCarthy, and Zald 1988). Social movements often start from small beginnings, such as neighborhood contacts, extended encounters, and groups (Gould 1993). Most of them probably never make it past their crises of newness and adolescence, especially when they compete with other movements over resources in the same niche (Hannan and Freeman 1989:chap. 10). Movements likely turn into organizations, with some bureaucracy, when they acquire permanent staff, files, and property.

The transformation from movement to organization is greatly accelerated when the movement negotiates with other movements, and especially with already established political organizations. Negotiating with the state is probably the single most critical transition between movements and organizations. Handling contacts with the environment is conducive to organization, because the environment expects someone at the top to be responsible enough to make binding decisions. Since not everyone can negotiate with everyone else at the same time, delegation of the authority to "speak for," and "on behalf of," the movement separates leaders from followers. The leaders sign documents, get interviewed and quoted in the media, maybe appear on TV. They soon monopolize the outside observers' attention space, and so concentrate representative agency at the top.

Short of radical resistance, silence, or violence, the only way for movement leaders to get anything done for their movements is to negotiate and compromise with the leaders of other movements or organizations. The more the leaders interact with other leaders in separate encounters and groups, the more they develop loyalties and obligations to each other. These newer obligations will, to some extent, conflict with the "original" mandates that the leaders carry from their constituencies. The more compromises are made, the more of the original agenda will be forsaken, replaced, watered down, and superseded by realpolitik. Radical rhetoric is then reserved for special occasions, such as emotional commemorations of the movement's heroic origins (Fuchs and Ward 1994).

Some followers may soon cry foul and complain about the "sellout" of the pure principles. The followers tend to attribute the compromises the leaders strike to the leaders' characters, to moral failure and corruptness. Some followers might leave the movement to join or start another one. Unsuccessful movements disband or shrink back into the local networks and modules from which they had emerged.

Organizations

How do organizations emerge from encounters, groups, and movements? It may be a bit misleading to suggest, with Perrow (1991), that modern Western societies *are* societies of organizations, since encounters, groups, and networks are still present as well, and they remain present also within and between organizations. It is also false to call organizations "artificial" constructs that replace "primordial"—or worse, "natural"—modes of association, since organizations house many encounters, groups, and informal systems (Coleman 1990:584–585, 597–598). To bemoan, from the vantage point of liberal humanism, that "purposive" organizations replace "natural" persons as dominant sources of agency will not do either, since both individual and corporate personhood are drastic simplifications and attributions by an observer, who takes the intentional stance to explain organizations as the result of corporate or managerial purposes, strategies, plans, and choices. But organizations are uniform "actors" only from very far away, and only for an observer who ignores their considerable internal diversity and complexity.

What is true, though, is that modern societies have many more organizations than do all other societies. Many organizations come from other or previous organizations as the result of spin-offs, mergers, or institutional copies. Hence new foundings tend to come in waves and bursts of organizational populations (Stinchcombe [1965] 1988:197). If they do not come from previous organizations or mergers, size and property are important variables in the transitions to organization. Ceteris paribus, size increases the degree of bureaucratic indifference toward persons. Organizations tend to observe persons as types, categories, cases, and numbers, although this tendency varies as well. (More on this variation later.) Organizations also distinguish between members and nonmembers, and then between various ranks and grids of members. Such distinctions are part of their formal structures, but we will see that formal structures occur on various levels within organizations and suborganizations.

Property and Payments

The most important suborganization in a science, for example, is the laboratory, which is typically housed within a larger structure, traditionally a department and university, but increasingly in corporations and government agencies. Laboratories condition and occasion the copresence of several workers. As the most immediate governance structure for an experimental science, labs are also the sites for local politics and advancement. A very important part of that structure is securing the material conditions for further scientific work, by doing and completing previous scientific work. Accumulating advantages over time, grants generate more grants, citations lead to more citations, and discoveries make more discoveries possible.

Scientific organizations compete intensely for funds, and manage that competition through peer-group networking with funding agencies. The bigger a science, the more intensive and extensive these contacts. An increasingly large part of scientific work is explaining the merits of that work to audiences, clients, and providers on the front-stages of the organization. The structural result is comparable to the "interlocking directorates" of major corporations, which reduce environmental dependency and risk by coopting and internalizing part of that environment into their internal structures and operations (Pfeffer and Salancik 1978:chaps. 6 and 7). Previous successes in this area make future successes more likely. Funding agencies tend to reduce the uncertainties of whom to fund—and, incomparably more likely and frequently, whom *not* to fund—by considering previous accomplishments and reputations.

Since funding agencies cannot do any science by themselves, and since they also have no independent way to judge any science's future potential for meritorious research, such agencies rely heavily on scientists and their reputations to make their decisions. But it is impossible for agencies and corporations to "finalize" science for assured, direct, and immediate payoffs or profits (van den Daele, Krohn, and Weingart 1979). They can predict the eventual outcomes of research even less than the scientists can. External hierarchies and agencies also cannot effectively decide and supervise how a piece of research is actually to be carried out, in the daily work of a laboratory or network of labs. If it were possible to "finalize" science, this would probably have been done a long time ago.

Organizations, rather than persons or households, now own most of the available wealth, including the material means of production and administration. Warriors turn into soldiers when the state owns and monopolizes the material means of violence. Gentlemen amateur scientists turn into research professionals when they no longer own the means of scientific production and depend on organizations and organizations' property to do their work. Organizations provide the material means of production, which means that one must be *there* to do one's work. One must be a member of some organization, or network of organizations, to do science, for example. If one is not in an organization that does science, it is also hard to become one of those scientists circulating in the networks between organizations, moving from lab to lab, and research center to research center. Whoever is not, in some way, a member of the organization cannot do research *there*. The material means are organizational, not private or personal, property.

In most cases, membership in some organization is a condition for payments. To receive payments, a lot of persons acquire membership and status in an organization. They now become its workers. Workers can be expected to show up and do their work. Their willingness to work there is construed as agreement to the organizational terms and parameters of membership, uncertain or controversial as these may be, or might become. If secretaries are expected to type, they are also expected to type whatever comes down the official line, even when some of the contents of some of the documents are not to the secretaries' liking. In turn, workers can expect their organizations not to expect just anything from them. Professors of literary criticism do not have to fear that their organizations will ask them to teach physics.

As a group or movement acquires property, it more likely turns into an organization, since the material and administrative nucleus of an organization keeps track of resource flows by means of files and records. This is done by accounting, where bureaucracy grows around record-keeping. But bureaucracy is not all there is to organizations. Organization is not incompatible with tradition or charisma, although organizations do tend to concentrate charisma at the top, where leaders with special properties and characters presumably make the decisions (Smith and Simmons 1983). Nor does organization replace "premodern" forms and modes of association, such as encounters and groups, or even Gemeinschaften, but actually provides them with workplaces and time to form.

Popular ideological and critical theories of organizations tend to hold them constant as oppressive iron cages, loci of instrumental reason, reified "systems," or fully disciplined sites of supervision and surveillance. Such metaphors exaggerate the ability of an organization to effectively control its internal and external environments. Organizations do sometimes coerce and supervise, but the actual degrees of hierarchy and discipline are variables that depend on other variables. The "integration" of an organization is a temporary and uncertain accomplishment of organizing, not a definitional steady state, default mode, or ground rule. Sometimes there may be more unity to an organization than at other times. Variations should also be expected in internal and external boundaries and differentiation, so that even unity and integration might be local and temporary, extending only as far as they do, and only until further notice.

Organizations appear as streamlined, orderly, and integrated rational machines from far away, perhaps to a philosopher or critic. Observing from a long distance tends to stereotype and simplify that which it observes. It observes that which is still observable from this distance. Outside observers likely take an organization's orderly and polished frontstage accounts of itself for granted. They have no time or opportunity to get much closer, maybe even inside, the organization, and hurriedly pick up the glossy brochures and glowing self-advertisements at the front door. Penetrate more deeply into the backstages of actual organizing, and order becomes more disorderly, ambivalent, and difficult to accomplish (Weick 1979:88). Discrepancies between front- and backstages become visible, and cracks appear in the masks of rationality. In these gaps and cracks, ironists and cynics reside, feeding off these very discrepancies.

Most organizations are only partly impersonal iron cages, dominated by the ubiquitous forces of instrumental and technical reason— and then only when seen from a distant outsider's or critic's point of view. Organizations are also "lifeworlds." For example, there is a lot of talk in organizations, and much of it concerns persons and their characteristic idiosyncrasies (Fuchs 1995). There are no strict distinctions between "systems" running on "delinguistified" media of exchange, and "lifeworlds" integrated through communicative action (Habermas [1984] 1987:153–197). From an insider's point of view, organizations *are* lifeworlds, not just formal and coercive mechanisms for coordination and control. The organizational lifeworlds consist of encounters, groups, and networks among both.

If they are not confined in extremely coercive total institutions, persons in organizations do not appear all that "alienated." They gossip a lot about personal drama and scandal. Organizations are frequently knots in enduring relationships that connect families and communities. While instrumental and technical rationality and efficiency are but a small part of Weber's classical theory of organizations, they have gained much more prominence in subsequent work, especially in "critical" theories. Rationality, however, is also best operationalized as a variable, not as a constant or a definitional steady state. That is, the degree to which an organization can appear "rational," in the Weberian sense, is variable and changing—it depends, for example, on routinization and closure of conflict. Rationality also surfaces when the organization turns outward, maybe in an attempt at securing support and legitimacy (Meyer and Rowan 1977). In the actual work of organizing, rationality is more likely bounded and failing, especially when this work is complex and uncertain.

With neo-institutionalism (Powell and DiMaggio 1991), the following observations on organizing and organization suggest that there is much less order, stability, and integration to them than frequently assumed. Any order and effective control is accomplished against resistance, inertia, or entropy. Order does not fall from the sky, and neither should it be made part of the very definition for organization. Instead, order emerges slowly and locally, and is not irreversible. A local order does not, all by itself, turn into a more global order, by the intrinsic force of its natural rationality and superiority. Rather, a local order must be extended to start mattering elsewhere as well, or at another time.

Turbulence Again

Organizations house encounters and groups, whose networks make up the informal system or systems. Encounters and groups emerge autopoietically under conditions of copresence. There is little that an organization can do to prevent this from happening, because it assembles and gathers persons repeatedly around workplaces. Expect organizing to be messy and disorderly because of this turbulence.

One might think that the top controls the rest, but the top is, after all, another part of the rest, not its conductor. No single encounter controls the processes and outcomes of all other encounters. Encounters are local and small. They are over soon and cannot be repeated. "Compatibility" between encounters and their results might be established later, and somewhere else, such as at the next higher levels of administration. Bureaucratic formalism and quantification accomplish a measure of aggregate or higher-level unity by summarizing and condensing the official outcomes of official encounters. But turbulence from encounters and groups occurs at upper levels of the organization as well, probably even more so, since much of what top executives do is talk with other top executives (Mintzberg 1973:44).

Another source of turbulence in the organization is its environment, especially that segment which is part of an organization's network, niche, or set. No two organizations have exactly the same environment, since they are part of each other's, but not their own, environments. Very turbulent environments pressure an organization into searching for and recognizing novel information (Hirsch 1972). Such organizations or suborganizations scan the world for surprises because they are rewarded for innovations.

Limits to Control

At a very abstract level, organizing is an attempt to convert uncertainty into routines. There are many sources of uncertainty, both internal and external. New uncertainties emerge all the time, together with technological and competitive challenges, for example. That organizing is risky can be seen in the low survival rate of organizations in their new or adolescent phases.

As bureaucracies, or in their bureaucratic parts, organizations cage complexity by formalism, standardization, and quantification. They assemble statistics from stories by averaging contexts and locales (Paulos 1998:12). This process holds some variations constant, which leads to a more simplified and digitized construct of organizational realities. Caging, though, is never complete or irreversible, since unprecedented uncertainties might emerge and since the caged or tamed complexity sometimes bursts out of its cage. This happens, for example, in the "normal accidents" that tend to occur in closely coupled and interactive networks (Perrow 1984). Statistics are not irreversible, either, but can be deconstructed—for example, by reopening and reintroducing the contexts, circumstances, and locales of their "raw" data. Some controversies in organizations concern alternative ways to compute the statistics.

Much administrating and managing is *not* doing something—inattention, indecision, or selectivity. This occurs even in centralized and absolutist bureaucracies, such as the one described by Musil as *Kakanien,* which is completely clueless most of the time, and not even aware of its own obsolescence and imminent demise. Offe (1972:74–76) has directed the theory of the state not to what it does, but to what it does not do, noting that the set of inactions is always very much larger than the set of actions. True to their liberal heritage and humanist pedigree, rationalist metaphors of organizations celebrate and exaggerate activity and agency. They focus attention on strategies, decisions, plans, actions, and purposes, and then on how all this can be rational, or made rational.

In competing for attention, problems push each other aside. For each issue before an administration, there are many more issues that do not make it there, or that get there only to face inattention or inaction. In their commonsense mode of observing, persons tend to attribute bureaucratic inaction to the intentional indifference or hostility of bureaucrats.

Administrations likely fare better at isolating a problem than doing something about it. There are many problems, but limited time. Not everything that comes into view can be dealt with, and the problems that are being addressed are being addressed one after another, while still more problems surface. Administrations also deal with problems in encounters or committees, where much happens that has little to do with the official business. Doing something about a problem may make things worse, especially in structures whose behavior is not well understood. Doing something also attracts more attention than not doing something and creates opportunities for resistance, criticism, or disagreement. Expect unexpected outcomes, revenge effects, and perverse incentives from planning and control, especially in complex and interactive organizing and organizations (Caplow 1994:7).

A university, for example, can schedule some encounters as seminars, but it cannot really regulate much of what goes on in these (Stinchcombe 1990:chap. 9). Much less is it possible to "effectively" control and coordinate all seminars in all universities. Further, seminars are but a tiny fraction of all the encounters that occur within the organization. The organization can, in its formal structures, codify expectations as to what should be taught and understood in its seminars, but it cannot make sure that the encounters will actually meet or satisfy such expectations. A university can have its departments formally assessed and evaluated, but what happens next, if anything, is much less certain. There are good reasons to punish the deadbeats, but good reasons also to see whether a resource increase might help improve morale, performance, and ranking. Maybe the reports of assessments are not being read or understood. Or maybe they are, but quickly forgotten. The reports just sit there and pile up. Much of administration is putting out immediate and local fires.

An administration can issue recommendations for, say, improvement in teaching or research, but whether anything actually improves or not no one knows—until the next assessment. The administration cannot teach the courses or write the articles itself. Neither does it know whether the research is any good, and so it counts the sheer quantity of the output, ignoring that which matters most to those who do it. Alternatively, the administration depends on academic reputations for making its decisions or indecisions, but academic reputations emerge from networks of faculty, not administration.

The university can close departments that it deems not worth keeping, but it cannot close all of them, and closing a department might cause more problems than it solves. Something must be done about those who were working and enrolled there. The university hires and fires persons, but both are tedious and depend on the encounters during a job interview, for example. The university has no idea what happened in these encounters. To a large extent, the administration depends on faculty to hire or fire faculty, although an administration's grip over faculty varies; for example, with size, status, and prestige.

The formal structure can declare that the official purpose of seminars is learning and knowledge, but official purposes tend to be coupled loosely to actual outcomes (Orton and Weick 1990). Whether or not anyone learns anything, how much they learn, and just what they learn are the result of encounters, not the formal structure. As a particular observer, the formal structure can measure learning in grades and sanction those who fail, but it is not clear exactly what gets measured in this way. Grading depends on encounters that involve not the administration, but teachers and students. Like all measures, grades depend on grids and metrics that are not caused by true scores or things in themselves. The formal structure might focus the attention of seminars according to curricula and "learning goals," but encounters generate and change their foci in response to their own history and contributions. In many cases, course syllabi and reading lists capture little of what actually transpires in the seminar, especially at doctorate and postgraduate levels, where more outcome uncertainty prevails. A seminar on Rorty can be expected to focus on Rorty, but that is about all that is known to those who do not attend.

Groups emerge and develop as well, without an organization being able to prevent or control much of this. Once a group is in place, destroying it from above might do more harm than good. Nothing guarantees that the doings of groups will be in line with the organization's official goals and purposes. As pockets of local solidarity and identity, groups build up their own cultures, rationales, loyalties, and relations to the world. There are many such groups, and networks of groups, within and between organizations. Not only is the organization unable to control and coordinate its many informal relations; it will also not even be aware of some or many of them.

To be sure, there are some total and coercive organizations that use heavy surveillance, physical confinement, constraints, and threats of violence. But prisons have their own informal relations and backstages. They also get little out of their inmates except dull compliance, resistance, or repetitive work without much initiative (Etzioni [1961] 1975:27–31, 388–391). Foucault's *panopticon* probably allows a hierarchy to see less than what critical theorists of power and discipline see. At least, the amount of that which an organization can effectively control and coordinate should be seen as variable. Turbulence from encounters, groups, and networks makes effective power an exaggeration—as observed by an outsider, for example, who takes closure and integration of organization for granted. Organizing as process is generally more disorderly than organization as selective and accomplished outcome.

The assumption here, again, is that organizing and organization are more improbable and uncertain than much organizational theory would expect. Challenges to order and stability come from within and without. Transaction cost theories of firms (Williamson 1975) see in this external turbulence and uncertainty a major cause of internalization, but they forget that internalization also adds more internal turbulence. Focusing on the *improbability of organizing* yields the puzzles of how organization is possible at all, how an organization manages to get anything done, and how it manufactures and displays a measure of unity and purpose. Organizing is, by and large, improbable, failure-ridden, and uncertain. It is never "finished." Much less should we posit, from the beginning, that organizations are effective and efficient in what they do, or rationally superior to alternatives. For one thing, the multiple observers within an organization will tend to have their own ways of assessing effectiveness and efficiency, thereby generating controversies over measurement and interpretation.

What Do Formal Structures Do?

Organizations are observers and contain observers, such as encounters and groups. They observe themselves and other observers, including other organizations. A formal structure frames and phrases an organization's "official" observations of itself, condensed and codified in charts, manuals, rules, regulations, and procedures. These official self-observations surface prominently on frontstages, when an organization explains and justifies its operations to novices, outsiders, audiences, critics, or public inspectors. On such occasions, organizations, and their internal divisions or units, prepare highly simplified and orderly maps, histories, and accounts of themselves (Herzfeld 1992:20, 65–66).

Such maps freeze the process of organizing into ready-made organization. They gloss over the complexities and uncertainties of organizing. In science studies, there is a useful distinction between ready-made science and science in the making (Latour 1987:4): Ready-made science is Kuhnian normal science, with a high degree of closure and routinization, while science in the making is more uncertain and controversial. Likewise, "organization" is the settled and simplified outcome and accomplishment of "organizing."

Observing organization only, one would exaggerate unity, coherence, and integration, much as observing nothing but textbook science would exaggerate scientific consensus and rationality. Organization is, for example, what outsiders see from a large distance. A formal structure is rarely a good predictor for "actual" behaviors and events.

There is, generally, a discrepancy between the formal and informal, although its degree varies. Formalism is not constant but variable; it varies both within and between organizations. Compare, for example, a research laboratory to the registrar's office in a college, or an elementary school to graduate education. The differences have to do with degrees of routinization and outcome predictability or uniformity. When these degrees are high, a formal structure tends to be a better empirical description and predictor for what is "actually" happening in an organization.

A formal structure contains imperfect devices for getting a grip on the turbulence from organizing as process. These devices include frontstages, leadership, bureaucratic observing, method or logic, and decoupling.

Decoupling

A formal structure defines which sorts of work organizations expect from their employees in various offices—though whether or not they will do their work is another matter entirely. Organizations expect their top executives to carry top credentials from top schools—although these executives might learn most of what they need to know on their jobs, not in schools. In accordance with the law of the land, a formal structure might include affirmative action offices—and once these are in place, an organization trusts that discrimination will disappear. If it does not, one knows which office to consult. Offices specify who is supposed to be in charge of certain tasks, but much uncertainty in organizing comes from ambiguity and controversy over just which office is in charge of which matters, and who is entitled to make certain sorts of decisions. Organizations decide at what levels certain kinds of decisions should be made—though they cannot make sure that the decisions will be understood and implemented as planned. They can communicate guidelines for promotion—though they cannot rule out that some people who deserve to be promoted get fired instead. A formal structure can establish who is expected to communicate what to which others in the chains of command and the division of labor—though it cannot rule out that people talk about other things as well.

By and large a formal structure, much like a biography, deals with events that have already occurred. More to the point, it deals with a selection of these, that is, those that are somehow brought to its attention. To get the formal structure's attention, one must activate it according to its own procedures and specifications. You file a complaint, for example, and there are guidelines for how this is done. A formal structure is a retrospective observer; it is sensitive to what it has done before, according to the records and files. It looks into the past to search for established rules or precedents. A formal structure also observes what a similar structure has done before or is doing elsewhere (DiMaggio and Powell 1983). A formal structure can change, but does so according to the relevant rules and protocols for change. This is why bureaucracies, once in place, tend to grow.

The formal structure does specify which encounters might be relevant to it, but it cannot legislate or determine how these encounters actually proceed, what their outcomes will be, or how this might eventually matter to the organization. The formal structure schedules some encounters for specific times, with a specific set of personnel, but it is a different matter who shows up, shows up late, or has to leave early. Organizations use scheduling, minutes, agendas, and protocols to get a grip on interactional turbulence, but encounters have a life of their own. Nothing guarantees that an encounter will somehow meet the expectations of the formal structure. The formal structure might contain antiharassment policies, but it cannot make sure that bodies in encounters will not feel attracted to some of the other bodies there.

Since encounters are autopoietic and turbulent, they frequently run out of time, so nothing much gets done in the meetings. Then one has to meet again. By that time, the "decision situation" may have changed. The formal structures can focus the attention of those encounters deemed officially relevant on the official business, but encounters can change that focus, as happens when someone present starts talking about unrelated matters. The encounter may try to refocus attention on the official business, but this takes time and may not work for long. The official results and decisions of an encounter are written up in minutes and memos, but those might disappear in the files or not be read, followed-up on, or interpreted in the "intended" way.

If all goes well and smoothly, rules and regulations tend to remain silently in the background of operations. In actual day-to-day organizing, a formal structure might rarely be activated. In many cases, the formal structure is the "last resort" for resolving a conflict or dealing with a grievance. It is more likely called into action when something goes wrong, when complaints are voiced, when conflicts erupt, or when someone blows the whistle (Fuchs and Westervelt 1996). Johns (1998:34) attributes an increased reliance on records and documents in the early modern printing culture to increasing conflicts over proper authorship and textual authenticity. A formal structure is what the organization constructs and perceives of itself when it searches for the "official" causes of accidents and failures.

Bureaucratic Observing

Like all observers, a formal structure or bureaucracy cannot deal with "raw" events in their full empirical and idiosyncratic complexity. Instead, a bureaucracy restructures and renormalizes that which it observes and deals with according to its own internal modes of operation. This mode depends on writing. If it is not in the files and records, it is not part of bureaucratic reality. Without the files, a bureaucracy has no memory.

To be relevant to the formal structure, or to be added to it, an encounter, for example, produces minutes and memos; otherwise, it just comes and goes. The minutes are much more selective and orderly than the encounters, whose official results they are supposed to summarize. Encounters have many more results, outcomes, and effects than contained in the minutes. By themselves, of course, no encounter's minutes and memos make any difference; they must be recognized by some other bureaucracy and *its* encounters, memos, and minutes.

A bureaucracy's mode of operation is "statistical" in a broad sense. It condenses and summarizes events and observations according to their relative frequency (Latour 1986:29). This is done by various methods and techniques of aggregation. Statistics cope with ambiguity, interpretive flexibility, or thick descriptions. The normal curve computes a central tendency from a large number of data and observations. Outliers and exceptions are transformed and reintegrated into the distribution. Bureaucracies search for the one single number that "says it all," and says it with convenience and ease (Miller 1992). Such numbers can be compared to other numbers gathered at different times and places by different offices and observers. In this way, a formal structure establishes some amount of continuity and compatibility. The registrar's office processes grades from all over the university, regardless of all the variations in courses, instructors, or terms.

Numbers can be aggregated at ever higher levels of comparison; one can compute the mean of means, and sets of sets. Statistical aggregation creates the "unity" and "order" characteristic of a formal structure. The levels or ranks in a bureaucracy can be seen as successive aggregations of aggregations accomplished at lower levels. It is these remote and abstract higher-level aggregates that most outsiders are left observing. As a result, they tend to exaggerate organizational order, unity, and rationality.

Like statistics, this bureaucratic aggregation and reaggregation removes the numbers and summaries more and more from their origins, which are more local, contextual, and historical. At higher and higher levels of aggregation and condensation, less and less of this original context and locale becomes visible. Statistics are remote from common sense, which prefers stories and plots involving persons in certain situations. Persons tend to blame other persons, bureaucrats, for what bureaucracies do to them.

At higher statistical and bureaucratic levels, the organizational reality is increasingly "constructed," that is, assembled from previous constructions at different times or levels in the administrative hierarchy. One result of this is that leaders often appear to those below them as out of touch with what "actually" goes on in their organizations—although, of course, the leaders are very much in touch with what goes on at the level of leadership. Nevertheless, leaders do depend on information that has been condensed, packaged, and abstracted several times and at several levels. At the same time, they seem to ignore much of this material as well, trusting more their own informal networks. Leaders seem to spend a lot more time talking than reading or writing (Mintzberg 1973:44).

Statistical and bureaucratic aggregations and constructs can—rather easily, in fact—be disaggregated and deconstructed. Much conflict in the formal structure concerns just what the numbers show and do not show, just whose numbers they are, and just how selective or "biased" they are. Another important set of conflicts in organizations is conflicts over what the rules mean, especially when something has occurred that indicates the rules may have been ignored or violated. But few people know the rules, still fewer know many of them, and different interpretations or implementations might be favored by different coalitions.

Nevertheless, once a formal structure is firmly in place, not anything is equally possible or likely anymore, and so some interpretations will prevail over others. These cease to be mere interpretations and acquire a stronger binding force. In philosophical terms, a formal structure is an actual or empirical solution to the problem of induction, which is irresolvable only in philosophy, not in organizations.

Organizational Frontstages

Once accomplished, higher-level unity and order can be displayed on frontstages, communicated as the "official" statistics and measures of performance, and mentioned to a public or critic as a warrant or token of the impartial and rational prudence, integrity, and responsibility of the organization. Enter the charts, histograms, pie graphs, and tables. They seek to impress the opposition. In addition to getting some of their work done, organizations assess and evaluate themselves and their performance, as do their divisions and departments. Such self-assessments become especially urgent when an organization is under public scrutiny, maybe in a drive for cost-cutting. Quantitative assessments present their impersonality as objectivity (Daston 1992). They are compared with other quantitative assessments—for example, with last year's performance, the performance of other divisions, or the performances of competing organizations. In this way, a coherent reality emerges, with measures for the position and location of an organization or suborganization in the networks of related and competing organizations.

None of this will likely silence the critics or opposition, but they are now under pressure to produce their *own* numbers, statistics, and aggregates. The costs of deconstruction have just been raised. From now on, conflicts include disagreements over statistics. These conflicts are very real; it is misleading to see the formal structure as myth only.

Calling a formal structure "myth" might suggest concealment of some true or actual underlying reality. But a formal structure is not a simple lie; rather, it is the reality of an organization as it condenses and summarizes its self-observations into a coherent overall account. To outsiders particularly, the formal structure *is* the organization; for insiders, it is that plus the informal system or systems.

When they appear on frontstages, persons behave in much the same way as a formal structure, especially when they find themselves under attack or criticism. Then they draw upon available cultural repertoires and scripts to make sense of their actions, to excuse themselves, or to blame someone else for what they have done. The result is that nothing is ever anyone's fault, really. Coherent stories likely surface when a person confronts expectations of rational or acceptable conduct. In fact, the common liberal understanding of "personhood" itself, of what it means to be a "person," is an understanding of persons as frontstage accomplishments.

Organizations are busy manufacturing reasons and rationales for why society is better off with than without the organization. Divisions within organizations do the same, sometimes in competition with other divisions. The result is many conflicting and uncertain rationales and rationalities, with no metaphysical guarantees of consensus, optimization, or integration into one "utility function."

Ceremonial occasions involving the entire organization are enacted by high-status frontstage officials. Such occasions celebrate the accomplishments, legends, rituals, and heroes of the organization. As opposed to more routine and everyday frontstages, ceremonies are special and rare events that might mark status transitions, anniversaries, the entry or exit of leaders, or commemorations of organizational history and origin. These extraordinary displays are carefully prepared, impressively orchestrated, and adorned with elaborate props. On such frontstages, the organization appears to have a clear mission and purpose. It speaks to larger cultural concerns and responds to broader public worries. Frontstage spectacles are displays of virtue and integrity designed to impress outsiders and restore the faith and enthusiasm of the ground troops.

The backstages are where "organizing" in Weick's (1979) sense takes place—the stage of organization-in-the-making, rather than readymade organization. Although backstages occur on all levels throughout the organization, they are more difficult to protect at lower levels, since more public exposure and more supervision make it difficult for groups there to turn away from inspection and inward. On its back-stages, the organization's informal systems handle surprises, excep-tions, issues of special urgency, problems requiring broader coopera-tion, and other unusual events. Such activities are much less rule- or method-driven, and rely more on initiative, judgment, and ad hoc pro-cedures. Grids and classifications are less prominent and rigid here, al-lowing for flexible adjustments and innovative suggestions. Member-ships are less defined and more fluid; between-unit "task forces" are the typical organizational modus operandi (Chisholm 1989:chap. 4). In science, interdisciplinary task forces are very common—for exam-ple, as new specialties emerge from several previous specialties, or as instruments migrate, together with their specialists, into different spe-cialties (Mulkay 1975).

Leadership

Power depends on situational impression management, or on present-ing and announcing a credible or impressive threat. The powerful must seem ready and willing to make good on their threats. If the threat is not credible, power might have to be backed up by coercion, but coercion is not a very effective way to get anyone to do anything, especially not tasks requiring initiative, discretion, or skill. A ruler can have everyone killed, but then there is no one to rule anymore. Coer-cion triggers perverse and revenge effects, such as resistance or dull compliance. Then still more force is needed and the situation might escalate into a prolonged and expensive spiral of mutual retaliations. Some states' fiscal order breaks up when they are unable to finance their coercive apparatus. Coercion also relies on noncoercive Durk-heimian solidarity within an executive or enforcement staff, which is why very coercive states are also very ritualistic, righteous, cultish, and dogmatically "pure" at the top. These are very "theatrical" states, which perform many impressive and captivating displays of their force. With Benjamin ([1921] 1977), a great deal of coercion turns power and politics into theater, spectacle, dramaturgy, and "aesthetics."

The powerful are powerless without the powerless. Hegel's master / slave dialectic acknowledges this. Decision-makers cannot themselves gather all the information they need to make their decisions; corpo-rate CEOs cannot tell their research and development personnel how to do their research better; local deans fire local faculty because other faculty at distant places have suggested that their work is not up to speed.

Power is also an exaggeration. When push comes to shove, many threats are called as the bluffs they were to begin with. The more you threaten, the more often you have to make good on your threats; if you do not, your power is revealed as the bluff it is. Power works most smoothly without threats, when it remains invisible. Once a power has to argue for its "legitimacy," it is no longer all that legitimate. One might say that power *is* this invisibility of a source of power. Power is not an original or primary source of events, but a drastically simplified explanation or account of these sources.

Generally, hierarchy is loosely coupled to actual organizational processes and behaviors. At least the extent to which hierarchy regulates outcomes is variable and depends on complexity and differentiation. Prisons are more hierarchical than biotech firms; this has to do with the uncertainty of tasks and the amount of discretion granted to workers. Hierarchies usually succeed in only the simplest of organizational structures and task technologies; as soon as uncertainty and surprises increase, hierarchy is quickly overwhelmed and starts delegating responsibilities decentrally to various divisions and their specialists.

In this sense, "hierarchy" is a simplified mode of observation that bundles expectations and directs them to the top of the organization. Now blame and merit can be allocated reliably, without extensive searches. An unchallenged assumption of leadership studies is that power is what executives "have" to get others to do something against their will. Executives have this power, while others do not, or have less of it. But how can it be known where the power is, or who has it, before its effects are observed?

Attributing power to persons is a commonsense routine that might work reasonably well in everyday life, but it will not do as a dogma of science. From a constructivist and second-order perspective, "power" is a label or attribution that makes sense of certain observed effects by locating their causal source in identifiable persons or concrete institutions—the powerful, the establishment, the ruling class, the state, and so on.

Such attributions do a lot of social, moral, and cultural work. They make it possible to blame and fire coaches for a loosing streak—

although coaching is, at best, only one of the many variables that explain winning and losing. "Hierarchy" makes it possible to observe certain persons as responsible for organizational outcomes—despite the fact that such outcomes are loosely coupled to the ideas and plans top managers might have. Hierarchy also makes it possible to relate the organization to other organizations; one knows the other leaders and thus whom to talk to and whom to negotiate with. Central states will find it easier to deal with other centralized states than with a bunch of feuding warlords or guerilla bands.

Method and Logic

An example for what a formal structure does is method in science. There is now much evidence suggesting loose coupling between the official rules of method and a science's actual operations (Shapin 1995). Method enters as research techniques and outcomes move out of the laboratory and onto the frontstages, such as public presentations, published papers, or rational reconstructions of a science's history. Method structures the official and public frontstage observations of how a science does its work. The repertoire of method is more orderly and systematic than actual research, which is not rule-driven or algorithmic. In the daily work of a science, logic and epistemology are conspicuously absent, much as a formal structure remains in the background of daily organizing, available in case something goes wrong.

Some philosophical critics of method conclude that there is no method to science at all, or that one should be against it (Feyerabend [1975] 1988:4). This is an essentialist mistake because it allows no variations. To be sure, the One Method or Logic of Science is a philosophical invention and fails to appreciate the considerable disunity of the sciences. But this does not mean that method is purely mythical or deceptive, or that a science could do just as well without method. The standard rational reconstructions in the history of a science are method-driven; they gloss over many actual complexities and uncertainties in telling a tale of cumulative progress and systematic advances. Method structures a science the more so as that science moves toward frontstages, where it meets, observes, and relates to other sciences or to different institutions.

This use of method happens regularly in courts, for example, where questioning a science's method also questions the reliability of its results and estimates, without having to question each and every result or estimate itself. Method economizes on both construction and deconstruction costs (Fuchs and Ward 1994). When writing a grant proposal, you cannot omit method either, or say that you chose not to have any method at all, given that postmodernists and anarchists have shown that there really is no such thing as method or logic. Published papers must also contain some legitimate method.

Method structures the aggregation and comparison of various contributions at higher and less local levels of abstraction and generality. A method might not determine, step by step, how a piece of research is actually accomplished, in the here and now of a site, but method does emerge later, when the outcomes of this work are related to the outcomes of similar work. Method suggests *violations of method* to be prime suspects for anomalous results, false predictions, and noisy results—not fraud, greed, or ethnicity. When this much is clear, the search for errors can start and remedial steps might be taken.

Method covaries with variables similar to the covariates of formal structure. For example, the more routinized or "normal" parts of a science tighten the coupling of method and actual process. Running a standard experiment with known outcomes in an undergraduate science lab is much more methodical and bureaucratic than innovative and controversial science. There is gradually more method to a science as it grows older, mature, and secure in its foundations and paradigms. In the beginning of a science, method may be borrowed from an already established science, maybe in a drive for institutional isomorphism and cultural legitimacy (DiMaggio and Powell 1983).

The significance of method also increases with size and distance, as a local and contextual practice slowly extends its radius and networks. Trust in the honor of gentlemen gradually gives way to trust in reputations and procedures (Shapin 1994). Method and measures facilitate mutual compatibility of observations within larger networks of scientific production and communication. Within the more idiosyncratic culture of a local lab, making method explicit and algorithmic may be redundant, but between a large number of such labs and local cultures, method emerges more readily as a common framing. Appeals to method and objectivity are also more likely when the virtue and integrity of a science are being questioned from outside. Then invocation of method signals that all is well and proper.

Trust in a science or organization is anchored by trust in methodological or formal propriety. Poovey (1998:chap. 2) shows how quantitative accuracy in early modern bookkeeping displayed legitimate trustworthiness in financial matters. That a scientific outcome is compatible with method, and that a decision is compatible with a formal structure, supports credence and credibility, and generalizes trust in procedures. Method and formal structure are not simply mythical; they do real work, just not the sort of work imagined by philosophers and their postist critics.

Variations in Organizational Cultures

Organizations and their cultures are not uniform and homogeneous. The Weberian legacy is a mixed blessing, since the ideal type has prejudiced the search for constants and fixed definitions. Whether organizations are rational, open, or natural systems, or maybe all of the above (Scott 1992:pt. 2), distracts from the more exciting problem of *when* they are these, as well as where, why, and how much. Organizations have been held constant as purposeful or rational instruments, impersonal iron cages, hierarchies, goal-driven formal structures, and closed systems. Much of this essentialism is due to the normative orientation of some organizational research as it is done prominently in business schools, managerial training academies, and popular how-to-run-your-business-better manuals. This applied work is mostly about leaders, decision-making, or human relations.

The components of the ideal type—formalism, bureaucracy, rationality, and hierarchy—have turned out to be variables, not constants (Pugh, Hickson, Hinings, and Turner 1969). Variations can be observed both between and within organizations, as well as over time. Rarely are organizations of one piece, since they frequently house multiple divisions, departments, clusters, and subcultures, which operate in different niches and environments. Subcultures depend on the number, boundedness, and connectivity of inside clusters and groups (Trice 1993:chap. 2).

Allowing for variation, quantification varies within and between organizations. In education, for example, the upper levels of graduate instruction are less bureaucratic than craftlike in their reliance on personal contacts and face-to-face guidance (Stinchcombe 1988:177–195). Smaller size contributes to this effect, as does status. Generally, the higher one climbs in the hierarchy, the less bureaucratic one's life, and the more discretion goes to workers dealing with more uncertain and complex tasks. This holds for relations between organizations as well; compare the more rigid and formalistic community college to the more discretionary and flexible ivy league university.

Organizational cultures vary accordingly. For example, small and innovative computer software firms that reward the creativity and imagination of those experts with credentials and reputations have different cultures from large public bureaucracies doing more routine and repetitive large-batch administration (Woodward [1965] 1980). The research department of a large corporation differs from its accounting division, and that division may itself be stratified according to varying degrees of task uncertainty.

Cultures and their symbolic textures covary with other variables, such as cohesion and coupling, task complexity, stratification, the external range of social networks, and the textures of organizational sets and environments.

Uncertainty

Ceteris paribus, the more complex, uncertain, and unpredictable the tasks and their outcomes, the more discretionary, individualistic, and liberal the work culture. Workers dealing with nonroutine and uncertain situations rely more on informal negotiations, personal judgment, and mutual consultation than official manuals and codified procedures. Task complexity correlates positively with stratification; upper-class cultures monopolize areas of uncertainty, which are less constrained by rules, regulations, and bureaucratic routines. Such groups are notoriously difficult to manage from above, because they have nothing to gain from providing administrators with the means of bureaucratic control. In the relationship between intellectual workers and administrators, for example, scientists behave "rationally" and incur agency costs because they have an interest in exaggerating their accomplishments.

Organizations practice more "hermeneutics" than "method" when dealing with problems that have many exceptions and unclear search procedures. In dealing with surprises and unusual cases, neither science, nor organizations generally, can follow established rules. Instead they rely more on informal and interpretive judgments and personal experience.

Conversely, lower task complexity, predictable outcomes, and standard operating routines invite more Weberian bureaucracy, Fordism, and centralized supervision. Persons are stuck more in their positions, and captured more securely in rigid grids and classifications. There is little or no room for modification and innovation (Douglas 1992a, 1992b). Lower-class cultures deal with tasks and situations that have been taylorized and rationalized as much as possible, making their workers more replaceable. There is, however, no linear deskilling over time. Rather, new technologies and branching effects may initially introduce more complexity, and so upgrade the skills and discretion of those specializing in them, until routinization sets in later.

This is often what happens upon the introduction of new instruments and technologies in a science. These upgrade the status and importance of skilled assistants, consultants, and technical personnel, until the equipment becomes more known and routinized over time. During technological innovations, technicians control vital areas of uncertainty, and so can, at least temporarily, rise in status until their work becomes more routine again (Galison 1997:37–40). Organizations routinize and taylorize as much as they can, but rely on skill, discretion, judgment, and experience where and when they cannot (yet) do so.

Highly routinized work does more closely follow the formal structure and explicit procedures. Such work can more easily be "algorithmically compressed," or reduced to a few standard and repetitive motions and operations. At this level, rationality and formalism are more than just frontstage myths, or a schema for allocating blame and responsibility. Rather, they monitor actual behaviors and events. When exceptions and unprecedented outcomes do occur at a more routine level, they are sent upward in the hierarchy, to higher-status specialists who claim such events as their unique cultural capital and opportunity for discovery.

Status

Status is multidimensional; it has formal and informal aspects, as well as different sources—such as internal organizational rank, rank of the organization, rank in one's profession or specialty, and rank of that specialty in the networks of related professions or specialties. Social status derives from (at least) three sources: position within the formal hierarchy of the organization, position in the informal networks and class cultures, and position of the organization in the larger formal and informal status systems among the organizations of a set. The first parameter captures status according to the classical determinants of formal structure (for example, power, income, education, seniority); the second parameter derives from location and reputation within the numerous informal systems and networks of an organization; and the third parameter combines formal and informal sources of status to arrange entire organizations in stratified networks of resource exchange, prestige, and reputation.

Within organizations, the formal sources of status act as constraints for the participation in, and composition of, informal systems. Among the most consequential structural constraints of the informal system are space and hierarchy. People in the same offices, floors, and buildings tend to interact more with each other than with outsiders. I am skeptical about email obviating the importance of physical space and social distance (McKenney, Zack, and Doherty 1992). Holders of comparable credentials often come from similar schools and tend to be placed in equivalent organizational niches, where they interact more with their own kind than with others. Such local ties seem to be more important for collective action and political mobilization than the formal parameters of class-in-itself (Gould 1993; Padgett and Ansell 1993).

This stratified arrangement of formal and informal status parameters applies as well to relations between organizations. There are core groups among organizations, and they behave in ways similar to informal networks of persons. High-status organizational cores consist of various participating organizations, such as SLAC, Desy, CERN, and KEK for high-energy physics. Organizations are controversially ranked in networks according to more official and measurable criteria, including property, profit, credit, or size. They are also informally ranked according to prestige, reputation, and distance from charisma. Ivy league universities more likely interact with other ivy league universities than with community colleges. Higher interaction density creates a common culture and coherent institutional habitus over time, resulting in a distinctive "style" that insiders can recognize at once.

Centrality

Centrality in informal systems or networks, either within or among organizations, means closeness to the core possessions of the network
and expressive, rather than just instrumental, association with those
who possess them (Milner 1994:34–36). There is much competition
over access to the core and its possessions. The best way to get in is to
be connected to someone who is already there. Compared to the entire network, core positions are very few in number. From the outside,
the core appears snobbish and arrogant, but this may or may not be
due to personal character. The core is very small, much smaller than
the rest of the network, and so cannot possibly reciprocate all the
exchange offers from outside (White, Boorman, and Breiger 1976).
Outsiders to the core attribute this failure to persons, to their "characteristic" arrogance, indifference, or elitism. But the numbers and pro-
portions alone, regardless of character, explain failures to reciprocate.

The core may also cultivate an esoteric and exclusive *Sendungs-
bewusstsein* or utopia that defines its larger cultural mission. This
agenda has a good chance of becoming the agenda of the network itself, since what happens in the core is observed throughout the network for clues as to where the advances and innovations are leading,
and where these are being made. Conflicts over priority are rampant
where the most prized possessions are breakthroughs, discoveries, and
major advances.

Networks without clear cores, or with very many separate cores, lose
their focus of attention and collapse into ideological camps. They
make no major advances, although minor and local improvements,
such as "advances in conversation analysis," might still occur within
a small school or perspective. In their reflexive and metatheoretical
clusters, however, networks without cores tend to consider philosophical arguments against the very possibility or desirability of "progress"
and "rationality."

Core positions are closely coupled to each other, but also are linked
to other, more distant, cores of networks anchored in different organizations of similar rank and set (Freeman [1978] 1979:226). This accounts for the frequently observed "cosmopolitanism" of upper-class
cultures. Bearman (1993) shows that in the century leading up to the
Civil War, the development of abstract and universalistic constitutional

and Puritan religious ideology followed the erosion of the localistic and kinship-based solidarities within networks among English gentry. Cosmopolitan networks have more social and cultural capital, which also enables them to define what cultural capital consists of, and so get yet more of it. The advantages and disadvantages from inclusion in and exclusion from core groups accumulate over time, and set the terms for future competitive accumulations. Giuffre (1999) finds photographers more likely to receive critical attention and high visibility when they have had longer tenure in loosely coupled and nonredundant networks with broad-ranging ties. The leading encounters and groups in such cosmopolitan networks behave much as the firms in White's (1988:228) markets: They form competitive social niches that monitor each other's performance.

Insofar as the core contains encounters and groups, stars more likely interact with each other than with nonstars, and nonstars have a hard time getting close to, and involved in, the core. This varies together with the core's exclusivity. In very exclusive and coherent groups, a communal dramaturgy signals the identity of this elite to itself and outsiders (Mullins 1972). Over time, networks can link generations among groups, as well as their encounters, into "dynasties" (Kanigel 1993).

Core groups are prominent and visible in dramatic cultural changes. On the verge of a breakthrough or innovation, the group is fueled by high emotional intensity. The ability to sense and define what the hot areas of a culture will be in the future must count as the most valuable possession of core groups (Holton 1996:60). They seem to follow their "noses" and "hunches," rather than rationally planning or programming an expected outcome according to formal methods. This "personal knowledge" and low level of procedural formalization make it even more difficult for outsiders to follow what goes on in core groups, let alone contribute to it. All these parameters of elite membership, and exclusion from it, are mutually reinforcing, which explains the surprising persistence of core groups—for example, in science since the seventeenth century, despite exponential increases in personnel, number of specialties, and other science indicators. Rudwick (1985: 426–428) maps this structure for a group of elite geologists involved in the Devonian controversy.

The cherished and coveted possessions in the core may be creativity (in science and the arts), charismatic authority (in politics), prophetic revelations (religion), or first-mover advantages (investment markets) (McGuire 1993:7). In all cases, core activities and positions involve access to innovations, novelties, risks, and promising or credible guesses of the future. In the biomedical sciences, the highest status practitioners are not the ones advancing treatments, but those augmenting uncertainties (Bensman and Lilienfeld 1991:221).

In all cases, core activities are the least routinized and bureaucratic, and rely most on performances that are difficult to formalize and standardize, such as skill, judgment, intuition, and discretion. Core activities are not algorithmic and method-driven; this escape from formalizations is part of, and reason for, the privilege and exclusivity of core groups. Their doings appear, and present themselves, as more esoteric, avant-garde, mysterious, and awe-inspiring than what transpires, for example, during high school lab class. One cannot seem to figure out how the leaders do what they do, and so resorts to "genius" or "creativity" to explain presumably "essential" differences among persons in their capacities or talents.

But excellence can be quite mundane (Chambliss 1989). When the genius is taken out of his natural habitat into a strange arena or stage, he can look helpless and incompetent. As Berger (1995) says, the mind thrives within a familiar ecology; transported to a very different context or setting, especially one in which the genius of the genius makes no difference, it may look hapless, foolish, and out of place. Behaviors, including mental creativity, need cues, reinforcers, natural settings, and stimuli. Nothing magical is going on. The cult of genius or, less spectacular, of special gifts and talents, is not an explanation for excellence, but a part of its very mystique.

Core groups are very selective in recruitment and self-reproduction; vacant positions are filled by mutual searches between masters and prospective apprentices, aided by recommendations circulating in the informal system (Zuckerman 1977:104). Core structures look more like crafts or guilds than factories (Galison 1987:244).

CHAPTER 6

Modes of Social Association II: Networks

In the beginning, there were fields of forces and relations. Then came the nodes, as outcomes of networks, not their independent or preexisting sources or causes. A node is anything that can become a component of a network, and that can be related to other such nodes, those that are already in place. Therefore, one cannot give a finite set or list of the components of a network. Whether or not something can become a node in *this* network is accomplished by the network itself—this is its "autopoiesis."

In and for the network in which they are nodes, the nodes are what they become as the result of their various and changing relations. They are not essential building blocks that remain the same over time and across network location. For as soon as they leave the networks that made them what they are, even the most powerful and self-assured nodes begin to look lost and out of place. Outside of their familiar surroundings, they are not what they used to be. Much like a charismatic hero or prophet without followers and listeners, they do not impress much anymore, and carry little weight. They may not even survive, because they lose the identity that came from sets of relations, not intrinsic or natural properties.

Consider some examples. Neurons can do what they do only as part of a brain. What made them neurons to begin with was the process of becoming embedded in neural networks, which led to selective activation of their blueprints. Embedding is the result of ontogenetic development, not the nodes themselves. This development gradually "pins

251

down" the possibilities of nodes, so that a mature neuron becomes very different from, say, skin tissue, although most cells share the same genetic blueprint. What matters for development is selective activation of DNA, not DNA itself. This selective activation is accomplished by embedding in emerging networks of self-similar relations. The result is livers separate from brains, and eyes separate from ears, though all comes from one zygote.

Likewise, a scientific finding is a communication that can never, all by itself, leave the network of scientific communication. By themselves, such findings do not matter, or even make sense, outside of their networks. Scientific findings start out locally and indexically. If they do make a difference, they do so within the local and narrow clusters of related findings, at least in the beginning. Even then, the vast majority of all scientific findings do not get much attention even from their surrounding networks. They make no, or very little, difference to what gets communicated next, or somewhere else in the network.

The sheer simultaneity of science means that a scientific finding cannot make a difference to findings that happen somewhere else at the same time, interactions between them notwithstanding. Such interactions do occur when the network condenses into coherent research clusters within a specialty, but these clusters are small and temporary, and there are very many of them at any time, within and across different specialties.

Much less likely is a scientific finding to make a difference outside of the networks of its science, to a different science, or even a nonscience, say religion. Commenting on the conflict between Galileo and the Church, Scheler (1924:62) points out that no scientific observation or experiment could, all by itself, bring down a strong institution. Why should the Church care about someone throwing stuff down from the Tower of Pisa? For Scheler, it was not Galileo's science, but his metaphysics, that challenged and provoked religious doctrine.

Nodes in a network become what they are, and remain what they have become, as soon, and as long, as they are held in position by the surrounding patterns of relationships. When they leave the network, they are no longer defined and stabilized by their relationships and start having trouble defining themselves. They may become part of another network, but will have to be restructured so as to fit into that network's operations.

To become part of a network, and make a difference in it, a node is "attended to" by the network. The network constructs a specific "format" or "version" of its nodes, as these nodes are embedded in patterns of relations. For example, a physical or mental sensation can become part of awareness only if it can be fed into the ongoing stream of consciousness. This requires attention—attending to *this,* rather than something else. What and how something is attended to is decided by the ongoing process of attention, not by that which the attention turns to next. For attention is finite and limited, while that which could be attended to in principle is infinite and unlimited. As a result, when the network of awareness, concentrating on the task at hand, is distracted by a sudden loud noise, concentration does not turn to that noise, but is broken.

Likewise, a piece of art becomes art after, not before, being fed into the network of other art. A piece of art becomes popular culture or elite culture not because of its intrinsic qualities; rather, these qualities result from being fed into the networks of either popular or elite art. It is not until this happens that the networks begin to reconstitute and redescribe a new element to make it fit with the other elements that are already there and in place. For the distinction between high and popular art, the networks of criticism and commentary are crucial, since art that draws the attention of critics becomes more "serious" in and through this very process. Drawing the attention and work of critics, curators, commentators, and other guardians, art is on its way toward becoming serious, and gradually acquires the "depth" expected from serious works of art. If its status consolidates, the network might retrospectively observe art's depth as the cause, not outcome, of this hardening.

The network of art scans and attends to its environment of potential art-to-be according to its own modes of operation. These operations include conflicts over what is, and what is not, art, or what is *this* art, as opposed to a different art. Pluralistic and competitive networks of art also allow for more internal diversity and opposition. But nothing that does not eventually become recognized as art can become part of it. An art will experience changes as catastrophic when they are enforced by the outside of nonart. As a result, when sociology studies art, art is being attended to by the network of sociology. In this process, it becomes a social fact, to be related to the established networks of similar or connected social facts. Only art, not sociology, can decide what is art, and only sociology, not art, can decide what is a social fact. At least this is so when both networks have high reputational autonomy, which supports internal professional closure and mutual demarcation. When science analyzes poetry or music, the result is science, not poetry or music.

Nodes are not, in themselves, fixed and stable. They are made so by embedding them in relations. Even then, nodes get moved around the network and, as a result, change their status, meanings, and implications. The meaning of a term is just the difference that it makes to other terms. The best empirical way to observe the meaning of a node or relationship is to modify or remove it, to see how the network reacts and adjusts to this modification or loss.

It is important to notice that, by getting linked to another node, a node also becomes indirectly linked to that node's relationships, increasing the structural constraints on meaning and behavior. Fixed and stable nodes, which seem to self-sufficiently exist in themselves, are *made* fixed and stable by becoming embedded in a cluster of relations, where they lose some of their former degrees of freedom to gain more identity or self-similarity. These nodes might, however, regain those freedoms upon moving out of their clusters into different sets of relationships, or even out of the network entirely. But these different clusters or networks will reduce degrees of freedom in their nodes as well, in their own special ways. A critical rule of method is that there are only variables, not constants. Constants are variables that are being *held* constant by the network in which they are constants. So constants are constants—until further notice.

Drift

Though they cannot really exist and survive outside of a network, think of an isolated node as a free-floating possibility, lacking definition and home, bouncing around in turbulence without constraints. Such a node is without qualities, much as the mathematician Ulrich in Musil's spectacularly modern novel. His profession is well chosen, since modern mathematics dissolves the essentialism and natural kinds of classical geometry, replacing them with processes and recursive operations (Spengler [1923] 1993:100–117, Bachelard [1934] 1984:22–25). Incidentally, a better translation of the title *Man without Qualities* would be *Man without Essence*.

Persons and nodes acquire qualities and definition as a result of becoming linked to other nodes and their relationships. To define something is to put it into "its" place, which is a position within relations to other nodes. There are as many definitions as possible or actual relations. If one of these definitions turns into *the* definition, more fundamental and, yes, essential than all others, then a node has had a long tenure within one exclusive set of relationships, and has thus lost a great deal of its freedoms, options, or alternatives. Such nodes are caged, tamed, or domesticated by very firm and durable embeddings in a stable and self-similar cluster of relations. They are held in the same place for a long time and so are more or less fully, and without rest, defined by this place and its history in the network.

In contrast, the more the nodes float and drift between and within networks, the less certain they become of who or what they are, and what they are supposed to do. Simmel's strangers and Bloor's anomalies behave much like this; they are always in between places, not really belonging comfortably anywhere. Strangers are outsiders both to where they came from and to where they are headed. They have yet to find the place where they belong. Strangers can be mysterious precisely because of this lack of definition and home. Likewise, anomalies remain anomalies until they are renormalized by the network to which they appear as anomalies.

An analogy for drift from mathematics would be differential equations, where symbols gain status and meaning from other symbols and their interrelationships, expressed as forces in a field of other forces. By themselves, these symbols do not refer to anything; any external reference they might acquire comes from internal closure and mutual stabilization in a *set* of symbols, itself part of another set, and so on. The question, then, is not whether mathematics refers—this is a false essentialist dualism. Rather, allowing for variation, reference is a matter of degree, and comes from mutual internal calibration, tuning, and closure within a set. Reference is the outcome, not cause, of coherence and self-similarity in a network. If a network does not cohere at all, it also produces no reference and no external reality. This happens to brains whose neural nets are damaged; they can no longer condense certain signals into a coherent representation or identification (Damasio 1994:54–56).

As a node enters the network, it is gradually fixed and determined by the relationships that link it to other nodes and relationships. When these links become very tight, repetitive, and redundant, as they do in a network core, the once undefined and free-floating node and its many possibilities are gradually pinned down and put into place. After some time, this place might appear as its "natural" place, where it belongs according to its true meaning and essential properties. Essentialism is the behavior of network cores. Tight internal closure and mutual stabilization of nodes in the core are what generate external reference and correspondence. In Durkheimian terms, reification—the projection of meaning onto the world itself—is the result of high network density and coherence.

Still, nodes drift out of their places, especially when they also have relations to different networks (Berg 1997). A group, for example, is less able to "contain" its members the more they have strong ties stretching outward to other groups. The identity of such a drifter is more uncertain and difficult to hold in place or define. A scientific instrument that is not solely or exclusively part of a science, but is also used, say, to produce the wondrous and entertaining effects of seventeenth-century popular magic, drifts from one network into another as well, changing its status and meaning in the process (Hankins and Silverman 1995:58, 114). The more such an instrument becomes embedded in a science, the longer it remains part of the science, and the more its ties to other networks are reduced or severed, the more this instrument acquires its "proper place" within that science, but not in popular magic or entertainment. This is especially so when this instrument becomes firmly linked to networks among the other instruments that have already found their firm and lasting place in this science.

Fields of Forces

Networks consist of relations, not nodes. That which is turned into a node of the network by the network may exist prior to the network in some form, but not (yet) in the form of *this* node in *this* network. To turn it into such a node, the network performs its net-work on this node. Nodes are outcomes, not sources or origins, of networks. Any stability, coherence, and identity a network might have do not result from the constancy of its elementary constituents, but from the web of mutually supporting and defining relations. The relations and the relations between them, or their patterns, hold the nodes in place, with variously strong or weak grips, and only until further notice.

Relations, not nodes, are how spiderwebs manage to withstand insults on their cohesion and integrity. By themselves, the knots in the web, no matter how firm and solid, get nothing done. A slight breeze will blow them every which way. In a geodesic dome, if one of the nodes is too rigid and solid, unable to give and take some insults, the "tensegrity" of the overall structure would be reduced (Ingber 1998). Were the nodes in a network constant and independent of the network, its stability and coherence would be much more fragile than when the nodes have some room and flexibility to adjust to changes in the overall structure. It is this structure that matters to the network, not its nodes by themselves.

Except for the brain, which is occasionally conscious of a tiny fraction of all it could be conscious of, or of that which other brains are conscious of at the moment, networks are not conscious. Only in exceptionally simple cases, such as thermostats or primitive reflexes, can they be directed or controlled from above, or from a center. One reason for this is that any steering center also adds more complexity to the network in the very process of reducing it. For in addition to the network's behavior, one now has that *plus* the behavior of the steering center, *plus* their multiple interconnections and interactions.

As a result, the network's behavior does not follow a unified plan or intention, though it may attribute intentions and agency to some of its nodes, as happens when it acknowledges authorship, puts the blame on some office, or celebrates reputation. But this is something that must be done by the network, if it is to happen at all. The nodes themselves "have" no agency. Authors are authors only when they are recognized as such, in relation to other such authors. No author can gain a reputation by himself, and any reputation he does have is what it is only within the networks of reputation.

There might be "ideas and beliefs" in a network, but these are temporary and selective condensations of some of the network's current states, as summarized by an observer, maybe for frontstage presentations. Often, frontstages explain what the network does in rational and meritocratic terms that celebrate the network's core virtues. For example, in networks that reward creativity, the basic notion is "talent" or "originality," which both explains and obscures the origins of change in and for the network. In contrast, outside scientific observers of the network do not explain its operations in the same way that it explains itself. They use their own attributions and distinctions, depending on what their cultures make or let them observe. For different observers, creativity appears as socially constructed or due to childhood, the genes, divine inspiration, accidents, and so on.

Network construction and extension are never finished, unless the network disappears or falls apart. The forces operating in a network do not "cause" the behavior of the network; rather, its behavior *is* that force, which might later, by an observer, be attributed to some cause or other. Sociologically, as an event that happens, causation is an empirical attribution by an empirical observer as well, and so varies between observers and over time. An observer can externalize causation, and attribute it to the world itself, but this is also something that must be done or not, and it must be done by an empirical observer in the here and now of a network. Externalization is attribution of the network's outcomes not to itself, but to the world as such. This happens in mature and advanced networks with much confidence and authority, or even monopoly (Chapter 7).

As an observer, a network constructs its chains of causation and history according to its own modes of observing. Causal and historical chains and series are selective accomplishments of networks as well. An important difference between networks is variations in how they assign causality, interrupt causal regresses, or simplify causal and historical links. As an observer of itself, a network tells abbreviated stories about itself, preferably stories with plots, purpose, logic, and sense.

As a network is colonized or replaced, however, one of the many discretionary abilities it loses is the ability to tell its own stories. More and more, the official stories are now being told by the successful invader. Invaders like to justify their invasion as a matter of superior morals, logic, truth, or rationality. In their version of history, the conquered and displaced specialty belongs to the prehistory of real science, or appears as an important step toward the invading specialty, maybe as a "special case" of the new network.

The more loosely coupled and pluralistic the network is, the more different internal observers it tends to accommodate, each constructing their own causes and histories. Levels of consensus and agreement vary accordingly, and together with the degrees of coupling and redundancy. In weak and loosely coupled specialties, there likely is no single official story or history.

No internal self-observation need, or indeed should, be accepted or taken for granted by observers outside the network, since these observers are the observers they have become in their own networks, not in the network they observe. Outsiders observe a network in terms of their own networks, those in which they are recognized insiders. These are the inside networks into which observations of an outside are to be fed, and in which these observations count on making a difference, gaining reputation, or drawing attention. Outsider's observations are not "arbitrary" or "relativistic." They are constrained by the network of related observations.

Power to the Networks

Power is constructed as the ability to make a difference, and as the cause for this difference. Common sense says that the actions of powerful persons make more difference than do actions of less powerful persons or persons without power altogether. Powerful persons get a lot done *because* they "have" much power. But the only way to find out where the power is is to observe its outcomes, not its source. Before power does indeed make a difference to society, it cannot be located, and so common sense commits a petitio principii. It infers power as a property or faculty of a powerful source from the very outcomes that this power is supposed to explain.

Which actions of powerful persons are the ones that make the difference, to which other actions do they make a difference, and how is this possible? Surely, it cannot be all actions of all persons. Most of the U.S. President's actions during a day make as little difference to anything as anyone's actions, say brushing one's teeth, tying one's shoes, or deciding what to eat for dinner. What spouses do makes more difference to what their spouses do than what Presidents do. Presidents cannot decide who watches what and when on TV. Much less can they influence how persons understand the news. They sign legislation, but cannot make law. Nor can they "control" what happens to the legislation once they have signed it, and once the legislation has left their desks, to be replaced by more legislation. Do Presidents "know" the legislation they sign, or would they have to know it for the legislation to make its difference? Hardly. They can declare wars, but not fight them or decide them. They cannot beat up their generals if the generals refuse to take orders.

The central point is that power is never "had," or not had, by a node in a network, regardless of whether this node is a scientific statement, a person, an office, an organization, or a state. No node in the network is without power, since all of the nodes that are part of the network are related to some other nodes, and since power is "in" these relationships. One might still say that some nodes are more powerful than others, but then it is this *difference*, not the power itself, that makes the difference in the network.

Power is the actual behavior of the network, whose outcomes are later, and by an observer, attributed to the powerful source. Power is the way in which an observer in or outside the network observes how the network is able to accomplish anything. But different observers attribute power to different sources—to the ruling class or the state, the President or the military, the First Lady, the stars, or the media. These attributions will be different for different observers, with no observer privileged enough to identify the one true source of power, once and for all. Power is not the cause for the behavior of the network; no single node in it, not even a central one, could ever understand, let alone steer, the behavior of an entire network. And the more complex and multicausal the network is, the more the possibilities of control decrease, and the more will attempts at control generate unpredicted and unintended effects.

Power is the juice that flows through the network, without ever being concentrated in a single source or reservoir. In this, power is much like electricity, which is also not "in" any of the components of a circuit. If it were possible to listen to it, one would hear power as the steady hum, sometimes hiss, of a network as it goes about its business. The *concept* of power is a simplified explanation for the behavior of a network. Neural network theories of the brain show that its behavior is massive parallel processing, without one conductor directing the entire symphony all by itself. A more fashionable way of saying this is that power—the ability to make a difference in a network of differences—is local, situational, temporary, and contextual.

Power depends on the task at hand. When Parsons theorized power as a generalized medium of exchange, he meant to decouple it from persons. But the extent to which power—or, indeed, any medium, including money—can be generalized is an empirical, not conceptual, problem. Such media become generalized when the networks in which they already are media expand into uncharted territory, or different networks. Money is good only where money is accepted, and the truth matters to those who care for and about it.

The power in a network does not initially occur outside of this network. It is restricted to the field of forces wherein it makes a difference to what happens next. Only with great difficulty can power be "translated" into different networks with different modes of operation. Physical strength makes a difference to social status only in social structures where physical strength matters. A scientific truth makes negligible difference to common sense. Even if it does make a difference, common sense still decides how this happens. For example, common sense might be told the scientific truth that persons do not really exist, but it will renormalize this information into something that persons say. Common sense can respond to some scientific fact or other, but just how this is done is up to common sense, not science. One might inform common sense that the moon is not a star, but persons will continue to see it "shine."

To take a different example, a science might inform policy making, but one cannot make any policy in the terms of a science. Sociologists especially should not be surprised when political organizations reconfigure the results and implications of their sociology in their own terms, which are not sociological, but political and ideological. It is possible to "feed" (some) sociology into (some) politics, but politics will restructure such feedings according to its own appetites and metabolism. Once some sociological observation or result is fed into politics, politics takes over and decides just how to handle its sociology. Then sociology can no longer control what happens next to its findings or advice. Sure, sociologists might still complain that the politicians misunderstand their findings, interpret them selectively, or draw the wrong conclusions. But such complaints remain idle and, on the remote possibility that they do get a second hearing in politics, will not make sure that from now on politics will understand better what a science is saying or doing. In any case, complaints about political misunderstandings of science are themselves based on the misunderstanding that politics is just science by other means, and that one network can control what another one does with its data, findings, and facts.

Generally, what different networks can handle and understand about each other is limited and restricted. How fully can a person, that is, a network of attributions to self, understand another one? And is there a way of understanding another person that does not depend on who we are ourselves, as observers of this person?

When a science gets dragged into the courts, yet another network outside of science, judges and juries who need to make a decision quickly cannot resolve the ambiguities and uncertainties of controversial and probabilistic scientific estimates. Since they are very remote from the networks and locations in which science is actually being made, outsiders exaggerate the certainty and consensus of science (Fleck [1935] 1979:106–108). In no way can outsiders contribute to the closure of scientific controversies, at least not anymore. An outsider might forbid, destroy, or outlaw a science, but these are not *scientific* acts. Doing law is not doing science; one cannot do both simultaneously, since legislatures or courts are not equipped to take measurements and test theories. As separate networks, they have different modes of operation, with their own invisibilities and inviolate levels. That which is taken for granted in one network is likely viewed as a more contingent, or even arbitrary, construction in another.

For example, modern law "naturally" assumes that persons are actors who are capable of acting otherwise, and thus can be "guilty" of something. For the law, as well as morality, this assumption is an inviolate level or foundational blind spot. These networks cannot do without the institution of personhood, which comes with moral or legal accountability. Law and morality might consider the situations and circumstances of persons, and cite these circumstances to alleviate guilt, but they cannot do what they do without personhood altogether. The law cannot consider the sociological possibility, for example, that by and large, cases are won by the more powerful parties. Instead, it assumes, officially at least, that cases are won on the basis of their "merits."

In contrast, a sociological science considers "personhood" as a variable and contingent outcome of certain social structures and cultures, such as modern law, which attribute legally relevant events and outcomes to natural or corporate persons. Without turning into part of the law, or into its rhetorical appendix, sociology cannot observe what the law observes, and so observes the *hows* of legal observation and operation instead of its *whats*.

What happens to science when it becomes part of the law is due to the law, not science, and vice versa. The law must eventually come to a decision based on assessments of responsibility, accountability, or guilt, while a sociological science views these as interruptions and simplifications of causal chains that are vastly more complex than any legal agency or decision could handle. Relations, nodes, and forces do not make a difference outside of a network—unless they reach and extend into new areas by forging new relationships or adding new nodes. A network and the events, relations, and forces in it make a direct and immediate difference only to this network, or to a cluster within it. The network is the field wherein something can make a difference. The only way for anything to matter in the network is through relationship. A node without any relations is not even really a node, since it makes no difference and gets nothing done. Neighbors are not neighbors to persons living in very distant neighborhoods, and vice versa. What happens in one neighborhood as part of this neighborhood makes, by itself, no difference to another neighborhood. Lovers are lovers to each other, not to strangers.

Power is relative to networks. Neurons cannot exist outside of a brain, and the neurons of your brain are not in someone else's head. Neither are your thoughts, emotions, or experiences. Therefore your neurons, perceptions, and thoughts remain your own until they enter a different network, say love, art, or communication. Then, love, art, or communication will restructure them through their own work and net-work. Networks are local, and so are their modes of operation. They can make a difference elsewhere, and at another time, but this is, on the face of it, rather improbable and requires the painstaking work of extending the network. Once this extension is accomplished, extension needs to be maintained, occasionally repaired, and adjusted to changing scenarios.

Metabolism

Neural networks operate electrochemically; they cannot switch their modes of operation and do something entirely different. They cannot do what livers or social movements do, and vice versa. They also cannot respond to that which cannot be translated and renormalized into electrochemical impulses. Brains can register something, but only if it finds its way into the brain. Even then, it is only in that brain, at that moment, not in all of them, and not all the time. Persons can, of course, report some of their experiences, express a few of their sensations, and talk about a sanitized selection of their feelings. But then a network of communication takes over, maybe a conversation, which is not a brain or brain state, and which does not "follow" from such states. What transpires in encounters or conversations is not due to brain states, but to encounters and conversations, including the previous encounters and conversations to which they are linked.

Likewise, bureaucracies can only perceive and deal with events that can be handled bureaucratically, that is, somehow made compatible with that which is already somewhere in the files, rules, and paperwork. If bureaucracies expand, they expand bureaucratically and renormalize new realities and information according to already established procedures. They can learn and change, but only according to bureaucratic procedures, not prophetic revelation or charismatic intuition. A revelation or intuition might be fed into a bureaucracy as raw material, but a bureaucracy cannot digest this material "as is," in its raw state. Rather, a bureaucracy will have to "cook" its raw materials to handle them in its own (bureaucratic) way. Bureaucracies cannot simply switch their modes of operation and start, say, loving people, or making them conscious.

Upon relating to the world outside of them, networks behave much as immune systems do. They have metabolism and resonance. That is, networks decompose and recombine an event or information according to their own blueprints. That which the metabolism cannot handle, or that which finds no resonance from the network, cannot become part of it in any way, and might not even be registered or noticed. Recognition depends on wavelengths and frequencies; if these are incompatible, two networks cannot communicate with each other. Much as a tuning fork, a network reacts to stimulations that make it vibrate according to its own resonance.

Any direct and unmediated influence of the world on a network that cannot renormalize this influence according to its own metabolism is likely catastrophic. An organism dies, or is taken over by another organism, when invaders enter it unnoticed and unreconstructed by its defensive immune system. One can turn art into politics, and science into ideology, but does so at the risk of destroying art or science altogether, as separate networks. This does not exclude empirical interdependencies between art and politics, or science and ideology. Far from it. To say that a science does not depend on politics is absurd. But such interdependencies must still be renormalized by the interdependent networks according to their own metabolisms. Politics can fund *this* science, rather than another one, but the science must still be done by the scientists, not the politicians. A science may be immoral, but its lack of morality says nothing about its quality as a science. When it is accused of being immoral, a science cannot do much with this accusation; in particular, it cannot make science with it.

Resonance means that a network of measures, for example, can measure something only in terms of its own mode of construction and specifications. It cannot measure anything in itself, or the *Ding an sich.* Nor can it measure "everything." Measures can be reliable and valid, but reliability means coherence or correlation within a network of measures, not correspondence between measures and measured things. A measure might be invalid, but only in relation to another, more valid measure, not in relation to the world as such. Reliability and validity are relations among measures, not between measures and their referents. A measure can be objective, but objectivity is the internal property and outcome of a network of measures as well, not of relations between measures and the world as it really is.

When they share metabolism and resonance, networks can interact and communicate, maybe even learn from each other. When there are actual relations and bridges between them, they might initiate "interdisciplinarity." But rarely does interdisciplinarity occur between, say, more than four or five specialties; more frequent are temporary task forces among two or three specialties. Still more frequent probably is interdisciplinarity as sheer rhetoric, window dressing, and promise. In any case, interdisciplinarity does not abandon specialty, but turns into yet another specialty of its own, administered by special centers, organizations, and institutes.

Two completely separate cultures, those without any links between them, are alien territory to each other. They do not observe each other, let alone feed any of their operations and results into the other's networks. An example is common sense and any advanced science, but also ethnomethodology and physics, or art and law. Various degrees of "incommensurability" result from such holes in the networks among networks. Incommensurability is not primarily a semantic difficulty with meanings, but a structural problem with network ties and holes. Commensurability varies; complete incommensurability is an extreme case. Holes vary also; they can be of various widths, depths, and durations (Burt 1992:42–44). The deeper, wider, and more durable a hole, the more incommensurability between that which the hole separates. There are deeper and more durable holes between the Two Cultures than between ethnomethodology and conversation analysis.

Two specialties separated by structural holes might still, however, have similar "codes," such as true / false, that allow them, at a minimum, to recognize each other as "sciences." But commonality or unity of codes occurs at a very abstract and general level. Two sciences may use the same code but still do very independent and different work, with very different outcomes. They might recognize a similarity in that they both are in the business of establishing matters of fact. But this may be as far as it goes, without any further mutual observation, cooperation, or joint venturing.

Renormalization

Internal resonance limits interactions and communications between separate networks. When they try to feed the results of their operations, or these operations themselves, into different networks, the target network restructures and recombines these results and operations to accommodate them into its own results and operations. If it cannot do this, the network cannot respond and react at all, and an observer might diagnose "incommensurability."

Theistic religions can respond to Darwinian evolution, but only by creating some hybrid, such as evolution "directed" by chief design and a master plan. Brains cannot swallow; livers cannot think. Organs can work "together" in the same body because they share the same basic blueprints, and because they decompose each other's outputs to recombine them into inputs that now can, indeed, be fed into their internal workings.

A science, for example, is not based on observations, least of all perceptions of the "just-open-your-eyes-and-watch" variety. It is not that the world at large entered the network through the doors of perception "as is." Rather, information that a network considers relevant is highly selective, prestructured, and "manufactured." It is not just that observations are "theory-laden," as some philosophers say. While this is true enough, it does not get at the heart of the matter. For even the very status and definitions of "observation," "fact," or "experience" depend on historical and cultural variations.

More radically, that which a network considers an observation is largely self-produced. To matter to a network, an observation is directed and renormalized by the attention and work of the network. It is the network that decides which sorts of observations matter to it, and in what shape or form they have to be to be recognized as observations that matter in the here and now of a network's current behavior. By far the most possible observations and events never receive any attention by a given network. No network can handle "pure" or "raw" events, only events that have been renormalized according to a network's own operations, including its instruments, measures, data-processing devices, and so on.

Most of the world is noise for most networks, including that which comes out of networks of different sorts. For example, neural networks cannot directly feed their events and states into networks that do not consist of neurons as well, such as science, art, or the world system. Since neural networks operate electrochemically, they can matter directly only to other neural networks that also operate electrochemically. This never happens directly between separate brains, only between linked networks within one brain. Neural networks can be researched scientifically, but how this is done follows from the networks that are neuroscience, not from those that are the brain. It is possible to communicate about brains and mental states, but communication is not a mental state and cannot "induce" any mental states, only subsequent communications.

The "codes" of a network accomplish much renormalization. A code is a general way to make sense of a contribution, and to attribute it to a certain source (Luhmann 1995:444). The true / false code of a science, for example, renormalizes any contribution to that science as something that can either be the case or not. Alternatively, Bayesian conditional probabilities can be assigned. The true / false distinction attributes the truth or falseness of a contribution to the actual state of the world, not to personal states, subjective desires, or class background. Whatever is fed into the network will be renormalized in this way, regardless of its "original meaning," intent, or context and circumstance. Once a contribution is fed into the network, this network takes over and structures or restructures this contribution according to its internal modes of operation. The result is that, "although the philosophy of Nietzsche, for instance, has a psychopathological motif, it generates social effects no different from those conditioned by a normal outlook on life" (Fleck [1935] 1979:37).

Likewise, networks of mass education translate students' mental and cognitive states into formal grades and credentials, which can be passed between various organizations in this network. In themselves, these states of mind are utterly inaccessible to networks of education. Therefore, the latter help themselves to a number of highly simplified and convenient fictions—that grades measure actual performance, that better grades are caused by better performance, that the same grade remains identical across different times and locations, and that employers should decide whom to hire on the basis of diplomas, because better diplomas mean better skills. These meritocratic fictions are not just fictions; like other myths, they become real when they start to make a real difference, which of course they do.

The science of education, however, another network different from education, deconstructs these myths and replaces them with the outcomes of actual research. But when that research is again fed into the networks of education and taught to students, the bureaucratic fictions become operative again, so that a paradox emerges: the science of education might teach classes in which students are graded on how well they understand that grades are fictions. Such paradoxes emerge whenever two separate networks come in contact with each other; paradoxes limit the direct and unmediated effect that one network can have on another's results and operations. Any such effect is mediated by renormalization.

Different networks construct their own chains of causality, their own perceptions of time and history, and their own basic elements or building blocks as those which they cannot do without or decompose any further—for now. To the extent that they are free to do this, different networks cannot "control" each other; they might find it difficult even to understand each other. As observers, networks will tend to model a foreign network not in terms of that network's own operations, but according to what matters at home. What else could they do? We can model the behavior of frogs according to the parameters of our frog science, but not according to how frogs appear to the grass in which they hop around. We can try to make sense of the classifications of tribal ethnobotany, but they can either be fed and renormalized into our own science, or not. If they can, they become part of the world according to our science. If they cannot, they are historical, cultural, and social facts. Understanding difference is possible, but only within the "horizons" (Gadamer [1960] 1975) of our own world.

The metaphor of horizons is useful, because horizons are not fixed and stable, but change with, and as a result of, the location and velocity of an observer. Observers with high velocity see changing horizons come and go at high speeds; slower observers see the world as more similar to itself over longer periods of time.

Networks go to work—not on the world at large, but on the outcomes of their previous operations. They have nothing to work with but the results of their previous work. They start again the next morning where they quit last night, so to speak. This does not imply repetition or conservation of tradition. But changes and innovations are also the results of previous or concurrent changes and innovations. There are usually many related previous changes that interact in some way to feed a discovery, innovation, or breakthrough. Such insights do not suddenly fall from the sky, but depend and interact with prior breakthroughs and related advances occurring somewhere else, or at another time. Even networks that specialize in innovations accomplish these innovations from their own previous results and operations, not from the world at large, the thing in itself, or the real object.

Self-similarity in networks is the result of this recursiveness in operations and outcomes, iterated over time. Recursive networks build up coherence and identity by going to work on their own previous results. In neural nets, this is called "learning by the back-propagation of error" (Churchland 1992:172). Learning does not occur from scratch each time; rather, a neural net is "trained up" by recursivity. As such networks "learn," their results become increasingly dissimilar to the original inputs, including the world at large, but more similar to *themselves*. The epistemological implication is that learning is not an increasing verisimilitude to the real world, but an increasing self-similarity. When they have practiced recursiveness for a while, networks become more similar and known to themselves, acquiring a distinctive identity, mode of self-observation, and history.

Autopoiesis

Network construction and extension take time and effort. They meet resistance from inertia and entropy. Still, over time, some nodes, and some relationships, become institutionalized—that is, they acquire a temporary stability that constrains further construction. This outcome is not necessary, or even likely, since a network faces both internal and external challenges to its integrity, especially when it is young and liable. As a network builds up, however, it gradually sets variable limits on what is possible next. It would still be a mistake to define what a network "is," for it is only what it has and will become. From the history of science we know that systematic definition and axiomatization come later in the evolution of a network, when it has settled into its niche and established some routines and basic certainties (Spengler [1923] 1993:43, 123). Then defining its identity is a critical part of what the network does to observe and distinguish itself from other networks, or from its previous identities.

A core puzzle is how networks emerge from unstructured complexity. On the face of it, successful emergence is rather improbable, for various reasons. First, the nodes-to-be might remain unrelated altogether—there are many more ways of being not connected than of being connected. The prospective nodes in an emerging network might also be nodes in a different network, and so experience a drift or pull from the forces within this other network. If they do become connected in a new network, there are many different ways in which this can be done. If a particular matrix or configuration of relations does emerge, it remains unstable and uncertain at first.

Network analyses of social movement emergence offer some clues as to how social structure emerges through autopoiesis. Social movements face grave challenges to organization, since they usually have no coercive apparatus or material incentives to secure participation. For the most part, they also cannot count on any prior rational motives and interests in the common or public goods to be provided eventually by the movement. Free riding remains a tempting option throughout movement emergence and consolidation, especially since future outcomes and benefits are uncertain and risky. Long delays in gratification are to be expected, as is an ultimate failure to provide any rewards whatever. Those who do participate also likely participate in other encounters, groups, organizations, and networks. In this situation, the odds are stacked high against movement emergence and continuation.

Kim and Bearman (1997) offer an autopoietic model of network emergence—against all odds. Their basic point is that nothing activates like activism. That which activates into participation is the structure of activism itself, iterating through time—not prior motives, intentions, or commitments. Activists "often discover that they are movement activists after extensive involvement in activist networks" (p. 74). Activism is more the result of movement participation than its antecedent cause. The emerging network pushes itself into the next level or wave of activism; it draws, recursively, on previous activism to ensure further activism. Still, the most likely next outcome is failure and dissolution, accounting for a widespread liability of newness in movements.

A condition for survival is the emergence of a "critical mass." The critical mass is in the core of the network, in its center of gravity. Here one finds a densely interlocking clique. The critical mass is held together, and in place, not by any special motivations or strong wills, but by its own interdependence. It is this strong interdependence that moves the critical mass to turn inward, toward its own connectivity, and away from opportunities and temptations to defect. Again, iterations consolidate this structure, taking previous levels of activity as inputs for subsequent activity.

The network core protects itself by buffering and enclosure. The dense and redundant ties in the core hold its nodes in place, reducing degrees of freedom by multiple and reinforcing connections. If anything, the leaders are less free and more constrained than the followers, since the longer they remain leaders, the fewer options and possibilities they have apart from continuing to be leaders. The movement's attention is focused on them, generating pressures to remain where they are. More peripheral or marginal followers can defect at any time.

The core produces an "envelope" around itself, distinguishing itself from the rest of the overall structure. It accomplishes a "symbiosis between identity and interest" (Kim and Bearman 1997:85) through its redundant pattern of ties. That is, the core now generates its own interests and identity, apart from any interests or identities its nodes may have. The nodes are what they become as part of the core. They become dedicated to a cause.

But this dedication comes from core membership, not the other way around. It is this pattern and interdependence that "activates," not any states in the nodes. In this way, networks can emerge and sustain themselves by means of interdependence without rational actors, coercion, and selective incentives: "Activism is enhanced through increasing embeddedness in an activist network" (Kim and Bearman 1997:73). This is network autopoiesis. Brym (1988:372) finds a similar pattern of movement activation and activism in the case of Jewish Marxist intellectuals in early twentieth-century Russia.

Self-Similarity

A working network accomplishes a measure of self-similarity as it focuses attention on itself, distinguishes its identity from other networks and from its own components, and draws boundaries around itself. Much as selves, a self-similar network has an identity, for itself and for others. Self-similarity is a variable accomplishment, not a steady state or ground rule. It changes over time and often consolidates over time, whereas young or novel networks in formation are not (yet) very similar to themselves. Ferguson (1998) analyzes the gradual emergence and formation of a separate and distinct "bourgeois" field of French gastronomy in the nineteenth century as the result of various demarcations—from the haute cuisine of the ancien régime, centered in pompous displays of courtly splendor, and from eating as sheer physiological necessity. The identity of a network consolidates as the result of distinctions from different identities.

The degree of self-similarity depends on how closely a network is coupled, and how strictly and rigidly its boundaries exclude the outside. Closely coupled or redundant networks or clusters with sharp and clear boundaries accomplish more self-similarity than do fragmented networks with weak boundaries.

Self-similarity has nothing to do with consensus or agreement. It does not imply that all the parts and components are alike or identical in some way. For example, the self-similarity of a brain, experienced as consciousness, does not imply that all its mental states are the same. Far from it. The contents of mental states change all the time. What remains is the ongoing process of distinction, which attributes mental states to self, not other. The difference between my self and your self is not in any actual mental state or conscious content, but in the attribution of such a state to my self or your self. Self-similarity refers to process and attribution, not content.

Self-similarity is an outcome of connectivity and ties, and then of higher internal than external connectivity and density. Within a network, ties and connections lead to "mattering." Networks are where something can matter in certain ways. Ties transport such mattering, not sheer information, in the sense of transporting a fixed and unchanging byte of information reliably, without changes in meaning. Mattering means that what happens in one part of the network is more likely to make a difference to related or strongly related parts than to unrelated or weakly related parts. Higher internal than external connectivity or density means that what happens in a network is more likely to matter to the network than to its environments, and vice versa.

It is the very relations that account for self-similarity, not just what these relations transport or transmit. Dissimilar nodes tend to become more similar over time, as a relationship between them is activated frequently and intensely. It is the relationship itself that shapes and forms the nodes to fit into the relationship. Dense clusters of nodes become more similar to themselves, as do the nodes within such clusters. Music produces the musician, and thinking produces the thinker—not the other way around.

The absence of ties across the structural holes in the network fabric means that nothing matters there. It is terra incognita. A node without any ties whatever matters to nothing, and makes no difference to anything. That which happens in or to it, if anything, happens only in or to it and remains contained there. For example, since there are no electrochemical ties between the brains of separate persons, nothing a brain experiences makes a difference to what any other brains experience at that time. There are, of course, ties between persons, but these are ties of interaction or communication, not electrochemistry. You can communicate your sensations or experiences to those very few persons who might care to hear about them, but then it is the communication that makes a difference, not the sensation itself. As the carriers of brains with sensations and qualia, persons are complete monads and strangers to each other, since there are no ties between them at this level.

Mattering is making a difference, but it is difficult to say just what sort, and how much, of a difference an event will make to a network. A contribution to a specialty, for example, might not matter at all to that specialty or, if it does, it might make an unintended or unexpected difference there. The self-similarity or identity of such a specialty only assures that the specialty can recognize a contribution to it and distinguish this contribution from the contributions to different specialties, for which the same is true. In contrast, specialties with weak identities and boundaries have less selective filters aiding in the recognition of contributions to themselves. Specialties undergoing major transformations, specialties in formation, or specialties about to disappear also have more uncertainty about what counts as a solid contribution. In networks with multiple bounded clusters, self-similarity also applies to such clusters. Networks are not of one piece. Most of them have various bounded parts, defined in terms of higher or different internal than external connectivity and activity. Citation clusters and interaction density can be seen as indicators approximately mapping such differential connectivity. If the bounded clusters become more similar to themselves than to the network within which they are clusters, this network might lose its identity and fall apart. Then this network no longer matters and makes no difference, except maybe to historians of it. To paraphrase Nietzsche, a network is in great trouble when the historians are the only ones paying any attention to it. For this means that the network is becoming a matter of the past, kept alive only in retrospect.

On the face of it, self-similarity of networks is an improbable accomplishment, since there are many more ways of not being connected than of being so connected. Why should anything matter or make a difference at all? How much of what matters now will still matter in the very long run? Connections take time and effort; they must be activated, reactivated, and maintained over time. It is much easier to let a connection fade out than to preserve a clear signal. Self-similarity faces challenges from turbulence, inertia, and entropy. The formation of a network depends more on accident and coincidence than on rational planning and strategy. It is up to the network itself to accomplish self-similarity; this cannot be legislated from above or outside. For example, encounters and groups form and disband all the time, without any God, fatherly prince, or rational administration able to do much about it.

In the literature, there are various concepts from different areas that describe self-similarity. In epistemology, there are coherence theories of truth, which attribute truth to the outcome of self-similarity among the components of theories as networks. Krieger (1992:102) observes a "congruence" between the handles, probes, and tools of physics. Pickering (1995) calls "interactive stabilization" the process by which several parts of a scientific network (models, theories, machines, observations) stay attuned to each other. Hacking (1992:44) attributes stability in cultures to mutual adjustments among "ideas, things, and marks." In cybernetics, the "eigen" or default values are the states a system produces when it is left to itself and its internal interactions. Fleck ([1935] 1979:28) refers to the consolidation of scientific facts as a "harmony of illusions" achieved by the mutual tuning and orchestration of the components within an increasingly self-similar science. Latour (1987:62) also sees solid facts emerging from the "heterogeneous engineering" of various parts in a network of science. In neural networks, a single sensation is the outcome of parallel processing; the recognition of identity, for example, is fed by multiple clues orchestrated to point at each other, and then to the "object," whose identity emerges from such mutual calibration and back-propagation.

These arguments point to mutual calibration, attunement, and disciplining of various components and connections in a network. How is this achieved despite disagreement, recalcitrance, and other kinds of resistance? How does a network "contain," and then make sure that that which has been contained does not get out, does not lose its structure and regularities? How does one go from a network with fuzzy boundaries and ambiguous unstable ties to a more solid and robust structure? And when do such structures collapse? To anticipate a bit: Networks with high self-similarity and a strong identity are more likely "realist"—they externalize their operations and outcomes to attribute them to the world itself. Networks with a weaker identity are more constructivist.

Unity

Advanced levels of self-similarity might construe unity, but unity is accomplished by the network itself, by means of coherence, demarcation, and closure. Unity and identity do not exist in themselves or by themselves. They are not logical but empirical properties, which is to say that unity and identity vary. A unity or identity is a variable outcome of a network's ongoing operations as it observes itself and is being observed. This includes the possibility that no unity can be secured, and that the network splits up or falls apart.

Unity requires a special sort of cultural work, akin to what Weber called systematization and rationalization of worldviews. The unity of a network comes fairly late in its development, if at all. Unity is the sign of a "mature" network—one that has had some time to find out, and define, what it "really is." Even then, unity cannot be taken for granted but must be maintained against further threats, insults, or alternatives. Definitions, firm extensions, strict reference, and logical coherence are late events in the institutionalization and consolidation of a network. No network starts out with its foundations secure and its definitions logically exhaustive and mutually exclusive.

Spengler ([1923] 1993:43) calls the unity of advanced cultures their "civilization." This term suggests a hardening and congealing of a mature network's "basic" relationships and "elementary" building blocks. But keep in mind that these relationships and building blocks are basic and elementary only for it, for this local network, until the network and its modes of construction and operation expand into other networks. Different networks have their own basic relationships and elementary building blocks—that which *they* cannot decompose and question any further, at least for the time being. Different networks "care" about different things, since what matters to them is different as well. If this network constructivism turned radical, it would say, for example, that particles are elementary building blocks—in the networks of today's particle physics.

The behavior of an advanced and established network tends to be essentialist—it has secured its foundations, institutionalized its referential niche, and reified its relationships into natural and obvious givens. In contrast, young cultures and emerging networks have not (yet) carved out their special and unique niches, established their unity, or settled on firm definitions of identity. The unity of a network is not a stable steady state, or an obvious given, but a variable accomplishment requiring time and institutionalization.

Boundaries

The limits or boundaries of a network are where its relations, forces, and nodes end, until the network expands or contracts. When the network disintegrates altogether, its boundaries, nodes, and forces disappear as well—although they might in some way be "conserved" in other networks. The former members of defunct groups might become members in new groups, but they are not the same members they used to be in the old group. Persons are not the same in their different groups; it is these different groups, as observers, that construct and observe their own members in their own different ways. A high degree of sameness or self-similarity of persons comes from a special kind of network—one that swallows its members whole, so that they are not members of any other group. A strong and persisting identity occurs in isolated and redundant networks; they are greedy and total.

A network has no fixed and stable boundaries, since boundaries result from, and vary together with, the behavior of the network. Networks and boundaries are coproduced as two resulting sides of the same operation that distinguishes the network from that which it is not. A stable and well-defined boundary is a special case of a network turning all of its attention inward, cutting off its ties to other networks and withdrawing from its environment. Rare cults do this.

The more frequent case is fuzzy boundaries with ambiguous membership and uncertain extensions and bridges into the network's surroundings. Such nervous and permeable boundaries might demarcate scientific specialties, for example, which cannot completely shut themselves off from related specialties, or only at the risk of eventual obsolescence or backwardness. Many innovations and discoveries come from the intersections and overlaps among sciences, and getting rid of these intersections risks blocking further advances.

Communities are bounded and local, not universal or global, though some are larger than others. But there is no global village. Who lives there? Only the communitarian philosophers of global village. But they have their own small villages—the networks among communitarians. A science makes a direct difference only to itself, and maybe to some other science, but not to all of them, all of the time. Much less does a science, by itself, make a difference to nonscience, including technology, common sense, religion, or dance. At least not when there is some differentiation between cultures.

Take technology. An observer might simplify the structures and processes of a science, but this should not obscure the fact that there is no straight logical path from, say, a theoretically justified scientific prediction to a working apparatus. The implications of experiments are usually not direct and obvious, and the observed events themselves are often ambiguous, controversial, and difficult to replicate. Even less is there a coherent deductive system of propositions that "implied" a working technology as the "truth" of its theory.

All networks are local to begin with; most remain local or disintegrate altogether. In the long run, disintegration is more likely than survival, since there are many more ways of being dead than alive. For every connection in a network, there are many different possibilities— of being connected in different ways, to different nodes, or not being connected at all.

A network with a boundary is thereby local. Boundaries are important for internal closure, demarcation, and self-similarity or identity. They vary in how selectively and rigidly they keep something in or out, and also in how strictly and meticulously they renormalize that which wants, or is pushed, to enter the network.

Network Expansions

As one network expands into another where it formerly did not matter, the "currency" of the target network is adjusted or converted into the currency of the expanding network. Convertibility of currencies or forms of capital does not occur by itself or naturally, however. There will likely be some resistance from the target network. If that can be overcome, the expanding network starts to matter more to the target network. The target's currency is devalued, so to speak, or maybe taken off the market entirely. It no longer matters in what is becoming the new network.

After invasion, the conquered specialty's indigenous distinctions matter less, or no more, if colonization is complete. The unique intellectual and material property of the target specialty is deflated, seen as a special case of the new science at best, and as pseudoscience at worst. The old theories, instruments, and technologies do not make a difference anymore, and nothing relevant follows from them for the future of science. They cease to generate fresh science and reputations, and gradually turn into history. Only a dead romance is colder than a dead science. Skills, problems, paradigms, technologies—they all begin to look inadequate, outdated, and antiquarian to the network that is now being established. The problems and puzzles of the old specialty are not finally "solved"; rather, they are displaced and replaced, debunked as "pseudo-problems," and relegated to the prehistory of true science.

But only in retrospect will a successful network be able to explain its expansion as the result of superior logic or rationality. At the time of conquest and conversion, reason and rationality are just part of the rhetoric of conflict. Whether an episode in science constitutes a "progressive" and cumulative improvement, or just a neutral and nondirectional problem shift, is decided with hindsight. The same is true in natural evolution; whether a new speciation is a dead end or a transition to a more advanced phase is unknowable at the time it happens. For one thing, at the time a speciation occurs, there is no observer, short of God, who had any such knowledge, since this would require that speciation had already occurred and, among other things, produced such a knowledgeable observer.

Hacking (1992) and Latour (1988:249) illustrate the microreality of network expansion. Basically, it consists of modifying the environment of the network in terms of what matters at home, so that part of the environment now becomes part of the network. Latour's case in point is how Pasteur managed to get his anthrax cure to work outside of his laboratory. This happened by transforming the farm into an extension of the lab. Extension is difficult and improbable, since farms are much dirtier and messier than laboratories. Farms also come with those recalcitrant and unsophisticated farmers who are hostile to folks from the city and have no understanding of the scientific method. Labs tame and domesticate complexity; nature is not as wild there. Experiments work outside of the lab where they originated only when the outside conditions have been modified according to the experimental conditions. In this way, an initially local network becomes gradually more macro and begins to matter elsewhere also. But this does not happen by itself, and can also be reversed, as happens when macro-networks, such as empires, collapse.

In the other direction, from the environment into the network, inputs are inspected and restructured before being admitted. The materials and substances in laboratories are very "unnatural"—that is, they are preprocessed by industrial engineering and often sold in large batches as black boxes by specialized corporations. Statistical programs are another example; they work with a fair amount of stability and predictability in different settings, thereby reducing localism and boundedness.

Another example of network restructuring of input or environment is survey research. Survey research restructures the conditions in its environment, which is some sort of relation to respondents, maybe a face-to-face interview. It cannot handle an encounter's raw complexity, and so tries to structure the interview as much as possible according to its own specifications, schedules, and formats. The more a survey does this, the more comparable it is to other surveys that do the same. For the survey, the interaction itself is a source of potential systematic error, and it accounts for such errors or biases by certain procedures. A reliable survey is one with a great deal of self-similarity across times, settings, and locales of interviewing, so that "1" means female, anywhere, at any time. Reliable and coherent surveys are fairly indifferent toward variations in context and circumstance.

Surveys can also restructure their inputs, or "responses." For one thing, such responses are measured in the way specified by the survey's operations. The data are correspondingly self-produced. They might have external referents, or true scores, but no referent or score enters the survey "as is," without renormalization according to measurement levels, grids, numbers, categories, boxes, and the like. True scores might be inferred or estimated in some way, but this inference or estimate remains based in the calculations of the survey.

This is true also for ethnographies, though maybe to a lesser extent, since ethnographies strive for more "naturalness" or closeness to the setting. Yet ethnographies have their own traditions, grids, and data-reduction devices as well; they can delay renormalization by using, for example, "grounded theory" or "sensitizing concepts," but eventually, to matter in more or less professionalized networks of related ethnographies, the ethnography will have to leave the field also, and attune itself to the ethnographies that are already in place.

Networks of Culture

Semantic Holism

The idea that cultures are networks goes back to the classics, specifically Durkheim, and then to such diverse authors as Fleck, Spengler, Wittgenstein, Duhem, Quine, Hesse, and Rorty. Thagard (1992) for example, sees science as "conceptual and propositional systems" (p. 7) that are "primarily structured via relations of explanatory coherence" (p. 9). In analytical philosophy, cultures are (too narrowly) reduced to theories, and theories are (again, too narrowly) reduced to webs of belief and networks of propositions. Analytical philosophy considers statements, propositions, concepts, and their logical relations to be the main components of cultural networks.

The epistemological point of semantic holism is that Vienna Circle inductivism and some "atomistic" Analytical Philosophy cannot account for the empirical or actual behavior of theories. Holists insist that the meaning and behavior of terms and propositions cannot be determined in isolation. For example, whether a term is observational or theoretical does not follow from its intrinsic semantic properties; rather, these properties follow from the kind of position a term holds in a larger structure. The structure decides what sorts of work a term will have to do on a given occasion; it is the usage of a term, and its relations to other terms, that give it "meaning."

Falsifications have attracted much attention from semantic holism. Since theories are networks, falsifications have no unique or necessary effects on what a theory does when it faces an anomaly or major contradiction. Rather, it is the network itself, as a whole, that reacts and responds to irritations and surprises. These ripple through the entire structure, which adjusts to anomaly on its own terms by, for example, making local modifications, ad hoc excuses, or promises of reconciliation in the near future of the theory, when it has learned more. If a term anchors a major or critical segment of the network, it will probably be saved in some way; if it occurs somewhere in the outskirts, making less of a difference to other terms and their relations, it might more easily be dropped.

That is, "characteristic properties" and "essential attributes" are not a cause, but an effect, of network location. When that location remains unchanged and stable for a long time, properties or attributes might turn into "intrinsic" and "essential" attributes. Conversely, when the location of a node in a network changes repeatedly, its attributes and characteristics will be seen as more contingent and accidental.

Quine (1964:42–43) distinguishes between cores and peripheries in the network of a theory. The core houses analytical statements, those that are true by definition or because of the meanings of words. Such truisms and tautologies are what I have been calling essences and natural kinds, held true in all possible worlds, forever, and for all possible observers. On its periphery, the network is more sensitive to empirical reality; this is where there occur synthetic statements—those which might be empirically false or in need of revision. The nodes in a theory move in and out of cores over time, and in different theories a node might have different status and location. *Themata* or paradigms, located in the core, can turn into falsifiable peripheral theories when they become controversial. In the other direction, empirical laws can turn into definitions when they consolidate firmly in the core. Likewise, what is used tacitly as a routine tool in one context or time might become a target for deconstruction in another science or time. All of this applies—for the time being, and until further notice.

Against semantic holism, it is never the *entire* network that responds to troubles, surprises, or exceptions. Rather, the differential internal connectivity of networks suggests that changes will respond to the patterns of relationships within networks. Revisions, for example, will have more direct and immediate consequences especially for closely related and coupled clusters of nodes, but less so for unrelated or weakly linked and remote corners of the network. Moreover, while Quine suggests that networks have only one core and a surrounding periphery, it is more realistic to expect some networks with multiple cores and peripheries. Many cultures have subcultures.

As it stands in philosophy, there are more problems with semantic holism. One is that networks are seen primarily as webs of explicit and codified beliefs and statements. This is a rather impoverished view of science and theory, because it captures only one side of science (statements), at only one point in time (after cultural closure), on only one kind of stage (the frontstage). Cultural networks include not only statements and propositions, but also the material means of cultural production, experiments, instruments, skills, and reputations. Cultures are networks among communications, but also among equipment, sites of production, encounters, groups, and organizations. Hacking (1992:44–50) offers a list of components organized into "ideas," "things," and "marks."

Frontstages are only one mode of observing a culture; cultures have backstages as well, which is culture-in-the-making as opposed to ready-made culture. Semantic holism does not allow for any, or enough, variation. It fails when encountering *differences* in network structures and behaviors. All networks are holistic—but that is just the beginning. The precise contours and structures of various networks and their bounded parts can be expected to differ considerably. "Holism" is not itself holistic, but variable. It should not simply mean that there is one undifferentiated and inscrutable "whole," as opposed to isolated and atomistic statements. Very rarely are all nodes and clusters directly linked to all other parts of the structure, in equal ways. Rather, there are distinct clusters and subcultures with higher internal than external connectivity.

Moreover, as a rule of method, expect many different *kinds* of connections and links, some stronger, others weaker. Variation matters. For example, minor changes that occur in weakly linked and isolated network sectors are more easily contained within these sectors. Other changes occur in areas that are strongly linked to many other areas. These will tend to reverberate through the entire structure, with surprising and unpredictable feedforward and feedback effects. Closely coupled networks are more likely to experience "normal accidents," especially when they also give rise to complex interactions and nonlinearity.

Another modification to Quine's model is to see the *proportion* of core to peripheral sectors itself as variable. Some networks will have relatively large cores, where most of what is thought, done, and believed could not be thought, done, or believed otherwise. In this frame of comparison, religions generally have larger cores than do modern sciences, but competitive and individualistic religions with high internal diversity and multiple changing markets presumably have smaller cores than state-supported and centralized bureaucratic monopolies. When such clerical monopolies are wrapped around the state's formal structure, cores become stronger and more hegemonic still.

Networks with large cores are well established, with a firm set of entrenched dogmas but little room for alternative interpretations. The neo-Durkheimians have shown that this sort of culture is likely crafted by rather isolated and localist groups, with high ritual density and little social capital or cosmopolitan connections across the boundaries. "High" groups and their cultures turn inward to consolidate their basic parameters, foundations, traditions, and institutions. Ceteris paribus, the more isolated and closely coupled the group, the larger its cultural core.

In contrast, cultures with small cores are more playful, experimental, and open to change. They have fewer dogmas and are more prepared to imagine different possibilities. They expect cognitively more than normatively, although they still do both. They welcome innovations and strangers as opportunities for discovery, and tolerate more diversity and ambiguity. Ceteris paribus, the more cosmopolitan and permeable a group and its boundaries, the smaller the proportion of core to periphery in its cultural network.

To transform semantic holism into a full-blown sociological network holism, we need a network theory of culture that does not restrict the nodes to explicit propositions and well-defined concepts, restrict the connections to formal logical relations, or freeze culture into a static picture of settled and closed normal culture.

Institutions

Each culture has its own black boxes, invisibilities, and natural kinds. I shall call them "institutions." The best theory of institutions we have, I think, comes from Gehlen's ([1956] 1964:40–44, 50–55, 59–60) philosophical anthropology. Institutions are not just rules, conventions, or norms, though explicit norms might summarize and simplify the behavior of an institution, maybe for the benefit of an observer of its frontstages. Norms and rules are part of the public and codified expression of what an institution does, but the institution itself is not merely a complex of rules, norms, and conventions.

Institutions are what a network cannot do without before dissolving or changing into another network. Mature networks have such core areas, but they are of various relative sizes and strengths compared with the other regions of the overall structure. Emerging networks do not yet have the critical mass to collapse into a core. At the same time, one network's basic and indispensable institutions might be another's contingent possibilities, and today's firm institutions may be tomorrow's conventional rules. Many networks have multiple institutions, themselves connected into their own networks and gravitating about their own cores. Institutions vary—although this variation is difficult, if not impossible, to observe from locations in the network in which they are institutions. Institutions are the blind spots of a network, that which it perceives and does when it perceives and does what comes naturally to it.

In cultural Quine-networks, the institutions are analytical truths, tautologies, natural kinds, and the elementary building blocks of the core's referential ecological niche. Institutions are never just beliefs, much less propositions, though beliefs and statements settle on the surface of an institution. Institutions are "just beliefs" only for another network observing them from outside. This outside network, however, has its own insides, including institutions, which are also more than "just beliefs" to this network.

Rather than just beliefs, institutions are *how* a network does what it does, not so much *what* it does. Hows remain longer than whats; how the brain manages to see something outlasts what it sees, at any particular time. Institutional modes of operation provide some unity and continuity to the ever-changing themes and referents of these operations themselves. Hows are not visible from within the core of the network. They become an explicit theme and subject only for another network, or for a rival location or subculture within the same network. Since networks often overlap, that which belongs to the periphery of one network may be part of another's core. That is, networks are linked to other networks—through networks, which have their own cores as well.

Institutions are the network's "default" mode of operation. They are how the network "sees" when it opens its eyes and goes about its routine business, undisturbed and unreflective. The core of administration, for example, is bureaucratic procedures and classifications condensed into files, which *are* the reality for administration. When the files are destroyed, the bureaucracy's world collapses, and with it the bureaucracy itself.

Cultures stratify, over time, into multiple layers of depth and invisibility, each with their own temporal frames of change, which do not necessarily move in lockstep. Drawing upon Braudel's distinction between various modes of historical time and change, Galison (1987:246–254) observes such layers in the culture of particle physics: in the core, there are long-term metaphysical and ontological worldviews; in the semiperiphery, models, while the outer or peripheral layer consists of networks among more or less explicit and formalized theories. Changes in one layer have no direct or immediate effects on the other layers.

A big part of a culture's core is its routine—though not its novel—instruments, tools, and materials. As a network goes about its business, it gradually sediments what will become its "essential" modes of operation into deeper layers in the network, where their status is consolidated by multiple reinforcing ties. The deeper such levels, the more resistant they are to change, and the more they are protected by the work of insulation, buffering, and ceteris paribus clauses. The nodes of a core strongly point to and support each other. They lose their individual independence and identity by firm enclosure into the identity of the core itself, much as cults secure strong group identity by reducing degrees of freedom for their individual members.

Consolidation and entailment happen when strongly recursive and closely coupled patterns of linkages make sure that repeated corroborations and confirmations create that "harmony of illusions" that Fleck calls a fact. The crucial point is that consolidation happens whenever a redundant pattern of relationships—social, cultural, or natural—is in place. For it is this very pattern itself that, regardless of what flows through the ties, causes convergence of various operations and outcomes in several locations throughout the core.

The core contains that which is taught to new generations as unproblematic and established fact. It includes Kuhnian exemplars, textbooks, demonstration experiments with predictable outcomes, and bureaucratic examination or grading rituals. These are all strongly and repetitively linked to each other, creating a stable and self-similar set of institutions that defines the network's reality and *Gestell* (frame). The ingredients of the core are held together by tautology and circularity, which come from repetitive and dense mutual ties in a coherent cluster of strong relationships. That is, the paths from one node in the core to another core node are direct, straight, well-worn, and obvious. This core stability comes not from its individual nodes, but from their dense and redundant mutual ties. The nodes draw their justification from all the other nodes in the core. Cores house strong logical and ontological necessity—for the network in which they are cores.

While the relative size and stability of cores vary from culture to culture, and nodes might move in and out of a core, the overall distinction between cores and peripheries in a network remains longer. Networks without cores collapse like bodies without skeletons, or scatter like fields without centripetal forces. Depending on its critical mass relative to other sectors of a network, the core exerts a stronger or weaker gravitational pull on the entire structure. This force is stronger the closer a network sector is related to it; it gets weaker as the distance from the core increases, as happens in the innovative, uncertain, and controversial areas in the network.

Cores are made, but seem to exist in themselves. They have a past, but this past and its contingencies gradually become invisible and irrelevant in the process of consolidation, caging, and taming. Cores are very presentist; they reconstruct the past as their prehistory and the future as a cumulative extension of the present. Very strong and hegemonic cores might declare that history itself has "ended."

A prominent core activity is classification. Classification is "how institutions think" (Douglas 1986:48). By means of classification, institutions confer identity, establish similarity and difference, and organize meaning in conceptual grids. In very strong, solid, and durable institutions, such grids tend to become naturalized or ontological over time. They cease to be mere constructs and turn into natural kinds or essences—as that which can no longer be imagined otherwise because it captures natural order itself.

Over time, as an institution consolidates, its classifications become more or less complete. Increasing completion entails the gradual closing or bridging of remaining structural holes in the core, by adding redundant and close relationships. Kuhnian normal science proceeds in this way, through piecemeal puzzle-solving, gradual improvements in working equipment, and filling in the missing links in theories. Increasing the resolution and reach of instruments is also part of this activity. In this way, higher degrees of circularity and tautology are established in the core, together with the invisible or blind spots in an institution. As long as they last, cores do not consider the possibility that there might be a world in which the core no longer applies. This unwillingness or inability to learn, however, is itself a condition for learning, especially for cumulative advances, since learning occurs only if not everything changes at the same time. If it does, there is not progress but breakdown.

The Physics of Cores

An entity belongs to the core not because of its intrinsic properties; its intrinsic properties are the result of prolonged embeddedness and tenure in the relationships that constitute the core. Cores temporarily "freeze" their entities by "fixing" their relationships or reducing their degrees of freedom. When degrees of freedom are reduced to zero, necessity reigns, whereas infinite degrees of freedom produce arbitrariness. Cores are like crystal lattices; peripheries are more like fluid dynamics. Reduction of degrees of freedom comes about as the result of increases in redundant tie patterns *alone:* "It is as if with the increase of the number of junction points, . . . free space were reduced" (Fleck [1935] 1979:83).

That is, regardless of what a core does, or what its entities are, the very redundancy and recursiveness of relations in cores lead to mutual stabilization and solid identity, with fewer degrees of freedom for the components. These are now "stuck" in their densely interwoven relations, held in place by the very pattern of connections. In physical terms, very strong and well-insulated cores house symmetries, invariances, and conservation laws (Krieger 1992:42–46, 77). This means that the overall identity of cores remains robust and intact longer, despite some insults, changes, and transformations.

Routine demonstration or teaching experiments with predictable outcomes, for example, are largely invariant to context, time, setting, or personnel. They are repeated again and again with highly stable results, although the specific tools and materials used might differ from occasion to occasion. Frequently, robustness is supported by standardized large-batch materials, tools, or equipment that vary little between locations. Any surprises that do occur are renormalized so as to not question the integrity of the core itself. Wherever one starts in the core, one ends up in the same position, no matter which path is chosen. Tautology and circularity assure that, remaining in the core, you can never leave home: "A rule is amended if it yields an inference we are unwilling to accept; an inference is rejected if it violates a rule we are unwilling to amend" (Goodman 1983:64).

In a core, we can find the stuff that much of philosophy is searching for, preferably universals, natural kinds, and basic or self-evident certainties. In the core, the network "naturally" converges on such stable and "obvious" behaviors as rationality, logic, and method. Much as institutions externalize their orders onto the world itself, in cores rigid designators refer to natural classifications and things-in-themselves. This is only possible through drastic simplifications and dramatic domestications of complexity. Outside of the core, the network's mode of operation tends to be more experimental and innovative. Cores and their nodes are tamed; peripheries allow more wildness, since they are less redundant and more loosely coupled. The French absolutist court is composed of domesticated mannerisms, while rawer passions reign the countryside (Elias [1939] 1982:258–261). Samurai warriors were domesticated into armies by being contained and enveloped within castles and courts, the cores of emerging modern states (Ikegami 1995:134–136, 144–145). Elias shows that such domestication was the result of increasingly dense interrelationships among court society that gravitated around a common center or core.

Cores do not exist by and of themselves; they are an outcome of the behavior of a network. They need work. Cores emerge when a network "folds into itself" to protect what are becoming its basic operations and modes of existence. The core is Being; the periphery is Becoming. The core has a very firm and highly selective boundary; the overall network's boundary shifts and expands, with no clear rules or criteria for extension or contraction.

In the peripheries, there is more uncertainty and ambivalence. Relations among nodes are more indirect, loosely coupled, and fragmented here. The paths extend into more unknown and uncertain territory, and there are fewer and fewer signs pointing home, to the core. This is where strange hybrids and anomalies occur, together with unfamiliar things that are difficult to tame, explain, classify, and replicate: "The less interconnected the system of knowledge . . . the less stable and more miracle-prone is its reality" (Fleck [1935] 1979:102). Novel instruments or techniques, for example, are notoriously unreliable and sensitive to context and setting. They are not, or not yet, domesticated or well understood. Like any novel node, or cluster of nodes, a new tool or device "drifts" away from its place, resisting attempts at freezing or caging the work it does. This provides opportunities for discovery and innovation.

Some of these instruments will eventually, upon being caged and routinized, become part of the core as well. Caging happens as degrees of freedom are reduced; then a device, instrument, or theory is more firmly held in place by reducing the variables that matter to it. Again, reducing degrees of freedom is possible by firm embedding in a recursive and redundant system of relationships. The longer this happens undisturbed, the more natural and obvious the status of core nodes, relations, and outcomes.

Core Protection

Buffer zones between cores and peripheries protect the core from insults to its integrity and identity. Organizations, for example, protect their cores through a variety of mechanisms and precautions, including stockpiling and various redundancies (Thompson 1967:20). The cores of theories are protected by ad hoc strategies, ceteris paribus clauses, and robust idealizations (Cartwright 1983). In groups, cores contain the sacred objects, rituals, and totems of the group, whose strength varies with the hold a group has on itself and its members. Here, taboos accomplish much core protection.

Buffer zones and walls around the core of a cultural network need net-work; they must be serviced, maintained, and repaired. One way of accomplishing this is through the taylorization and standardization of inputs. Initiation rites do this for groups; they deconstruct and reconstruct novices to make them fit into collective identity. Buffers and walls inspect the instruments and materials that a culture uses in its core. This core cannot handle raw or unstructured complexity, only preprocessed and packaged standard tools, materials, and substances.

Core Changes

One operational criterion for network location is degrees of resistance to change. Moving closer to the core, this resistance increases. Cores remain compact and self-similar longer than do other structures of a network. They still change and adjust to some surprises, but not to major ones, those that seem to suggest a totally different world. Major surprises seem unthinkable inside the core. Exceptions, contradictions, and unexplained events remain, but they do not challenge the structural integrity of the core's institutions. Cores are very confident and realist, especially when they are the only cores in the network, and especially when this network is very authoritative itself. In more decentralized and pluralistic networks, with more and mutually competitive cores, there is less realism, and this realism is more pragmatic than ontological.

The chances are that when a core does change, it collapses altogether; this happens in revolutions. But the prophets and ideologues of revolutions tend to exaggerate incommensurability and breaks in continuity. The older cultures and networks may persist in some way, even after the revolution. In any case, cores do not change as much as they just fall apart—under a very massive blow from outside, for example, or from another core. Core dissolution is more likely still when several such blows strike at several strategic locations at the same time, leading to multiple and interacting system failures, or "normal accidents." Apparently, this is the scenario for state breakdowns; these are fed by multiple interacting failures, including fiscal crises, conflicts among the elite, military defeat, and the collapse of central taxation (Skocpol 1979:chap. 1).

In less dramatic cases, a core might also be invaded from outside, say by an imperialist network and culture. This is the scenario in empirical episodes of actual scientific reduction, for example, when one specialty is wholly conquered and absorbed into an expanding one (Spear 1999). Some corporate mergers and takeovers may also belong to that scenario, although complete mergers are probably rarer than a more or less tense alliance.

The most surprisingly stable and resistant core is probably that of common sense, the natural attitude, or the everyday lifeworld. To repeat, there are many problems with these concepts, such as extension, but if there is such a thing as common sense, then it has remained fairly unchanged since Aristotle. This common sense is not what is believed, but how it is believed, whatever the content. This "how" is essences and natural kinds. Common sense is the world as it appears, in whatever concrete form it does so. Certainty in appearance, or in the belief that this world is the real world, separates the "spirit" of common sense from the "spirit" of a modern science (Bachelard [1934] 1984:30), although it should be added that no science can do without its *own* common sense—as and at the core of its own networks.

The core is the common sense of a network, its hows and modes. When a more peripheral segment decays, the resulting effects remain more local, while core changes ripple through the entire structure. In structural terms, cores have high betweenness, degree, and range (Freeman [1978] 1979): To get from any one point in a network to any other one, core positions and locations must likely be passed through, since they have strong centrality. Peripheral sectors are also anchored in cores; from there, they draw their "ultimate" institutional support and justification. Probing and questioning a peripheral element of a culture, this element will trace its links farther and farther into the core, depending on how stubbornly the attempt at deconstruction persists.

Cores might also decay from overextension or stagnation, thereby turning success into failure. As a core swallows larger and larger parts of the network, this network no longer generates interesting, or non-routine, puzzles. Its nodes and links become brittle with age, and the entire structure "freezes" in the winter of a dying civilization (Spengler [1923] 1993:145).

CHAPTER 7

Realism Explained

In the philosophical tradition, the problem of realism has to do with the ontological referents of abstract concepts or theoretical entities. Do they exist or not? Does "car" have a referent, or is it only a word? What about the ontological status of numbers and mathematics? In much of medieval philosophy, realism's opposite was nominalism, or the doctrine that only particulars exist, but not abstract universals or general categories. In nominalism, universals are nothing more than *flatus vocis,* hollow sounds of speech, or just "names." One cannot confirm them by any of the senses and in this sense they are not "real."

In more modern times, one rival of realism has become positivism, which is skeptical about the existence of referents for theoretical terms or constructs. In positivism, and also in instrumentalism and conventionalism, theories might economize on explanation and description costs, but they do not refer to anything "real," at least not in the same way as statements about particular observations do. Rather, theories are more or less convenient labels to organize and "save" the experiences. The only way for theoretical and abstract entities to acquire a measure of actual reality and empirical existence is by a series of careful inductive steps, from basic observations "up" to more general notions. This was "logical" positivism, which found its most ambitious version in Carnap. But largely due to Popper's ([1934] 1976:4–5) and Goodman's (1983:72–81) critiques, much skepticism now also extends to systems of inductive logic since, simply put, one never knows when to stop counting and observing, and start generalizing. Are ten white swans enough to venture that all swans are white, or a thousand, or millions? According to which rule or algorithm?

As with realism, there is no consistent philosophical doctrine of "skepticism" either (Frede 1979:102). In fact, some skepticisms hold that the very idea of "consistent philosophical doctrine" is a chimera. One commonality, however, is withholding judgment about invisible properties and things in themselves. Traditional skepticist themes include the thing in itself, the possibility of knowing other minds, the justifiability of induction, and the reality of the past (Strawson 1985:2–3). As a rule, skeptics do not deny that we can ever know anything, but certainty is unattainable except, maybe, in common sense (Ayer [1956] 1990:chap. 2). Skeptics are less skeptical about belief itself, but more skeptical when it comes to strong reasons and justifications for why we believe what we do.

There are various degrees of skepticist radicalness. For example, there is a moderate or "mitigated" skepticism that pervades philosophical justifications of the Scientific Revolution, as in Mersenne or Gassendi, or Chillingsworth and Tillotson (Shapiro 1983:26; Dear 1984:190–193; van Leeuwen 1963:chap. 2). In a gesture of demarcation and distinction, this probabilistic sort of skepticism extends primarily to metaphysics and religion. It does not go very far or deep, and is perfectly compatible with advances in natural philosophy or experimental science. Two more contemporary versions of mitigated skepticism are Popperian falsificationism and Quine's naturalism.

A more radical skepticism can be found in postmodernism, for example, where the very idea or possibility of representation is doubted, regardless of what these representations claim to represent. This sort of skepticism has affinities with relativism. It is antifoundational, up to the point of anarchism. Skeptical or constructivist networks emphasize context, locale, history, and the constructive operations of a particular observer (Douglas 1985:19). Constructivist cultures have many insides and outsides, with multiple and more or less equal observers, who can only see what they can see from their particular position and location. Constructivist observing is democratic and pluralist; realist observing is hierarchical and exclusive. Constructivist observing admits many observers, while realist observing admits only one observer, one who transcends variation and time. Realist and transcendental observers remain invisible while, in constructivism, there is much doubt about truth, reference, and universals.

Frequently, the realism / skepticism controversy is mapped onto the great divide between the Two Cultures. Philosophers are, by and large, less skeptical when it comes to physics or biology than when sociology or history are considered. Philosophers are willing to grant realism wholesale to particles or genes, or whatever entities natural science posits, but remain skeptical about the independent reality of things social. Realism is the preferred philosophical explanation for the "success" of modern science—it works because it is true, and we know it is true because it works. When it comes to things social, the usual reason offered for skepticism is that things social are "obviously" constructed, while natural science discovers things as they really are, without any constructive operations. Since philosophers have no unique way to assess the objective reality of natural things, however, their realism about physics or biology amounts to little more than a gesture of respect and deference to these sciences.

Sociology does not join this apologetic ritual of affirmation, but reconsiders the entire division between the Two Cultures. The problem of realism cuts across the social / natural dichotomy. The fact that, by and large, physics runs into less opposition to realism about itself is just that—an empirical or contingent fact, not a deep or universal ontological necessity. Expect realist cultures to emerge whenever certain social structures are in place, regardless of ontology and the referential niche of the cultures considered. There is realism in Greek tragedy, in natural law, and in state socialist art. There is more realism to surveys than to textually reflexive ethnographies, and more realism to normal science than controversial science. Platonism is realist about universal ideas, while modern philosophical realism is realist about particles, forces, and DNA. Likewise, there is more positivist skepticism about radical innovations in cosmological theory, but less skepticism when it comes to the reality of persons.

Regardless of the particular items that cultures might be realist about, these variations do not reflect ontology, but social structure. Cultures can be realist or skepticist about many different things, and they can be realist or skepticist to varying degrees. The underlying commonality of realism and skepticism is not content, but the mode of attribution of content, which I argue depends on observers in the social structure—that is, on encounters, groups, organizations, and networks. This assumes, however, that social structure is real, although there is no consensus on this point in sociology at large.

In any case, I am not interested in the philosophical problem of realism, nor will I offer any solutions to the "general problem" of representation or correspondence associated with it. There do not seem to be any "general problems" with knowledge as such, except for those posed by philosophers, who have not "solved" any of them, despite centuries of effort. Rather, a problem with knowledge exists only for a particular culture or observer, at a particular time, when they run into contradictions, anomalies, exceptions, and puzzles that they cannot solve for now, given their present states, tools, and abilities (Dewey 1970:32). When this happens, however, a culture does not search for philosophical solutions, but is content with pragmatic and local adjustments or modifications. No culture ceases its work altogether because it cannot solve general problems with representation. It does not face such general problems and difficulties, only its own problems and difficulties, and these do not get solved as the result of philosophical methods or analyses.

Much of what follows, then, is premised on the suspicion that the philosophical problem of realism is a pseudo-problem and cannot be solved by general or epistemological means. Despite postmodern caricatures of positivism, this suspicion actually goes back to the Vienna Circle (Carnap [1928] 1961:326; Schlick 1938:115). Carnap's (1956:207) later framework relativism distinguishes between "internal" and "external" realism; in internal realism, "to recognize something as a real thing or event means to succeed in incorporating it into the system of things at a particular space-time position so that it fits together with the other things recognized as real, according to the rules of the framework." In contrast, external realism is metaphysical and irresolvable speculation about things in themselves.

In what follows, "realism" means externalization and attribution of a network's outcomes not to the network, but to the world itself, or that part of the world which constitutes the network's referential niche. In terms of the theory of observers, realist cultures curb or prohibit second-order observing. The major empirical puzzle is when and why realism is more or less likely to happen. "Realism" is operationalized as something that can vary, so that some cultures are expected to be more realist than others. This includes variations in a culture over time; the consolidation of a network as it ages might produce more realistic confidence than the beginning phases of a young network about to be formed.

Expect, then, a continuum of externalization. Some cultures will have a great deal of confidence in the ontological reality of their constructs, up to the point where these are no longer seen as "constructs" at all, but as the way the world is, always has been, and always will be. Other cultures will be less sure that their outcomes map the actual fabric of the world and will attribute them more to themselves—to their activities, behaviors, and modes of observation. Still other cultures will subscribe to an even more radically reflexive constructivism, questioning the very idea of a reality out there, or the very possibility of correspondence and representation.

Instead of treating realism as an either / or option, as something that "knowledge as such" either has or does not have (to be decided in philosophy), a sociological theory of realism allows for variation, and explains this variation as the result of corresponding variations in networks and social structures. Variation does not solve, but dis-solves, realism as a problem in epistemology. Sociologically, it is not that some terms of a culture, say observations of particulars, can correspond to reality, while other terms, say theoretical entities, do not, and cannot ever correspond, for intrinsic reasons. Sociologically, we cannot divide a culture, or a set of cultures, into items that are real and items that are not. Only a culture itself can do this, but it is not up to sociology to decide whether anything in a culture other than its own corresponds to reality or not. For this decision would entail practicing such a culture, instead of doing sociology.

At this point, a paradox emerges. If sociology explains realism and skepticism as dependent variables, are its own observations realist or constructivist? That depends on the structure of its own networks. At present, these networks are very fragmented, multicultural, and perspectivist; such loose coupling makes the observer highly visible, since there are many such observers, separated by gaping structural holes. Such conditions make realism less likely. In a minimal sense, however, even constructivism makes some realist assumptions—for example, that networks, observers, and constructs actually "exist." But they exist only weakly, amid much controversy and uncertainty.

Sociology is neither constructivist nor realist but, given its currently fragmented state, uses constructivism to explain both constructivism and realism as cultural outcomes of networks. That is, it explains when constructs appear as such, as constructs, and when they appear unconstructed—for the networks and cultures that do the constructing.

A Continuum of Realism

"Realist" are networks and observers, or areas in networks, that have managed to render themselves invisible, for themselves and possibly for other observers as well. It is critical to remember that networks and cultures are not of one piece, so that realism and skepticism can coexist within one overall network, and can also vary in degree.

For purposes of illustration, I will ignore these variations for now and describe realism and its opposites in their extremes. Realist networks externalize their outcomes, attributing them to the order of things in themselves. They cannot imagine a world in which their universal truth is not true, or they fear such worlds as barbarian threats to culturedness itself. Realism is comparatively static and constant. It can change, but does so by completing itself into more and more "perfection" (Panofsky 1951:44–45). Realist networks, or realist clusters within networks, allow little or no variation between observers and over time, and make these observers more or less invisible. Authors of realist textbooks in normal science withdraw behind the observations that they repeat, reaffirm, and consolidate through exercises. They step aside to let the truth speak for itself. In contrast, the observers behind major breakthroughs in innovative science are much more visible as agents and authors. They are celebrated and credited with vision and creativity.

Realist observers are passive receptacles or mirrors of an independent reality. They have little or no "agency," and whatever agency they do retain is discouraged as vanity, idle temptation, bias, or systematic error. Therefore, any remaining agency effects on culture must be controlled, accounted for, or eradicated. Observers in a realist culture do what seems, to them, to come "naturally"; they move through the network with ease and confidence in arriving back home, where the foundational and basic truths wait to be confirmed and affirmed yet again, regardless of which particular path is chosen. Otherwise, an observer has just made a mistake, maybe under the influence of sin, impropriety, or a fall from grace. But there can be no major and persistent surprises or anomalies imagined as shaking these very foundations. The minor surprises that do still occur will, eventually, turn out to conform to the first principles as well.

To a large extent, the observers in a realist network are interchangeable once they have acquired their status as "official" observers. They have little or no autonomy and independence. Their identity is firmly enclosed within the institutions that make them the observers they are in the first place. They are not creators of culture, but its faithful servants, commentators, or loyal guardians. Observers disappear behind realism into an invisibility and anonymity. They might still be recognized and identified, but any reputation they do have is derived from the sacred founding fathers in whose name they speak, not from their originality or creativity. The culture itself is just there; it may have a beginning, but no end, and is part of an eternal cosmological order. Therefore, there is also no location outside the network from which this network could be observed as a "fact," as one culture among others, or as an empirical phenomenon. That is, realist cultures are also transcendental and a priori.

Realist cultures are presentist about pasts and futures. The more recent past appears as an incomplete version of the present, and the future is a gradual extension and completion of what has already been achieved. In the more distant past lies the glorious origin of the Truth that needs to be recovered, preserved, and remembered. The ontological security provided by realism has emotional dimensions as well, since spiritual comfort comes from being convinced and assured that there is just one right order, this order, and it must not be upset. Fear and anxiety result from interruptions and cracks in this order. Garfinkel (1967:55) has shown how panic spreads from disruptions in the taken-for-granted certainties of commonsense observers. Gehlen ([1956] 1964:43) traces the "grand peur" during the French Revolution to a collapse of institutions.

In Ward's (1990:143) terms, realist cultures develop a "logical," as opposed to "rhetorical," mode of operation. A strong emphasis on logic, codification, and consistent conceptual closure with "minimal authorial self-reference" is the mark of secure institutional embedding. Meaning is more likely literal than figurative or metaphorical. When meaning becomes "purely symbolic," dissociated from things and objects, a "rhetorical" mode emerges, signaling much weaker authority.

Likewise, Turner (1974:54–55) contrasts two modes of making culture, the "orderly" (or realist) and the "liminal" (or constructivist). The first mode employs formal analysis, which treats cultural relations as rule-driven, atemporal, and synchronic. Logic is rigorous and un-compromising in its insistence on method and procedure. It is also in-different to who, specifically, offers reasons and makes arguments ac-cording to its universal rules. "Liminal" modes of culture, in contrast, value creativity and discretion more than systematic closure and axi-omatic completion of a coherent system.

Contrast realism with its opposites on the underlying continuum of variation. "Skepticist" or "constructivist" networks are those that attrib-ute cultural outcomes more to their own behaviors and operations, not to the world at large. They promote reflexive self-observation and ideological critique or debunking and deconstruction. They allow for multiple observers and more possible worlds, making their own con-structions more visible as constructions, as something that could as well be done otherwise, or not at all. The multiple observers in loosely coupled networks start observing from different locations and come up with different outcomes as well, separated by wide and deep struc-tural holes in the fabric of culture. Various degrees of "incommen-surability" result—between what come to be seen as practices, forms of life, perspectives, and standpoints. These constructs bear the stamp of origin, context, and locale. One can tell where they came from, how they were accomplished, and which particular perspective biases these observations. Constructivist networks and cultures have a relativist his-torical eye for other cultures and themselves. They are less serious and confident, and more ironic or playful.

In some skepticism, representations lose their innocence and be-come suspicious, since they have something to hide—the standpoints, locations, and interests of their observers. One task of interpretation is now to uncover the boundedness and localism of all interpretations, none of which is privileged, superior, or exempt from ideology. While the Marxist critique of ideology is still realist about Marxism, the soci-ology of knowledge gradually turns reflexive and applies its construc-tivism to itself as well, abandoning any privileged exemption from con-struction. The culture "refers"—back to itself, not to the world of facts, objects, and things in themselves. "Meaning" comes not from things, but from other words and texts, arrayed and related to each other in loose discourse, narrative, and semiotics. Semantic ambiguity and in-terpretive flexibility become the network's mode of operation. In sum, and in the extreme, when skepticist networks observe themselves, they perceive variable constructions, driven by local ideologies, interests, and biases. When realist networks observe themselves, they see the gradual unfolding or recovery of an eternal and external truth that always shines.

Core Expansions and Time

All other things being equal, a culture becomes more realist as the core of its networks expands, growing disproportionately larger and faster than noncore areas. One empirical indication for this pattern is the growth curves that Mullins (1973) has observed for scientific specialties, curves that show gradual consolidation into normality and routine. Recall that cores house institutions and invisibilities, or the established foundations of a network, where the network does what comes "naturally" to it. Realism tends to increase further when an expanding core is very redundant, closely coupled, and complete, so that there are few, if any, holes and uncharted territory. Realist cultures accomplish high degrees of self-similarity and coherence. They are rather complete and closed. They expect the rest of the world, including pasts and futures, to be similar to themselves.

Self-similarity and institutionalization take time. They are outcomes of a network and its recursive operations, feeding its previous results into further work. Self-similarity and coherence are gradual outcomes of iterated recursivity. Networks go to work on the outcomes and results of their previous operations. Upon doing this for a while, they build up a world and history. When the network is left "undisturbed" for some time, it consolidates parts of itself into firmer institutions, which are then mapped onto the very fabric of the world, as it "really" is.

It is possible that cores grow to the point where they swallow much of the entire network, including its more restless, turbulent, or innovative parts. When this happens, there is little or no more opportunity for cultural turnover and change. The velocity of the network decreases, and time seems to slow down. The observer remains in place and stationary for a long time, and with him stay the culture's horizons. The longer a horizon remains in the same place, limiting and bounding the field of vision where it does, the more does that horizon appear observer-independent altogether, seemingly marking the very boundaries of the world itself.

Such networks tend to conserve cultural traditions; they look backward through time, longing to return home to sacred and ancient origins. With Spengler ([1923] 1993:43), such networks arrive at the "winter" of a culture. A network at this stage has completed its edifice and is now completely exhausted. There are no further fresh starts and departures. The network cannot excite itself into activity anymore. No pressures from inside or outside the network stimulate the culture into creativity. There is nothing much left to do except continue to preserve that which has already been accomplished. Stagnation and backwardness settle in, and weariness. The culture ossifies and tires of itself, up to the point of nihilism. Cultures about to die of old age might reach a point where the realism and confidence of an earlier period of expansion and consolidation give way to a senile longing for death.

Realism is the result of success; nihilism results from too much success. Success breeds realism, and realism justifies it philosophically, that is, not as the result of an empirical or contingent climb to superiority, but as a culture being in close touch with the Truth. Successful and expanding cultures are realist about themselves, and reductionist about the cultures that they invade or conquer. Frequently, reduction and expansion are driven by successful tools, instruments, and devices; to a large part, it is their machines that are driving the current expansion of the neurosciences (Spear 1999). Tools for imaging and computing the brain are what philosophers of mind, for example, lack, and so the philosophers have very little that measures up to the accomplishments of neuroscience. Philosophers can only talk and write about the brain, while neuroscience can map and manipulate it.

Reductionism is the by-product of an expanding and confident realism. The expanding culture deems itself "real," while the cultures targeted for invasion appear secondary and derivative, without any independent or foundational status. The higher a culture is positioned in a hierarchy among cultures, the more confident it is about the realism of its First Principles, and its abilities to do everything better than the cultures below it. Conversely, lower-status cultures tend to negate or deconstruct themselves. They have little confidence in their facts and theories. Sometimes, they may be left with little than admiration and imitation of the top. Camic (1992:211) traces the early history of American psychology to the high status of Darwinism and experimental physiology.

All other things being equal, very young networks are more turbulent and uncertain. At any time, they are as likely, or more likely, to disband than to continue. Much like new firms or movements, most new specialties probably never take off, and disappear before they can make a difference. They have not had much time to consolidate their accomplishments through close coupling and redundancy. Young networks have small and weak cores, particularly when they are not spin-offs from already existing networks. They have fragile identities and are not sure about their nodes and relations. Young networks are in flux, subject to frequent recombinations of nodes and relations. They cannot rely on a long and continuous history of accomplishments and successes. Young networks are liable and centrifugal. They have not yet settled into default or routine modes of operation, and they admit more possibilities and alternatives.

If there are any subsequent generations, however, these will receive a network or cultural core more as established fact; they attribute more realism to it than was present at the time of inception (Berger and Luckman 1967). Those who arrive later see what is there, take some of it as given and for granted, and start from these premises. As time passes and others repeat what has been done before, traditions "sediment." Hanson ([1958] 1969:98) shows how this occurred for Newtonian mechanics: "In 1687 the law of inertia was apparently nothing but an empirical extrapolation; but in 1894 it functioned mostly in an *a priori* way." Duhem ([1906] 1991:24–27) argues, in the same direction, that two factors are crucial for producing realism about theory: a theory must be "completed" by making it internally consistent and orderly, and time must pass. The more this happens, the more we "apprehend that the logical order in which theory orders experimental laws is the reflection of an ontological order, the more we suspect that the relations it establishes among the data of observation correspond to real relations among things, and the more we feel that theory tends to be a natural classification" (pp. 26–27). One might summarize this transition in the formula realism = positivism + time.

Accomplishing a degree of realism and transcendence takes work and time, much as it takes time to make official statistics converge on the same numbers in the various heterogeneous and dissimilar provinces of an emerging national state, and just as it takes time to make a measure standard and uniform beyond the setting and occasion in which it was originally conceived and introduced. Since everything that exists starts out locally and at a particular point in time, practical or innerworldly transcendence requires separating numbers and measures from their original contexts and circumstances. Wise (1995:98) notices that the uniformity of standards and measures depends "on the existence of large numbers of travellers." Hence the importance of net-work, of forging relationships that reach into the surroundings so that something that used to matter *here* now matters *there* as well. Otherwise, an event remains just this—an event, gone when it is over.

Such extensions do not happen by themselves, or overnight. They do not fall from the sky, or follow from the intrinsic and essential rationality or superiority of the expanding culture, although rational reconstructions explain extensions in this way with the benefit of hindsight. Neither are successful extensions immune to subsequent failures and reversals of extension. There always remains the possibility of refeudalization and decentering. Empires collapse, as do systems of transportation, communication, and mathematics. Some empires collapse so quickly and readily that doubts emerge as to how stable, strong, integrated, and imperial they were to begin with (for example, Odom 1998:390–392).

Machines

Ceteris paribus, realism clusters and coalesces around working machines and routine technologies of various kinds. There is a family resemblance between bureaucracies, machines, Quine-cores, and rituals in that they contain and constrain many degrees of freedom by firm embeddings and "caging." Realism increases as degrees of freedom decrease. When cages operate in their routine or default modes, they tame alternative interpretations, discretion, and interpretive flexibility.

Machines are cages that wire operations into their hardware. To a great extent, they isolate and insulate their inner workings against variations in materials, personnel, or circumstance of operation. The output of a machine can then be attributed to the machine itself, not to actors or subjective discretion (Daston and Galison 1992:83). The "ethos" of the scientific machine is a "mechanical objectivity" that reduces variations between observers by rendering them replaceable and interchangeable (Daston 1995:19–22; Swijtink 1987:267). Machines work when the number of operative variables that might affect an outcome is low; for example, by standardizing or randomizing that which is fed into the machine as "input." The working of a machine depends on the networks around it; sever the ties in this network, and the machine does nothing. A working machine is usually part of a larger network, which contains links among machines, materials, sites, and organizations. These links are not just "technical," in the narrower sense of the term, but also social and organizational. Cut off any set of these links, remove the machine from the organization in which it is housed, and chances are the machine can no longer do what it did before.

As part of a network, a machine becomes more insensitive to differences in context, locale, or situation, and generates highly self-similar, coherent, and repetitive outcomes across a variety of settings and occasions. Repetition is important for realism, especially repetition across various sites and times (Heilbron 1993:15–16; Griffith and Miller 1970:129). Bureaucracies work in much the same way in that their performance is decoupled from accidental and contingent variations. Bureaucracies can communicate with each other so well because they ignore most things that might matter—they simplify and standardize their constructions and representations of the world around them. A powerful ritual is powerful precisely because it focuses the attention of the group on itself, and thereby reduces personal discretion and attention to other things.

Once a machine is in place, it tends to "machinate" its surroundings as well, since a machine can handle only that which is, or is made, machine-compatible. Moralism observes machination as "alienation"; the workers are absorbed by the rhythm of the machine and become its "appendices." Machines, much as rituals, do have their own "rhythms," which draw that which is close to them into their own performance and modes of operation. In this way, degrees of freedom are constrained and a performance consolidates, or becomes "real." Machines no longer work, or work well, when they are removed from the familiar ecology of related machines, materials, and inputs. A car travels well on a paved road with gas stations and repair shops.

To get a new and unfamiliar machine to work, it helps to have some machines in place already, to which the newcomer can be linked. In this way, a new, unfamiliar, and erratic machine loses some of its degrees of freedom. It becomes connected and embedded in the network of machines that have already been tamed and domesticated. Recall that it is the connections, and the patterns among connections, that reduce a node's degrees of freedom. Link several unfamiliar and erratic machines to each other, however, and observe an increase in complexity through interaction effects and breakdowns, rather than increased outcome predictability and uniformity.

Caging takes time and is not irreversible. Major accidents and disasters reveal this; they are caged complexity bursting out of its cage. Accidents happen even with seemingly well-understood technologies, such as aircraft, and they often result from nonlinearity and higher-order interaction effects. Strong and catastrophic effects from outside can trigger such accidents as well; an example is the military defeat of states, which can trigger state breakdowns and revolutions. "Normal" accidents are generated in highly complex and closely coupled technosystems.

When a core contains black boxes and routine machines or technologies, the network is anchored and held together not just by words, symbols, and conventions, but also by material things and tangible objects. These are the tools of Kuhnian normal science. While they are being used as resources, tools remain unproblematic, although they might be problematic in another context, or at another time. Tangible tools make little room for skepticism, especially when they generate rather predictable and uniform outcomes across a variety of settings, occasions, times, or operating personnel. To produce such similar outcomes on repeated occasions, regardless of personnel, locale, or circumstance, a culture requires stability in its nodes and relations. Realism comes from mutual consolidation of the nodes and relations in a network, which are trained, tamed, and orchestrated into convergent self-similarity and coherence.

What makes a culture "hard" and realist, rather than "soft" and constructivist, is hardware, among other things. Bennett (1992:2, 13) shows that astronomy turned into a hard science when, in the eighteenth century, institutional observatories across Europe were linked into an extensive network that circulated standard astronomical instruments in large batches of routine equipment. When a culture contains mostly texts, its mode of construction is more likely conversational and discursive. All other things being equal, in textual cultures there is little or nothing beyond texts and their authors, whereas cultures with hardware also have equipment and apparatus, in addition to texts. When pushed to do so, hard cultures can ground texts in things, in materials and objects, which give the text some ontological security. Textual cultures can only point at further levels and networks of texts, including the networks among authors, commentary, criticism, and exegesis.

Frequently, black boxes are produced in large batches with little variation between units. When the materials and tools are very standardized, cultural outcomes can be produced and reproduced with a great deal of regularity and certainty, across various settings and times. Such standardized materials and tools are prominently used in instructional or demonstrational contexts, when the network repeats and affirms its central accomplishments, maybe in an effort at socializing novices and training future generations. In such contexts, a culture has achieved greater control over the conditions for producing its core results and achievements. There is much repetition and drill here, with little or no room for surprises. The surprises that do occur tend to be attributed to accidents and contingent circumstances, such as incompetence or inexperience, not to any faults in normal science as such. As we have seen from organizations, very unusual and promising exceptions and surprises might be delegated "upward" to high-status specialists in exceptions.

Novel instruments and machines, in contrast, are less well known and harder to tame. They travel less well across contexts and are more sensitive to variations in inputs, connections, and personnel. "Bugs" make them erratic, and it takes time and work to get rid of the bugs. Novel machines, tools, or programs are not yet well connected to machines, tools, and programs that are already there, more firmly in their place. Closure and consolidation settle in as a machine or tool becomes more and more densely connected to the other nodes and relations in the network. Then the machines and tools acquire a more robust identity, which comes from firm embeddedness in a network of relations. But in the beginning, a novel tool or instrument is not yet caged and domesticated by its relations to the already working parts of a culture.

A culture feels more confident about itself when it is at home, in its familiar settings, performing routine work with familiar outcomes. For the academic cultures, this happens in the visible colleges of lecture halls, classrooms, and teaching labs (Berger 1995:82). Away from home, a culture has less control over the conditions that make it successful. It enters separate and different networks, where different things matter, and things matter in different ways. Lacking its familiar territory and material ecology, a culture has more trouble recreating its central results and outcomes.

Successful network expansion is by no means certain or given. Outside of its origins and home, a culture is no longer playing on its own field, and on its own terms. This also happened when Pasteurian laboratory science first moved into the farms in the French countryside (Latour 1988).

Instruction

One cannot socialize persons into a "language game" while teaching at the same time that the game is not really real. Talk of "language games" suggests a degree of skepticist erosion and ironic withdrawal. "Irony" about cultures flourishes in positions with considerable structural autonomy from routines, mass instruction, and normal science. Ironists prosper in positions affording much individualist discretion, as happens in conversational and essayistic fields with little closure and consolidation on core accomplishments. Irony is not at home around textbooks, demonstration experiments, or multiple-choice exams. It is the attitude of removed and detached elite virtuosity. But the registrar's office is not equipped to handle much irony or reflexivity. There it is assumed that the matter tested is closed and adequately measured in grades and numbers. Realism prospers in, and around, the core of a bureaucratic apparatus.

Tendencies toward realism get stronger as the numbers increase, whereas fewer participants in private and expensive liberal arts education encourage more discretion and individualism. Teaching and grading large numbers of students in standard examinations is more constrained by bureaucratic formulas and administrative requirements. At this level, doctrine and dogma receive strong and uncompromising institutional support from the organization, which relies on routines, and routinized inputs, to do its own work. A bureaucracy is variably indifferent to the exit and entry of the personnel who enforce it. Rather than discretion and creativity, it is concerned about standardization, quantification, and repetitiveness.

To some extent, instruction is also hierarchical, reducing the opportunities for innovation and dissent further while, at the same time, increasing confidence in realism. Dear (1992:628) traces the pragmatic skepticism in philosophies of the Scientific Revolution to the dissolution of corporate hierarchy in the medieval universities. In the hierarchy, teachers and their assistants look over the shoulders of their students, checking whether they are doing it right. As a "grid," hierarchy contributes to the closure and rigidity of classifications. With a hierarchy firmly in place, the teachers are rarely, if ever, wrong. Through hierarchy, and the rituals of instruction and grading, normal culture connects with bureaucratic order-giving and rule enforcement.

Socialization produces more realism still, when it consists also of doing, rather than mere saying, or of a confluence and coemergence of saying exactly what one is doing, and vice versa. Demonstrations and rituals accomplish such confluence in a merging of words, worlds, and deeds. One does what one says one does and, by and large, the events predicted do actually happen. This magic increases the neophyte's confidence that reality is what is being demonstrated and ritually enacted.

Density

Normal or bureaucratic culture is more localistic and "high group." It is contained more in a local organization and is concerned more about intellectual administration. Workers in such cultures have less social and cultural capital than do those in the more cosmopolitan and extensive networks of innovative culture-in-the-making. The closer a culture, or one of its areas, is to bureaucratic and administrative routines, and the farther it is from the frontiers, the more it tends to support realism about its core institutions, practices, and instruments or technologies. Schneider (1997) links the emergence of literary realism to the institutional prominence of literature teachers in search of a method of interpretation. In marked contrast, elite professionals emphasize discretion and openness.

More localistic cultures enforce the formal structure. They have many facts and foundations, or large and redundant Quine-cores. They focus inward, on past achievements seen as in need of completion, systematization, and gradual extension. No major surprises are conceivable here, and it is not in localized networks that breakthroughs occur. According to the Durkheimian principles, these cultures respond to innovative and skeptical challenges by monster-barring, or by reaffirming the central certainties of dogma (Bloor 1983:142). Such cultures are suspicious of strangers and anomalies; they tend to protect cores against challenges and insults by means of buffering and renormalization.

At the frontiers of a culture, realism is likely more pragmatic and opportunistic than ontological or cosmological, as rapid advances and frequent turnovers make ultimate truths, final closure, and universal foundations unstable and changing. In fact, such foundations are an impediment to innovation, which is the most prestigious form of cultural capital here. It is at the frontiers that novel culture is being made, by high-status workers with extensive networks stretching beyond any local group or organization. These invisible colleges are more remote from bureaucratic settings and organizational routines, with uncertain extensions, shifting participation, and fluctuating boundaries.

This cultural elite prides itself on avant-garde virtuosity, "personal knowledge," and skills unavailable through formal training alone. In this culture, there is a disdain for quantification, standardization, and bureaucratic planning (Porter 1992a:28). Among this elite, we find "genius" and the mysteries of creativity, of not being able to tell how one gets one's ideas. In Weber's and Schneider's (1993:7) terms, innovative or avant-garde culture, as it is being made, is more charismatic and "enchanted" than ready-made or normal culture. The latter allows fewer agency effects, whereas novel culture attributes discoveries and breakthroughs to the unusual faculties and talents of extraordinary persons. Charismatic and enchanted culture is methodologically elusive about itself, whereas normal culture rationalizes and accounts for itself as rule-driven and methodical.

A similar difference appears in the opposition between "skill" and "method." The reliability of an observation depends either on the skills of an observer, or on a method of observation, such as least squares (Obesko 1995:114, 119). Skill is personal and elitist; method is more democratic, since it reduces discretion. For example, in least square techniques, the assumption is that all observations have equal status and reliability. In contrast, virtuosi claim, and grant each other, a special discretionary and personal "nose" or "hunch" for the great problems and their solutions.

Expect, then, more realism in groups closer to the formal structure, in lower-prestige areas that are concentrated around the material and symbolic means of intellectual administration—bureaucracies, textbooks, official instruction and examinations, or normal science. These are high-density groups with little social capital and few ties to the centers of innovation. The farther a position in a network is from where novel culture is actually being made, the more realism this position tends to attribute to culture (Collins 1981). Ossification and routinization occur at the network rims, while the innovative centers move forward. Fleck ([1935] 1979:108) notes that the most dedicated followers and believers in fashion are far removed from the centers where fashion is actually being made.

Monopoly and Hegemony

Monopolies are rarely so strong and solid that they exclude all competition and pluralism. The centrality of a state, or the universality of a Church, are, to some extent, local and restricted as well; they extend their rule and grip only as far as they do, and only until further notice. Nothing is fully transcendental. There are pockets of heresy, resistance, and dissent even in the strongest of organizational monopolies. In fact, institutional realism might increase as the result of conflict with rival positions and competing philosophies; it is a sociological commonplace that a common enemy tends to close the ranks of the faithful. Novick (1988:286) attributes the decline of relativism in the American historical profession to precisely this regularity. White and McCann (1988:392–394) also trace increases in the coherence of rival camps during the "oxygen revolution" to paradigmatic conflict.

Still, realism increases as a culture becomes the "official" culture of a dominant or hegemonic organization. Mannheim's ([1928] 1971:233–234) examples include the Chinese mandarin literati, Prussian civil service, military academies, and the golden age of high medieval scholasticism, before humanism, printing, and the Reformation. We might add orthodox and dogmatic Marxism under Stalin, when intellectuals and artists became official spokespersons for the party and could do little work apart from the state academies, short of going underground. In such situations, a more or less closed status group appropriates the means of the mind. The truth is the possession and privilege of this group. The truth does not have to be "found," really, but is always and already "had" by the group.

An elite's control over culture becomes even stronger when its members possess an exclusive ability to read and write, do so in an esoteric and nonvernacular language, or limit access to sacred texts. Observers are the more privileged the closer they are to the core of the political or clerical organization. Observers more remote from the core have a hard time escaping the force of its gravitational pull. There are few opportunities for culture outside of the official channels. The material means of cultural production are highly concentrated in the center or core, in a palace, temple, court, or party. To do any work at all one must be there, but the ways of getting there are very restricted, elitist, and closed to most. The means for deciding which cultures are illegitimate, dangerous, and to be eradicated are also concentrated in the core, backed up by a coercive apparatus. For Feyerabend (1987:11), realism and universalism are "leftover from times when important matters were run from a single center, a king or a jealous god, supporting and giving authority to a single world view."

The workers in such cultures tend to be servants of a state or church, drawing their livelihoods from the work they do for the organization. They have little autonomy and discretion, and no independent networks apart from the center or hegemonic organization. Their work is not innovation, but repetition and preservation.

An example comes from the sacred Cathedral schools of the Middle Ages, whose main business was instruction in the liturgical rituals (see Znaniecki [1940] 1975:96–100). Most philosophical material from this period is teaching material, or associated with official instruction in preparation for service. Even the staged disputations, which later drew much scorn from the advocates of experimental natural philosophy, proceed repetitively, through a fixed sequence of highly ritualized and standard rhetorical moves. Teaching is almost exclusively oral; the mnemonics of oral instruction give rise to "formulas, stock arguments, and standard moves" that facilitate remembering and repeating (Kenny and Pinborg 1982:17). The actual teaching proceeds by explicating the true meaning of an authoritative text or commentary "line by line and word by word" (Grafton 1992:23). The true meaning is already there in the authoritative text, waiting to be affirmed once again, with predictable results. Often a canonical text is surrounded on the page by its official commentary, whose main mode of demonstration is the formal syllogism, with outcomes logically implied in the premises (Dear 1985:148). Any remaining contradictions or inconsistencies are smoothed over by the textual techniques of metaphor and analogy. Such are the cultural technologies of strong realism: completion and affirmation within a highly redundant and firmly institutionalized network, mapped onto the order of the cosmos itself.

Textual cultures, then, are not in themselves, or by necessity, constructivist or skepticist. When texts are largely contained within an organizational monopoly, such as a church, reading and writing are also part of the organization and are backed up by its apparatus, authority, and traditions. The monopoly might protect its exclusive cultural possessions by means of secrecy, arcana, and esoteric language, accessible only to a few select initiates (Eamon 1985:325). Readers or writers of such esoteric texts have little interpretive leeway. They write commentaries on authoritative or sacred scriptures, and instruct novices in the proper understanding and appreciation of the classics: "The monks did not observe and discover, but remembered and participated in an oral tradition bound by religious law" (Troll 1990:114).

Frequently, workers in realist cultures are copyists rather than authors, constrained within a strict organizational or liturgical regimen. To change that which is being copied is considered vain, frivolous, or sinful (Drogin 1983:12). The copyists' reading is not a solitary communication with distant others, but the oral and manual exercise of a craft, carried out under close surveillance by the authorities. The Church owns all or most books; to get to the library, one must pass through the church and its officials first. Clerics monopolize literacy, and there is no or little room outside the church for reading and writing. "Knowledge" is the "spiritual property of a sacred school" (Znaniecki [1940] 1975:100). Under these constraints, textual cultures move toward realism as well. Textual cultures are more constructivist when they reside in fragmented networks.

When the work of political or clerical servants of a state or church contains much formal and official instruction and examination, maybe in preparation for official service, realism increases further, since instruction and examination discipline a culture into repetition and predictability, especially when the numbers get larger, and testing becomes more standardized and large batch (DeWulf 1922:159). Bureaucratic rituals of instruction and examination constrain a culture into repeating and confirming its core institutions. Under these circumstances, cultural work is, to a large part, intellectual administration, or completion and codification of an already "perfect" edifice. There might still be scattered and isolated virtuosi engaged in making, rather than teaching, culture, but their independence decreases with closeness to the core, especially when they are separated from other such virtuosos.

Competition and Decentralization

Realism decreases when multiple and decentral cultures and networks compete against each other. Honigsheim (1923:175–187, esp. 185–187) explains the Franciscan nominalism from Duns Scotus to Occam as the result of a breakdown in clerical monopoly over culture and philosophy. The very fact of competition drives home the point that there are many observers who can, and do, observe in terms of their own cultures or subcultures. Competition introduces the possibility of attributing observations to an observer, not to the world at large or to the referential niche that this observer observes (Bloor 1984:239). Attributions to observers can yield a measure of constructivism, maybe even ideological observing, where observations lose their innocence and become rooted in class position, interests, and hidden agendas. Once a culture is seen as the outcome of construction, that culture has a much harder time claiming realism. The sheer number of observers in competitive cultures makes it obvious that there are only empirical observers, who can only observe that which can be seen from where they are located. Collins (1998:101) notes that "Aristotle's contemporary Pyrrho took the disagreement of the schools as explicit warrant for relativism." Once observers arrive in large numbers, the number of observations increases as well and, with it, suspicion of transcendental or privileged observers: "Wasn't it this process of upward social mobility in Athenian democracy that triggered the first big wave of skepticism in the history of occidental thought?" (Mannheim [1929] 1969:10).

Sheer size is not the only factor, however. Much depends on whether society is more hierarchical and authoritarian than pluralistic and decentral. Lloyd (1996:24–40) compares astronomy, mathematics, and medicine in the Greco-Roman world, before Christianity, with China before the rise of Buddhism. More specifically, the contrast is between classical Greece and the Han Dynasty in China, after the period of Warring States, when Confucianism became the official ritual and religion of a centralized state. Lloyd sets in opposition two basic social structures and modes of cultural and intellectual production: in Greece, intellectual life comes closer to a competitive "market," while Chinese intellectual networks are focused and concentrated on a "temple." Greek intellectual production comes out of a variety of rival schools, academies, and masters, while intellectual outcomes in China are memorials and tributes to a throne. By and large, Chinese astronomers were official servants to the imperial astronomical bureau. Their reputations depended on closeness to the ruler or emperor, while the reputations of the Greek intellectuals were driven more by peers and pupils. Greek pupils generally paid for instruction, had no lifelong commitment to a particular school, and could move between different masters. In contrast, Chinese intellectual communities were patterned after religious sects, with unquestioned allegiance to a patrimonial authority. Here, the main mode of instruction was memorizing and reciting the *Jing*, which aimed at consolidation of orthodoxy. The Greek schools used lectures and public debates modeled after the adversarial exchanges in law courts and political assemblies, while Chinese intellectuals preserved and recovered the ancient wisdom from the Sage Kings. The result of monopoly is stagnation and uniformity; DiMaggio (1997:438) attributes periods of little creative ferment in music to high levels of market concentration.

Competition and pluralism drive intellectual work toward innovation, while monopolies restrict work to official service and intellectual administration of a state or church. Competition allows for more observers, and thus for the possibility of conflict and constructivist observing, where truth is not "possessed" by a central ruler from the beginning of time, but must be found in an adversarial process of trial and error.

The constructivism of many observers differs from the realism of one observer, or a privileged observer, but also from the more radical skepticism of fragmented observers in "anarchistic" cultures with extremely loose coupling. In very loosely coupled networks, little coherence and convergence can be obtained across observers, with the possible result of incommensurability and relativism. Then observations more or less completely, without rest, refer back to observers, not to what they observe. An extreme form of constructivism is radical standpoint epistemologies that question the very possibility of truth, objectivity, and coherence, or see these as vices rather than virtues.

Competition varies between the extremes of radical skepticist decentralization and full-blown realist monopoly. Both extremes are rare and unstable. Expect a normal curve, with most cultures falling somewhere between the extremes and changing their relative locations on the curve over time.

As independent networks of intellectuals develop outside the Church—for example, in the cities of the Italian and European Renaissance—the intellectuals begin to address each other, creating their own foci of attention (Hale 1977:32, 37–38). Kaelber (1998:129) confirms that many medieval heresies, including those promoted by Waldensians and Cathars, spread among urban civic strata more remote from the centers of clerical control. With growing independence and self-reference, and supported by independent means of cultural production, reputation begins to go to innovators, not curators, and reputation starts to be decided by peers, rather than political or clerical authorities. This takes conflict, and does not happen overnight. But hegemonic orthodoxy decreases as a result of increasing independence and self-reference of cultural networks, since such networks increase competition over innovation as the most desired source of cultural and reputational capital.

An example comes from the twelfth-century Renaissance, when migrant intellectual masters achieved a degree of independence from the established clerical and monastic institutions of learning and from preparation for official or religious service (Haskins 1957:28, 48, 302; Ward 1990:142, 151). The wandering masters had their own students and "schools," and they observed each other, gaining "professional" reputations that were less strongly linked to affiliations with hegemonic organizations. Migrating from location to location, the wandering masters were also "in between," not just "within," the established sites of culture.

In-betweenness and marginality breed dissent and skepticism in locations outside the established sites and institutions of truth. Ward (1990:151) observes that competition and the rise of literacy produced a great number of "marginal intellectuals" who could not be absorbed by the established institutions of learning, and so formed a satirical opposition to the canonical university establishment and its official regime of truth: "The antidiscourse of the nonestablishment intellectuals of the twelfth century, situated outside or on the margins of the developing nodes, centers, and institutions of truth and authority, is what we have come to know as 'humanism,' as the so-called 'Renaissance' feature of twelfth-century society" (p. 142). In the same vein, Stock (1984:16–17) attributes hereticism and reform in the twelfth century to novel "textual communities" that developed apart from the established Church. Likewise, Mizruchi (1983:2, 11) observes that skepticism tends to occur in "abeyance" processes—for example, when demographic growth exceeds the absorption and carrying capacity of established institutions and organizations. This creates marginal movements as temporary reservoirs for the unattached and floating surplus. A novel culture might emerge in these margins and interstices and, with it, a weakening of official dogma and orthodoxy might occur. Mulkay and Turner (1971) attribute skepticism and innovation to marginality as well; their examples include Islamic saints and French impressionistic painting.

Literacy and Printing

The controversy about the effects of literacy and printing on culture has oscillated between determinism and revisionism (Thomas 1992). In the deterministic account, literacy and printing cause large-scale and global changes, such as societal rationalization, state-building, and modernization. Literacy paves the way for the transition from small societies with oral cultures to empires and advanced civilization. Printing leads to the Renaissance, Reformation, and ultimately, the Scientific Revolution as well, since print emancipates culture from the stronghold of the church.

Revisionists counter that the effects of literacy and printing depend on other factors and cannot cause any global changes in culture, at least not by themselves. For a long time, literacy remained a tool and appendix to oral culture. It was concentrated among elites, and served magical and religious purposes. Likewise, printing changed culture only slowly, and only when interacting with other changes. At first, print simply meant that more copies of the old books were available.

The revisionist account seems more in line with the historical evidence, including research on the changes brought about by other technologies, such as household appliances, PCs, the telephone, or the Internet (Fischer 1992:5; Wellman and Gulia 1995). What a technology can do depends very much on what is actually done with it, and what is actually done with a technology usually differs from the original design purposes or engineering intentions. The effects of literacy and print on culture depend on social structure; for example, on the degree to which literacy and print are concentrated within an organizational or status group monopoly, or are introduced into more decentral and pluralistic networks. Literacy and printing are not magic wands, transforming society and culture by means of their intrinsic or essential forces. Rather, their effects depend on what is already there in society and culture, and what is already there decides whether, how, and how fast a new technology or tool generates changes. Therefore, literacy and print do different things to different societies and cultures, and their effects also depend on historical time. Further, expect any changes that do occur as the result of literacy and print to be local and gradual at first.

With these revisionist cautions in mind, what are the differences between oral and written communication, and then between preprint and print cultures (Ong 1982:42, 49; Havelock 1982:185–206, 1986:63–78; Eisenstein 1993:56)? Reading and writing increase the social and temporal distance over which communication can travel. Literacy increases the chances for communication to separate from copresence and encounters. In primarily oral cultures, communication is more restricted to the here and now of the spoken word, and documents and records are not used to help remember the past. Oral communication is firmly embedded in the location and situation where it happens. Speakers and listeners are there for each other to see and hear. They can use ostension and perception of something in the world, *this* world, which is here in the immediate surroundings of an encounter, to aid understanding. This world is given and present in the reality of the moment.

In written communication, the contexts and horizons of readers and writers begin to diverge, both socially and over time. Keep in mind, though, that this divergence is not an automatic or necessary consequence of literacy since, at first, many or most texts were probably read aloud to listeners, who were there when this happened. But literacy does increase the probability of abstracting communication from a shared setting or occasion. Readers and writers may not know each other, and may never encounter each other in the here and now of a shared context and setting. Reading and writing allow for communication in solitude; one can go back and forth in a text, read it again, and observe inconsistencies or contradictions. Authors can no longer expect and rely on their readers, if any, to live in the same world, at the same time, in the here and now of a shared location. Once a text is completed, maybe stored and circulated, an author loses control over how it is being read, as well as by whom, when, and in which context.

Authorial loss of control means increased discretion for readers. As a listener in a conversation, you cannot really avoid hearing that something is being said; you cannot deny that the speakers are here, in the flesh, and you also have a harder time denying that things exist in the world around you. The conversation can point and refer to these things. As a reader of a text, you cannot even be sure that the author actually exists or existed, that it is this author who actually wrote it, or that the text was written at a certain time and place. Thus, reading and writing introduce more abstractness and contingency into communication. There are increased possibilities for "misunderstanding"—that is, for interpreting a text in ways different from their authors *and* other readers. It is not just that readers may never encounter authors, but also that readers may never encounter each other.

Written communication, then, separates authors from readers, and readers from other readers, over larger social, cultural, and temporal distances. This increases the possibilities for disagreement and skepticism, compared to encounters, which are more realist about themselves. Encounters occur in the world as it actually happens around the encounter. But it is up to readers to understand what is written in their own way, because there are no authors, or other readers, present. Readers can observe that different readers understand a text differently, and they can expect that future readings of a text will place it in different contexts and horizons. To be sure, listeners can also understand what is being said in different ways, but conversations can react more readily and quickly to misunderstandings and interpretive divergence. Conversations focus attention more narrowly than reading on what is being talked about here and now. Unlike textual communication, they can observe disagreement "at once" and "repair" it, generating more convergence on meaning than can reading and writing.

With the introduction of the printing press, more texts, and copies of texts, became available. Much depends, however, on how many presses there are, who owns them, who decides what is being printed, and what is to be done with the printed texts. If printing is fully confined and contained within a monopoly, such as a state, party, or church, the organization becomes even more powerful and present, since it can now use printing in addition to its other tools to help multiply and disseminate official decrees and dogmas. In contrast, if there is a general market for printed materials, an organization has a much harder time controlling and regulating what is being printed, by whom, and for which audience (Weimann 1996:32).

In the case of general market demand, printed materials are fed into more decentral and competitive networks and cultures. There are more books available than before, and some books come from distant locations and times. One can buy books and does not have to pass through the authorities in charge of the library. These authorities loosen their grip on the books; they can outlaw some of them, but not all of them, and outlawing them generates so much more curiosity. Since more copies of the same texts are made available, networks among readers can correspond with each other, and focus the attention space on an emerging republic of letters. When texts are also printed in the vernacular, and not just the official language of a state, church, or educated elite, the culture of print becomes still more "democratic" and pluralistic.

As the number of texts increase, and as more texts come in from more different backgrounds, contradictions and inconsistencies between them become more obvious than if a political or clerical hegemony had been able to appropriate and contain this cross-fertilization. Grafton (1991:25–30) argues that such contradictions and inconsistencies were what drove Renaissance humanism into opposition to scholasticism. Unlike the scholastics, humanist readers did not paper over, or suppress, inconsistencies among texts to preserve a central authoritative tradition. They rather used such inconsistencies to elevate historical methods of reading and exegesis over doctrinal and moral systematics. The "historical method" of the humanists took inconsistencies among texts to indicate actual and empirical cultural diversity, while scholastic reading aimed at unity and coherence to consolidate and cement a core dogma, which could not have a genuine history.

As more books became available, and as epistolary networks among scholars and wealthy urban literati developed outside of the Church and the medieval universities, these networks became more independent and autonomous, selecting their own foci of attention. Rowland (1998:10–24) describes this changing scenario for the Roman Academy. As more texts arrived on the scene, coming in from more diverse sources, novel and creative permutations and combinations among texts and traditions emerged (Eisenstein 1993:44). The number of observers increased as well, introducing the possibility of second-order observation and "constructivism." That is, observations were attributable to observers and their locations and positions in society, culture, and history. There was more room for skepticism toward a unified and universal tradition and cosmology. The sheer diversity of texts and their observers drove home the realization that all observation is empirical, that is, part of the actual world.

With the coming of printing, the materials of culture proliferated and traveled over larger distances. One must be careful, however, not to exaggerate the dramatic effects of printing on culture, as if the printing press transformed culture by its own logic or force, independent of social structure. A printing press is not a magic wand; its effects are more long-term and constrained by continuities that remain in place. At first, printing simply meant more copies of the same old materials, rather than dramatic innovations and rapid cultural change. By itself, a printing press just sits there, or stands around, at some local site, little more than another invention among others. It begins to have an effect when it is placed into networks, such as networks between printers and their clients or customers. Then the place where the press is located might become a new center for intellectual activity, one difficult to control or regulate from above.

The effects of printing on culture depend on interaction with other forces, including changes in social structure. Johns (1998:11–19) argues that Eisenstein (and also McLuhan) exaggerate the force of print culture, particularly its degree of standardization, dissemination, and fixity, together with its role in bringing about secular humanism, Protestantism, and the Scientific Revolution.

With these cautions in mind, print culture did make more written materials available, and it did so on a wider scale. In the humanist scholar's study, there were now more books than before, and these came from a larger variety of sources, sometimes traveling over large distances and reporting on remote cultures. One sixteenth-century device to handle the increasing number of books in the study was the book wheel, which enabled a reader to "spin from text to text, compare authority with authority, [and] seek rapidly for truth in the bedlam of competing voices" (Grafton 1992:117). The mechanics of the book wheel match the altered conditions of reading during this era, as scholars struggled to consider more sources of learning. The grip of the Church on the book became looser, and reading and writing moved, to a greater extent, away from the Church and its control into a more cosmopolitan network of literary markets. Simplifying a bit, Ward (1990:148) contrasts "monopolist versus pluralist control of the location, production, and consumption of writing," and identifies monopoly with scholasticism and the Renaissance with pluralism. The more books appear, and the less contained they are within an ecclesiastical monopoly, the more inconsistencies and contradictions between them become visible, and the more questionable becomes the notion of a single and unified tradition.

Orality, Perception, and Copresence

By and large, and ceteris paribus, laboratory sciences occasion more copresence and encounters among workers than nonexperimental and bookish or textual cultures. With Knorr-Cetina (1999:27), a "laboratory" is a space where objects differ from the way they are outside. A laboratory object does not have to be accommodated in its "natural" settings. Events are made to happen, regardless of when they happen in nature. On this account, much of astronomy has, of late, been transformed into a laboratory science.

Laboratories are, among other things, sites of prolonged and repeated encounters and groups. Textual cultures, in contrast, are more "bookish"; they rely more on reading and writing, rather than on manipulations of tangible objects and material things. Textual cultures relate texts to other texts, producing more remoteness to physical things and materials. Laboratories also deal with texts, and also with texts that relate to other texts, but that which is "behind" the text is a more tangible and physical reality—the presence of instruments, machines, and apparatus. A critic who doubts the reality behind the text can be referred back to the laboratory, which is much more difficult to doubt (Latour 1987:64–74). A critic who disagrees with a statement in a textual culture can only be referred to other texts, resulting in layers of commentary and exegesis, which are ever more removed from any reality that could in some way be "perceived." Such elaborate layers of textual commentary and exegesis are absent from experimental sciences.

In textual fields, "perception" and "observation" are more remote from tangible or measurable things and objects. When reading, one sees the words and symbols on the page, nothing more. When writing a text in such a culture, one is not, or not as much, surrounded by machines and instruments and their outputs. Instead, one is surrounded by other texts only, which makes it more difficult to assume that texts refer to anything nontextual.

The material ecology of the scholar's study, as well as its everyday phenomenology, differ from the ecology of a laboratory (Gaston 1973:25). Texts can report or describe observations, but this is also done within, and as part of, the text, maybe in the footnotes. Cultures that are to a large extent networks among texts are further removed from perception and measurement. Thus there is a constructivism about textual cultures absent from laboratory sciences although, as we have seen, this constructivism varies as well; for example, with the pluralism of networks. There is much less constructivism when reading and writing are contained and confined within hegemonic organizations.

Inasmuch as laboratories are sites for encounters and groups, they allow for the "duality of perception and communication" typical of face-to-face interactions and oral communication. As Luhmann wrote (1992:229): "Daraus ergeben sich in jeder Situation kommunikative Unbestreitbarkeiten, die dann der Kommunikation als Sicherheitsquelle dienen können. Man kann in der Situation von etwas immer schon Akzeptiertem ausgehen." (From this duality, certain undeniable facts emerge in each situation that can provide communication with a source of certainty. In a situation, one can assume that certain things will be agreed upon.) Encounters happen in the here and now among copresent persons. Textual cultures also have encounters and groups, of course, but here, the prominence of writing and reading means that much more work is done in discretionary solitude, away from others. By himself, a reader can "imagine" more, and may imagine more alternative possibilities than when checked and observed in the copresence of others. Solitary readers "wander" more, and their wanderings are less disciplined by the company of others who are engaged in similar or related work and tasks. In laboratory sciences, more work occurs in actual copresence and interaction with others. Coauthorship is also much more frequent here than in the humanities.

The communication that is embedded in physical interventions and manipulations of things in the laboratory is more oral than the written communication through and about texts. Ethnographies of laboratory life observe a "talking science" (Lynch 1985:147–150). Talk occurs among workers gathered around experimental sites, workbenches, detectors, and other apparatus. In the common here and now of encounters, the laboratory is available as a primordial and tangible reality that can be perceived and manipulated by those who are present (Amann and Knorr 1990). There are "hands-on" interventions in the material world. As Hacking (1983:23) remarks, "If you can spray [electrons], then they are real." This reality offers a degree of resistance to some interventions and manipulations, which constrains the remaining degrees of freedom in interpretations and solves "underdetermination" in practice, if not in "theory."

Nothing similar occurs in textual and bookish modes of production. They communicate more than they perceive anything behind, or underneath, the written or printed symbol. Textual fields perform few, if any, physical or material operations and interventions on tangible objects. They have a hard time escaping the word. They do not show or demonstrate much, in the way this is done in laboratories. They have fewer tools and devices to make their claims and representations "stick."

In textual fields, communication is more abstract and remote from any reality outside of itself. It is more "semiotic" and self-referential. In purely written, as opposed to oral, communication, one does not usually even know whether a text is a forgery. Oral communication among copresent persons, as occurs more frequently in laboratories drawing workers together in the here and now of a physical setting, has fewer or no such problems. Ong (1982) distinguishes a primarily oral from a literate or textual "mentality," and concludes that orality increases the concreteness of culture—the extent to which it seems linked to an external reality, there for all to see who are also present. It is clear who speaks and who listens. It is also clear who is there and not. Oral communication is part of a here and now provided by the immediate setting and surrounding. One can assume that the others, those who are also there, perceive more or less the same world. If they are not here right now, but in the cafeteria, they will be back later, and then can be shown what transpired during their absence. Upon returning, they can also see for themselves. Others can see, feel, touch, or smell something. One might question this or that perception, but not perception as such, in its rendering of that which it perceives. The objects perceived are right here, available by ostension.

Encounters are much more alert and sensitive to their surroundings than are texts. Encounters can use and rely on many more visible and tangible clues for meaning. As encounters occur, the world around them, and the persons in this world, occur as well. Of course, as empirical events that either happen or not, reading and writing occur in the world as well, but their "horizons" are not the same as they are for persons copresent in an encounter. Readers and authors are not usually in an encounter, in the shared here and now. Readers and writers might exist for each other, but they do so more as possibilities and abstract expectations.

One can, of course, describe or display in writing what one has seen. The technique of "virtual witnessing" of an experiment by readers who were not present when it happened is an important part of the novel seventeenth-century genre of the experimental report (Shapin 1984). Such reports use drawings, pictures, and graphs, in addition to words, to convince readers that things actually happened as reported. But the reader's perception is then of a representation of reality, not that reality itself. "Trust" in honor or reputation is then required. One must trust that the reported observations were actually observed by those in whom one trusts.

Two important caveats are in order now, though. First, as Ravetz (1971:77, 109) noted, probably for the first time, the material ecology of a laboratory consists not of "primordial" things and entities, as they appear naturally. Rather, laboratory work is performed on highly pre-processed and "artificial" objects and substances, which are the result of previous work and operations. Second, the observations in a science are, to various degrees, inferential. Pinch (1986:43) documents such a complex chain for solar neutrino research. That which is eventually "seen" and recorded represents one end and outcome of a long and multilayered network of measures, detectors, indicators, and indirect interpolations. The distance between the object or referent of observation, and that which is actually observed in some way, varies from science to science, and also over the course of a science's history, as it acquires more advanced instruments, techniques, and devices. Much "progress" in a science is reducing the number of intermediaries, indirect links, and passage points between an observation and its referent or source (Galison 1987:259).

By and large, though, textual and bookish cultures take more time and steps to reach the reality they are about, if they ever do so, or even doubt they are about any "reality" outside of culture itself. This happens the more a textual culture is based in fragmented and decentral networks. Since they have no, or few, nontextual and nondiscursive operations, they also lack any means to closely couple the word to the world. Textual cultures have only still more words to do this, and so tend to end up where they started, within the word.

Consensus

It has often been observed that "harder" sciences generate more consensus than "softer" ones, although at the innovative frontiers of the harder sciences there is much controversy as well. One possible explanation for this difference is that laboratory sciences, whether they deal with things social or natural, occasion more copresence, encounters, and conversations. Referring to "houses of experiment" in seventeenth-century England, Shapin (1988:397) notes that "the obligation to tell the truth, like the consequences of questioning that one was being told the truth, were intensified when one looked the other 'in the face,' and particularly when it was done in the public rooms of the other's house." There is some evidence, from conversation analysis, that the formal structure of conversations generates pressures for agreement. Reading, in contrast, is done in discretionary solitude, which increases the opportunities for disagreement, especially when the networks of reading and writing have become pluralistic, decentralized, and competitive. Hence textual and bookish cultures, where work is done less among copresent others, may be expected to generate less consensus than laboratory sciences—all other things being equal.

What is it about interaction and conversation among copresent persons that makes disagreement less likely? First, as Luhmann (1984:560–562) notes, interactions are not complex enough to handle much disagreement. They can either avoid conflict or turn into conflicts, but not both. They cannot split into two interactions—one that proceeds with the interaction before erupting into conflict, and one that is the conflict. Conflict turns an interaction into conflict; the conflict is then all the interaction can process and handle. Further, disagreement is more costly and risky than agreement, since the dissenter has to propose an alternative to what has been said or communicated. Disagreement may raise the expectation that the dissenter knows more and can offer a better solution. Disagreement draws the attention of the encounter to the deviant, who is now scrutinized.

Unlike agreeing, disagreements usually require an explanation. If one says "no," one has to explain why one is doing so, since a sheer "no" might be seen as mere stubbornness or provocation. Hence, in conversations, disagreements are frequently delayed or qualified, maybe even interpreted away as "really" or "underneath" signaling agreement. Alternatively, a disagreement triggers a revision in a conversational offer, which now carries the expectation of being more acceptable than the statement or utterance drawing the disagreement. Persistent and frequent disagreement may be considered rude or impolite, and interpreted as an obnoxious refusal to communicate at all. Conversational tact and etiquette might be employed to buffer or soften the embarrassment of such rudeness. As Wittgenstein (1953:50) remarks, "The civil status of a contradiction, or its status in civil life: there is the philosophical problem."

Conversations also employ "funneling" devices that make disagreement less likely. The conversation starts with something highly agree-

328 · AGAINST ESSENTIALISM

able, and then proceeds as if the next step "followed" from the premise. In this way, persons are gradually "caged" into the ongoing flow of the conversation. The longer one goes along with this flow, the more one is "trapped" into explicit or expected assent, and the more the impression hardens that those present more or less agree with the bulk of what is going on. That is, the time to disagree is early on in the conversation, not when it has proceeded for some time. Or at least later disagreements are expected to be more narrow and easy to reconcile. One cannot really go along with the conversational flow for a long time and then suddenly question the premises from which it all started. If one disagrees early on, one still has a better option of exiting the encounter altogether, without raising any eyebrows.

Conversations also draw upon "no fault" explanations to mitigate or reconcile disagreements (Schegloff 1992). That is, disagreement might be interpreted as the dissenter not being able to see what the others have seen, or not having learned what the others have experienced. In this way, disagreement can be excused and renormalized as actual agreement—if I had seen or learned or experienced what you have, I would agree as well. One form of this mechanism to avoid disagreement is deference to authority and expertise. Disagreement with presumed or acknowledged experts risks being exposed as foolish or incompetent. When there is a good chance that others might know more, the safest strategy is to go along with the conversational flow, avoiding embarrassing damages to reputation and credibility. What is more, there always is a good chance that the others do know more, especially in those scholarly conversations where knowing more is the name of the game, and where the perception of intellectual superiority triggers admiration and deference. Since there is so much more to know than any person can know, however, even those who know it all do not know the half of it and risk having their own ignorance exposed eventually, especially when they flaunt their knowledge all the time. Therefore, many scholarly conversations are not that scholarly, and rely on a polite abstention from exposing and digging into each others' ignorance.

In sum, "there is a 'bias' intrinsic to many aspects of the organization of talk which is generally favorable to the maintenance of bonds of solidarity between actors which promotes the avoidance of conflict" (Heritage 1984:265). The implication is that specialties with a lot of experimental work, which make room for extended copresence and groups together at work settings over long periods of time, institution-alize stronger pressures for agreement and consensus than do special-ties with more solitary intellectual production, such as social theory or literary criticism.

Distance and Frontstages

Harry Collins (1988:726) observes that the more remote an observer of a culture is from it, the more rationality, certainty, closure, and real-ism he attributes to that culture. Actually, one can also find this point in Reichenbach (1951:43), who muses that "it is a strange matter of fact that those who watch and admire scientific research from the out-side frequently have more confidence in its results than the men who cooperate in its progress." In part, this may be because distant observ-ers tend to observe the frontstages, rather than backstages, of a culture and its organizations. Frontstages simplify, condense, and abbreviate the processes and outcomes of a culture. They account for its be-haviors by means of rational reconstructions and systematic method. Move closer to where culture is being made, to its backstages, and cul-ture appears less orderly, method-driven, or clearly defined.

Frontstage work is the work of summary and condensation; in the case of outside suspicions or inspections, a frontstage is where rational legitimacy is communicated. As a cultural product moves frontstage, its coherence or self-similarity gradually increases as the result of or-dering and juxtaposition of mutually supporting meanings and repre-sentations (Latour 1986:22). The trained and accomplished conver-gence of many nodes and relations is what gives a network its stability and objectivity. With the benefit of hindsight, frontstages tell stories of cumulation, rationality, and progress. In so doing, they gloss over and repair the many inconsistencies, errors, and contradictions endemic to culture-in-the-making (Ziman [1978] 1991:86; Shapin 1990:207).

Realism and rationality are outcomes of frontstage work. A good ex-ample comes from the analysis of scientific texts. They are "frauds" in Medawar's ([1963] 1990) sense of the term; that is, they do not report what actually happened when the research was being done. Instead, they present a coherent and teleological account of a gradual unfold-ing of truth according to method, logic, and rationality. Scientific papers are highly selective condensations and simplifications of a science (Star 1983:207). Reading a science's literature, especially its textbooks, suggests more closure, consolidation, and certainty than obtains backstage. A distant observer relying exclusively on frontstage documents tends to attribute more realism to the observed culture.

In sum, realism increases as the result of many interacting variables, not as the result of any one force. It increases when a culture is grounded in routine machines, tools, and instruments, around the formal and technical cores of organizations. This effect is strengthened further as the material means of culture are monopolized by an organizational hegemony. Realism occurs more frequently than skepticism in large-batch and standardized instruction of the official doctrines and dogmas. It is more at home on frontstages, which exaggerate closure, coherence, and consolidation. In laboratory sciences that occasion more copresence, encounters, and groups, realism is anchored in the tangible reality of a here and now, with its physical interventions and manipulations. When these scientific workplaces also occasion much conversation among copresent workers, there are structural pressures for agreement and consensus, whereas more textual and bookish fields allow a higher degree of individualistic discretion.

Conclusion

Where can we go from here? Much remains and needs to be done, but here are what I see as the most important next moves. The first is empirical tests of the book's propositions, which I have done only in a cursory and sketchy way. One empirical focus might be the theory of realism and cultural closure, which offers concrete predictions as to when a culture externalizes and attributes its outcomes to a transcendental or universal source. What is needed here is a comparative analysis of observers and the conditions of their observing. The critical variables have been identified, but it remains to be seen how well the theory stands up to detailed case studies, such as high medieval scholasticism or socialist art. The sociology of culture is advancing into the center of the field, and studies of individual cultures will have important contributions to make to the general theory.

From science studies, we have excellent materials on how the culture of science behaves. It should be possible to compare science to other cultures to venture some generalizations as to how various cultures and cultured observers do their work. When the similarities and differences emerge, we will be in a better position to offer a general theory of culture, which is now in its beginning stages. We need to know what makes something an art, as opposed to a science or music, and how a culture assimilates a contribution into its internal fabric. To assert, as I have done, that culture has a "metabolism" remains metaphorical until we have a good description of how this happens—a "social physiology."

I am unhappy with my fuzzy distinctions between observers, cultures, and networks. Much more conceptual precision is required. The theory of observers and second-order observing is a very promising track for the sociology of culture, but more work should go into analyzing what makes an observer the observer he is. Observing is not passive but active and constructive, and persons are but one kind of observer. An observer is also a doer or, better, a doing—the drawing of a distinction, according to which something can matter. If this is acceptable, the next step is to explore how observers emerge, when they end, and how other observers react to this. A very important observer in modern society is the mass media, and I think the theory of observers, together with organizational sociology, is in a good position to explain how the mass media construct a world out of distinctions, a world that is both real and not.

Another area of work concerns the theory of networks and systems. I believe that this is where the greatest promise for explanatory sociology lies. I am impressed by the sophistication of systems theory and by network theory's exceptional empirical record. We need to move beyond thinking of networks in terms of persons and agency, and apply relationalism to networks whose nodes are not persons. The field of neural networks is making great progress in modeling the mind as parallel and distributed processing; maybe we can find some similarities in the workings of networks, regardless of whether these networks are in brains, states, or world systems. I suspect that one such basic mode of net-work is the involution of a core or several cores in the network, where it houses its institutions and blind spots. Cores are gravitational centers of networks; the gravitational force decreases in proportion to distance from the core. Is there an inverse-square law to be found here?

Chapters 5 and 6 make the rather strong argument that all society takes place in four basic modes of association. To see how well this idea resonates with the evidence, studies of encounters, groups, organizations, and networks will have to be mined much more systematically to see how these levels emerge, change into each other, and relate to the other levels. I have done this only metaphorically, with talk of "nesting." But nesting is too vague and ambivalent to capture just how an encounter, for example, becomes a group, and just how a group survives the end of its encounters. The specialty of social movements is critical in this context, since it deals with transformations in levels of social associations.

My own current efforts are mostly in the direction of a sociological theory of mind; sociology has made few advances in this area, and it is ruled by standard Mead. The cognitive neurosciences have the strongest grip on the mind, but I believe that computational models are far too rationalist to account for what minds do, including thinking, talking, and writing. Researchers talk about folk psychology without ever talking to any folk. They believe that persons have beliefs and desires, and that these explain what people do. When we know what people do, we know all there is to know about society and culture. But computers are not very good at common sense. A computer is a mind formatting itself in terms of discrete mental states and precise rules for manipulating such states. The mind "is" not a computer or, if it is, is not so good at computing and does much else besides deal with propositions and deductions.

Thinking is not internal conversation, and writing is not the realization of thought. Consciousness is overrated, since it proceeds without robust awareness. Consciousness is but the tip of the iceberg of mental life. We are not so much conscious but moody animals. There is a mood for thinking also. One can be in the mood for thinking. A mood is nonintentional—one is "in" it, rather than "having" it. Likewise, we are "in" thought; thinking "has" us. The distinction between feeling and thought ignores that thoughts have feelings as well. We are not very transparent to ourselves, much less to others.

A core problem in this context, raised by Luhmann, is how communication is possible at all. Communication is not shared meaning or significant symbols. Meadian social psychology is too intellectualist. Put sharply, we can never say what we mean or mean what we say. When you say, "I do not understand what you are saying," my response is not to point at my head, referring you to an intention there. Rather, I say something else and hope this will make clearer what I mean, but the same problem emerges for this communication, and so on. Problems of communication and meaning are not settled in minds, but in further communication. What transpires in communication is not ideas, thoughts, or intentions. Rather, these are convenient shorthands for summarizing communications and attributing them to a source, which can now be blamed or credited for them.

When it comes to matters of mind, very little is certain. I exist; there are others and a world. I see and sense part of it, and do not question that I do so. What exactly I see I am not sure; I cannot describe it very well. I do not see discrete objects or things; Merleau-Ponty's phenomenology comes a lot closer to "actual experience" than does cognitive science. What others see and sense I know even less. I am someone, not someone else, but there might not be an I who "has" experiences. Heidegger once remarked that it was very fortunate that the Greeks had no experiences.

I have great faith in sociology's potential to become a great science, one that is far superior to its competitors when it comes to explaining culture, society, or even the mind. Unfortunately, the discipline's strengths are not visible to other sciences, and they are obscured within sociology as well. We come across as a field not to be taken too seriously. The other sciences pay very little attention to what happens in our field, which means that absurd misconceptions and flaws emerge when these sciences address culture and society. I think the gravest of these flaws is to think of culture as something that resides in the mind, and of society as something that happens between persons. When it comes to society and culture, disciplines outside of sociology tend to endorse a naive and commonsensical individualism.

APPENDIX

REFERENCES

INDEX

Appendix: Theses

1. In the beginning, there were networks. Networks are fields of forces. They do not consist of nodes. Nodes are outcomes of networks. Nodes without relationships are nodes without qualities.

2. Society occurs in encounters, groups, organizations, and networks. Networks link these, and themselves, into larger networks. Nothing controls society or even holds it together. It has no "order," or only that temporary and fragile order which it makes and remakes for itself.

3. The boundaries of networks shift together with their own velocities and those of related networks.

4. Society is a massively plural and parallel occurrence or happening. There is no master- or mega-encounter that could regulate all the other encounters.

5. Everything that happens happens locally, at a certain place and time. All that exists exists empirically, and only until further notice.

6. Transcendence and universality are innerworldly, temporary, and variable outcomes of expanding networks. These outcomes are improbable and reversible. They require the painstaking work of network.

7. A core rule of method is to allow for variation. There are no natural kinds, essential properties, or things-in-themselves. But a network can condense and converge into kinds and properties that appear natural and essential to it.

8. Natural kinds and stable objects appear when an increasingly self-similar network hums to itself. They both take time.

9. Explaining is not action, but interaction at a distance. As the distance closes, explanation turns into understanding and finally into love.

10. There is no logical relationship between scientific explanation and technological control. Science augments complexity; engineering cages it, but only for the time being. Sometimes, complexity bursts out of its cage.

11. That science is instrumental reason is an invention of philosophy, not science.

12. The unity of science extends only as far as actual mergers and unions between sciences. There is no "science as such." No scientist does "science in general."

13. The subject or actor is part of the explanandum, not the explanans, of sociological science. Agency is a variable at-tribute to personhood, not an essential fact about natural persons. Consciousness is overrated.

14. Persons do not act, much less act rationally. "Action" is how some observers make sense of some events. Personhood is an institution.

15. Free will is the residual from failed attempts at explanation and domestication.

16. What persons say is not the cause, but the outcome, of communication. Nothing communicates like communication.

17. A culture or science has nothing to work with but the results of its previous operations. No science or culture goes to work on "reality" or "nature."

18. What makes science special is not truth, but time out from ideological suspicion.

19. Constructivism is adequate only if it can explain why some constructions appear unconstructed. Otherwise it is an arrogance and imposition.

20. Sociology is not about social facts, but about how and when such facts emerge, and when not. All facts are constructs, but some are weaker, others stronger. All cultures are constructed, but only some of them are constructivist.

21. A culture is not in the mind. It does not consist of ideas, although ideas summarize and simplify some cultural results.

22. Realism and relativism are not opposites, but are linked by a continuum of cultural closure and settlement.

23. The limits of an observer are where he stops (for now) asking further questions. An observer is always a cultured observer, or no observer at all.

24. Everything is what it is in relation to what it is not, not yet, or not anymore.

25. A culture or science cares—for itself. It is interested—in itself. It values—itself. A disinterested observer is careless.

References

Abbott, Andrew. 1988. *The System of Professions.* Chicago: University of Chicago Press.

Adorno, Theodor W. 1951. *Minima Moralia.* Frankfurt, Germany: Suhrkamp.

Amann, Klaus, and Karin Knorr. 1990. "The Fixation of Visual Evidence." Pp. 85–121 in *Representation in Scientific Practice,* edited by Michael Lynch and Steve Woolgar. Cambridge, Mass.: MIT Press.

Arditi, Jorge. 1998. *A Genealogy of Manners: Transformations in Social Relations in France and England from the Fourteenth to the Eighteenth Century.* Chicago: University of Chicago Press.

Arrow, Kenneth. 1992. "Rationality of Self and Others in an Economic System." Pp. 63–88 in *Decision Making: Alternatives to Rational Choice Models,* edited by Mary Zey. Newbury Park, Calif.: Sage.

Ashmore, Malcolm. 1989. *The Reflexive Thesis.* Chicago: University of Chicago Press.

Ayer, Alfred J. [1956] 1990. *The Problem of Knowledge.* New York: Penguin.

Bachelard, Gaston. [1934] 1984. *The New Scientific Spirit.* Boston: Beacon Press.

Baldwin, John W. 1982. "Masters at Paris from 1179 to 1215: A Social Perspective." Pp. 138–172 in *Renaissance and Renewal in the Twelfth Century,* edited by Robert L. Benson and Giles Constable. Cambridge, Mass.: Harvard University Press.

Barnes, Barry. 1974. *Scientific Knowledge and Sociological Theory.* London: Routledge.

———. 1992. "How Not to Do the Sociology of Knowledge." *Annals of Scholarship* 8:321–335.

Bearman, Peter S. 1993. *Relations into Rhetoric.* New Brunswick, N.J.: Rutgers University Press.

Becker, Howard S. 1982. *Art Worlds.* Berkeley: University of California Press.

Beckermann, Ansgar, ed. 1977. *Analytische Handlungstheorie.* Frankfurt, Germany: Suhrkamp.

Ben-David, Joseph. [1960] 1991. "Scientific Productivity and Academic Organization in Nineteenth-Century Medicine." Pp. 103–124 in his *Scientific Growth.* Berkeley: University of California Press.

———. [1972] 1991. "The Profession of Science and Its Powers." Pp. 187–209 in his *Scientific Growth.* Berkeley: University of California Press.

Ben-David, Joseph, and Randall Collins. 1966. "Social Factors in the Origins of a New Science: The Case of Psychology." *American Sociological Review* 31:451–465.

Benjamin, Walter. [1921] 1977. "Zur Kritik der Gewalt." Pp. 179–247 in *Gesammelte Schriften.* Frankfurt, Germany: Suhrkamp.

Bennett, J. A. 1992. "The English Quadrant in Europe: Instruments and the Growth of Consensus in Practical Astronomy." *Journal for the History of Astronomy* 23:1–14.

Bensman, Joseph, and Robert Lilienfeld. 1991. *Craft and Consciousness.* New York: Aldine de Gruyter.

Berg, Marc. 1997. "Of Forms, Containers, and the Electronic Medical Record: Some Tools for a Sociology of the Formal." *Science, Technology, and Human Values* 22:403–433.

Berger, Bennett M. 1995. *An Essay on Culture.* Berkeley: University of California Press.

Berger, Peter, and Thomas Luckman. 1967. *The Social Construction of Reality.* New York: Doubleday.

Bernstein, Basil. 1974–1977. *Class, Codes, and Control.* London: Routledge & Kegan Paul.

Black, Donald. 1976. *The Behavior of Law.* New York: Academic Press.

———. 1993. *The Social Structure of Right and Wrong.* New York: Academic Press.

Blau, Peter M., and Joseph E. Schwartz. 1984. *Crosscutting Social Circles: Testing a Macrostructural Theory of Intergroup Relations.* New York: Academic Press.

Bloor, David. 1976. *Knowledge and Social Imagery.* London: Routledge.

———. 1983. *Wittgenstein: A Social Theory of Knowledge.* New York: Columbia University Press.

———. 1984. "A Sociological Theory of Objectivity." Pp. 229–245 in *Objectivity and Cultural Divergence,* edited by S. C. Brown. Cambridge: Cambridge University Press.

Bloor, M. J. 1983. "Notes on Member Validation." Pp. 156–172 in *Contemporary Field Research*, edited by Richard Emerson. Boston: Little, Brown.

Boden, Deirdre, and Don H. Zimmerman, eds. 1991. *Talk and Social Structure: Studies in Ethnomethodology and Conversation Analysis*. Berkeley: University of California Press.

Bohman, James. 1991. *New Philosophy of Social Science*. Cambridge, Mass.: MIT Press.

Bourdieu, Pierre. 1980. *Le Sens Pratique*. Paris: Minuit.

———. 1984. *Distinction*. Cambridge, Mass.: Harvard University Press.

———. 1989. "Social Space and Symbolic Power." *Sociological Theory* 7:14–25.

———. 1991. *Language and Symbolic Power*. Cambridge: Polity Press.

———. 1993. *The Field of Cultural Production: Essays on Art and Literature*. New York: Columbia University Press.

Bridgman, Percy W. 1950. *Reflections of a Physicist*. New York: Philosophical Library.

Brym, Robert. 1988. "Structural Location and Ideological Divergence: Jewish Marxist Intellectuals in Turn-of-the-Century Russia." Pp. 359–379 in *Social Structures: A Network Approach*, edited by Barry Wellman and S. D. Berkowitz. Cambridge: Cambridge University Press.

Burnyeat, M. F. 1984. "The Sceptic in His Place and Time." Pp. 225–254 in *Philosophy in History: Essays on the Historiography of Philosophy*, edited by Richard Rorty, J. B. Schneewind, and Quentin Skinner. Cambridge: Cambridge University Press.

Burt, Ronald S. 1992. *Structural Holes: The Social Structure of Competition*. Cambridge, Mass.: Harvard University Press.

Callebaut, Werner, ed. 1993. *Taking the Naturalistic Turn, or How Real Philosophy of Science Is Done*. Chicago: University of Chicago Press.

Camic, Charles. 1992. "The Matter of Habit." Pp. 185–232 in *Decision Making: Alternatives to Rational Choice Models*, edited by Mary Zey. Newbury Park, Calif.: Sage.

Campbell, Karen E., and Barrett A. Lee. 1992. "Sources of Personal Neighbor Networks: Social Integration, Need, or Time?" *Social Forces* 70:1077–1100.

Caplow, Theodore. 1994. *Perverse Incentives: The Neglect of Social Technology in the Public Sector*. Westport, Conn.: Praeger.

Carnap, Rudolf. [1928] 1961. *Der Logische Aufbau der Welt/Scheinprobleme in der Philosophie*. Hamburg, Germany: Meiner.

———. 1956. "Empiricism, Semantics, and Ontology." Pp. 205–221 in his *Meaning and Necessity*. Chicago: University of Chicago Press.

Cartwright, Nancy. 1983. *How the Laws of Physics Lie*. Oxford: Oxford University Press.

Cassirer, Ernst. [1910] 1969. *Substanzbegriff and Funktionsbegriff.* Darmstadt, Germany: Wissenschaftliche Buchgesellschaft.

Chalmers, David J. 1996. *The Conscious Mind.* New York: Oxford University Press.

Chambliss, Daniel F. 1989. "The Mundanity of Excellence: An Ethnographic Report on Stratification and Olympic Swimmers." *Sociological Theory* 7:70–86.

Chandrasekhar, Subrahmanyan. 1987. *Truth and Beauty: Aesthetics and Motivation in Science.* Chicago: University of Chicago Press.

Chisholm, Donald. 1989. *Coordination without Hierarchy: Informal Structures in Multiorganizational Systems.* Berkeley: University of California Press.

Chokr, Nader. 1993. "Cluster's Last Stand." *Social Epistemology* 7:329–353.

Churchland, Paul. 1992. *A Neurocomputational Perspective.* Cambridge, Mass.: MIT Press.

Churchland, Paul, and Patricia Churchland. 1999. *On the Contrary.* Cambridge, Mass.: MIT Press.

Cicourel, Aaron V. 1981. "Notes on the Integration of Micro- and Macro-levels of Analysis." Pp. 51–80 in *Advances in Social Theory and Methodology: Toward an Integration of Micro- and Macro-Sociologies,* edited by Karin Knorr-Cetina and Aaron V. Cicourel. Boston: Routledge & Kegan Paul.

Clarke, Lee. 1992. "Context Dependency and Risk Decision Making." Pp. 27–38 in *Organizations, Uncertainties, and Risk,* edited by James Short and Lee Clarke. Boulder, Colo.: Westview.

Cole, Jonathan R., and Stephen Cole. 1973. *Social Stratification in Science.* Chicago: University of Chicago Press.

Cole, Stephen. 1992. *Making Science: Between Nature and Society.* Cambridge, Mass.: Harvard University Press.

Coleman, James S. 1990. *Foundations of Social Theory.* Cambridge, Mass.: Belknap Press of Harvard University Press.

Collins, Harry M. 1981. "The Place of the 'Core-Set' in Modern Science." *History of Science* 19:6–19.

———. 1983. "An Empirical Relativist Programme in the Sociology of Scientific Knowledge." Pp. 85–113 in *Science Observed,* edited by Karin Knorr-Cetina and Michael Mulkay. London: Sage.

———. 1985. *Changing Order: Replication and Induction in Scientific Practice.* London: Sage.

———. 1988. "Public Experiments and Displays of Virtuosity: The Core-Set Revisited." *Social Studies of Science* 18:725–748.

———. 1990. *Artificial Experts: Social Knowledge and Intelligent Machines.* Cambridge, Mass.: MIT Press.

———. 1998. "Socialness and the Undersocialized Conception of Society." *Science, Technology, and Human Values* 23:494–516.

Collins, Randall. 1975. *Conflict Sociology*. New York: Academic Press.

———. 1979. *The Credential Society*. New York: Academic Press.

———. 1988. *Theoretical Sociology*. San Diego: Harcourt Brace Jovanovich.

———. 1993. "The Rationality of Avoiding Choice." *Rationality and Society* 5:58–67.

———. 1998. *The Sociology of Philosophies: A Global Theory of Intellectual Change*. Cambridge, Mass.: Belknap Press of Harvard University Press.

Collins, Randall, and David Waller. 1994. "Did Social Science Break Down in the 1970s?" Pp. 15–40 in *Formal Theory in Sociology: Opportunity or Pitfall?* edited by Jerald Hage. Albany: State University of New York Press.

Cook, Karen S., ed. 1987. *Social Exchange Theory*. Newbury Park, Calif.: Sage.

Coser, Lewis A. 1974. *Greedy Institutions: Patterns of Undivided Commitment*. New York: Free Press.

Coulter, Jeff. 1989. *Mind in Action*. Cambridge: Polity Press.

Cozzens, Susan E. 1989. *Social Control and Multiple Discovery in Science*. Albany: State University of New York Press.

Crane, Diana. 1972. *Invisible Colleges*. Chicago: University of Chicago Press.

———. 1987. *The Transformation of the Avant-Garde*. Chicago: University of Chicago Press.

———. 1992. *The Production of Culture*. Newbury Park, Calif.: Sage.

Csikszentmihalyi, Mihalyi. 1990. *Flow: The Psychology of Optimal Experience*. New York: Harper & Row.

Damasio, Antonio R. 1994. *Descartes' Error: Emotion, Reason, and the Human Brain*. New York: Grosset & Dunlap.

Danto, Arthur C. 1968. *Analytical Philosophy of History*, 2d ed. Cambridge: Cambridge University Press.

Daston, Lorraine. 1991a. "Baconian Facts, Academic Civility, and the Prehistory of Objectivity." *Annals of Scholarship* 8:337–363.

———. 1991b. "The Ideal and Reality of the Republic of Letters in the Enlightenment." *Science in Context* 4:367–386.

———. 1992. "Objectivity and the Escape from Perspective." *Social Studies of Science* 22:597–618.

———. 1995. "The Moral Economy of Science." *Osiris* 10:3–24.

Daston, Lorraine, and Peter Galison. 1992. "Images of Objectivity." *Representations* 40:81–128.

Dawes, Robyn M. 1991. "Social Dilemmas, Economic Self-Interest, and Evolutionary Theory." Pp. 17–40 in *Morality, Rationality, and Efficiency: New Perspectives on Socioeconomics*, edited by Richard M. Coughlin. Armonk, N.Y.: M. E. Sharpe.

Dawkins, Richard. 1995. *River out of Eden: A Darwinian View of Life*. New York: Basic Books.

Dear, Peter. 1984. "Marin Mersenne and the Probabilistic Roots of 'Mitigated Skepticism.'" *Journal of the History of Philosophy* 22:173–205.

———. 1985. "Totius in Verba: Rhetoric and Authority in the Early Royal Society." *Isis* 76:145–161.

———. 1988. *Mersenne and the Learning of the Schools.* Ithaca, N.Y.: Cornell University Press.

———. 1992. "From Truth to Disinterestedness in the Seventeenth Century." *Social Studies of Science* 22:619–631.

———. 1995. *Discipline and Experience: The Mathematical Way in the Scientific Revolution.* Chicago: University of Chicago Press.

Dennett, Daniel C. 1984. *Elbow Room: The Varieties of Free Will Worth Wanting.* Cambridge, Mass.: MIT Press.

———. 1987. *The Intentional Stance.* Cambridge, Mass.: MIT Press.

———. 1996. *Darwin's Dangerous Idea: Evolution and the Meanings of Life.* New York: Touchstone.

DeNora, Tia. 1991. "Musical Patronage and Social Change in Beethoven's Vienna." *American Journal of Sociology* 97:310–346.

Dewey, John. 1970. "The Need for a Recovery of Philosophy." Pp. 3–69 in *Creative Intelligence.* New York: Octagon.

DeWulf, Maurice. 1922. *Philosophy and Civilization in the Middle Ages.* New York: Dover.

Dietrich, Michael R. 1993. "Underdetermination and the Limits of Interpretative Flexibility." *Perspectives on Science* 1:109–126.

DiMaggio, Paul. 1977. "Market Structure, the Creative Process, and Popular Culture." *Journal of Popular Culture* 11:436–452.

———. 1987. "Classification in Art." *American Sociological Review* 52:440–455.

DiMaggio, Paul J., and Walter W. Powell. 1983. "The Iron Cage Revisited: Institutional Isomorphism and Collective Rationality in Organizational Fields." *American Sociological Review* 48:147–160.

Douglas, Mary. 1966. *Purity and Danger.* London: Routledge & Kegan Paul.

———. 1970. *Natural Symbols.* New York: Pantheon.

———. 1985. "Pascal's Great Wager." *L'Homme* 93:13–30.

———. 1986. *How Institutions Think.* Syracuse, N.Y.: Syracuse University Press.

———. 1992a. "Institutions of the Third Kind." Pp. 167–186 in her *Risk and Blame.* London: Routledge.

———. 1992b. "Muffled Ears." Pp. 55–82 in her *Risk and Blame: Essays in Cultural Theory.* London: Routledge.

Dreyfus, Hubert L. [1972] 1992. *What Computers Still Can't Do.* Cambridge, Mass.: MIT Press.

Drogin, Marc. 1983. *Anathema! Medieval Scribes and the History of Book Curses.* Totowa, N.J.: Allanheld and Schram.

Droogers, André. 1980. "Symbols of Marginality in the Biographies of Religious and Secular Innovators." *Numen* 27:105–121.

Duhem, Pierre. [1906] 1991. *The Aim and Structure of Physical Theory*. Princeton, N.J.: Princeton University Press.

Durkheim, Emile. [1912] 1965. *The Elementary Forms of the Religious Life*. New York: Free Press.

Dunbar, Robin I. M. 1996. *Grooming, Gossip, and the Evolution of Language*. Cambridge, Mass.: Harvard University Press.

Dyson, Freeman. 1988. *Infinite in All Directions*. New York: Harper & Row.

Eamon, William. 1985. "From the Secrets of Nature to Public Knowledge: The Origins of the Concept of Openness in Science." *Minerva* 23:321–347.

Eisenstein, Elizabeth L. 1993. *The Printing Revolution in Early Modern Europe*. Cambridge: Cambridge University Press.

Elias, Norbert. [1939] 1982. *Power and Civility*. New York: Pantheon.

Elster, Jon. 1989. *Nuts and Bolts for the Social Sciences*. Cambridge: Cambridge University Press.

Emirbayer, Mustafa, and Ann Mische. 1998. "What Is Agency?" *American Journal of Sociology* 103:962–1023.

Etzioni, Amitai. [1961] 1975. *A Comparative Analysis of Complex Organizations*, 2d ed. New York: Free Press.

Ferguson, Priscilla P. 1998. "A Cultural Field in the Making: Gastronomy in Nineteenth-Century France." *American Journal of Sociology* 104:597–641.

Feyerabend, Paul. [1975] 1988. *Against Method*. London: Verso.

———. 1987. "Progress in Philosophy, the Sciences, and the Arts." Pp. 143–161 in his *Farewell to Reason*. London: Verso.

Fischer, Claude S. 1992. *America Calling: A Social History of the Telephone to 1940*. Berkeley: University of California Press.

Fleck, Ludwik. [1935] 1979. *Genesis and Development of a Scientific Fact*. Chicago: University of Chicago Press.

Flood, John. 1991. "Doing Business: The Management of Uncertainty in Lawyers' Work." *Law and Society Review* 25:41–71.

Forman, Paul. 1995. "Truth and Objectivity." *Science* 269:565–567, 707–710.

Frangsmyr, Tore, J. L. Heilbron, and Robin E. Rider, eds. 1990. *The Quantifying Spirit in the Eighteenth Century*. Berkeley: University of California Press.

Franklin, Allan. 1997. "Calibration." *Perspectives on Science* 5:31–80.

Frede, Michael. 1979. "Des Skeptikers Meinungen." *Neue Hefte für Philosophie* 15/16:102–129.

Freeman, Linton C. [1978] 1979. "Centrality in Social Networks: Conceptual Clarification." *Social Networks* 1:215–239.

Freeman, Linton C., Douglas Roeder, and Robert R. Mulholland. [1979]

1980. "Centrality in Social Networks II: Experimental Results." *Social Networks* 2:119–141.

Frost, Peter J., et al., eds. 1991. *Reframing Organizational Culture.* Newbury Park, Calif.: Sage.

Fuchs, Stephan. 1995. "The Stratified Order of Gossip: Informal Communication in Organizations and Science." *Soziale Systeme* 1:47–72.

———. 1996. "The New Wars of Truth." *Social Science Information* 35:307–326.

Fuchs, Stephan, and Saundra Westervelt. 1996. "Fraud and Trust in Science." *Perspectives in Biology and Medicine* 39:248–269.

Fuchs, Stephan, and Steven Ward. 1994. "What Is Deconstruction, and Where and When Does It Take Place? Making Facts in Science; Building Cases in Law." *American Sociological Review* 59:481–500.

Gadamer, Hans-Georg. [1960] 1975. *Wahrheit und Methode.* Tübingen, Germany: Mohr.

Galison, Peter. 1985. "Bubble Chambers and the Experimental Workplace." Pp. 309–373 in *Observation, Experiment, and Hypothesis in Modern Physical Science,* edited by Peter Achinstein and Owen Hannaway. Cambridge, Mass.: MIT Press.

———. 1987. *How Experiments End.* Chicago: University of Chicago Press.

———. 1997. *Image and Logic: A Material Culture of Microphysics.* Chicago: University of Chicago Press.

Garfinkel, Harold. 1967. *Studies in Ethnomethodology.* Englewood Cliffs, N.J.: Prentice Hall.

Garfinkel, Harold, Michael Lynch, and Eric Livingston. 1981. "The Work of a Discovering Science Construed with Materials from the Optically Discovered Pulsar." *Philosophy of the Social Sciences* 11:131–158.

Garvey, William D., and Belver C. Griffith. 1971. "Scientific Communication: Its Role in the Conduct of Research and Creation of Knowledge." *American Psychologist* 26:349–362.

Gaston, Jerry. 1973. *Originality and Competition in Science: A Study of the British High Energy Physics Community.* Chicago: University of Chicago Press.

Gehlen, Arnold. [1956] 1964. *Urmensch und Spätkultur,* 2d ed. Frankfurt, Germany: Athenäum.

Gell-Mann, Murray. 1994. *The Quark and the Jaguar: Adventures in the Simple and the Complex.* New York: W. H. Freeman.

Gellner, Ernest. 1992. *Reason and Culture: The Historic Role of Rationality and Reason.* Oxford: Blackwell.

Giddens, Anthony. 1984. *The Constitution of Society.* London: Polity.

Gilbert, G. Nigel, and Michael J. Mulkay. 1984. *Opening Pandora's Box.* Cambridge: Cambridge University Press.

Gillispie, Charles C. 1960. *The Edge of Objectivity.* Princeton, N.J.: Princeton University Press.

Gimpel, Jean. 1976. *The Medieval Machine: The Industrial Revolution of the Middle Ages.* New York: Penguin.

Giuffre, Katherine. 1999. "Sandpiles of Opportunity: Success in the Art World." *Social Forces* 77:815–832.

Goffman, Erving. 1961. *Asylums.* New York: Doubleday.

———. 1974. *Frame Analysis.* New York: Harper & Row.

———. 1981. *Forms of Talk.* Philadelphia: University of Pennsylvania Press.

Gombrich, E. H. 1980. "Standards of Truth: The Arrested Image and the Moving Eye." *Critical Inquiry* 7:237–273.

Goodman, Nelson. 1978. *Ways of Worldmaking.* Indianapolis, Ind.: Hackett.

———. 1983. *Fact, Fiction, and Forecast,* 4th ed. Cambridge, Mass.: Harvard University Press.

Gould, Roger V. 1993. "Trade Cohesion, Class Unity, and Urban Insurrection: Artisanal Activism in the Paris Commune." *American Journal of Sociology* 4:721–754.

Gould, Stephen Jay. 1993. *Eight Little Piggies: Reflections in Natural History.* New York: W. W. Norton.

Grafton, Anthony. 1991. *Defenders of the Text: The Traditions of Scholarship in an Age of Science, 1450–1800.* Cambridge, Mass.: Harvard University Press.

———. 1992. *New Worlds, Ancient Texts: The Power of Tradition and the Shock of Discovery.* Cambridge, Mass.: Belknap Press of Harvard University Press.

Granovetter, Mark. 1974. *Getting a Job.* Cambridge, Mass.: Harvard University Press.

———. 1985. "Economic Action and Social Structure: The Problem of Embeddedness." *American Journal of Sociology* 91:481–510.

Griffith, Belver C., and A. James Miller. 1970. "Networks of Informal Communication among Scientifically Productive Scientists." Pp. 125–140 in *Communication among Scientists and Engineers,* edited by Carnot E. Nelson and Donald K. Pollock. Lexington, Mass.: Heath Lexington Books.

Gross, Paul R., and Norman Leavitt. 1994. *Higher Superstition: The Academic Left and Its Quarrels with Science.* Baltimore, Md.: Johns Hopkins University Press.

Habermas, Jürgen. 1968a. *Erkenntnis und Interesse.* Frankfurt, Germany: Suhrkamp.

———. 1968b. *Technik und Wissenschaft als "Ideologie."* Frankfurt, Germany: Suhrkamp.

———. [1984] 1987. *The Theory of Communicative Action.* 2 vols. Boston: Beacon Press.

———. 1990. *The Philosophical Discourse of Modernity: Twelve Lectures.* Cambridge, Mass.: MIT Press.

Hacking, Ian. 1983. *Representing and Intervening.* Cambridge: Cambridge University Press.

———. 1992. "The Self-Vindication of the Laboratory Sciences." Pp. 29–64 in *Science as Practice and Culture,* edited by Andrew Pickering. Chicago: University of Chicago Press.

Hagstrom, Warren O. 1965. *The Scientific Community.* Carbondale: Southern Illinois University Press.

Hale, J. R. 1977. *Renaissance Europe.* Berkeley: University of California Press.

Hall, Richard H. 1991. *Organizations: Structures, Processes, and Outcomes.* Englewood Cliffs, N.J.: Prentice Hall.

Halle, David. 1984. *America's Working Man.* Chicago: University of Chicago Press.

Hallett, Garth L. 1991. *Essentialism: A Wittgensteinian Critique.* Albany: State University of New York Press.

Hankins, Thomas L., and Robert J. Silverman. 1995. *Instruments and the Imagination.* Princeton, N.J.: Princeton University Press.

Hannan, Michael T., and John Freeman. 1989. *Organizational Ecology.* Cambridge, Mass.: Harvard University Press.

Hannerz, Ulf. 1992. *Cultural Complexity: Studies in the Social Organization of Meaning.* New York: Columbia University Press.

Hanson, Norwood Russell. [1958] 1969. *Patterns of Discovery: An Inquiry into the Conceptual Foundations of Science.* Cambridge: Cambridge University Press.

Harré, Rom. 1983. *Great Scientific Experiments.* Oxford: Oxford University Press.

Haskins, Charles H. 1957. *The Renaissance of the Twelfth Century.* New York: Meridian.

Havelock, Eric. 1982. *The Literate Revolution in Greece and Its Cultural Consequences.* Princeton, N.J.: Princeton University Press.

———. 1986. *The Muse Learns to Write.* New Haven, Conn.: Yale University Press.

Heidegger, Martin. [1927] 1979. *Sein und Zeit.* 15th ed. Tübingen: Max Niemeyer.

Heilbron, J. L. 1993. "Some Uses for Catalogues of Old Scientific Instruments." Pp. 1–16 in *Making Instruments Count,* edited by R. G. W. Anderson, J. A. Bennett, and W. F. Ryan. Cambridge: Variorum.

Heinich, Nathalie. 1996. *The Glory of Van Gogh: An Anthropology of Admiration.* Princeton, N.J.: Princeton University Press.

Heritage, John. 1984. *Garfinkel and Ethnomethodology.* Cambridge: Polity Press.

Heritage, John, and David Greatbatch. 1991. "On the Institutional Character of Institutional Talk: The Case of News Interviews." Pp. 93–137 in *Talk and Social Structure*, edited by Deidre Boden and Don H. Zimmerman.

Herzfeld, Michael. 1992. *The Social Production of Indifference: Exploring the Symbolic Roots of Western Bureaucracy*. Chicago: University of Chicago Press.

Hesse, Mary. 1980. *Revolutions and Reconstructions in the Philosophy of Science*. Bloomington: Indiana University Press.

Hilts, Philip J. 1982. *Scientific Temperaments: Three Lives in Contemporary Science*. New York: Simon and Schuster.

Hirsch, Paul M. 1972. "Processing Fads and Fashions: An Organization-Set Analysis of Cultural Industry Systems." *American Journal of Sociology* 77:639–659.

Hirsch, Paul M., Stuart Michaels, and Ray Friedman. 1990. "Clean Models vs. Dirty Hands." Pp. 39–56 in *Structures of Capital*, edited by Sharon Zukin and Paul DiMaggio. Cambridge: Cambridge University Press.

Hirschman, Albert O. 1977. *The Passions and the Interests*. Princeton, N.J.: Princeton University Press.

Hofstadter, Douglas R. 1979. *Gödel, Escher, Bach: An Eternal Golden Braid*. New York: Basic Books.

Hollier, Robert. 1985. "Introduction: Hermeneutics and Pragmatism." Pp. ix–xx in *Hermeneutics and Praxis*, edited by Robert Hollier. Notre Dame, Ind.: University of Notre Dame Press.

Hollis, Martin, and Steven Lukes, eds. 1982. *Rationality and Relativism*. Cambridge, Mass.: MIT Press.

Holton, Gerald. 1973. *Thematic Origins of Scientific Thought*. Cambridge, Mass.: Harvard University Press.

———. 1996. "'Doing One's Damnedest': The Evolution of Trust in Scientific Findings." Pp. 58–77 in his *Einstein, History, and Other Passions*. Reading, Mass.: Addison-Wesley.

———. 1998. *The Scientific Imagination*. Cambridge, Mass.: Harvard University Press.

Honigsheim, Paul. 1923. "Zur Soziologie der mittelalterlichen Scholastik: Die soziologische Bedeutung der nominalistischen Philosophie." Pp. 175–218 in *Hauptprobleme der Soziologie: Erinnerungsgabe an Max Weber*, vol. 2. Munich, Germany: Duncker & Humblot.

———. 1924. "Zur Soziologie des realistischen und nominalistischen Denkens." Pp. 308–322 in *Versuche zu einer Soziologie des Wissens*, edited by Max Scheler. Munich, Germany: Duncker & Humblot.

Hooker, Clifford A. 1995. *Reason, Regulation, and Realism: Toward a Regulatory Systems Theory of Reason and Evolutionary Epistemology*. Albany: State University of New York Press.

Ikegami, Eiko. 1995. *The Taming of the Samurai: Honorific Individualism and the Making of Modern Japan*. Cambridge, Mass.: Harvard University Press.

Ingber, Donald E. 1998. "The Architecture of Life." *Scientific American* January:48–57.

Johns, Adrian. 1998. *The Nature of the Book: Print and Knowledge in the Making*. Chicago: University of Chicago Press.

Kaelber, Lutz. 1998. *Schools of Asceticism: Ideology and Organization in Medieval Religious Communities*. University Park: Pennsylvania State University Press.

Kahneman, Daniel, and Amos Tversky. 1990. "Prospect Theory: An Analysis of Decision under Risk." Pp. 140–170 in *Rationality in Action*, edited by Paul K. Moser. Cambridge: Cambridge University Press.

Kanigel, Robert. 1993. *Apprentice to Genius: The Making of a Scientific Dynasty*. Baltimore, Md.: Johns Hopkins University Press.

Kenny, Anthony, and Jan Pinborg. 1982. "Medieval Philosophical Literature." Pp. 11–42 in *The Cambridge History of Later Medieval Philosophy*, edited by Norman Kretzman, Anthony Kenny, and Jan Pinborg. Cambridge: Cambridge University Press.

Kim, Hyojoung, and Peter S. Bearman. 1997. "The Structure and Dynamics of Movement Participation." *American Sociological Review* 62:70–93.

Knorr-Cetina, Karin D. 1981. *The Manufacture of Knowledge*. Oxford: Pergamon.

———. 1999. *Epistemic Cultures: How the Sciences Make Knowledge*. Cambridge, Mass.: Harvard University Press.

Knorr-Cetina, Karin D., and Aaron V. Cicourel, eds. 1981. *Advances in Social Theory and Methodology: Toward an Integration of Micro- and Macro-Sociologies*. Boston: Routledge & Kegan Paul.

Knorr-Cetina, Karin D., and Michael Mulkay. 1983. "Introduction: Emerging Principles in Social Studies of Science." Pp. 1–17 in *Science Observed*, edited by Karin Knorr-Cetina and Michael Mulkay. London: Sage.

Kollock, Peter. 1994. "The Emergence of Exchange Structures: An Experimental Study of Uncertainty, Commitment, and Trust." *American Journal of Sociology* 100:313–345.

Krieger, Martin. 1992. *Doing Physics: How Physicists Take Hold of the World*. Bloomington: Indiana University Press.

Kripke, Saul. 1980. *Naming and Necessity*. Cambridge, Mass.: Harvard University Press.

Kuhn, Thomas S. [1962] 1970. *The Structure of Scientific Revolutions*, 2d ed. Chicago: University of Chicago Press.

———. 1977. *The Essential Tension*. Chicago: University of Chicago Press.

Lakatos, Imre. 1970. "Falsification and the Methodology of Scientific Research Programmes." Pp. 91–196 in *Criticism and the Growth of Knowledge*, edited by Imre Lakatos and Alan Musgrave. Cambridge: Cambridge University Press.

Lamont, Michele. 1992. *Money, Morals, and Manners: The Culture of the French and American Upper-Middle Class*. Chicago: University of Chicago Press.

Latour, Bruno. 1986. "Visualization and Cognition: Thinking with Eyes and Hands." *Knowledge and Society* 6:1–40.

———. 1987. *Science in Action*. Cambridge, Mass.: Harvard University Press.

———. 1988. *The Pasteurization of France*. Cambridge, Mass.: Harvard University Press.

———. 1990. "Drawing Things Together." Pp. 19–68 in *Representation in Scientific Practice*, edited by Michael Lynch and Steve Woolgar. Cambridge, Mass.: MIT Press.

———. 1993. *We Have Never Been Modern*. Cambridge, Mass.: Harvard University Press.

Laudan, Larry. 1990. "Demystifying Underdetermination." Pp. 267–297 in *Scientific Theories*, edited by C. Wade Savage. Minneapolis: University of Minnesota Press.

———. 1996. *Beyond Positivism and Relativism*. Boulder, Colo.: Westview.

Laumann, Edward O., and David Knoke. 1987. *The Organizational State*. Madison: University of Wisconsin Press.

Lawrence, Paul R., and Jay W. Lorsch. [1967] 1986. *Organizations and Environment*. Cambridge, Mass.: Harvard University Press.

Leslie, Stuart W. 1993. *The Cold War and American Science: The Military-Industrial-Academic Complex at MIT and Stanford*. New York: Columbia University Press.

Levitt, Barbara, and Clifford Nass. 1989. "The Lid on the Garbage Can." *Administrative Science Quarterly* 34:190–207.

Lloyd, Geoffrey. 1996. *Adversaries and Authorities: Investigations into Ancient Greek and Chinese Science*. Cambridge: Cambridge University Press.

Lohr, C. H. 1982. "The Medieval Interpretation of Aristotle." Pp. 80–98 in *The Cambridge History of Later Medieval Philosophy*, edited by Norman Kretzman, Anthony Kenny, and Jan Pinborg. Cambridge: Cambridge University Press.

Luhmann, Niklas. 1976. "Generalized Media and the Problem of Contingency." Pp. 507–532 in *Explorations in General Theory in Social Science*, edited by J. J. Loubser et al. New York: Free Press.

———. 1979. *Trust and Power*. New York: Wiley.

———. 1984. *Soziale Systeme*. Frankfurt, Germany: Suhrkamp.

———. 1986. *Love as Passion*. Cambridge, Mass.: Harvard University Press.

————. 1989. *Ecological Communication.* Chicago: University of Chicago Press.

————. 1990. *Essays on Self-Reference.* New York: Columbia University Press.

————. 1992. *Die Wissenschaft der Gesellschaft.* Frankfurt, Germany: Suhrkamp.

————. 1995. *Social Systems.* Stanford, Calif.: Stanford University Press.

————. 1997. *Die Gesellschaft der Gesellschaft.* Frankfurt, Germany: Suhrkamp.

Lynch, Michael. 1985. *Art and Artifact in Laboratory Science.* London: Routledge.

————. 1992. "Extending Wittgenstein: The Pivotal Move from Epistemology to Sociology of Science." Pp. 215–265 in *Science as Practice and Culture,* edited by Andrew Pickering. Chicago: University of Chicago Press.

Lyotard, Jean-François. 1984. *The Postmodern Condition.* Minneapolis: University of Minnesota Press.

Macdonald, Stuart. 1992. "Information Networks and the Exchange of Information." Pp. 51–69 in *The Economics of Information Networks,* edited by Cristiano Antonelli. Amsterdam: Elsevier.

Maffesoli, Michel. [1988] 1996. *The Time of the Tribes.* London: Sage.

Mannheim, Karl. [1928] 1971. "Competition as a Cultural Phenomenon." Pp. 223–261 in *From Karl Mannheim,* edited by Kurt H. Wolff. New York: Oxford University Press.

————. [1929] 1969. *Ideologie und Utopie.* Frankfurt, Germany: Schulte-Bulmke.

————. [1933] 1956. *Essays on the Sociology of Culture.* New York: Oxford University Press.

March, James G., and Herbert A. Simon. 1958. *Organizations.* New York: Wiley.

March, James G., and Johan P. Olsen. 1976. *Ambiguity and Choice in Organizations.* Bergen, Norway: Universitetsforlaget.

————. 1984. "The New Institutionalism." *American Political Science Review* 3:734–749.

March, James G., and Zur Shapira. 1992. "Behavioral Decision Theory and Organizational Decision Theory." Pp. 273–303 in *Decision Making: Alternatives to Rational Choice Models,* edited by Mary Zey. Newbury Park, Calif.: Sage.

Marcuse, Herbert. 1964. *One-Dimensional Man.* Boston: Beacon Press.

Margolis, Howard. 1993. *Paradigms and Barriers: How Habits of Mind Govern Scientific Beliefs.* Chicago: University of Chicago Press.

Margolis, Joseph. 1991. *The Truth about Relativism.* Oxford: Blackwell.

Marsden, Peter. 1983. "Restricted Access in Markets and Models of Power." *American Journal of Sociology* 88:686–717.

Marshall, Douglas. 1999. "Beyond Rational Choice Sociology." Paper presented at the American Sociological Association meetings in Chicago.

Marx, Karl. [1939–1941] 1972. *Grundrisse*. Pp. 221–293 in *The Marx-Engels Reader*, edited by Robert C. Tucker. New York: W. W. Norton.

Marx, Karl, and Friedrich Engels. [1932] 1972. *The German Ideology*. Pp. 146–200 in *The Marx-Engels Reader*, edited by Robert C. Tucker. New York: W. W. Norton.

Matthews, Robert A. J. 1997. "The Science of Murphy's Law." *Scientific American* April:88–91.

Mayr, Ernst. 1976. *Evolution and the Diversity of Life*. Cambridge, Mass.: Belknap Press of Harvard University Press.

———. 1997. *This Is Biology: The Science of the Living World*. Cambridge, Mass.: Belknap Press of Harvard University Press.

McAdam, Doug, John D. McCarthy, and Mayer N. Zald. 1988. "Social Movements." Pp. 695–737 in *Handbook of Sociology*, edited by Neil J. Smelser. Newbury Park, Calif.: Sage.

McCarthy, E. Doyle. 1996. *Knowledge as Culture*. London: Routledge.

McClellan, James E. 1985. *Science Reorganized: Scientific Societies in the Eighteenth Century*. New York: Columbia University Press.

McGuire, Kevin T. 1993. *The Supreme Court Bar*. Charlottesville: University Press of Virginia.

McKenney, James, Michael Zack, and Victor Doherty. 1992. "Complementary Communication Media: A Comparison of Electronic Mail and Face-to-Face Communication in a Programming Team." Pp. 262–287 in *Networks and Organizations*, edited by Nitin Nohria and Robert C. Eccles. Boston: Harvard Business School Press.

Medawar, Peter. [1963] 1990. "Is the Scientific Paper a Fraud?" Pp. 228–233 in his *The Threat and the Glory*. New York: Harper Collins.

Megill, Allan. 1991. "Introduction: Four Senses of Objectivity." *Annals of Scholarship* 8:301–320.

Merton, Robert K. 1973a. "The Matthew Effect in Science." Pp. 439–459 in his *The Sociology of Science*. Chicago: University of Chicago Press.

———. 1973b. "Priorities in Scientific Discovery." Pp. 286–324 in his *The Sociology of Science*. Chicago: University of Chicago Press.

———. 1988. "The Matthew Effect in Science, II." *Isis* 79:606–623.

Meyer, John W., and Brian Rowan. 1977. "Institutionalized Organizations: Formal Structure as Myth and Ceremony." *American Journal of Sociology* 83:340–363.

Meyer, Marshall W., and Lynne G. Zucker. 1989. *Permanently Failing Organizations*. Newbury Park, Calif.: Sage.

Miller, Peter. 1992. "Accounting and Objectivity: The Invention of Calculable Selves and Calculable Spaces." *Annals of Scholarship* 9:61–86.

Mills, C. Wright. 1940. "Situated Actions and Vocabularies of Motive." *American Sociological Review* 5:904–913.

Milner, Murray Jr. 1994. *Status and Sacredness*. New York: Oxford University Press.

Mintzberg, Henry. 1973. *The Nature of Managerial Work*. New York: Harper and Row.

Mitcham, Carl. 1994. *Thinking through Technology*. Chicago: University of Chicago Press.

Mizruchi, Ephraim H. 1983. *Regulating Society: Marginality and Social Control in Historical Perspective*. New York: Free Press.

Moore, Gwen. 1990. "Structural Determinants of Men's and Women's Personal Networks." *American Sociological Review* 55:726–735.

Morrill, Calvin. 1995. *The Executive Way: Conflict Management in Corporations*. Chicago: University of Chicago Press.

Mulkay, Michael J. 1975. "Three Models of Scientific Development." *The Sociological Review* 23:509–526.

———. 1979. *Science and the Sociology of Knowledge*. London: Allen & Unwin.

———. 1985. *The Word and the World*. London: Allen & Unwin.

Mulkay, Michael J., and Bryan S. Turner. 1971. "Over-Production of Personnel and Innovation in Three Social Settings." *Sociology* 5:47–61.

Mullen, Brian, Craig Johnson, and Eduardo Salas. 1991. "Effects of Communication Network Structure: Components of Positional Centrality." *Social Networks* 13:169–186.

Mullins, Nicholas C. 1972. "The Development of a Scientific Specialty: The Phage Group and the Origins of Molecular Biology." *Minerva* 19:52–82.

———. 1973. *Theories and Theory Groups in Contemporary American Sociology*. New York: Harper & Row.

Mullins, Nicholas C., Lowell L. Hargens, Pamela K. Hecht, and Edward L. Kick. 1977. "The Group Structure of Cocitation Clusters: A Comparative Study." *American Sociological Review* 42:552–562.

Nagel, Thomas. 1986. *The View from Nowhere*. New York: Oxford University Press.

Newbold, R. F. 1979. "Boundaries and Bodies in Late Antiquity." *Arethusa* 12:93–114.

Novick, Peter. 1988. *That Noble Dream: The 'Objectivity Question' and the American Historical Profession*. Cambridge: Cambridge University Press.

Nozick, Robert. 1993. *The Nature of Rationality*. Princeton, N.J.: Princeton University Press.

Obesko, Kathryn. 1995. "The Meaning of Precision: The Exact Sensibility in Early Nineteenth-Century Germany." Pp. 103–134 in M. Norton Wise, ed., *The Value of Precision*. Princeton, N.J.: Princeton University Press.

Odom, William E. 1998. *The Collapse of the Soviet Military*. New Haven, Conn.: Yale University Press.

Offe, Claus. 1972. *Strukturprobleme des kapitalistischen Staates*. Frankfurt, Germany: Suhrkamp.

Ong, Walter J. 1982. *Orality and Literacy*. London: Methuen.

Orbell, John. 1993. "*Hamlet* and the Psychology of Rational Choice under Uncertainty." *Rationality and Society* 5:127–140.

Orton, J. Douglas, and Karl E. Weick. 1990. "Loosely Coupled Systems." *Academy of Management Review* 15:203–223.

Padgett, John F., and Christopher K. Ansell. 1993. "Robust Action and the Rise of the Medici, 1400–1434." *American Journal of Sociology* 98:1259–1319.

Panofsky, Erwin. 1951. *Gothic Architecture and Scholasticism*. New York: Meridian.

Parsons, Talcott. 1971. *The System of Modern Societies*. Englewood Cliffs, N.J.: Prentice Hall.

Paulos, John Allen. 1998. *Once upon a Number: The Hidden Mathematical Logic of Stories*. New York: Basic Books.

Perinbanayagam, R. S. 1991. *Discursive Acts*. New York: Aldine de Gruyter.

Perrow, Charles. 1967. "A Framework for the Comparative Analysis of Organizations." *American Sociological Review* 32:194–208.

———. 1984. *Normal Accidents*. New York: Basic Books.

———. 1986a. *Complex Organizations: A Critical Essay*, 3d ed. New York: Random House.

———. 1986b. "Economic Theories of Organization." *Theory and Society* 15:11–45.

———. 1991. "A Society of Organizations." *Theory and Society* 20:725–762.

Peterson, Richard A. 1994. "Culture Studies through the Production Perspective: Progress and Prospects." Pp. 163–189 in *The Sociology of Culture: Emerging Theoretical Perspectives*, edited by Diana Crane. Oxford: Blackwell.

Peterson, Richard A., and D. Berger. 1975. "Cycles in Symbol Production: The Case of Popular Music." *American Sociological Review* 40:158–173.

Pfeffer, Jeffrey, and Gerald R. Salancik. 1978. *The External Control of Organizations: A Resource Dependency Perspective*. New York: Harper & Row.

Pickering, Andrew. 1984. *Constructing Quarks: A Sociological History of Particle Physics*. Chicago: University of Chicago Press.

———. 1991. "Objectivity and the Mangle of Practice." *Annals of Scholarship* 8:409–425.

———. 1995. *The Mangle of Practice: Time, Agency, and Science*. Chicago: University of Chicago Press.

Pinch, Trevor J. 1986. *Confronting Nature: The Sociology of Solar Neutrino Detection*. Dordrecht, The Netherlands: Reidel.

Polanyi, Michael. [1958] 1964. *Personal Knowledge: Towards a Post-Critical Philosophy*. New York: Harper and Row.

Poovey, Mary. 1998. *A History of the Modern Fact*. Chicago: University of Chicago Press.

Popper, Karl R. [1934] 1976. *Logik der Forschung*. Tübingen, Germany: Mohr.

———. 1972. *Objective Knowledge: An Evolutionary Approach*. Oxford: Clarendon.

Porter, Theodore M. 1992a. "Objectivity as Standardization: The Rhetoric of Impersonality in Measurement, Statistics, and Cost-Benefit Analysis." *Annals of Scholarship* 9:19–59.

———. 1992b. "Quantification and the Accounting Ideal in Science." *Social Studies of Science* 22:633–652.

———. 1995. *Trust in Numbers: The Pursuit of Objectivity in Science and Public Life*. Princeton, N.J.: Princeton University Press.

Powell, Walter W. 1985. *Getting into Print*. Chicago: University of Chicago Press.

Powell, Walter W., and Paul J. DiMaggio, eds. 1991. *The New Institutionalism in Organizational Analysis*. Chicago: University of Chicago Press.

Price, Derek J. de Solla. 1979. "Philosophical Mechanism and Mechanical Philosophy." Paper presented at Clark Library, University of California, Los Angeles.

———. 1986. *Little Science, Big Science . . . and Beyond*. New York: Columbia University Press.

Pugh, Derek S., David J. Hickson, C. R. Hinings, and C. Turner. 1969. "The Context of Organizational Structures." *Administrative Science Quarterly* 14:91–114.

Quine, Willard van Ornam. 1964. "Two Dogmas of Empiricism." Pp. 20–46 in his *From a Logical Point of View*. Cambridge, Mass.: Harvard University Press.

———. 1969a. "Epistemology Naturalized." Pp. 69–90 in his *Ontological Relativity and Other Essays*. New York: Columbia University Press.

———. 1969b. "Ontological Relativity." Pp. 26–68 in his *Ontological Relativity and Other Essays*. New York: Columbia University Press.

———. 1969c. "Speaking of Objects." Pp. 1–25 in his *Ontological Relativity and Other Essays*. New York: Columbia University Press.

———. 1992. "Structure and Nature." *The Journal of Philosophy* 89:5–9.

Raub, Werner, and Jeroen Weesie. 1990. "Reputation and Efficiency in Social Interactions: An Example of Network Effects." *American Journal of Sociology* 96:626–654.

Ravetz, Jerome R. 1971. *Scientific Knowledge and Its Social Problems*. Oxford: Clarendon.

Reichenbach, Hans. 1951. *The Rise of Scientific Philosophy*. Berkeley: University of California Press.

Rescher, Nicholas. 1988. *Rationality*. Oxford: Clarendon.

Rorty, Richard. 1979. *Philosophy and the Mirror of Nature*. Princeton, N.J.: Princeton University Press.

———. 1989. "The Contingency of a Liberal Community." Pp. 44–69 in his *Contingency, Irony, and Solidarity*. Cambridge: Cambridge University Press.

———. 1991. "Solidarity or Objectivity?" Pp. 21–34 in his *Objectivity, Relativism, and Truth*. Cambridge: Cambridge University Press.

Rosen, Charles. 1998. *Romantic Poets, Critics, and Other Madmen*. Cambridge, Mass.: Harvard University Press.

Rosenau, Pauline M. 1992. *Postmodernism and the Social Sciences*. Princeton, N.J.: Princeton University Press.

Rosenberg, Alexander. 1995. *Philosophy of Social Science*. Boulder, Colo.: Westview.

Rowland, Ingrid D. 1998. *The Culture of the High Renaissance: Ancients and Moderns in Sixteenth-Century Rome*. Cambridge: Cambridge University Press.

Rudder Baker, Lynne. 1987. *Saving Belief: A Critique of Physicalism*. Princeton, N.J.: Princeton University Press.

Rudwick, Martin J. 1985. *The Great Devonian Controversy*. Chicago: University of Chicago Press.

Rummel, Erika. 1995. *The Humanist-Scholastic Debate in the Renaissance and Reformation*. Cambridge, Mass.: Harvard University Press.

Ryle, Gilbert. [1949] 1984. *The Concept of Mind*. Chicago: University of Chicago Press.

Salmon, Wesley C. 1989. "Four Decades of Scientific Explanation." Pp. 3–219 in *Scientific Explanation*, edited by Philip Kitcher and Wesley C. Salmon. Minneapolis: University of Minnesota Press.

Scarry, Elaine. 1985. *The Body in Pain*. New York: Oxford University Press.

Schegloff, Emanuel. 1992. "Repair after Next Turn." *American Journal of Sociology* 95:1295–1345.

Scheler, Max. 1924. "Probleme einer Soziologie des Wissens." Pp. 5–146 in *Versuche zu einer Soziologie des Wissens*, edited by Max Scheler. Munich, Germany: Duncker & Humblot.

Schlick, Moritz. 1938. "Positivismus und Realismus." Pp. 83–115 in his *Gesammelte Aufsätze*, 1926–1936. Vienna, Austria: Gerold.

Schmitt, Frederick F. 1995. *Truth: A Primer*. Boulder, Colo.: Westview.

Schneider, Mark. 1993. *Culture and Enchantment.* Chicago: University of Chicago Press.

———. 1997. "Social Dimensions of Epistemological Disputes: The Case of Literary Theory." *Sociological Perspectives* 40:243–263.

Scott, W. Richard. 1992. *Organizations: Rational, Natural, and Open Systems,* 3d ed. Englewood Cliffs, N.J.: Prentice Hall.

Searle, John R. 1992. *The Rediscovery of the Mind.* Cambridge, Mass.: MIT Press.

———. 1995. *The Construction of Social Reality.* New York: Free Press.

Sen, Amartya K. 1990. "Rational Fools: A Critique of the Behavioral Foundations of Economic Theory." Pp. 25–43 in *Beyond Self-Interest,* edited by Jane J. Mansbridge. Chicago: University of Chicago Press.

Shapin, Steven. 1984. "Pump and Circumstance: Robert Boyle's Literary Technology." *Social Studies of Science* 14:481–520.

———. 1986. "History of Science and Its Sociological Reconstructions." Pp. 325–386 in *Cognition and Fact,* edited by R. S. Cohen and T. Schnelle. Dordrecht, The Netherlands: Reidel.

———. 1988. "The House of Experiment in Seventeenth-Century England." *Isis* 79:373–404.

———. 1990. "The Mind Is Its Own Place: Science and Solitude in Seventeenth-Century England." *Science in Context* 4:191–218.

———. 1994. *A Social History of Truth.* Chicago: University of Chicago Press.

———. 1995. "Here and Everywhere: Sociology of Scientific Knowledge." *Annual Review of Sociology* 21:289–321.

———. 1996. *The Scientific Revolution.* Chicago: University of Chicago Press.

Shapiro, Barbara J. 1983. *Probability and Certainty in Seventeenth-Century England.* Princeton, N.J.: Princeton University Press.

Shermer, Michael. 1997. *Why People Believe Weird Things.* New York: Freeman.

Shils, Edward. 1975. *Centre and Periphery.* Chicago: University of Chicago Press.

Shrum, Wesley. 1991. "Critics and Publics: Cultural Mediation in Highbrow and Popular Performing Arts." *American Journal of Sociology* 97:347–375.

Simmel, Georg. [1908] 1971. "Group Expansion and the Development of Individuality." Pp. 251–293 in his *On Individuality and Social Forms.* Chicago: University of Chicago Press.

———. [1908] 1977. *Philosophie des Geldes.* Berlin: Duncker & Humblot.

Simon, Herbert A. [1945] 1976. *Administrative Behavior.* New York: Free Press.

———. 1990. "Alternative Visions of Rationality." Pp. 189–204 in *Rationality in Action,* edited by Paul Moser. Cambridge: Cambridge University Press.

Skirbekk, Gunnar, ed. 1980. *Wahrheitstheorien.* Frankfurt, Germany: Suhrkamp.

Skocpol, Theda. 1979. *States and Social Revolutions.* Cambridge: Cambridge University Press.

Smiley, Marion. 1992. *Moral Responsibility and the Boundaries of Community.* Chicago: University of Chicago Press.

Smith, Kenwyn K., and Valerie M. Simmons. 1983. "A Rumpelstiltskin Organization." *Administrative Science Quarterly* 28:377–392.

Smith, Roger, and Brian Wynne, eds. 1989. *Expert Evidence.* London: Routledge.

Smith, Thomas S. 1992. *Strong Interaction.* Chicago: University of Chicago Press.

Southern, Richard W. 1982. "The Schools of Paris and the School of Chartres." Pp. 113–137 in *Renaissance and Renewal in the Twelfth Century,* edited by Robert L. Benson and Giles Constable. Cambridge, Mass.: Harvard University Press.

Spear, Joseph H. 1999. *The Sociology of Reductionism.* Ph.D. diss., Department of Sociology, University of Virginia.

Spengler, Oswald. [1923] 1993. *Der Untergang des Abendlandes: Umrisse einer Morphologie der Weltgeschichte.* Munich, Germany: DTV.

Sperber, Dan. 1996. *Explaining Culture: A Naturalistic Approach.* Oxford: Blackwell.

Star, Susan Leigh. 1983. "Simplification in Scientific Work." *Social Studies of Science* 13:205–228.

Staudenmaier, John M. 1985. *Technology's Storytellers: Reweaving the Human Fabric.* Cambridge, Mass.: MIT Press.

Stephan, Paula E., and Sharon G. Levin. 1992. *Striking the Mother Lode in Science.* New York: Oxford University Press.

Stiefel, Tina. 1985. *The Intellectual Revolution in Twelfth-Century Europe.* New York: St. Martin's.

Stigler, George J., and Gary S. Becker. 1990. "De Gustibus Non Est Disputandum." Pp. 191–221 in *The Limits of Rationality,* edited by Karen S. Cook and Margaret Levi. Chicago: University of Chicago Press.

Stinchcombe, Arthur L. 1965. "Social Structure and Organizations." Pp. 142–193 in *Handbook of Organizations,* edited by James G. March. Chicago: Rand McNally.

———. 1988. *Stratification and Organization.* Cambridge: Cambridge University Press.

———. 1990. *Information and Organization.* Berkeley: University of California Press.

Stock, Brian. 1984. "Medieval Literacy, Linguistic Theory, and Social Organization." *New Literary History* 16:13–29.

Strawson, P. F. 1985. *Skepticism and Naturalism.* New York: Columbia University Press.

Sulloway, Frank J. 1996. *Born to Rebel.* New York: Pantheon Books.

Swijtink, Zeno. 1987. "The Objectification of Observation: Measurement and Statistical Methods in the Nineteenth Century." Pp. 261–285 in *The Probabilistic Revolution,* Vol. 1: *Ideas in History,* edited by Lorenz Krüger, Lorraine Daston, and Michael Heidelberger. Cambridge, Mass.: MIT Press.

Tambiah, Stanley J. 1979. "A Performative Approach to Ritual." *Proceedings of the British Academy* 65:113–169.

Taylor, Charles. 1971. "Interpretation and the Sciences of Man." *Review of Metaphysics* 25:1–51.

Tenner, Edward. 1997. *Why Things Bite Back: Technology and the Revenge of Unintended Consequences.* New York: Vintage Books.

Thagard, Paul. 1992. *Conceptual Revolutions.* Princeton, N.J.: Princeton University Press.

Thomas, Rosalind. 1992. *Literacy and Orality in Ancient Greece.* Cambridge: Cambridge University Press.

Thompson, James D. 1967. *Organizations in Action.* New York: McGraw Hill.

Thorne, Kip S. 1994. *Black Holes and Time Warps: Einstein's Outrageous Legacy.* New York: W. W. Norton.

Tolbert, Pamela S., and Lynne G. Zucker. 1995. "Institutional Analyses of Organizations." Paper presented at the American Sociological Association meetings in Washington, D.C.

Trice, Harrison M. 1993. *Occupational Subcultures in the Workplace.* Ithaca, N.Y.: ILR Press.

Troll, Denise A. 1990. "The Illiterate Mode of Written Communication: The Work of the Medieval Scribe." Pp. 96–125 in *Oral and Written Communication: Historical Approaches,* edited by Richard Leo Enos. Newbury Park, Calif.: Sage.

Tuchman, Gaye. 1978. *Making News: A Study in the Social Construction of Reality.* New York: Free Press.

———. 1988. "Mass Media Institutions." Pp. 601–628 in *Handbook of Sociology,* edited by Neil J. Smelser. Newbury Park, Calif.: Sage.

Turner, Stephen. 1994. *The Social Theory of Practices.* Chicago: University of Chicago Press.

Turner, Victor. 1974. "Liminal to Liminoid, in Play, Flow, and Ritual: An Essay in Comparative Symbology." *Rice University Studies* 60:53–92.

Tversky, Amos, and Daniel Kahneman. 1990a. "Judgment under Uncertainty." Pp. 145–178 in *Rationality in Action,* edited by Paul Moser. Cambridge: Cambridge University Press.

———. 1990b. "Rational Choice and the Framing of Decisions." Pp. 60–89 in *The Limits of Rationality*, edited by Karen S. Cook and Margaret Levi. Chicago: University of Chicago Press.

van Brakel, J. 1992. "Natural Kinds and Manifest Forms of Life." *Dialectica* 46:243–259.

van den Daele, Wolfgang, Wolfgang Krohn, and Peter Weingart, eds. 1979. *Geplante Forschung*. Frankfurt, Germany: Suhrkamp.

van Helden, Albert. 1994. "Telescopes and Authority from Galileo to Cassini." *Osiris* 9:9–29.

van Leeuwen, Henry G. 1963. *The Problem of Certainty in English Thought, 1630–1690*. The Hague, Netherlands: Martinus Nijhoff.

Van Rees, Kees, and Jeroen Vermunt. 1995. "Event History Analysis of Authors' Reputation." Paper presented at the American Sociological Association meetings in Washington, D.C.

Ward, John O. 1990. "Rhetoric, Truth, and Literacy in the Renaissance of the Twelfth Century." Pp. 126–157 in *Oral and Written Communication: Historical Approaches*, edited by Richard L. Enos. Newbury Park, Calif.: Sage.

Ward, Steven. 1996. *Reconfiguring Truth*. Lanham, Md.: Rowman & Littlefield.

Watson, James D. 1968. *The Double Helix*. New York: Atheneum.

Weber, Max. [1904] 1982. "Die 'Objektivität' sozialwissenschaftlicher und sozialpolitischer Erkenntnis." Pp. 146–214 in his *Gesammelte Aufsätze zur Wissenschaftslehre*. Tübingen, Germany: Mohr.

———. [1906] 1982. "Objektive Möglichkeit und adäquate Verursachung in der historischen Kausalbetrachtung." Pp. 266–290 in his *Gesammelte Aufsätze zur Wissenschaftslehre*. Tübingen, Germany: Mohr.

———. [1919] 1982. "Wissenschaft als Beruf." Pp. 582–613 in his *Gesammelte Aufsätze zur Wissenschaftslehre*. Tübingen, Germany: Mohr.

———. [1922] 1980. *Wirtschaft und Gesellschaft*. Tübingen: Mohr.

———. 1978. *Economy and Society*. Berkeley: University of California Press.

Weick, Karl E. 1979. *The Social Psychology of Organizing*. Reading, Mass.: Addison-Wesley.

Weimann, Robert. 1996. *Authority and Representation in Early Modern Discourse*. Baltimore, Md.: Johns Hopkins University Press.

Wellman, Barry, and S. D. Berkowitz, eds. 1988. *Social Structures: A Network Approach*. Cambridge: Cambridge University Press.

Wellman, Barry, Peter J. Carrington, and Alan Hall. 1988. "Networks as Personal Communities." Pp. 130–184 in *Social Structures: A Network Approach*, edited by Barry Wellman and S. D. Berkowitz. Cambridge: Cambridge University Press.

Wellman, Barry, and Milena Gulia. 1995. "Net Surfers Don't Ride Alone."

Paper presented to the American Sociological Association meetings in Washington, D.C.

Westrum, Ron. 1978. "Science and Social Intelligence about Anomalies: The Case of Meteorites." *Social Studies of Science* 8:461–493.

White, Douglas R., and H. Gilman McCann. 1988. "Cites and Fights: Material Entailment Analysis of the Eighteenth-Century Chemical Revolution." Pp. 380–404 in *Social Structures,* edited by Barry Wellman and S. D. Berkowitz. Cambridge: Cambridge University Press.

White, Harrison C. 1988. "Where Do Markets Come From?" *American Journal of Sociology* 87:517–547.

———. 1992. *Identity and Control: A Structural Theory of Social Action.* Princeton, N.J.: Princeton University Press.

White, Harrison C., Scott A. Boorman, and Ronald L. Breiger. 1976. "Social Structure from Multiple Networks I: Blockmodels of Roles and Positions." *American Journal of Sociology* 81:730–780.

Whitley, Richard. 1984. *The Intellectual and Social Organization of the Sciences.* Oxford: Clarendon.

Wiley, Norbert. 1994. *The Semiotic Self.* Chicago: University of Chicago Press.

Williamson, Oliver. 1975. *Markets and Hierarchies.* New York: Free Press.

Wilson, Brian R., ed. 1970. *Rationality.* Oxford: Blackwell.

Wilson, Robert. 1988. "Reputations in Games and Markets." Pp. 27–62 in *Game-Theoretic Models of Bargaining,* edited by Alvin E. Roth. Cambridge: Cambridge University Press.

Wise, M. Norton. 1995. "Precision: Agent of Unity and Product of Agreement." Pp. 92–100 in M. Norton Wise, ed., *The Values of Precision.* Princeton, N.J.: Princeton University Press.

Wittgenstein, Ludwig. 1953. *Philosophical Investigations.* New York: Macmillan.

———. 1969. *On Certainty.* New York: J. & J. Harper.

Wolfe, Tom. 1998. *A Man in Full.* New York: Farrar, Straus & Giroux.

Wolpert, Lewis. 1992. *The Unnatural Science of Science: Why Science Does Not Make (Common) Sense.* London: Faber & Faber.

Woodward, Joan. [1965] 1980. *Industrial Organization.* London: Oxford University Press.

Woolgar, Steve, ed. 1988. *Knowledge and Reflexivity: New Frontiers in the Sociology of Knowledge.* London: Sage.

Zerubavel, Eviatar. 1991. *The Fine Line: Making Distinctions in Everyday Life.* New York: Free Press.

Ziman, John. [1978] 1991. *Reliable Knowledge: An Exploration of the Grounds for Belief in Science.* Cambridge: Cambridge University Press.

Znaniecki, Florian. [1940] 1975. *The Social Role of the Man of Knowledge.* New York: Octagon.

Zuckerman, Harriet. 1977. *Scientific Elite.* New York: Free Press.

———. 1988. "The Sociology of Science." Pp. 511–574 in *Handbook of Sociology,* edited by Neil J. Smelser. Newbury Park, Calif.: Sage.

Index

Abbott, Andrew, 165, 166
Abeyance, 317
Abstract concepts, 135, 293
Academia, 36, 43, 44, 83, 230–231
Accidents, normal, 229, 283, 291, 306
Accumulation, 170
Action, 13–14, 16, 66, 99, 123, 230; theory of, 44, 49; rationality of, 112–113. *See also* Rationality
Actors, 63–64, 113–114, 116–119
Administration, 180–182, 230–231, 285
Adorno, Theodor, 30, 136, 178
Aesthetics, 240
Agency, 5, 8–9, 21, 52, 137, 151, 257, 332; persons as constructs, 63–64; free will, 103–104; uncertainty and, 106–107; rational choice theory and, 117–118
Agency framework, 21–22, 63, 98
Aggregation, 98, 236–237
Albert, Hans, 115
Algorithms, 76, 101, 108, 118, 243, 246
Alienation, 305
Amann, Klaus, 324
Amateurs, 90, 147, 165, 190
Analytical philosophy, 12, 44, 62, 281
Anarchy, 92, 294, 315–316
Anomalies, 14, 75, 255, 289, 298
Ansell, Christopher K., 247
Anthropology, 81, 155, 284

Antiessentialism, 15–16, 64, 104, 161. *See also* Relationalism
Antifoundationalism, 2, 8, 73, 294
Antihumanism, 63
Apprentices, 68
Arditi, Jorge, 213
Aristotelian metaphysics, 12, 15–16
Aristotle, 15–16, 314
Arrow, Kenneth, 124
Art, 9–10, 30, 52, 152, 157–159; criticism, 35–36, 39, 170, 176, 253; sociology of, 39–40, 159, 167, 253–254; relation to institutions, 53, 56, 57; innovation and, 60, 181–185; professionalization of, 165–170; reputation and, 166, 169–170; meaning of, 166–168; status and, 166–169, 177; contexts and clues, 170–178; networks, 172–175; artists' signatures, 174–175; displays and performances, 179–180; administered, 180–182; production of, 180–182; independents, 182–183. *See also* Avantgarde
Artificial intelligence, 101, 118–119
Ashmore, Malcolm, 88
Association, modes of, 4
Associations, 191
Atomism, 281
Attention, 59, 253
Audience, 183–184

Sociology, 67, 88; tools of, 1, 8, 297; of culture, 1–2, 9–10, 27–29, 32, 58, 154, 162–164; science and, 6–7, 27; of knowledge, 29, 32, 69, 74, 164; of art, 39–40, 159, 167, 253–254; ethnomethodology, 43–47, 56, 99, 121, 124; causation and, 117–119
Solidarity, 52, 56, 137, 154, 213, 240
Spear, Joseph H., 60, 291, 302
Specialization, 10, 85, 147
Specialty, 60, 83, 89–92, 185, 265; knowledge and, 147–148
Speech acts, 30–31
Spengler, Oswald, 21, 189, 254, 270, 276, 292, 302
Sperber, Dan, 139
Stabilization, 17, 77, 212–213, 254
Standardization, 134, 229, 288, 290, 305, 307
Standpoints, 29, 35, 73, 88, 92, 94
Star, Susan Leigh, 330
State, 53, 98, 174, 230, 291
Statistics, 134–135, 198–199, 229–230, 236–238; expansion and, 279–280
Status, 56, 64, 88; organizations and, 39, 246–247; art and, 166–169, 177; avant-garde and, 177–178
Stigler, George J., 123
Stinchcombe, Arthur L., 148, 224, 230, 245
Stock, Brian, 317
Strangers, 255
Stratification, 19, 60, 159–164, 285
Strawson, P. F., 294
Strong Program, 32
Strong theories, 58, 115
Structural constructivism, 7–8
Structural equivalence, 21–22
Structural fortification, 220–221
Structuralism, 2, 176
Structure, 66, 233–240, 242, 309–311, 327
Studies in Ethnomethodology, 43
Subcultures, 3, 10, 51, 61, 149, 155, 244
Subject, death of, 2–3, 99
Subjectivity, 100
Surveys, 103–104, 121, 280
Swijtink, Zeno, 305

Symbols, 255
Systems theories, 3, 4, 7–8, 63–67, 332

Taboos, 61, 62, 111, 140, 197, 290
Tautology, 12, 157–158, 160–161, 217, 282, 286, 288
Taylor, Charles, 96–97
Taylorization, 103, 135, 151, 165, 180, 290; instrumentation and, 76, 246
Technical cores, 217–218
Technical values, 41
Technology, 221–222, 277–278, 318. *See also* Instrumentation; Machines
Television, 136, 182
Temporalization, 159, 181
Tensegrity, 63, 257
Text, 306–307, 312–313, 318–320; in laboratory, 322–323; frontstages and, 329–330
Textual cultures, 306–307, 312–313, 322–326
Thagard, Paul, 281
Themata, 218, 282
Theory-ladenness, 18, 74–78, 267
Thick description, 47, 108
Things-in-themselves, 6, 12, 101, 288. *See also* Natural kinds
Thinking, 209–210, 333
Thomas, Rosalind, 121, 317
Thompson, James D., 171, 217–218, 290
Time, 50–51, 88–89, 301–304
Tolbert, Pamela S., 93, 115
Topics, 23, 27
Totalitarianism, 112
Totems, 175, 215, 220
Trading zones, 93
Traditional philosophy, 73–74, 92
Transaction cost theories, 232–233
Transcendence, 11, 69, 303–304, 331
Translation, 78–84
Tribal ritual, 179
Tribes, 52, 56
Trice, Harrison M., 244
Troll, Denise A., 313
True/false code, 267
Truth, 23, 28–29, 35, 46, 82, 87, 302; pragmatism and, 68–69; representation and, 72, 74; rational choice the-

ory and, 124–125; text and, 312–313.
See also Ideology
Turbulence, 4, 10, 11, 210–211; in organizations, 228–229, 232–233, 235, 303
Turner, Bryan S., 317
Turner, C., 244
Turner, Stephen, 92, 119
Turner, Victor, 53, 124, 299
Tversky, Amos, 126
Two Cultures, 56, 294
Typologies, 50, 55

Ulysses (Joyce), 143
Uncertainty, 60, 75–76, 109, 125, 135, 229, 241; agency and, 106–107; in art, 176–177; organizations and, 245–246
Underdetermination, 74–79, 324
Unit act, 49
Unity, 9, 19, 119–123, 237, 275–276; organizations and, 120–121, 227
Universality, 61, 69, 81, 293, 331
University, 230–232, 317, 321
Utility, 113, 125–126
Utopianism, 222, 248

Value-freedom, 7, 40–43
Van Brakel, J., 12, 13
Van Leeuwen, Henry G., 294
Van Rees, Kees, 170
Variables, 3–4, 11, 49, 254; dependent variables, 4–5, 8; natural kinds as, 17, 50, 55; time as, 50–51; distance, 104–105, 163; rationality as, 115–116, 137
Variation, 6, 8, 9; qualitative and quantitative, 49, 158; method and, 49–58; in cultural forms, 58–59; translation and, 79–80, 83–84; in organizational cultures, 244–250. *See also* Continuum
Velocity, 36, 55–56, 62, 184, 301
Vermunt, Jeroen, 170

Verstehen, 104
Vienna Circle, 281, 296
Virtual witnessing, 325

Waller, David, 73
Walls, 216–217, 290
Wants, 123–127
Ward, John O., 316, 317, 322
Ward, Steven, 53, 71, 223, 243
Weber, Max, 41, 49, 59–60, 111, 112, 115, 116, 130, 146, 276, 310
Weick, Karl E., 121, 227, 231, 239
Weimann, Robert, 73, 320
Weingart, Peter, 225
Wellman, Barry, 66, 203–204, 318
Westervelt, Saundra, 62
White, Douglas R., 311
White, Harrison C., 16, 21, 51, 191, 248, 249
Whitley, Richard, 55
Wiley, Norbert, 118
Williamson, Oliver, 132, 232
Wilson, Brian R., 81
Winch, Peter, 81
Wise, M. Norton, 304
Wittgenstein, Ludwig, 23, 71, 327
Woodward, Joan, 181, 245
Woolgar, Steve, 25
Workers, 226, 309
World systems, 63, 98
Worldviews, 276
Writing, 125, 236, 318–320, 325, 333

Zack, Michael, 247
Zald, Mayer N., 14, 223
Zerubavel, Eviatar, 216
Zetterburg, Hans, 23
Ziman, John, 190, 329
Znaniecki, Florian, 312, 313
Zucker, Lynne G., 93, 98, 115
Zuckerman, Harriet, 250